Maike Oergel
Culture and Identity

Maike Oergel

Culture and Identity

Historicity in German Literature
and Thought 1770–1815

Walter de Gruyter · Berlin · New York

The completion of this project was supported by a grant
from the *Arts and Humanities Research Board*.

♾ Printed on acid-free paper which falls within guidelines,
on the ANSI to ensure permanence and durability

Library of Congress – Cataloging-in-Publication Data

Oergel, Maike, 1964–
  Culture and identity : historicity in German literature and thought 1770–1815 / by
Maike Oergel.
    p. cm.
  Includes bibliographical references and index.
  ISBN-13: 978-3-11-018933-9 (alk. paper)
  ISBN-10: 3-11-018933-X (alk. paper)
  1. German literature – 18th century – History and criticism. 2. German literature – 19th
century – History and criticism. 3. Germany – Civilization – 18th century 4. Germany –
Civilization– 19th century. 5. Literature and history – Germany. 6. Collective memory –
Germany – History – 18th century. 7. Collective memory – Germany – History : 19th cen-
tury. I. Title.
  PT313.O47 2006
  830.9'006–dc22

                                                                      2006021275

ISBN-13: 978-3-11-018933-9
ISBN-10: 3-11-018933-X

Bibliographic information published by Die Deutsche Bibliothek

Die Deutsche Bibliothek lists this publication in the Deutsche Nationalbibliografie;
detailed bibliographic data is available in the Internet at <http://dnb.ddb.de>

Printed in Germany
Cover Design: Christopher Schneider, Berlin
Typesetting: Dörlemann Satz GmbH & Co. KG, Lemförde
Printing and binding: Hubert & Co. GmbH & Co. KG, Göttingen

For my mother
and in memory of my father

Contents

Introduction

Historicity, Modernity and the Germans: The Historical Dialectic and New Concepts of Culture, Consciousness and Identity

It is a cultural commonplace that the period of roughly one generation either side of 1800 was crucial for the definition of modern German identity. During this period unprecedented intellectual and literary creativity generated a cultural canon that retained its status for a long time: the literary, critical and theoretical works of what is traditionally known as *Sturm und Drang*, *Klassik*, *Romantik*, and the philosophical systems of German Idealism. It is equally well established that this period forms the "Sattelzeit" of modernity (Koselleck), the age of a paradigm shift regarding the nature and purpose of the individual, society, history, culture. But despite long-standing critical interest there has been little emphasis on what arguably constitutes a key intellectual framework crucial to modern and German identity: the destabilising as well as productive force of the growing awareness of historicity, to which, incidentally, most contemporary debates on modernity, national identity and cultural expression related. The effect the emergent notion of historicity has had on the experience of intellectual, physical and social reality is well recognised. But little attention has been given to how it influenced the German understanding of identity in general and the literary concepts in which specific identities found conscious expression. This investigation aims to show how the increasing awareness of historicity crucially influenced the German concept of modernity and how these two concepts shaped modern German identity and underpinned cultural and intellectual activity. They are in fact responsible for the link between modern German identity and the conception of culture which a century later enabled Friedrich Meinecke to define the *Kulturnation*. Any enquiry into German national identity that places culture at its centre is also an enquiry into the theory of the German cultural and intellectual

Sonderweg. And this study is no exception. The *Sonderweg*-theory hinges on the idea of a discontinuity within Enlightenment thinking. The relationship between the emergent German concept of modernity and key tenets of Enlightenment thinking forms the interface from which the notion of historicity developed. By focusing upon this meeting point, it is possible to assess the continuities and discontinuities of Enlightenment ideas in the crucial period around 1800.

The German contribution to modern European thought has long been linked to historicism: the identity-builders of the early 20th century, who defined the "Entstehung des Historismus" (Meinecke)[1], the "Goethezeit" (Korff)[2] and the "Deutsche Bewegung" (Nohl)[3], relied largely on an assumed opposition between Enlightenment ideas and historicist perspectives. Invariably, their definitions centred on a rejection, or an overcoming, of the Enlightenment, which was cast as Franco-British, i.e. foreign, in origin. This rejection was not simply an expression of xenophobia, but of a belief that the Enlightenment was *not theirs,* that it was the intellectual and cultural property of other nations and expressed the genius of a different mentality. They believed that a genuinely German tradition had to rely on other things. While the following underlines that a particularly advanced awareness of historicity emerged among German thinkers towards the end of the 18th century, it equally clearly demonstrates that Enlightenment ideas laid the basis for this awareness, even as they provided an opposing pole, which is something the thinkers involved were quite conscious of.[4] In this respect my investigation contributes to the understanding of the dialectic of the En-

---

[1] Friedrich Meinecke, *Die Entstehung des Historismus*, (1st 1936) ed. by Carl Hinrichs, vol. 3 of *Werke*, Munich: Oldenbourg, 1959.

[2] H.A. Korff, *Geist der Goethezeit. Versuch einer ideellen Entwicklung der klassisch-romantischen Literaturgeschichte*, 5 vols, Leipzig: Weber, 1923–57.

[3] Hermann Nohl, *Die deutsche Bewegung. Vorlesungen und Aufsätze zur Geistesgeschichte 1770–1830*, ed. by O.F. Bollnow and F. Rodi, Göttingen: Vandenhoek & Ruprecht, 1970.

[4] The suggestion of a link between Enlightenment and *Sturm-und-Drang* thought was put forward as long ago as 1963 by Werner Krauss ("Französische Aufklärung und deutsche Romantik", *Wissenschaftliche Zeitschrift der Karl-Marx-Universität Leipzig* 12 (1963), quoted in H.R. Jauss, *Literaturgeschichte als Provokation*, Frankfurt aM: Suhrkamp, 1970, p. 81), who was not coincidentally a critic working in the GDR, the political self-understanding of which was congenial to establishing a rationalist tradition for the German cultural heyday around 1800. A similar interest in the intellectual continuity of the German Enlightenment is not evident in West Germany until the 1980s.

lightenment in general as well as to the understanding of the continuity of Enlightenment ideas in German thought.[5]

As the awareness of historicity emerges at the very interface of Enlightenment thought and post-Enlightenment thinking, my purpose here must be to identify how thinkers who are taken to be representatives of *Sturm und Drang*, *Klassik*, and *Romantik* respectively dealt with a gradually more and more fluid intellectual framework when they defined concepts of modernity and national identity, i.e. how they amended or discarded the Enlightenment notions of universality and constancy. The claim that the modern German self-definition derives from a multi-facetted reassessment of Enlightenment notions, which has always been the basis of any kind of *Sonderweg*-theory, will not be disputed. But the premises, results and governing factors of this German reassessment will appear in a new light. This study argues the following: The period from 1770 to 1815 forms an intellectually coherent phase in terms of the intellectual problems addressed and intellectual and cultural objectives to be achieved, even if the ways in which these objectives are approached vary.[6] The central intellectual problem is the histo-

---

[5] German *Klassik*, or Weimar classicism, has been repeatedly singled out as the place where the German Enlightenment continued, and found a refuge. Cf. T.J. Reed, "Die Geburt der Klassik aus dem Geist der Mündigkeit" *Jahrbuch der deutschen Schillergesellschaft* 32 (1988) 367–374 or Gottfried Willems, "Goethe – ein Überwinder der Aufklärung?" *Germanisch-Romanische Monatsschrift* 40 (1990) 22–40. It will become evident that, on the one hand, this idea requires qualification, while on the other hand the Enlightenment's influence also permeates *Sturm und Drang* and *Romantik*. In this respect the findings of this investigation relate to the discussions of the nature of the *Spätaufklärung*, in which *Sturm und Drang* becomes (dialectically) integrated into the Enlightenment (cf. G. Frank, "*Sturm und Drang*: Towards a new Logic of Passion", *Counter-Cultures in Germany and Central Europe*, ed. by Steve Giles & Maike Oergel, Bern/Oxford: Peter Lang, 2003, pp. 25–42) or in which *Klassik* is seen as an expression of the final self-awareness of *Aufklärung* (cf. Dieter Borchmeyer, "Wie aufgeklärt ist die Klassik?" *Jahrbuch der deutschen Schillergesellschaft* 36 (1992) 433–440).

[6] The strict adherence to the periodisation *Sturm und Drang*, *Klassik* and *Romantik* is being debated, and has long been undermined, but no attempt has so far been made to integrate all three "periods" into one context that is conditioned by historicity, to integrate them on the basis that the engagement with Enlightenment ideas takes place on the premise of this conditioning by historicity. Any such attempt could of course be seen as aiming at the "terminologische Unifizierung" of *Klassik* and *Romantik* that Dieter Borchmeyer has warned against. Borchmeyer wishes to safeguard Weimar classicism as a unique and distinct entity, although he is clearly aware of the impossibility of any true classicism at this point in European intellectual history and of the shared ground between *Klassik* and *Frühromantik* (cf. D. Borchmeyer, *Weimarer Klassik. Portait einer Epoche*,

ricity of values, including moral and philosophical categories. The central objective is the accommodation of once universal values within a framework of temporality. The aim can no longer be to make them time-resistant, but to integrate the notion of change into any new value system. The result is invariably a process of growth and decline within time that is driven by a self-prompting dynamic. This self-prompting dynamic tends to be based on an assumed internal dialectic. The dialectical process in time allows for the continuity of values through assimilation and absorption by creating an historical perspective based on succession, while leaving room for discontinuity and difference by relying on oppositional successions, which create the "new". Thus static dichotomous structures are replaced by triadic dialectical movements. The problem of historicity produced the dialectical process as a key intellectual methodology.

These problems and objectives are evident in philosophical, aesthetic and cultural discourses of the time, as well as in literary practice. The self-prompting dialectical process is the engine of cultural development in "Classical" cultural theory, such as that of Schiller, as well as in "Romantic" thinking, such as that of the Schlegel brothers. In the philosophical field it drives the reassessment and development of Kant's work by Fichte, Schelling and Hegel. The historical dynamic, which relies on the dialectical process, is derived, either directly or obliquely, from the debates about the differences between ancient and modern culture. Far from being an invention by Hegel, or even Fichte, the origin of the modern idea of the dialectical process lies in the *Querelle des Anciens et des Modernes*, which after its conclusion in France in the early 18th-century fell on fertile ground in late 18th-century Germany. Debate over the difference, and the relationship, between ancient and modern is the basis for the discussion from which a clear awareness of historicity develops, and this difference emerges as the pivot on which the concepts of modernity (and modern identity) hinge. Thus considerations derived from the *Querelle* form the basis for Herder's *Sturm-und-Drang* reassessment of Shakespeare, Schiller's "Classical" aesthetic and cultural theories as well as Friedrich Schlegel's Romantic literary theory. At one remove, they inform the Idealist theories of the development of knowledge and consciousness, which endeavour to give theory a historical framework, or put differently, to put

---

Studienausgabe, Weinheim: Beltz Atheäum, 1998, pp. 13–44). However, any unique distinctiveness must not blind the critic to the common intellectual ground inherited, shared and worked on by two generations of German thinkers between 1770 and 1815.

rationalism on a historical footing. The accommodation of historicity in areas of cultural identity and human cognition produced a definition that attached a special significance to the German contribution to modernity (which was still to be made, or completed, at any rate). This study argues that the national identity which results from this intellectual and cultural background is inherently *post-national* in that it conceives of itself as succeeding the other, already sharply defined national identities with an awareness of their (dialectical) individualities and contributions. This post-national understanding of nationality aims at a potential synthesis of (national) identities. This synthetic identity was to rely on *culture*, in its broadest sense. Culture was to supersede (power-)politics in the course of the historical process towards a state of human affairs when freedom would be genuinely integrated with reason and necessity (which was the Holy Grail of nearly all philosophical thought of the time). Such a historical-cultural project turns the German lack of national definition into potential human universality, turning particularity into a function of universality, and abandons the priority of a *particular* national identity. This process of identity creation is unthinkable without the contemporary discussions about the nature and purpose of modern art and modern thought, which equally pivot on the notion of historical relativity and how this relativity relates to (and shapes) cognitive reflexivity.

The awareness of historicity also had a crucial impact on the *literary* activities of the *Goethezeit*. The question of what a literature that adequately expressed (German) modernity would *be like* produced, from different quarters, the different answers of "Volkspoesie" (Herder), "ästhetische Erziehung" towards an integration of the sensual-physical and the rational-conceptual (Schiller) and "progressive Universalpoesie" (Friedrich Schlegel). All three of these concepts of literature not only share an unflinching awareness of historicity, but also the unwavering conviction that the altering effect of time can only be accommodated, never denied, and that this accommodation can only take place through an enhanced understanding of the relation between individual self and its surrounding world and past, which closely links them with the philosophical activities of the time. Schiller's and Schlegel's concepts already indicate a *process* in their names, all three suggest in their terminology a synthesis of potential opposites. As regards *literary practice*, the historically evolved difference between ancient and modern and the resulting modern (German) identity, based on dialectical historical developments, is presented with great complexity in two of the most innovative works of the period, Goethe's *Wilhelm Meisters Lehrjahre* and his *Faust I*.

The German concepts of modernity and national identity are conditioned by the above problems and objectives. The *theory of modernity* that emerges from this intellectual orbit defines modernity as the opposite *as well as* the successor to antiquity. It opposes as well as assimilates and transforms ancient values, making the connection between ancient and modern dialectical in nature. At the same time modernity is defined to have its own internal dialectic, which is responsible for its restless dynamic and which makes it so profoundly different from what is defined as antiquity. The internal dialectic of modernity is powered by two distinct but related dynamics. The modern mind is restless because, as the successor to antiquity, it retains a conscious or unconscious memory of ancient conditions, which are perceived as different and hence present an alternative manner of intellectual existence. Modernity places itself in a dialectical relationship to antiquity. This represents the historical dialectic of modernity as successor (to antiquity), which is a re-working of the original *Querelle* under historicist conditions. On the other hand, modernity is constructed as based on a hybrid origin, which fused two very different elements: a Northern (non-classical) antiquity and the abstract and spiritual religion of Christianity. This is the independent dialectic of modernity, derived from an original historical dichotomy, which rests on the polar opposition between worldliness and spirituality. (These opposites also interact under historicist conditions and form the basis from which modern identity evolves.) So as well as forming part of the universal dialectic of history, modernity has its own, clearly visible internal dialectic between its indigenous antiquity (which shares the key feature of naturalness with classical antiquity) and an intellectual progress towards abstraction. The double dialectic of modernity appears either as the difference between freedom-loving, war-like, honour-bound Northernness and Christian intellectualism or between remembered (ancient) wholeness and unity and experienced (modern) incompleteness and striving. These two can overlap. Unlike antiquity, modernity is openly and immediately dialectical; the modern mind is conscious of its dialectic and this knowledge is defined as a key characteristic of its identity.

One might have assumed that any exploration of the impact of the awareness of historicity in a German context would turn to the beginnings of German historicism, which was so integral to German self-definition in the 19th and early 20th centuries, rather than the (German) Quarrel of the Ancients and the Moderns and German Idealism. This, however, would be extremely limiting. The awareness of historicity does not immediately equal the Historicist outlook. An instance of this awareness does not constitute fully-fledged Historicism. The awareness of historicity first and foremost poses questions, to which the concept of historicism gives one particular answer. Historicism is one application of the results of this awareness. Herder's awareness of historicity, for example, remained curiously neutral, because he continued to grapple, throughout his life, with the questions his awareness posed. An analysis of the *Querelle* helps to shed light on the emergence of this awareness in a way that the classical treatments of the emergence of German Historicism do not. While the literature on historicism is voluminous, there is very little to be found on what caused this outlook to arise in the first place. Georg Iggers noted some time ago that the history of the emergence of the historicist outlook still needed to be written.[7] This emergence is frequently only presented as a new trend in intellectual history that simply *appeared*, and succeeded the doctrines of natural law by countermanding them. Friedrich Meinecke, who of course produced the trend-setting ("classical") investigation into the origins of historicism, set the scene when he contented himself with suggesting that new concepts, such as historicism, simply "spring up" in history, evincing the unpredictable individuality of historical developments.[8] Since Thomas Kuhn defined such historical sea-changes that alter the cultural and intellectual outlook as "paradigm shifts" in 1962,[9] the dialectical process has been closely linked to such historical changes. It gives the historical process method and structure. (It is worth noting, however, that Meinecke had already implied as much himself when he put his study of the emergence of historicism under the auspices of a dialectic of the doctrine of natural law.)[10] This investigation shows that historical dialectics

7 Georg Iggers, *The German Conception of History: The National Tradition of Historical Thought from Herder to the Present*, Middletown CT: Wesleyan University Press, 1968, p. 31, rev. edn. 1983.
8 Meinecke, *Die Entstehung des Historismus*, 355.
9 Thomas Kuhn, *The Structure of Scientific Revolutions*, Chicago/London: Chicago University Press, 1962.
10 Natural law engendered its own downfall and the rise of historicism. Pinpointing the "spingende Punkt" of the origin of historicism he points to Descartes as "allererstes Vorzeichen einer kommenden Revolution des Denkens" (*Historismus*, 13). Meineke noted further: "Aber nun geschieht es nicht selten in der Vorgeschichte von Revolutionen, daß eben die Wendungen, die sie in der Tiefe schon insgeheim vorbereiten, den alten bisherigen Zustand zunächst [...] gerade befestigen. Das erkennende Subjekt, das Descartes und unter seinen Nachwirkungen die französische Aufklärung vor Augen hatten, war ja noch nicht das individuelle Subjekt in der Mannigfaltigkeit seiner geschicht-

were recognised considerably earlier, that they were in fact part and parcel of the emerging awareness of historicity.

Idealism and Historicism tend to be defined as opposites. And they clearly tend towards different ends: historicism towards relativism and idealism towards a framework of universal ideals.[11] However, this investigation shows that German Idealism endeavours to integrate the two in order to avoid being trapped by the extremes of either tendency, since pure idealism was no longer intellectually viable and relativism considered undesirable. In this, German Idealism is clearly a historicised idealism. But it equally clearly remains an idealism since the ideal, or the complete closing of the gap between the higher (ideal) reality and the lower reality, which is the hallmark of the historicist approach to reality, is only achieved at the end of the historical process rather than during it. Accomplishing a closing of the gap has so far only been claimed to be the achievement of Historicism.[12] What links German Idealism and Ger-

---

lichen Erscheinungen, sondern das allgemeine Subjekt, der abstrakte Mensch des Naturrechts. […] So ging, soweit die französische Aufklärung herrschte, dem Historismus voran, nicht etwa eine Abschwächung, sondern gerade die Steigerung des naturrechtlichen Denkens, die freilich […] den verborgenen Keim des Verfalls in sich trug." (*Historismus*, 13–4)

[11] Meinecke, again among the first to comment on this difference, excluded from the historicist camp those late 18th-century thinkers who posited an ideal, albeit on the distant horizon of historical development, or who suggested that history followed a grand design. He was critical of Hegel, who in his view "das geschichtliche Leben zu gängeln versuchte durch einen erratbaren Heilsplan" (*Historismus*, 584), when history simply happens. Iggers, however, suggested three decades later, and quite correctly in my view, that the "common roots in the philosophy of German Idealism" were responsible for a relatively uniform tradition of historical conception in German historiography (*German Conception*, 3). I would add to this that the temporal framework formulated in German Idealist theory, which is responsible for engendering this uniform German historical conception, is conditioned by the late 18th-century awareness of historicity.

[12] Ulrich Muhlack claims: "Die immanente Geschichtsbetrachtung des Historismus leugnet diese Zweiteilung der Realität. Sie kennt nur eine einzige Realität: die historische, in der die beiden bisher als getrennte Realitäten als identisch erscheinen. Sie erhebt nicht die Welt der Ideen und der Werte über die niedere Welt, sondern vereinigt beide Welten. Sie holt die Welt der Ideen und der Werte in die niedere Welt herab, oder umgekehrt: sie hebt die niedere Welt zur Welt der Ideen und der Werte empor, aber nicht im Sinne einer Annäherung oder Anpassung, sondern in dem Sinne, daß sie immer schon Welt der Ideen und der Werte ist." (Muhlack, *Geschichtswissenschaft im Humanismus und in der Aufklärung: Die Vorgeschichte des Historismus*, Munich: Beck, 1992, p. 20) In Muhlack's study, Humanism and the Enlightenment come across as the ancients and the moderns respectively. Only historicism proper, which emerges at the end of the 18th century, manages to overcome the split between them by uniting the two into "im-

man historicism is, again, the dialectical process, which both intellectual approaches to existence use to accommodate and explain impermanence. Dialectics is a ubiquitous solution when it is necessary to cope with continuous historical change without giving in to absolute relativism. It embeds each individual phase within an overall process without detracting from its uniqueness, making this uniqueness its supreme value. It allows for the generation of the genuinely new, but reduces the haphazardness of coincidence in historical development by giving the process of generation a definite, but open-ended shape. The new has to be different to be new, and in the dialectical process the different becomes defined as productive. Due to its productive nature dialectics avoids any cause and effect-mechanism. The mechanistic process, derived from physics and championed by Enlightenment thought, had retained the laws of the constancy of matter and force and proved incapable of coping with the new "inconstancy". The dialectical process leaves open exactly the question to which Idealism and Historicism give different answers. It leaves room for either placing the achievement of perfection at the end, as Idealism does, or placing it as an ever-present option within the historical process, as the (classical) historicists, such as Meinecke and Ranke, did.

In the first three (theoretical) chapters of this investigation the authors treated have been chosen to present the new ideas regarding historicity and the problems and opportunities they created for definitions of cultural and intellectual values and identities, including different endeavours to set up historicised theories and identities. The investigation begins with Herder and moves from his groundbreaking *Sturm-und-Drang* ideas on historicity to answers to the crisis of values from Romantic (Friedrich and August Wilhelm Schlegel), Classical (Schiller) and Idealist (Fichte, Schelling, Hegel) sources in order to evaluate their similarities and differences. Against the background of a dialectical historical process it becomes possible to illuminate the ubiquitously important function of what might be summarised as the concept of the "original-natural", which is a crucial feature in all cultural and intellectual theories discussed here. It appears in different guises, such as the "ancient", the

---

manente Geschichtsbetrachung", whereby everything is historical and the gap between reality and meta-historical immutable ideals is closed. In this, Muhlack follows Meinecke and also Benedetto Croce, whose "absolute historicism" he refers to as an example of how to avoid the pitfalls of total relativism: the absolute in not abolished, but at last made concrete, appearing as real in reality (ibid.).

"naïve", popular traditions, even the beautiful and the unconscious, but in every context it represents a past intellectual and cultural condition that needed to be overcome and yet must not be completely lost, if further progress is to occur. Finally the works by Goethe, the protracted creative geneses of which spanned the entire period in question here, contain intricate and detailed reflections of the issues discussed here, blurring the boundaries between Classical and Romantic, Idealist and historicist, national and "reinmenschlich", the natural and the intellectual.

To be sure, the fields which this investigation brings together – the impact of the awareness of historicity, the intellectual diversity of the *Goethezeit*, German identity – have, individually, rich research histories. But the debates in all these areas have frequently been argued on an ideological basis, either for or against German "badness" (for want of a better word) by identifying certain areas or elements of German history or culture as suspect, i.e. responsible for National Socialism and the "German catastrophe" of the mid-20th century, and consequently disparaging or suppressing them. Examples of this can be found in the debates about the German *Sonderweg*, German *Klassik* or German Romanticism, and about the turn from left to right in German nationalism.[13]

The idea of the German political, historical and cultural *Sonderweg*, initially formulated as part of the definition of a modern German identity, then utilised to explain German political (and ethical) deviance, was sanitised in the 1960s by the Bielefeld School when under structuralist influences national historiography turned into social historiography, then denounced by neo-conservatives as an undesirable rod with which to beat the Germans. It was finally denied altogether by post-modernist approaches to history.[14] Yet the *Sonderweg*-idea has remained rather pervasive in intellectual and cultural analyses of things German.[15] Perhaps the reason lies in the fact that there *is* something characteristically different from "Western" approaches to modern historical and political development in German culture that is less deviant than the result of the particular timing of its emergence. However, in the context of this investigation any notion of "lateness" should not be read as meaning "belatedness", which Helmut Plessner so influentially defined as the reason

---

[13] Cf. Dieter Langewiesche, "Nation, Nationalismus, Nationalstaat: Forschungsstand und Forschungsperspektiven", *Neue Politische Literatur* 40 (1995) 190–236.

[14] Cf. Stefan Berger, "The German Tradition of Historiography, 1800–1995", *German History since 1800*, ed. by Mary Fulbrook, London: Arnold, 1997, pp. 477–92, esp. 487–91.

[15] Cf. Karin Friedrich, "Cultural and Intellectual Trends", ibid., pp. 88–105.

for the "German misery" over 50 years ago.[16] This contextualisation shows that the "lateness" merely indicates the German position as *succeeding* to ideas that have gone before, which enabled the German thinkers of the time to engage in productive and creative work with these ideas.

The definition of Classical and Romantic concepts and characteristics remains, notwithstanding its venerable history, an area of intense debate and disagreement. The heated academic discussions of 1988 and 1992 argued over the positioning of *Klassik* in relation to Enlightenment and Romanticism, and focused on the perceived anomaly of German classicism – and by extension German thought and culture – compared to other (Western) national literary histories.[17] *Klassik* and *Romantik* studies are of course the birthplace of *Germanistik* as a modern academic discipline, classical and romantic literary products were the first indigenous and contemporary objects of discussion in the emerging field of *Germanistik* and classical and romantic literary and cultural theories the first conceptual frameworks for these discussions. Originally *Germanistik* was also the discipline that defined a German identity. So it is not surprising that the interpretation of this period and its contents is still accorded a high priority.

An inter-connectedness, rather than polar opposition, between *Klassik* and *Romantik* has long been recognised (Mandelkow),[18] as has the historicity of *Klassik*[19] and the crucial nature of the awareness of historicity in Romantic thought (Manfred Frank)[20]. That the problematic of time was a constitutive element in both the Romantic and Classical mindset has perhaps never been in doubt. It was already clearly recognised by

---

[16] Cf. Helmut Plessner, *Die verspätete Nation. Über die Verführbarkeit des bürgerlichen Geistes*, (1st 1935/1959) Frankfurt aM: Suhrkamp, 1992.

[17] Cf. *Jahrbuch der deutschen Schillergesellschaft* 32 (1988) 347–374 and again 36 (1992) 409–454.

[18] Cf. Karl Robert Mandelkow, "Kunst- und Literaturtheorie der Klassik und Romantik", *Europäische Romantik I,* ed. by K.R. Mandelkow, Wiesbaden: Athenaion, 1982, pp. 49–82.

[19] Implicitly from the denunciation of the *Klassiklegende* in the early 1970s onwards (cf. Reinhold Grimm, Jost Hermand, eds., *Die Klassiklegende. 2nd Wisconsin Workshop*, Frankfurt aM: Athenäum, 1971) via Müller-Seidel's collected essays in *Die Geschichtlichkeit der deutschen Klassik. Literatur und Denkformen um 1800,* (Stuttgart: Metzler) in 1983 to Wilhelm Voßkamp's edited volume *Klassik im Vergleich* of 1993 (Stuttgart/Weimar: Metzler).

[20] M. Frank, *Das Problem "Zeit" in der deutschen Romantik: Zeitbewußtsein und Bewußtsein von Zeitlichkeit in der frühromantischen Philosophie und in Tiecks Dichtung*, (1st edn 1972) Paderborn: Schönigh, 1990.

Fritz Strich, the early 20th-century critic whose highly influential *Klassik und Romantik oder Vollendung und Unendlichkeit* (1922) did so much to establish the fundamental difference between these two "movements". Yet all of these studies focus on the intellectual efforts around 1800 as attempts to countermand the effects of temporality, to set up bulwarks against the passage of time and the force of history, against the anxieties and uncertainties sparked, not least, by the increasingly unsettling course of the French Revolution. They are not considered as efforts to consciously *accommodate* the new experience of historicity, to *adapt* theory and concepts of universality to the experience of change and impermanence. This study takes a different approach: deliberately side-stepping the puzzling dichotomy between the desire for normativity and the experience of historicity,[21] which has dominated scholarly discussion of Weimar classicism – and by extension of the entire *Goethezeit* – over the last twenty years, it shows how in the minds of Goethe's contemporaries historicity was in fact the only norm possible. This approach, inevitably, contributes to integrating the cultural activities in Germany around this time into a European context by suggesting that the general outlook of the *Goethezeit* was, broadly speaking and for want of a better term, "Romantic". But more importantly it argues against the notion of *profound* otherness (or belatedness) of modern German thought, *without* negating the evident particularity of these German cultural activities, which lies in their particular sensitivity to the dialectical structures of the modern intellectual situation.

The most profitable pointers towards the artistic and intellectual significance of temporality in this period come from Reinhart Herzog and Reinhart Koselleck's influential *Epochenschwelle und Epochenbewußtsein* which seeks to formulate a hermeneutic theory of historicity and periodisation.[22] Here Koselleck identified historicity as the underlying structural definition of (post-18th century) "Neuzeit", which for him constitutes modernity.[23] Yet nowhere have these fragments of the *Goethezeit* – the awareness of historicity, its accommodation (rather than denial) in contemporary literary, philosophical and cultural theory, and its in-

21 Cf. W. Voßkamp, "Normativität und Historizität europäischer Klassiken", *Klassik im Vergleich*, pp. 5–7. This collection serves as useful point of entry into this debate.
22 Reinhart Herzog/Reinhart Koselleck, eds., *Epochenschwelle und Epochenbewußtsein*, Munich: Fink, 1987, p. VIII.
23 Reinhart Koselleck, "Das 18. Jahrhundert als Beginn der Neuzeit", *Epochenschwelle und Epochenbewußtsein*, 269–82, esp. 278–81.

fluence on the shaping of modern German identity – been investigated in conjunction and systematically related to each other. This means that the way in which the problematic of historicity has shaped modern German literature, thought, and identity has been consistently underestimated, despite the fact that it is widely acknowledged as constitutive of modernity. Yet the preoccupation with changeability and impermanence, which turn former constants into a process, which in turn posits a long-lost beginning and projects a distant consummation, goes a long way to explain what became crucial features of German identity, such as projected universality and projected consummateness. Its preoccupation with the integration of particulars suggests that there is an awareness right at the point of conception that German national identity is the result of a process of *construction*, which makes it a case of particular interest for research on nationalism and the definition of national identity, which over the last twenty years has replaced the idea of the natural essence of national identity with that of the constructed nature of national identities.[24] This investigation thus feeds into the ongoing discussion of the genesis and maintenance of national identities in general while at the same time illuminating the particularities of German identity in particular.[25]

Note on the Translations: English translations of the primary sources are provided in the footnotes. Where no published translation is cited, the translations are my own.

---

[24] Cf. Ernest Gellner, *Nations and Nationalism*, Oxford: Blackwell, 1983; Eric Hobsbawm, Terence Ranger, eds., *The Invention of Tradition*, Cambridge: Cambridge University Press, 1983 and Benedict Anderson, *Imagined Communities: Reflections on the Origin and Spread of Nationalism*, London: Verso, 1983.

[25] Cf. for a summary Hans-Ulrich Wehler, *Nationalismus. Geschichte, Formen, Folgen*, Munich: Beck, 2001, especially pp. 7–13.

Chapter 1

Historicity and the Definition of Modern Culture: The German *Querelle des Anciens et des Modernes* and the New Concepts of Literature

The *Querelle des Anciens et des Modernes* will serve as a starting-point, because it marks the beginning of the developments in historical understanding, literary aesthetics and identity construction under discussion here. In the course of the 18th century the concepts of the ancient and the modern had come to represent a general historical contrast: between nature, beauty and cultural origin on the one hand and reason, reflexivity, analysis and progress on the other. In the late 18th-century debates surrounding the merits and demerits of ancient and modern culture one can trace the developing historical understanding from a limited awareness of the historicity of culture and science to the full recognition of the historical nature of art and knowledge. This chapter defines the position modern art is assigned in human history in these debates and discusses the new concepts of literature that emerge in the orbit of this definition between 1770 and 1800. The following two chapters investigate how cognition was being related to the historical process and how cultural and intellectual progression proved seminal for defining a modern German identity, which emerges out of the definition of (European) modernity.

The battle-positions of the original French *Querelle* can be summarised as the state of achieved perfection versus the process of achieving perfectibility. On the one side the ancients represented an unsurpassable ideal that one could only hope to emulate, which is a position that allows for historical development only in the form of deterioration. On the other side the argument runs that the moderns have attained superiority over their ancient forebears through the process of augmenting knowledge, a position that conceives of historical development as improvement by increase. The quarrel was settled in a preliminary way when the opponents agreed on a historicising solution that proclaimed the existence of a *beau relatif* appertaining to each culture. Here lies indeed the origin of modern historicism.[1] But this Enlightenment historicism is limited, because its *beau relatif* does not impinge on the existence of a *beau universel*, a universally valid ideal. Such an ideal presupposes the existence of universally valid standards for assessing culture and constancy in the nature of human understanding. These two presuppositions negate a thoroughly historicist approach.[2] The following traces the gradual reduction of universal ideals, such as the *beau universel*.

Initially it appears as if limiting cultural and aesthetic relativity by the existence of a universal ideal was necessary to keep the *anciens* on board in this settlement, if it was not to be a victory of the *modernes*, because the notion of perfectibility propagated by the *modernes* seemed to entail the relativity of values *eo ipso*. But on closer inspection it becomes evident that the retention of the *beau universel*, the constancy of values, was integral to the position of the early eighteenth-century *modernes*, too. Their modern superiority is based on exactly such a constancy of values. It makes possible the measuring of progress. Although dependent on change, perfectibility relies on the notion of sameness. Only if things are broadly the same can uniform standards of assessment be sensibly applied and improvements be expected to have similar success rates. If things are profoundly different, they can neither be measured by the

---

[1] As Hans Robert Jauss suggested in his *Literaturgeschichte als Provokation*, Frankfurt aM: Suhrkamp, 1970, pp. 29–33.

[2] The debate about the historical and historicist acumen of the Enlightenment continues. Thirty years ago Peter Hanns Reill argued that the Enlightenment understanding of history was already historicist (cf. *The German Enlightenment and the Rise of Historicism*, Berkeley/L.A./London: University of California Press, 1975), while more recently Ulrich Muhlack has defended the deep division in historical understanding between the Enlightenment and Historicism as defined by Friedrich Meinecke in his groundbreaking *Die Entstehung des Historismus* (1936) (cf. *Geschichtswissenschaft im Humanismus und in der Aufklärung. Die Vorgeschichte des Historismus*, Munich: Beck, 1991). Even more recently a consensus has been suggested which locates the gradual emergence of new historistically minded paradigms broadly in the second half of the 18th century and considers this counter-discourse as part of the Enlightenment's own self-analysis (cf. P.H. Reill, "Herder's Historical Practice and the Discourse of Late Enlightenment Science", *Johann Gottfried Herder: Academic Disciplines and the Pursuit of Knowledge*, ed. by W. Koepke, Columbia SC: Camden House, 1996, pp. 13–21). From this perspective the new discourses form part of the internal dialectic of the Enlightenment, which has occupied thinkers from Kant to Adorno and Horkheimer and which in recent interpretations embraces most counter-Enlightenment movements towards the end of the 18th century.

same standards, (nor be expected to respond to the same measures of improvement). It follows that Enlightenment historicism achieves only a partial historicising, because it does not part with irreducible absolutes. Natural law, as ascertained by reason, is such a supreme absolute: it is constant in nature and in human understanding, and discovering its workings in all provinces of knowledge is the task of the enlightened mind. This gradual comprehending of the truth and previously unknown aspects of reality marks the process of progress. It is the discovery of what has been assumed to already exist. Modern superiority amounts to an *increase* in knowledge. Progress is strictly quantitative; hence it can be accurately measured. The increase in perfection is a mechanical process.

Enlightenment historicism historicises culture and science quantitatively, i.e. in relation to the complexity of its cultural and scientific products and accompanying understanding. Qualitative historicising is left to post-Enlightenment thought. Its origin lies in the concept of organic growth, which comes to the fore during the *Sturm und Drang*-movement, in Herder's work. The notion of organic development replaces that of the mechanistic processes of Enlightenment understanding. Frederic Beiser has shown how Herder's third way of the organic principle negotiated between the supernaturalism of a divine origin and the reductionist mechanisms of materialism to prepare a way ahead that allowed natural law, and reason, to become adaptable to historical processes.[3] Without abandoning the naturalistic and rational approach, Herder derived ideas from the science of biology, which was advancing at the time, to replace those of physics, which had dominated earlier Enlightenment thinking. In contrast to the mechanistic laws of physics based on cause and effect and on the constancy of matter and force, the investigation of organic processes revealed the latter to be self-prompting, to be independently productive, which opens the door to the possibility of qualitative difference, to transformation and discontinuity, without supernatural intervention.

Herder conceived of the historical process in analogy to natural processes. But the nature he referred to was not the nature of the mechanical processes of the eternally constant natural (physical) law, but a generative complex that relied on *growth* from one stage to the next. The impermanence rather than the constancy of parameters lies thus at the

---

[3] Beiser, *The Fate of Reason: German Philosophy from Kant to Fichte*, Cambridge MA: Harvard University Press, 1987, pp. 127 ff.

heart of natural as well as historical processes. Change becomes defined as driven by internal productivity rather than external factors: Change brings about the genuinely new, rather than adjusts the sum of knowledge in the wake of discovering what already exists, albeit previously unknown.

Inspired by the impetus stemming from Rousseau to seek salvation in pre-civilised humanity, Herder had familiarised himself with the past, particularly with previously ridiculed eras and cultural products, and (famously) sought empathy with them. Due to this empathy he developed his view that all phases of human history have their intrinsic value, thus laying the basis for another crucial tenet of historicist thought: all values are independently conditioned by their historical situation. Herder does not abandon the idea of meaningful progress, – he does not even fully abandon the idea of the constancy of human nature[4] – but he modifies the appreciation of how succeeding phases of human history are connected. If these connections are based on self-prompting organic growth rather than mechanistic clockwork, an element of unpredictability and mutability results that was inconceivable before. This has far-reaching consequences for the adherence to (immutable) absolutes. Classical antiquity can no longer be an absolute ideal, only a relational one, a point Herder will make. Reason may not be constant and universal at all, but subject to historical conditions that alter not just its appearance, but also its nature, in different phases. If this is the case, it cannot be the first principle that governs everything, world and mind, as it is subject to change. Instead change itself becomes the first principle.

Against this background the discussion about the relation between antiquity and modernity is taken up in Germany. This discussion entails a consideration of the problem of how an ideal is related to, and can be integrated into, the historical process. The German *Querelle* is, unlike its French predecessor, characterised by the effort to *relate*, rather than *oppose*, the concepts of ancient and modern to each other. Considering Herder's, Schiller's and Friedrich Schlegel's essays on this topic in conjunction makes it possible to trace the emergence of the (well-known) cultural theory of modernity based on accelerating impermanence *across*

---

[4] "Zu allen Zeiten war der Mensch derselbe, nur äußerte er sich jedesmal nach der Verfassung, in der er lebte." Herder, *Briefe zur Beförderung der Humanität*, Achte Sammlung, *Sämmtliche Werke*, vol. 18, ed. by Bernhard Suphan, Berlin: Weidmannsche Buchhandlung, 1883, pp. 67–140, 139. "Human nature has been the same at all times, but every time it expressed itself according to the constitution in which it existed."

the "schools" of *Sturm und Drang, Klassik* and *Frühromantik*. This approach shows very clearly that all three thinkers display a crucial similarity: all three define modernity in close relation to a notion of the ancient-natural.

The Structural Ideal of Original Culture: Herder's "Shakespear" as a Modern Ancient

Herder takes up the discussion about the relation between ancient and modern literature in his Shakespeare-essay, published in the programmatic manifesto of *Sturm-und-Drang* thought *Von deutscher Art und Kunst* in 1773. The genesis of the piece goes back to 1771 and thus lies at the very beginning of his Storm and Stress-phase.[5] In his opening paragraph, Herder asserts that all recent treatments of Shakespeare, whether in praise or condemnation, are flawed, because they all operate with inappropriate criteria.

> Die kühnsten Feinde Shakespears haben ihn […] beschuldigt und verspottet, daß er, wenn auch ein grosser Dichter, doch kein guter Schauspieldichter, und wenn auch dies, doch wahrlich kein so klassischer Trauerspieler sey, als Sophokles, Euripides, Corneille und Voltaire […]. Und die kühnsten Freunde Shakespears haben sich meistens nur begnüget, ihn hierüber zu entschuldigen, zu retten: seine Schönheiten nur immer mit Anstoß gegen die Regeln zu wägen, zu kompensiren.[6]

Both approaches rest on the same prejudice: a belief in the constancy of artistic ideals, either criticising or excusing Shakespeare for not abiding by the rules. The novelty of his own approach, which, Herder claims, will reveal the real Shakespeare, lies in the fact that he does not assume any such (universal) rules, but intends to assess the dramatist indepen-

---

5 Cf. Nachwort by Hans Dietrich Irmscher in the Reclam-edition of *Von deutscher Art und Kunst*, (Herder, Goethe, Frisi, Möser, *Von deutscher Art und Kunst. Einige fliegende Blätter*, Stuttgart: Reclam, 1968, 2nd edn 1988, repr. 1995), p. 149.

6 Herder, "Shakespear", *Sämmtliche Werke*, vol. 5, ed. by Bernhard Suphan, Berlin: Weidmannsche Buchhandlung, 1897, pp. 208–231, 208. Forthwith "Shakespear". "Shakespeare's fiercest enemies have […] mocked him and accused him, even if he is a great poet, of being no great dramatist, and even if he is this, of being no classical tragic dramatist, like Sophocles, Euripides, Corneille and Voltaire […]. And Shakespeare's most committed friends have mostly been content to excuse him, to rescue him: to consider his achievements only in relation to his offences against the rules, to compensate."

dently according to his time, i.e. in historicist fashion, by examining his cultural conditions "Wie ist der Boden? [...] Was ist in ihn gesäet? was sollte er tragen können?" ("Shakespear", 217).[7] As Shakespeare and Sophocles originate from profoundly different cultures, they cannot be expected to have produced the same drama. This cultural divide is caused by the intervention of history.

> In Griechenland entstand das Drama, wie es in Norden nicht entstehen konnte. [...] In Norden ists also nicht und darf nicht seyn, was es in Griechenland gewesen. Also Sophokles Drama und Shakespears Drama sind zwei Dinge, die in gewissem Betracht kaum den Namen gemeinsam haben. [...] Wie sich Alles in der Welt ändert: so mußte sich auch die Natur ändern, die eigentlich das Griechische Drama schuf. ("Shakespear", 209/210, 213)[8]

At first sight this approach does not go much beyond the insights achieved at the end of the French *Querelle*: art works are conditioned by the culture which produces them and hence different. At second glance, however, it emerges that Herder extends the limited historicist approach he inherited to effectively reduce the universal ideal (the *beau universel*) to the level of a structural ideal: he defines Shakespeare as what might be called a *modern ancient*. No longer is ancient perfection irreconcilably pitted against modern perfectibility, or the ancient ideal set against modern superiority. Now an ancient ideal that is truly representative of its culture is compared with an original modern ideal that is its structural equivalent. Both occupy the same position in the development of their respective cultures and fulfil the same function, but are distinct regarding content. If Sophocles is the epitome of true Greek art in its state of nature, then Shakespeare is just that for modern drama. "Eben da ist also Shakespear Sophokles Bruder, wo er ihm dem Anschein nach so unähnlich ist, um im Innern, ganz wie er zu seyn. Da alle Täuschung durch das Urkundliche, das Wahre, das Schöpferische der Geschichte erreicht wird." ("Shakespear", 225)[9] In this definition of equivalence lies the

---

[7] "How is the soil? [...] What has been sown into this soil? What should it be able to yield?"

[8] "In Greece a dramatic art developed that could never develop in the North. [...] In the North dramatic art is not, and must not be, what it was in Greece. Thus the plays of Sophocles and the plays of Shakespeare are so different that in certain respects they can hardly be compared. [...] Everything in the world changes: thus also the world which was responsible for creating Greek drama changed."

[9] "Exactly where Shakespeare, according to appearances, is so very different from Sophocles lies the basis for their brotherly similarity: in essence they are alike. Because all (artistic) illusion is achieved through the original, the true and the creative in history."

basis for the curious double vision of the late 18th-century *Querelle* in Germany that has (famously) struck readers of Schiller's *Naïve und Sentimentalische Dichtung*, where the naïve appears as the sentimental.[10] For the first time (structural) features of ancient culture are traced in modern culture, which provides the basis for defining the heterogeneity of modernity, which Schiller and Schlegel will make their task.

Herder defines perfection in art as the state when the artwork perfectly expresses and represents the culture it originates from, when culture is first crystallised into art, creating identity, and eventually tradition. So it is not a case of perfection, or perfectibility, but of perfect particularity, which occurs at specific points in cultural history. Herder locates this point early on in cultural development. Such "ideals" retain their normative value only for the duration of that cultural period, *but* their structural value as a representative ideal of that culture for all of human history (which is why there is still a point in studying Sophocles). Art, for Herder, only makes sense in a particular and concrete context. The only constancy he allows for in history is the general structure of cultural development, which he conceives of as analogous to nature, e.g. analogous to the growing of a plant or the maturing of a living creature.

The search for and definition of such a representative ideal of modern art lies at the heart of *Sturm-und-Drang* intentions. It was to be the foundation on which a new relevant contemporary art and culture could be based. It had to derive from the first fully representative period of modern culture close to its origin, in the terminology used above, it had to be an ideal drawn from the "ancient" period of modernity, when modern culture shared the structural features of originality with the earlier cultural ideal: ancient culture. In their rebellion against what they considered the stuffy regime of universalist (i.e. meaningless) and over-civilised (i.e. lifeless) dogma, the *Stürmer und Dränger* sought to identify a relevant original art and culture that could point the way out of what they considered the artificial greenhouse of refined mid-18th-century taste. In suggesting parallels between an original phase in Greek culture, which for them stood at the beginning of the history of cultural identities and de-

---

[10] Cf. Peter Szondi, "Das Naïve ist das Sentimentalische: Zur Begriffsdialektik in Schillers Abhandlung" *Euphorion* 66 (1972) 174–206. The problem is still being discussed: M.A. Hewitt has recently spoken in this context of an unstable conceptual construction, in which the two concepts have complete reversibility. Cf. "(Re)zoning the Naïve: Schiller's construction of Auto-Historiography" *European Romantic Review* 14 (2003) 197–202.

fines this identity *in nuce*, and a structural counterpart at the beginning of modern history, Herder builds on "Pre-Romantic" work done in France and England. Such structural equivalence had already been cautiously suggested for the Greek heroic period and the European medieval phase by de la Curne de St. Palaye and Richard Hurd respectively.[11]

To illustrate his points, Herder proceeds to sketch three different moments in European cultural history: the ancient one (the Greece of Sophocles) and two modern ones, one good (the drama of Elizabethan England) and one bad (the classicism of France). Sophocles and Shakespeare are different but equally admirable because both of them produced drama that was relevant to their time and audience, "natural" in Herder's terminology, because it had grown from and represented their respective cultures. Relevant drama, which "achieves its dramatic purpose for [a] people" (75), i.e. moves the spectator, is informed by a people's "history, *Zeitgeist*, customs, opinions, language, national prejudices, traditions and pastimes" (ibid.).[12] French classical drama is meaningless because, according to Herder, it imitates classical rules that have no relevance in the modern world and do not achieve any dramatic purpose.

> Alles was Puppe des Griechischen Theaters ist, kann ohne Zweifel kaum vollkommner gedacht und gemacht werden, als es in Frankreich geworden. [...] Bei alle dem ists aber doch ein drückendes, unwiderstrebliches Gefühl "das ist keine Griechische Tragödie! von Zweck, Würkung, Art, Wesen kein Griechisches Drama!" [...] Warum? weil im Innern nichts von ihm Dasselbe mit Jenem ist, nicht Handlung, Sitten, Sprache, Zweck, nichts – und was hülfe also alles Äussere so genau erhaltene Einerlei? [...] Es sind Gemälde der Empfindung von dritter fremder Hand. ("Shakespear", 213–215)[13]

In what do the specific particularities of ancient and modern art consist? Herder defines Sophocles' cultural background as conditioned by sim-

---

[11] Cf. De la Curne de St. Palaye, *Memoirs sur l'ancienne Chevalrie considérée comme un établissement politique et militaire* (1759) and Richard Hurd, *Letters on Chivalry and Romance* (1762).

[12] "bei [einem] Volk Dramatischen Zweck erreicht"; "Geschichte, nach Zeitgeist, Sitten, Meinungen, Sprache, Nationalvorurtheilen, Traditionen und Liebhabereien".

[13] "The exterior of Greek theatre can without a doubt hardly be more perfectly be rethought and re-created as it has been in France. [...] And yet there remains an oppressive, irresistible feeling that this is no Greek tragedy, no Greek drama according to its original purpose, effect, nature and essence! [...] Why? Because in essence the two are profoundly different, in terms of plot, customs, language, purpose – so the carefully reconstructed exterior is of no use. [...] They are representations of foreign and third-hand emotions."

plicity and unity, whereas Shakespeare's is characterised by multiplicity and the experience of fast-moving time. This difference lays the basis for all subsequent definitions of modernity in contrast to antiquity. The experience of simplicity and unity is reflected in the three dramatic unities and the straightforward and linear structure of the plot in Greek drama.

> Tretet in die Kindheit der damaligen Zeit zurück: Simplicität der Fabel lag würklich so sehr in dem, was Handlung der Vorzeit, der Republik, des Vaterlandes, der Religion, was Heldenhandlung hieß, daß der Dichter eher Mühe hatte, in dieser einfältigen Grösse Theile zu endecken, Anfang, Mittel und Ende Dramatisch hineinzubringen. [...] Einheit der Fabel – war Einheit der Handlung, die vor ihnen lag; die nach ihren Zeit- Vaterlands- Religions- Sittenumständen, nicht anders als solch ein Eins seyn konnte. Einheit des Orts – war Einheit des Orts; denn die Eine, kurze feierliche Handlung ging nur an Einem Ort, im Tempel, Pallast, gleichsam auf einem Markt des Vaterlandes vor. ("Shakespear", 210–211)[14]

While the Greek rules of unity are entirely natural for Greek drama, (*that* key feature of good art in *Sturm-und-Drang* thought), because they have evolved out of the Greek cultural situation: "Das Künstliche ihrer Regeln war – keine Kunst! war Natur!" (68),[15] they are, according to Herder, nonsense for Shakespeare. Since multiplicity and the experience of time conditioned his cultural background, Shakespeare dramatised complex events which take place against the backdrop of the experience of "history". This makes the unity of time and place impossible.

> [Shakespeare] fand keinen so einfachen Volks- und Vaterlandscharakter, sondern ein Vielfaches von Ständen, Lebensarten, Gesinnungen, Völkern und Spracharten [...]. Er fand keinen so einfachen Geist der Geschichte, der Fabel, der Handlung. [...] Wenn bei diesem das Eine einer Handlung herrscht: so arbeitet Jener auf das Ganze eines Eräugnisses, einer Begebenheit. ("Shakespear", 218/219) [...] Sophokles blieb der Natur treu, da er Eine Handlung Eines Ortes und Einer Zeit bearbeitete: Shakespear konnt ihr allein treu blei-

---

[14] "Step back into the childhood of that long-gone period: the simplicity of the plot was so much part of the way things were done in that early period, in the republic, the fatherland, the religion, the activities of the heroes that the poet had difficulty to discover distinct parts in this uniform greatness, to distinguish dramatically between a beginning, a middle and an end. [...] The unity of the plot was the unity of the actions which lay before them and which could according to the historical conditions of their time, their fatherland, their religion and their morals be no other than uniform. The unity of place was the unity of place because the one short solemn activity only occurred in one place, the temple, the palace, the marketplace of their homeland."
[15] "The artificial in their rules was – no art, it was nature!"

ben, wenn er seine Weltbegebenheit und Menschenschicksal durch alle die Örter und Zeiten wälzte, wo sie […] geschehen. (ibid., 226)[16]

Shakespeare's genius makes it possible to create wholeness out of this chaos. "Fand Shakespear den Göttergriff eine ganze Welt der Disparatesten Auftritte zu Einer Begebenheit zu erfassen." ("Shakespear", 222)[17] And this, for Herder, identifies Shakespeare's drama as representing history. "Kein Stück wäre doch Griechische *Tragedy*, […]. Jedes Stück ist *History* im weitesten Verstande." (230)[18] Historical drama is seen as the modern equivalent to ancient Greek tragedy. Sophocles and Shakespeare may occupy the same position structurally in their respective cultural histories, but Shakespeare belongs not just to a different, but to a *later* culture, due to the progress of time, which results in the greater complexity of his world. History itself had become more evident and conditioned, and continues to condition, the experience of existence. The artistic management of this complex condition and the conscious experience of history require the specific Shakespearean genius. That Herder identifies the experience of the historical existence (and its intellectual management), which he finds in Shakespeare, as the modern condition becomes obvious when the description of Shakespeare's "divine grasp" of the conditions of modern culture resurfaces in his *Auch eine Philosophie*, published a year later, as the ideal of history-writing.

Wenn's mir gelänge, die disparatsten Szenen zu binden, ohne sie zu verwirren – zu zeigen, wie sie sich auf einander beziehen, aus einander erwachsen, sich ineinander verlieren, alle im Einzelnen nur Momente, durch den Fortgang allein Mitteln zu Zwecken – welch ein Anblick! welch edle Anwendung der menschlichen Geschichte! welche Aufmunterung zu hoffen, zu handeln, zu glauben, selbst wo man nichts, oder nicht alles sieht![19]

---

[16] "[Shakespeare] found no such uniform national character, but instead a multiplicity of social classes, ways of life, attitudes, nations and languages […]. He found no such simple spirit of history, of plot, of actions. […] When in Sophocles the single aspect of an action dominates, Shakespeare works towards the wholeness of an event, or occurrence. […] Sophocles stayed true to his nature when he worked on one action in one place at one time: Shakespeare could only stay true to his by rolling his international event and the fate of man through all the places and times in which they had occurred."

[17] "Shakespeare discovered the divine move to compress an entire world of the most disparate scenes into one occurrence."

[18] "No play would be a Greek tragedy. […] Each play is History in the broadest sense."

[19] *Auch eine Philosophie der Geschichte zur Bildung der Menschheit, Sämmtliche Werke*, vol. 5, ed. by Bernhard Suphan, 475–594, 513. "If I could succeed in connecting the most disparate scenes without confusing them – to show how they relate to each other, develop from each other, fade into each other. How they are individually only moments, through

Herder does not actually speak of Shakespeare as "modern" as such. No doubt, because he did not wish to identify him with the features of modernity as defined by the *Querelle*, i.e. cultural advancement over the ancients. This would have run counter to his aim of establishing him as a natural original genius who represents his culture, the notions on which Herder had based Shakespeare's kinship with Sophocles. Instead of temporal positioning he prefers a spatial one: Shakespeare is a "Northern" (Nordic) writer, "Dichter der Nordischen Menschheit" ("Shakespear", 220).[20] That this is nevertheless a clear identification as post-classical, as modern, is evident, again, from *Auch eine Philosophie*, where Herder has the "North" succeed antiquity in history (514). Herder identifies Shakespeare's culture as part of his own: "Man laße mich als Ausleger [...] fortfahren: denn ich bin Shakespear näher als dem Griechen". ("Shakespear", 219)[21]

In the differentiation of simplicity and multiplicity Herder does adhere to some aspects of the notion of advancement, which the moderns have achieved over the Greeks, as defined by the French *Querelle*. This may be thought to clash with his notion of the independent individual value of each phase of human development. Herder's thinking remains indebted to the Enlightenment notion of progress, but he imagines this progress as an organic process. While holding on to the possibility of linear development, within one culture and to some extend also in the history of human cultures as a whole, he introduces the idea of unqualified independent self-worth. A succession of individual ideals, although independent, are linked in a chain of reciprocal relations. Moreover, "more complicated" does for Herder not at all mean closer to perfection. He was too dissatisfied with the current state of culture to subscribe to a simple notion of progressive perfectibility, and too influenced by Rousseau not to believe that progress may go wrong, and lead to debilitation. While he believed that humanity was capable of progress, progress was not inevitable. In fact, there is little sense of perfectibility in his contemporaneous work on the nature of history. In keeping with his view that all phases of human history are equal in value and existing for their own end, the difference between simplicity and multiplicity seems to be

---

the progression of time only means to an end – what a spectacle! What noble use of human history! What an encouragement to hope, to act, to believe, even there where one does not see anything, or not everything!"

[20] "poet of the northern race of humanity".

[21] "May I continue as exegete: for I am closer to Shakespeare than I am to the Greek (poet)."

caused by a straightforward "more" of history. This produces a different quality of existence, but no feeling of superiority. In *Auch eine Philosophie* he concluded:

> Niemand ist in seinem Alter allein, er bauet auf das vorige, dies wird nichts als Grundlage der Zukunft, will nichts als solche seyn. [...] Der Ägypter konnte nicht ohne den Orientaler seyn, der Grieche bauete auf jene, der Römer hob sich auf den Rücken der ganzen Welt – wahrhaftig Fortgang, fortgehende Entwicklung, wenn auch kein einzelnes dabei gewönne! (512–513)[22]

At this stage, Herder shrinks from attempting to define the final purpose of history. *Auch eine Philosophie* is full of awed references to the magnitude of the historical process, of which the human mind is too small a part to presume to uncover its meaning. History, like nature, is a revelations of the divine, ordered and purposeful but nevertheless forever ahead of human understanding, simply because of its vast scope. This, however, should not deter the human being from understanding as much as possible. Human history is a continuing process that, from the human perspective, simply goes on. But by conceiving of history as structurally similar cycles of civilisations, which build on each other, Herder does introduce an ordering element into the historical process and foreshadows a key aspect of the Idealist conception of history: that of relational progression. Herder's interpretation of cultural history establishes three key notions that lay the basis for the discussions of antiquity and modernity to come: *difference*, yet *analogy* between the two, as well as *relational historical progression* from one to the other. Sophocles and Shakespeare represent the same stages in their respective cultures, but the modern poet *succeeds* the ancient one, Shakespeare has to deal with a "more" of history.

In Herder's insistence on *structural* ideals the difference between his historicism and that of the early Enlightenment becomes visible: while the latter acknowledged the influence of different cultural and historical situations on culture and understanding, it tended to view the past as closed, in line with its notion of ever-advancing progress, in which a mechanistic and quantitative passing on of knowledge occurred. For Herder, the past remains a vital ingredient of the present, to which it is

---

22 "No era stands alone, each builds on what went before, each becomes the foundation of the future, does not intend to be anything else. [...] The Egyptian could not exist without the Oriental, the Greek built on both, the Roman lifted himself onto the top of the entire world – indeed progression, continuing development, even if no single element gains (any lasting advantage) in the process."

linked through an understood and experienced tradition. This tradition in turn creates cultural identity, a particularity of culture without which the human being cannot understand (anything). The Enlightenment view of history focuses on what has been overcome, while Herder's view focuses on what has survived (and still has a cultural function to fulfil).

So the imitation of ancient Greek drama in modern Europe is pointless on two counts: it assumes a static ideal, when human culture is dynamic, has moved on, and it comes from the wrong past, the past of a culture too different from modern France and Germany, which is only in a diluted and fragmentary fashion responsible for the younger nations' cultural development. According to Herder, the French and the Germans, unlike the English, do not properly recognise their cultural tradition and identity, nor do they truly understand cultural history as such. Herder's criticism of what he presents as French practices in this essay is two-pronged: on the one hand he attacks French classicism, which continued to influence the German literary scene, and on the other hand he attacks the arrogance of the French Enlightenment, which entertained a blinkered belief in its own superiority.[23] He considers its exclusive orientation towards the future dangerous because it disconnects human thought from its own past and traditions, which to Herder are the lifeblood of human conception and understanding. The result is lifeless, meaningless abstraction, which does not speak to the senses. In terms of the *Querelle* Herder necessarily ends up rejecting both sides, because both take ahistorical approaches. The *anciens* incur his wrath because of their ossifying adherence to a static formula, the *modernes* because of their misplaced sense of superiority. Instead Herder attempts a full synthesis of the original counter-points of the French *Querelle*. He accepts the existence of admirable ideals as well as the notion of progress and tries to connect the two in a meaningful manner by defining an ideal that is not cast in stone, either in an inaccessible past nor in a perfect future, but that is, in concrete terms, relevant to his own cultural present and that can at the same time, in abstract terms, remain relevant throughout the entire history of human cultural development because it

---

[23] Herder's invective against French drama is clearly not scholarly objective. Driven to polemics by what he considered an overpowering French influence and a slavish adherence to it by much of the German audience, he chooses to ignore much of the contemporary French criticism concerning the inappropriateness of continuing classicism. Cf. Barbara Belhalfaoui, "Johann Gottfried Herder: Shakespeare – ein Vergleich der alten und neuen Tragödie" *DVjs* 61 (1987) 89–124, 91/2.

is a structural ideal, a type. As such he is an *ancien* who has learnt (or taught himself) the lesson of historicism.

Hans Robert Jauss criticised Herder for his unwillingness to set modernity into a clear – dialectical – relationship to antiquity, which would make visible not just a process, but the progress of the whole of history towards an end. Jauss holds Herder's radical historicist views, each period has absolute value for and in itself, responsible for his lack of overarching categories, which are necessary to develop a clearly defined relation between the two. Herder does indeed refrain from providing a mechanism, other than organic growth, according to which one phase arises out of its predecessor and according to which future developments will occur. But curiously, Jauss considers this as evidence for Herder's inability to progress beyond the position of the early 18th-century *Querelle*, when it was Herder's historicist endeavour to limit nearly *all* norms that constitutes his intellectual advance beyond the *Querelle*. The *new* theoretical, yet historicist thinking on these matters, which emerges in the 1790s with Schiller and Friedrich Schlegel, with whom Jauss compares Herder, was only possible *after* Herder's modifying of naturalistic and classicist norms.[24] Herder's differentiation between Sophocles and Shakespeare in terms of unity and multiplicity anticipates the distinctions that will dominate in what has come to be considered as the German *Querelle* proper, i.e. the reflections of Schiller and Schlegel on this matter twenty years later. Here the modern condition becomes defined as the experience of striving in time, which is contrasted with a (supposed) achieved fulfilment on the part of the ancients. In his Shakespeare-essay Herder was primarily interested in analogous parallelism, which describes a difference of equals, not a complementary contrast. This makes it possible for him to view ancient antiquity and ancient modernity as equivalent originals on level terms. This equality lays the crucial basis for Schiller's subsequent positive definition of modernity.[25]

---

[24] Cf. Jauss, *Literatur als Provokation*, 72–75.

[25] Jauss (*Provokation*, p. 81) and Heinz-Dieter Weber (in *Friedrich Schlegels Transzendentalpoesie*, Munich: Fink, 1973, p. 164) insist that Schiller was the first to define modernity positively. But in my view Schiller and Herder merely have different viewpoints: Herder is origin-oriented, Schiller future-oriented in their respective positive evaluations.

From Structural Equivalence to Dialectical Integration: The Ancient and Modern in Schiller's *Naïve und Sentimentalische Dichtung* and Friedrich Schlegel's *Studium der Griechischen Poesie*

To fully appreciate the relations between the ideas of these three writers it is necessary to look at the texts in some detail. Like Herder, both Schiller and Schlegel search for a way of establishing a meaningful relation between ancient and modern culture. When Schiller and Schlegel take up the discussion about the respective definitions and merits of ancient and modern culture in the mid-1790s, the historicist approach is integral to their argument. Schiller's essay *Über Naive und Sentimentalische Dichtung* (1795/96) is based on the idea that art is profoundly different in different historical periods because it is deeply affected by changing intellectual conditions. Ancient and modern poetry, and their conditions, can only be compared on a structural level. Universal yardsticks, still commonly applied, are useless.

> Man hätte deßwegen alte und moderne – naive und sentimentalische – Dichter entweder gar nicht oder nur unter einem gemeinschaftlichen höheren Begriff [...] mit einander vergleichen sollen. Denn freylich, wenn man den Gattungsbegriff der Poesie zuvor einseitig aus den alten Poeten abstrahirt hat, so ist nichts leichter, aber auch nichts trivialer, als die modernen gegen sie herabzusetzen.[26]

Schiller's assessment of the key features of ancient Greek culture, the epitome of naive art, and modern culture is also similar to Herder's. Characterised by simplicity and unity, ancient art and culture are based on concreteness, while modern culture, and sentimental art, which have lost this simplicity, are characterised by a wealth of material, which tends to be abstract in nature.

---

[26] Schiller, *Über Naïve und Sentimentalische Dichtung*, *Schillers Werke. Nationalausgabe*, vol. 20.I, Weimar: Böhlau Nachfolger, 1962, pp. 413–503, 439. Forthwith *NSD*. "Perhaps on this account one should not compare ancient with modern – naïve with sentimental – poets either at all, or only by reference to some higher concept common to both [...]. For clearly, if one has first abstracted the concept of those species [concept of the genre of poetry] one-sidedly from the ancient poets, nothing is easier, but nothing is also more trivial, than to depreciate the moderns by comparison." *Friedrich von Schiller, Naïve and Sentimental Poetry and On the Sublime. Two Essays.* Translated, with Introduction and notes by Julius A. Elias, New York: Frederick Ungar, 1966, pp. 113–14. My version in brackets. Forthwith NSP.

> Siegen gleich die alten Dichter auch hier in der Einfalt der Formen und in dem,
> was sinnlich darstellbar und körperlich ist, so kann der neuere sie wieder im
> Reichthum des Stoffes, in dem, was undarstellbar und unaussprechlich ist, kurz,
> in dem, was man in Kunstwerken Geist nennt, hinter sich lassen. (*NSD*, 440)[27]

Schiller, too, sees a parallel between the early ancient Greek art and Shakespeare, a parallel that for him is based on impersonal, concrete direct-
ness, which Schiller experiences as unsentimental insensitivity.

> Die trockene Wahrheit, womit er den Gegenstand behandelt, erscheint nicht
> selten als Unempfindlichkeit. Das Objekt besitzt ihn gänzlich. [...] Wie die
> Gottheit hinter dem Weltgebäude, so steht er hinter seinem Werk; Er ist das
> Werk, und das Werk ist Er. [...] So zeigt sich z.B. Homer unter den Alten und
> Shakespeare unter den Neuern; zwey höchst verschiedene, durch den uner-
> meßlichen Abstand der Zeitalter getrennte Naturen, aber gerade in diesem
> Charakterzuge völlig eins. (*NSD*, 433)[28]

As for Herder, Shakespeare represents also for Schiller an ideal of representative cultural achievement that is on a par with ancient cultural
achievements, although the cultures these poets represent are profoundly different. Both Homer and Shakespeare are to Schiller natural
geniuses, "poets of a naïve youthful world rich in spirit"[29] and conform
to the same structural ideal of a poet. Thus for Schiller, too, Shakespeare
represents an ideal of originality that is similar to Herder's evaluation of
the "modern ancient" because features first identified and idealised in
ancient culture are traced in modern culture. Schiller even seems to subscribe to a fully-fledged cultural equivalence, when he suggests that
ancient Greek culture has had its own sentimental phase, treating both
cultures as independent cultural cycles. Evidently Schiller has taken on
board Herder's ideas.

Much research has been focused on the "difficulty" of Schiller's essay,
which comes from his parallel use of the same categories as aesthetic

---

[27] "And even if the ancient poets are victorious too in the simplicity of forms and in whatever is sensuously representable and corporeal, the modern can nonetheless leave them
behind in richness of material in whatever is unsusceptible of representation and inef-
fable, in a word, in whatever in the work of art is called spirit." NSP, 115.

[28] "The dry truth with which he deals with the object seems not infrequently like insensitivity. The object possesses him entirely. [...] Like divinity behind the world's structure
he stands behind his work; he is the work and the work is he. [...] Thus, for example,
Homer among the ancients and Shakespeare among the moderns reveal themselves;
two vastly different natures separated by the immeasurable distance of the years, but
one in precisely this trait of character." NSP, 106.

[29] "Dichter einer naiven und geistreichen Jugendwelt", *NSD*, 432.

ideals on the one hand and as historical phenomena on the other. The conditions of naivety occurred in purity only in (early) Greek history, yet they apply to any "geistreiche Jugendwelt". Sentimental poetry is the mark of modernity, but also the result of advanced cultural development in Greece.[30] That this difficulty results from the two distinct relations – oppositional *as well as* successive – between the ancient and the modern has only been partially recognised. To integrate these had become the (great historical) challenge. Schiller's essay illustrates the difficult interlocking of the dichotomous relation between ancient and modern (they are different but equal) and the successive relation between them, which indicates that modern conditions result from developments beyond and after antiquity. Schiller addresses the challenge by employing a dialectical approach.[31] The analogous relation defined by Herder is turned into an antithetical one, which takes care of the oppositional relation and at the same time provides a model for sequential succession, and even a prospective resolution. This preserves the equality between the two, but also offers the opportunity to establish aim and purpose for (modern) history and gives the relational progression of history an engine.

---

[30] Cf. Georg Lukacs "Schillers Theorie der modernen Literatur" (1935), and, again, Peter Szondi, "Das Naïve ist das Sentimentalische" (1972) and M.A. Hewitt, "(Re)zoning the Naïve", (2003).

[31] Not least because of their pre-Hegelian date, Schiller's dialectics have been considered in need of qualification. The commentary on *Naïve und Sentimentalische Dichtung* in the *Nationalausgabe* speaks of a "besondere Art" (quoted by Peter Szondi, "Das Naïve ist das Sentimentalische", 201); more recently Bernhard Fischer called it a "Vorform" in his article "Goethes Klassizismus und Schillers Poetologie der Moderne: *Über Naïve und Sentimentalische Dichtung*" *Zeitschrift für deutsche Philologie* 113 (1994), 225–245, 226. Peter Szondi pointed out the difference between triadic argumentation in Kant and Hegel and placed Schiller in-between. ("Das Naïve ist das Sentimentalische", 202/3). Peter-André Alt finally speaks in this context of "a dialektisches Verfahren, das jedoch nicht mit letzter Entschiedenheit zur Anwendung gelangt" (Alt, *Schiller. Leben-Werk-Zeit*, 2 vols, Munich: Beck, 2000, II, 210), although he later uses the "gelenkige Dialektik Schillers" (ibid., 224) without qualification. M.A. Hewitt, on the other hand, has recently argued that any dialectical structures, especially a dialectical synthesis, are a misreading of Schiller; they are prevented in Schiller's thinking due to an insistence on a perpetual interplay between seemingly oppositional concepts. ("(Re)zoning the Naïve", 197–202) As the following will make clear, to me it seems obvious that, as Szondi points out, the dynamic of the Hegelian structure, which differentiates Hegel's thinking from Kant's, is already fully evident in Schiller's, and indeed Schlegel's, essay. Hewitt is correct to stress the importance of the structural dynamic. But the synthesis is only denied in the present, not as a future potential.

Like Herder, Schiller wishes to promote a better understanding of the nature of modern art and the conditions that produce it. Such an understanding is vital because it is the basis for realising the potential of (modern) humanity. "Unsere Kultur soll uns, auf dem Wege der Vernunft und der Freiheit, zur Natur zurückführen." (*NSD*, 414)[32] While Herder was concerned with improving contemporary art for the benefit of contemporary society, Schiller's scope is far greater. By naming a specific aim for the process of human history, he directly anticipates the conceptions of German Idealism. This future-oriented scope and structure cause him some difficulty.

Schiller's essay *does* display indecision. His desire to relate the concepts of ancient and modern to each other in a way that accords modernity equality conflicts with his deep-rooted penchant for concepts related to the natural, which is the signature of ancient culture. His essay rests on the dichotomy of nature and art, or nature and culture. It demonstrates the clash between Schiller's ("modernist") conception of the historical process as improvement (which feeds into his developing notion of a transcendental philosophy of history) and his worship of nature and the natural in aesthetic and philosophical terms. Herder managed to settle the *Querelle* for himself through the notion of equivalence. Schiller seems to relive the confrontation: an original ideal competes with the notion of progress. For Herder, who shares this penchant for the natural-original, it is absorbed in his focus on the origin and the originality of (any) culture. For Schiller this penchant complicates his future-oriented approach focused on purposeful historical progress. Like Herder, Schiller strives to reconcile positions akin to those of the French *Querelle*.

Schiller's preference for the natural does not simply signal a nascent leaning towards a concept of classicism (understood as an unquestioned veneration for things ancient). Instead it is clearly a remnant of his *Sturm-und-Drang* aesthetics. Parts of the essay read as if they were lifted straight out of Goethe's *Werther*. Both *Sturm und Drang* and old-fashioned classicism are indebted to the notion of an ancient natural ideal. Nature, prioritised and elevated, is the pivot of Schiller's considerations. Nature was as much the key concept for the new (modern) culture the *Stürmer und Dränger* wanted to create as it was a regulative idea in the views of an *ancien*, or indeed in the definition of classical art as it emerges in the 1790s. "Der Dichter, sagte ich, ist entweder Natur, oder er

---

[32] "Our culture, by means of reason and freedom, should lead us back to nature." NSP, 85.

wird sie suchen. Jenes macht den naiven, diesen den sentimentalischen Dichter." (*NSD*, 436).[33] *Kunst*, art as well as artifice, and *Kultur*, although named in the opening paragraphs as the (only) path towards reattaining naturalness, are suspect, tainted with the notion of debilitation, destruction and divisiveness. "Unsre Kindheit ist die einzige unverstümmelte Natur, die wir in der kultivirten Menschheit noch antreffen." (*NSD*, 430)[34] "Die Natur macht [den Menschen] mit sich eins, die Kunst trennt und entzweyet ihn." (*NSD*, 438)[35] Nature is the only true guide for the poet. "Auch jetzt ist die Natur noch die einzige Flamme, an der sich der Dichtergeist nährt, [...] zu ihr allein spricht er auch in dem künstlichen, in der Kultur begriffenen Menschen." (*NSD*, 436)[36] This is Wertheresque *Zivilisationskritik* indeed. Here as there, (true) art and nature are intricately linked.

> Die Dichter sind überall [...] die Bewahrer der Natur. Wo sie dieses nicht ganz mehr seyn können und schon in sich selbst den zerstörenden Einfluß willkürlicher und künstlicher Form erfahren oder doch mit demselben zu kämpfen gehabt haben, da werden sie als die Zeugen und die Rächer der Natur auftreten. (*NSD*, 432)[37]

All poets he truly considers great, from Homer to Goethe, are, at least in tendency, naive. His concept of genius is inseparably linked to naivity.

> Naiv muß jedes Genie seyn, oder es ist keines. [...] Unbekannt mit den Regeln, den Krücken der Schwachheit und den Zuchtmeistern der Verkehrtheit, bloß von der Natur oder dem Instinkt, seinem schützenden Engel, geleitet, geht es ruhig und sicher durch alle Schlingen des falschen Geschmackes. [...] Die verwickelsten Aufgaben muß das Genie mit anspruchsloser Simplicität und Leichtigkeit lösen; [...] Dadurch allein legitimiert es sich als Genie, daß es durch Einfalt über die verwickelte Kunst triumphiert. (*NSD*, 424)[38]

---

33 "The poet, I said, either is nature or he will seek her. The former is the naïve, the latter the sentimental poet." NSP, 110.

34 "Our childhood is the only undisfigured nature that we still encounter in civilised mankind." NSP, 103.

35 "Nature sets him at one with himself, art divides and cleaves him in two." NSP, 112.

36 "Even now, nature is the sole flame at which the poetic spirit nourishes itself; [...] to her alone it speaks even in the artificial man entoiled by civilisation." NSP, 110–11.

37 The poets are everywhere [...] the guardians of nature. Where they can no longer quite be so and have already felt within themselves the destructive influence of arbitrary and artificial forms or have had to struggle with them, then they will appear as the witnesses and avengers of nature." NSP, 106.

38 "Every true genius must be naïve, or it is not genius. [...] Unacquainted with the rules, those crutches for weakness and taskmasters of awkwardness, led only by nature or by instinct, its guardian angel, it goes calmly and surely through all the snares of false taste.

Schiller's *Sturm-und-Drang* convictions run deep. His definition of
poetic genius is very similar to Herder's in his *Ossianbriefe* in *Von deutscher Art und Kunst*, from which it is no doubt derived:

> Immer die Sache, die sie sagen wollen, sinnlich, klar, lebendig anschauend:
> den Zweck, zu dem sie reden, unmittelbar und genau fühlend: nicht durch
> Schattenbegriffe, Halbideen und symbolischen Letternverstand [...] zer-
> streuet: noch minder durch Künsteleien, sklavische Erwartungen, furchtsam-
> schleichende Politik, und verwirrende Prämeditationen verdorben – über all
> diese Schwächungen des Geistes seligunwissend, erfassen sie den ganzen Ge-
> danken mit einem ganzen Worte, und dies mit jenem. Sie schweigen entweder
> oder reden im Moment des Interesses mit einer unvorbedachten Festigkeit,
> Sicherheit und Schönheit. [...] Bis endlich die Kunst kam und die Natur aus-
> löschte. [...] Nach Regeln zu arbeiten, deren wenigste ein Genie als Naturre-
> geln anerkennet; über Gegenstände zu dichten, über die sich nichts denken,
> noch weniger sinnen, noch weniger imaginieren läßt [...] und endlich wurde
> alles Falschheit, Schwäche und Künstelei.[39]

To square the circle of the original ideal and the future consummation
of human art and existence Schiller needs to relate the natural to progress and posit a future naturalness. He moves from assuming equivalence between the phases of ancient and modern naturalness (Herder's
view) to a projected synthesis of the two. Consequently Schiller's concept of nature is differentiated into two parts, one referring to what
could be termed original nature and the other to what might be called
consummate nature. The first is split again into two distinct concepts:
on the one hand it relates to the world extraneous to humans, from

---

[...] The genius must solve the most complex tasks with unpretentious simplicity and
facility. [...] And only thus does genius identify itself as such, by triumphing over the
complications of art by simplicity." NSP, 96.

[39] Herder, *Auszug aus einem Briefwechsel über Oßian und die Lieder alter Völker*, *Sämmtliche
Werke* vol. 5, ed. by Bernhard Suphan, 159–207, 181–183. "They always have in their
mind's eye a lifelike, sensuous, clear picture of the thing they want to say: they clearly
feel the purpose for which they speak: they are not distracted by [...] shadowy concepts, half-ideas, symbolic understanding of empty letters; even less are they spoilt by
artifice, slavish expectations, fearfully creeping politics, and confusing premeditations,
they are blessedly ignorant of all these debilitations of the mind, and they grasp the
whole thought in one word. Either they are silent or they speak in the moment of interest with an unspoilt firmness, sureness and beauty. [...] Until, in the end, art came
and extinguished nature. [...] To work according to rules of which the fewest a genius
recognises as natural, to write poetry on matters which do not inspire thought, less
sense and even less the imagination [...] and in the end all became falseness, weakness
and artifice."

minerals to animals, which is characterised by the absence of (human) reason and freedom as well as the presence of an existential harmony free from doubts. The contemplation of this kind of nature moves the modern human to sentimental feelings of pleasure mixed with wistful yearning.[40]

> Wir lieben in ihnen [these elements of extra-human nature] das stille schaf-fende Leben, das ruhige Wirken aus sich selbst, das Daseyn nach eignen Ge-setzen, die innere Nothwendigkeit, die ewige Einheit mit sich selbst. (*NSD*, 414)[41]

On the other hand the concept of original nature also refers to the natu-ral in the human being, who is, as rational creature, by definition separ-ate from the non-rational entities in nature, but has retained a link with the natural state from which humanity emerged. The full realisation (i.e. conscious resurrection) of this currently submerged and stunted ("ver-stümmelt") natural side within a rational framework is the mark of true humanity.

> Denn entfernt sich gleich der Mensch durch die Freyheit seiner Phantasie und seines Verstandes von der Einfalt, Wahrheit und Nothwendigkeit der Natur, so steht ihm doch nicht nur der Pfad zu derselben immer offen, sondern ein mächtiger und unvertilgbarer Trieb, der moralische, treibt ihn auch unaufhör-lich zu ihr zurück. (*NSD*, 436)[42]

The natural quality of humanity in its un-stunted form is the mark of naive art, which is perfectly exemplified by the ancient Greeks. "Bei [den alten Griechen] artete die Kultur nicht so weit aus, daß die Natur darüber verlassen wurde." (*NSD*, 430–31)[43] The modern human is moved at the sight of (extra-human) nature in a way the Greek human is not, because it represents an ideal he can, under current conditions, only view as an external observer, because it is too obscured inside him. "Weil die Natur bey uns [Modernen] aus der Menschheit verschwunden

---

[40] Variously referred to as "Wohlgefallen", "Wehmut", "erhabene Rührung".

[41] "We love in them the tacitly creative life, the serene spontaneity of their activity, exist-ence in accordance with their own laws, the inner necessity, the eternal unity with themselves." NSP, 85.

[42] "For even if man should separate himself by the freedom of his fantasy and his under-standing from the simplicity, truth and necessity of nature, yet not only does the way back to her remain open always, but also a powerful and ineradicable impulse, the moral, drives him ceaselessly back to her." NSP, 110.

[43] "With them [the ancient Greeks] civilisation did not manifest itself to such an extent that nature was abandoned in consequence." NSP, 104.

ist, [treffen] wir sie nur außerhalb dieser, in der unbeseelten Welt, in ihrer Wahrheit wieder an." (*NSD*, 430)[44]

The creator of sentimental art has lost this naturalness through exposure to over-civilisation, but, by virtue of his (moral) humanity, is perpetually compelled to strive to re-achieve this lost naturalness. Here the internal dialectic of modernity, along with its dynamic, emerges.

> Wir erblicken in ihnen [elements and non-human creatures of nature] also ewig das, was uns abgeht, aber wonach wir aufgefodert sind zu ringen, und dem wir uns, wenn wir es gleich niemals erreichen, doch in einem unendlichen Fortschritt zu nähern hoffen dürfen. (*NSD*, 415)[45]

Schiller's definitions of the natural, and of modern humanity's need to recapture it, cannot be conceived as a regaining of a paradise lost and a return to an original state, if progress is supposed to be meaningful and human rationality is not supposed to be an aberration. So the natural in its consummate state is distinct from its original version. In its original form the natural is, in its extra-human and human forms, limited and limiting because it is based on necessity, not freedom.

> Aber ihre Vollkommenheit ist nicht ihr Verdienst, weil sie nicht das Werk ihrer Wahl ist. [...] Was ihren Charakter ausmacht, ist gerade das, was dem unsrigen zu seiner Vollendung mangelt; was uns von ihnen unterscheidet, ist gerade das, was ihnen selbst zur Göttlichkeit fehlt. Wir sind frei, sie sind nothwendig. (*NSD*, 414–415)[46]

Watching extra-human nature going about its business may move the modern human to tears of wistful yearning, but it is an inappropriate objective for modern humanity to aim at.

> Jene Natur, die du dem Vernunftlosen beneidest, ist [...] keiner Sehnsucht wert. Sie liegt hinter dir [...]. Verlassen von der Leiter, die dich trug, bleibt dir jetzt keine andere Wahl mehr, als mit freyem Bewußtsein und Willen das Gesetz zu ergreifen. [...] Laß dir nicht mehr einfallen, mit ihr [der Natur] tau-

---

[44] "It is because nature in us has disappeared from humanity and we discover her in her truth only outside it, in the inanimate world." NSP, 103.

[45] "In them, then, we see eternally that which escapes us, but for which we are challenged to strive, and which, even if we never attain to it, we may still hope to approach in endless progress." NSP, 85.

[46] "Yet their perfection is not to their credit, because it is not the product of their choice. [...] What determines their character is precisely what is lacking for the perfection of our own; what distinguishes us from them, is precisely what they themselves lack for divinity. We are free, they are necessary." NSP, 85.

schen zu wollen, aber nimm sie in dich auf und strebe, ihren unendlichen Vorzug mit deinem eigenen unendlichen Prärogativ zu vermählen und aus beydem das Göttliche zu erzeugen. (*NSD*, 428–29)[47]

The loss of the state of nature is irreversible, which may be painful and frightening, but in this lies the hope: the loss is caused by the advancing human powers of abstraction and reflexion. These represent an unfolding of the rational side of the human being, and are as such *also* intrinsic to human nature. Any attempt at regression would amount to denying the very nature of humanity. The capacity for reflexion and the resulting freedom are the human "prerogative". Reflexion is crucial in the overall progress of humanity. When at first it appeared as the curse of human development, destroying the natural state, it turns out to be the redeeming feature of culture, which will ultimately make reattaining (some kind of) enlightened naturalness possible. The sentimental poet's desire to strive beyond the given – and unsatisfactory – reality creates the perspective for the progressive ideal of consummate naturalness. This is the basis for a positive evaluation of modern culture, which links Schiller with the ideas of the French *modernes* who championed progress and improvement.

From this perspective, original human naturalness, as achieved by the ancients, appears almost as limiting as the natural of extra-human nature. The achievement of the Greeks must now seem preliminary to the modern cultured mind which has progressed along the path of increasing reflexion.

Solange der Mensch noch reine, [...] nicht rohe Natur ist, wirkt er als ungetheilte sinnliche Einheit und als ein harmonirendes Ganze. Sinne und Vernunft, empfangendes und selbstthätiges Vermögen, haben sich in ihrem Geschäfte noch nicht getrennt [...]. Seine Empfindungen [gehen] [...] aus dem Gesetz der Nothwendigkeit, [seine Gedanken] aus der Wirklichkeit hervor. Ist der Mensch in den Stand der Kultur getreten, und hat die Kunst ihre Hand an ihn gelegt, so ist jene sinnliche Harmonie in ihm aufgehoben, und er kann nur noch als moralische Einheit, d.h. als nach Einheit strebend sich äußern. Die Übereinstimmung zwischen seinem Empfinden und Denken, die in dem ersten Zustande wirklich stattfand, existiert jetzt bloß idealisch; sie ist nicht

---

[47] "That nature which you envy in the irrational [non-rational, MO] is worthy of no respect [...]. It lies behind you [...]. Abandoned by the ladder that supported you, no other choice now lies open to you, but with free consciousness and will to grasp the law. [...] Let it no longer occur to you to want to exchange with her [nature], but take her up within yourself and strive to wed her eternal advantage with your eternal prerogative, and from both produce the divine." NSP, 101–02.

mehr in ihm, sondern außer ihm; als ein Gedanke, der erst realisirt werden soll. (*NSD*, 436–37) [...] Durch das Ideal kehrt er zu Einheit zurück. (*NSD*, 438)[48]

The realisation of the ideal as such is unachievable. "Weil aber das Ideal ein Unendliches ist, das er niemals erreicht, so kann der kultivierte Mensch in seiner Art niemals vollkommen werden, wie doch der natürliche Mensch es in seiner zu werden vermag." (*NSD*, 438)[49] Despite this ongoing imperfection the modern condition is ultimately superior to the ancient one.

> Das Ziel, zu welchem der Mensch durch Kultur strebt, [ist] demjenigen, welches er durch Natur erreicht, unendlich vorzuziehen. [...] Insofern aber das letzte Ziel der Menschheit nicht anders als durch jene Fortschreitung zu erreichen ist, und der letztere nicht anders fortschreiten kann, als indem er sich kultiviert und folglich in den erstern übergeht, so ist keine Frage, welchem von beyden in Rücksicht auf jenes letzte Ziel der Vorzug gebühre. (*NSD*, 438)[50]

Modern sentimental poetry has a key role to play in approximating to the ideal.

> Dem sentimentalischen [Dichter] hat sie [die Natur] [...] einen lebendigen Trieb eingeprägt, jene Einheit, die durch Abstraktion in ihm aufgehoben worden, aus sich selbst wieder herzustellen, die Menschheit in sich vollständig zu machen und aus einem beschränkten Zustand zu einem unendlichen überzugehen. (*NSD*, 473)[51]

---

48 "So long as man is pure – not, of course, crude – nature, he functions as an undivided sensuous unity and as a unifying whole. Sense and reason, passive and active faculties, are not separated in their activities [...]. His perceptions [...] proceed out of the law of necessity, the latter [his thoughts] out of actuality. Once man has passed into the state of civilisation and art has laid her hand upon him, that sensuous harmony in him is withdrawn, and he can express himself now only as a moral unity, i.e. as striving after unity. The correspondence between his feeling and thought which in his first condition actually took place, exists now only ideally; it is no longer within him, but outside of him as an idea still to be realised. [...] Through the idea he returns to unity." NSP, 111–12.

49 "But because the ideal is an infinitude to which he never attains, the civilised man can never become perfect in his own wise, while the natural man can in his." NSP, 112–13.

50 "The goal to which man in [through, MO] civilisation strives is infinitely preferable to that which he attains in nature. [...] But insofar as the ultimate object of mankind is not otherwise to be attained than by that progress, and man cannot progress other than by civilising himself and hence passing over into the first category, there cannot therefore be any question to which of the two the advantage accrues with reference to this ultimate object." NSP, 113.

51 "Upon the sentimental poet she [nature] has [...] impressed a lively impulse, to restore out of him that unity that has been disrupted by abstraction, to complete the humanity within himself, and from a limited condition to pass over into an infinite one." NSP, 154.

Imperfection works as a spur. The ancients had ceased to progress because they had achieved what they could, within their limitations. "Einig mit sich selbst und glücklich im Gefühle seiner Menschheit, mußte er bey dieser als seinem Maximum stillestehen." (*NSD*, 431)[52] The internal dialectic of modernity, which is based on the memory of harmony and the experience of loss, produces its own dynamic, which is realised as constant striving. It will become a key feature in all subsequent definitions of modernity. Schiller's assertion that nature was the only proper inspiration for the poet is now qualified: "Die Natur [...] ist es auch noch jetzt, in dem künstlichen Zustande der Kultur, wodurch der Dichtergeist mächtig ist; nur steht er jetzt in einem ganz andern Verhältnis zu derselben." (*NSD*, 436)[53] Schiller's twofold view of nature and the natural, in its original and its consummate forms, make his synthesis of original ideal and progress towards (near-)perfection possible. He outlines a non-regressive model for the integration of ancient features into modern culture, not just in the modern past as did Herder, but in the future of modernity without compromising the original identity of modernity.

Schiller develops further Herder's definition of modern literature as coping with complexity by giving it a clear purpose and direction. Because modern poetry uses reflexive abstraction to cope with the complexity of modern existence, it is not only able to adequately represent its complex existence, but also to gradually approach the ideal of humanity. Schiller unfolds a panoramic picture of human striving, which also characterises the contemporaneous philosophy of Fichte, and later that of Schelling and Hegel, in which every succeeding stage takes priority over, but still relates to, the preceding one. Unlike Herder, Schiller explicitly endorses the modern frame of mind as more advanced, not just in quantity but as containing the potential of further progress. But, to return to the "difficulty" of the essay, despite Schiller's confident assertion in the opening paragraphs that "unsere Kultur soll uns auf dem Wege der Vernunft und Freiheit zur Natur zurückführen" (*NSD*, 414), the undercurrent of lament over the loss of original naturalness never quite ceases. There is more than a hint of making the most of a bad situ-

---

[52] "At one with himself and happy in the sense of his humanity he was obliged to remain with it as his maximum." NSP, 104.

[53] "And it is still nature [...] even now in the artificial condition of civilisation, in virtue of which the poetic spirit is powerful; but now it stands in quite a different relation to nature." NSP, 111.

ation, a sort of intellectual brave face, in Schiller's championing of the sentimental and the reflexive. By necessity, it must be the answer to the modern problem. "Verlassen von der Leiter, die dich trug, bleibt dir jetzt keine andere Wahl mehr, als mit freiem Bewußtsein und Willen das Gesetz zu ergreifen."

The *Sturm-und-Drang* concept of the true art and genius shares many features of the *anciens'* appreciation of original perfection. Both Herder and Schiller agreed on the misery of the present and yet, unlike the defenders of the *anciens*, both wanted to promote modernity, because, historically minded, they considered it *their* culture and reality. They saw a clearer understanding of the conditions of modernity, and of its potential, as the key to facilitating a better (modern) literature, aesthetics, and humanity. The difference between them is that Herder approached understanding modernity by investigating its origin, its own "antiquity", while Schiller's approach focused on the potential inherent in the modern condition. In the 1770s it was Herder's aim to assist in the creation of a positive, independently grounded self-image of "Nordische Menschheit", which would see itself as different but equal to the humanity of antiquity. Schiller's divided loyalties between nature and progress eventually produce a synthesis that paves the way for the superiority of modernity. Both their approaches to the difference between ancient and modern are driven by the wish to create a historically meaningful relationship between ancient and modern, which they achieve by integrating the ancient into modernity, Herder by structural analogy, Schiller by historical dialectics.

The close proximity of date and content of Schiller's essay and Friedrich Schlegel's *Studium-Aufsatz* (1795–7) has given rise to considerable critical attention in recent decades. Some of the common ground the two writers share, which had long been obscured by the entrenched division between *Klassik* and *Romantik* bequeathed by later 19th-century German criticism[54] and the well-known antipathy between the two men during

---

[54] It is no coincidence that the earliest suggestion of an intellectual closeness between the classicist Schiller and the Romantic Schlegel came from a non-German critic. O.A. Lovejoy linked Schiller to the *Frühromantik* in 1920 ("Schiller and the Genesis of German Romanticism" *Modern Languages Notes* 35, repr. in O.A. Lovejoy, *Essays in the History of Ideas*, Baltimore: John Hopkins Press, 1948, pp. 228–253). Outside Germany, where the definition of Romanticism is wider in scope, the distinction between *Klassik* and *Romantik* was never taken very seriously.

Schiller's lifetime, has been repeatedly pointed out, as have the differences.[55] Both consider art and poetry as the truest expressions of humanity and contrast ancient Greek and modern art as natural versus artificial. Both consider striving an essentially human trait that is spurred on
particularly by the modern condition. The latter is an imperfect unsatisfactory situation, based on stunted debility, which nevertheless has the
potential for progressive redemption. The modern condition has the capability to be redeemed by striving for an ideal, which, however, can
only be approximated. The ancient condition is set in a double relation
to its modern counterpart, which combines the original two approaches
of the *Querelle*. Firstly the ancient condition looms large on the historical
horizon because it allowed the achievement of its particular perfection.
Within an historically minded outlook, however, this makes it as an
ideal which can only function in a structural rather than normative fashion. Its (particular) perfection is defined as limited because it is, secondly, an historical predecessor to the modern, which is capable of sur-
passing it in terms of human achievement because it has the potential to
integrate the two identities or conditions. Like Schiller, Schlegel exhibits
a dual approach to nature in relation to humanity: the natural is considered irrevocably lost, but it remains the basis for an ideal that is to be
(re-) approximated to in the future. It has not been fully appreciated that
Schlegel, despite his extremely negative view of modern conditions, also
puts forward a positive definition of modernity. Instead he is frequently
presented as engaging in its unmitigated damnation.[56]

Herder and Schiller were quick to express their dissatisfaction with the
present in artistic and intellectual terms and clear in defining the problems that beset the modern condition. But, it is true, neither quite
reaches the depressive depths of Friedrich Schlegel who considers the
modern experience as disjointed, disharmonious and desperate. Schlegel, too, uses Shakespeare to define the modern condition. Indeed his
art represents the "pinnacle of modern poetry"[57], but this time Shake-

---

[55] Cf. Richard Brinkmann, "Romantische Dichtungstheorie in Friedrich Schlegels
Frühschriften und Schillers Begriffe des Naiven und Sentimentalischen" *DVjs* 32 (1958)
344–71, also Franz Norbert Mennemeier, *Friedrich Schlegels Poesiebegriff dargestellt anhand
der literaturkritischen Schriften*, Munich: Fink, 1971, pp. 108–116; Jauss, *Provokation* (1970),
67–106; Alt, *Schiller* vol. 2 (2000), 224–230.

[56] Cf. recently Alt, *Schiller*, 224 ff. Also Jauss, *Provokation*, 81.

[57] "Gipfel der modernen Poesie", Friedrich Schlegel, *Über das Studium der Griechischen Poesie*, *Kritische Friedrich-Schlegel-Ausgabe* vol. 1, ed. by Ernst Behler, Paderborn/Munich/
Vienna: Schönigh/Thomas Verlag, 1979, pp. 217–367, 249. Forthwith *Studium*.

speare's *Hamlet* is seen to represent a "Maximum der Verzweiflung" caused by the "ewige[n] Kolossale[n] Dissonanz, welche Menschheit und Schicksal unendlich trennt".[58] Like Herder and Schiller, Schlegel picks up on the starkness of Shakespearean tragedy, and he repeats what Herder first suggested when he rejects the classical rules of drama in relation to Shakespeare's plays on the grounds that Shakespeare was modern and that the theory of modern poetry and art (which he describes as "characteristic poetry" and "philosophical art") has yet to be fully worked out.

> Das gewöhnliche Urteil, Shakespeares Inkorrektheit sündige wider die Regeln der Kunst, ist […] sehr voreilig, so lange noch keine objektive Theorie existiert. Überdem hat ja noch kaum irgendein Theoretiker auch nur versucht, die Gesetze der charakteristischen Poesie und philosophischen Kunst überhaupt etwas vollständiger zu entwickeln. (*Studium*, 250)[59]

Schlegel, too, subscribes to the notion of the natural art of the genius, as originally propounded by Herder and longed for by Werther. Only the weak artist follows rules:

> Eine unwiderstehliche Sympathie befreundet nämlich den Kenner ohne Takt und treffenden Blick mit den ordentlichen Dichtern, die zu schwach sind, um ausschweifen zu können. Es ist daher wenig mehr als die Mittelmäßigkeit derjenigen Künstler, […] welche unter dem Namen der Korrektkeit gestempelt und geheiligt worden ist. (*Studium*, 249–50)[60]

Schlegel's assessment of the ills of the current situation is very similar to Schiller's. The modern condition is defined as alienated from a natural state by what he considers the modern excess of reflection and abstraction, and as yearning for a reunion with what has been lost. For Schlegel, modern culture is defined by artificiality. From its beginnings, governing

---

58 *Studium*, 248. "Maximum of despair" caused by the "eternal colossal dissonance that ceaselessly separates humanity and fate". Friedrich Schlegel, *On the Study of Greek Poetry*, translated, edited, and with a critical introduction by Stuart Barnett, Albany, NY: State University of New York Press, 2001, p. 33. Forthwith *Study of Greek Poetry*.

59 "The typical judgement that Shakespeare's incorrectness sins against the rules of art […] is very premature as long as no objective theory about art exists. Moreover, there has hardly been any theoretician who has even attempted to develop more completely the rules of characteristic poetry and philosophical art." *Study of Greek Poetry*, 34.

60 "An irresistible sympathy befriends the expert that lacks sensitivity and a keen eye with respectable poets who are too weak to be capable of excesses. It is thus not much more than the mediocrity of those artists […] that has been certified and made sacrosanct under the name of correctness." *Study of Greek Poetry*, 34.

concepts ("dirigierende Begriffe") and acts of free will have been the guiding principles of modern aesthetics. (*Studium*, 232/3) Schlegel points the finger at a preoccupation with truth and morality ("Wahrheit und Sittlichkeit", *Studium*, 218) instead of with the beautiful, which makes the experience of art painfully dissatisfactory: "Die trefflichsten Gedichte der Modernen [...] lassen einen verwundenden Stachel in der Seele zurück, und nehmen mehr als sie geben." (*Studium*, 217)[61] His evaluation of modern poetry sounds predominantly negative: The modern condition has produced poetry that, in its anarchic disjointedness, resembles an "aesthetic junkshop".[62] It is confused, lawless and skeptical, it lacks universality. For Schlegel, all these attributes explain what he sees as the key feature of modern poetry, "das Interessante". There is an "Übergewicht des Individuellen, Charakteristischen und Philosophischen" (*Studium*, 241),[63] which so far has prevented the evolution of any form of epochal or artistic coherence. Modernity is particularised, whereas ancient culture expressed universality. Modern culture only causes dissatisfaction, because the disconnected particulars lack any systematic relation to each other. The individual quality (das Individuelle) has never yet been raised to the level of any form of universality. It is between these concepts that dialectical tension develops.

Consequently, modern poetry evinces undeniable greatness, but in a seemingly pointless and unordered fashion.

> Wenn man diese Zwecklosigkeit und Gesetzlosigkeit des Ganzen der modernen Poesie, und die hohe Trefflichkeit der einzelnen Teile gleich aufmerksam beobachtet: so erscheint ihre Masse wie ein Meer streitender Kräfte, wo die Teilchen der aufgelösten Schönheit, die Bruchstücke der zerschmetterten Kunst, in trüber Mischung sich verworren durcheinander regen. (*Studium*, 223–4)[64]

---

[61] "The most splendid poems of the moderns [...] leave a thorn in the soul and take more than they give." *Study of Greek Poetry*, 17.

[62] "Ästhetischer Kramladen", *Studium*, 222. Barnett translates this phrase as "general store of aesthetics" (*Study of Greek Poetry*, 20), which in my view is a translation of the more neutral "Krämerladen". To my mind "Kramladen" suggests a disjointed collection of objects and has a slightly judgmental ring.

[63] "Predominance of the individual, the characteristic and the philosophical", *Study of Greek Poetry*, 30.

[64] "When one considers with equal care the purposelessness and lawlessness of the whole of modern poetry as well as the true excellence of its individual parts then the sum of it appears like an ocean of warring forces, where the parts of the dissipated beauty, the fragments of shattered art, move confusedly through one another in a lugubrious mixture." *Study of Greek Poetry*, 21.

Here the multiplicity and complexity of the modern condition that was first defined by Herder return. Schlegel's characterisation of modern poetry as a chaotic mix closely resembles Herder's description of the contents of Shakespeare's plays.

> Lauter einzelne im Sturm der Zeiten wehende Blätter aus dem Buch der Begebenheiten [...] einzelne Gepräge der Völker, Stände, Seelen! die alle die verschiedenartigsten und abgetrenntest handelnden Maschinen [...] sind. [...] Wie vor einem Meere von Begebenheit, wo Wogen in Wogen rauschen, so tritt vor seine [Shakespeare's] Bühne. Die Auftritte der Natur rücken vor und ab; würken ineinander, so Disparat sie scheinen, bringen sich hervor, und zerstören sich, damit die Absicht des Schöpfers, der alle im Plan der Trunkenheit und Unordnung gesellet zu haben schien, erfüllt werde. ("Shakespear", 219–220)[65]

For both Herder and Schlegel, Shakespeare is a quintessentially modern poet, whose work expresses the character of modernity, marked by (seeming) dissolution and disparateness and dominated by the characteristic and individual, i.e. the particular. But while Herder was awed and impressed by this complex wealth of individual particulars, and remains convinced there is a point to them (which Shakespeare was able to grasp), to Schlegel the modern multiplicity seems to be a disturbing chaos of lawlessness that produces a frantic search for order and perfection.

> Unter den verschiedensten Formen und Richtungen [...] äußert sich in der ganzen Masse der modernen Poesie durchgängig das Bedürfnis nach einer vollständigen Befriedigung, ein gleiches Streben nach einem absoluten Maximum der Kunst. [...] Je öfter das in der menschlichen Natur gegründete Verlangen nach vollständiger Befriedigung durch das Einzelne und Veränderliche (auf deren Darstellung die Kunst bisher ausschließend gerichtet war) getäuscht wurde, je heftiger und rastloser ward es. (*Studium*, 253)[66]

---

[65] "All individual leaves from the book of history, blowing in the storm of history [...] individual features of nations, classes, souls! Which are all very different machines acting most individually [...]. Approach his [Shakespeare's] stage as if you approach a sea of events, where waves crash into waves. The scenes of nature move forward and back; work into one another, as disparate as they appear, they create each other and destroy each other, so that the Creator's intention, who seems to have put them all together according to a drunken and disorderly plan, be fulfilled."

[66] "Through the most varied forms and orientations [...] the same need for a complete satisfaction, a consistent striving for an absolute maximum of art expresses itself in all modern poetry. [...] The more often the longing for a complete satisfaction [which is] grounded in human nature was disappointed by the individual and mutable [(to the representation of which art has up to now been exclusively geared)] the more ardent

The "absolute maximum of art" is for Schlegel the "ne plus ultra of the aesthetic",[67] that is to say the beautiful, which still eludes modern art. Again, modernity is characterised by striving, but the accelerating striving he describes appears blind and almost pointless. If Schiller's account was marked by an intellectual brave face that had to make the best of a bad lot but never quite got over its attachment to the natural ideal that has been lost, this is true of Schlegel's essay to an even greater extent. And yet, from a damning assessment of modernity's ills, he too moves on to the promise of modern greatness to come. And to construct his lifeline out of the dark chaos of modernity he, too, uses the historicist concept of the structural ideal, which provides the blueprint of originality that needs to be first rediscovered in modernity and then appropriately and progressively developed in modern culture, achieving the same sort of integration of ancient features into modernity.

Historical analysis is the key. "Vielleicht gelingt es uns, aus dem Geist ihrer bisherigen Geschichte [of modern poetry] zugleich auch den Sinn ihres jetzigen Strebens, die Richtung ihrer fernern Laufbahn und ihr künftiges Ziel aufzufinden."[68] There is a point, and an aim, and this aim will turn out to be positive. Schlegel considers historical analysis vital, because theory, the theory of modern poetics and aesthetics he is after, needs history.

> Reine Wissenschaft bestimmt nur die Ordnung der Erfahrung, die Fächer für den Inhalt der Anschauung. Sie allein würde leer sein – wie Erfahrung allein verworren, ohne Sinn und Zweck – und nur in Verbindung mit einer vollkommnen Geschichte würde sie die Natur der Kunst und ihrer Arten vollständig kennen lernen. (*Studium*, 273)[69]

---

and restless it became." *Study of Greek Poetry*, 35. Translation in brackets mine, in the first case replacing "that would be", which in my view is not correct, in the second case adding a section that is missing in the translation.

67 "ästhetisch Höchste", *Studium*, 253; *Study of Greek Poetry*, 35.

68 *Studium*, 224. "Perhaps it is possible for us to discover from the spirit of its previous history [of modern poetry] the meaning of its current efforts, the direction of its further course, and its future goal." *Study of Greek Poetry*, 21.

69 "Pure science only determines the organization of experience, the pigeonholes for the contents of intuition. By itself it would be empty – just as experience would be confused, without sense or purpose – and it is only in connection with a perfect history that it would be able to truly impart lessons about the nature of art and its genres." *Study of Greek Poetry*, 47.

The history of poetry will reveal the theory of poetry. But the history of modern poetry must be considered in comparison with the original model of cultural history, that of the ancient Greeks, and in relation to the prototype of poetic perfection, Greek literature.

> Nur bei einem Volke entsprach die schöne Kunst der hohen Würde ihrer Be-stimmung. Bei den Griechen allein war die Kunst von dem Zwange des Be-dürfnisses und der Herrschaft des Verstandes immer gleich frei. [...] Allen Bar-baren hingegen ist die Schönheit an sich selbst nicht genug. Ohne Sinn für die unbedingte Zweckmäßigkeit ihres zwecklosen Spiels bedarf sie bei ihnen einer fremden Hülfe, einer äußern Empfehlung. Bei rohen wie bei verfeinerten Nichtgriechen ist die Kunst nur eine Sklavin der Sinnlichkeit oder der Ver-nunft. [...] Schon auf der ersten Stufe der Bildung und noch unter der Vor-mundschaft der Natur umfaßte die Griechische Poesie in gleichmäßiger Voll-ständigkeit [...] das Ganze der menschlichen Natur. [...] Ihr goldenes Zeitalter erreichte den höchsten Gipfel der Idealität (vollständiger Selbstbestimmung der Kunst) und der Schönheit, welcher in irgendeiner natürlichen Bildung möglich ist. Ihre Eigentümlichkeit ist der [...] vollständigste Abdruck der all-gemeinen Menschennatur. Die Geschichte der griechischen Dichtkunst ist eine allgemeine Naturgeschichte der Dichtkunst. (*Studium*, 275–6)[70]

Greek art furnishes the prototype of the beautiful, the aesthetically high-est, because it successfully linked the particular and the universal. But it remains a prototype, its achievements remain on the natural level. Modern art must achieve its own (advanced) ideal on the level of reflec-tion. At first this seems difficult, because the beautiful can only be achieved under natural conditions:

> Nur da ist das höchste Schöne möglich, wo alle Bestandteile der Kunst und des Geschmacks sich gleichmäßig entwickeln, ausbilden und vollenden; in der natürlichen Bildung. In der künstlichen Bildung geht diese Gleichmäßig-

---

[70] "Only in the case of one people did fine art correspond to the great dignity of its des-tiny. Only in the case of the Greeks was art equally free from the constraints of necessity and the rule of the understanding. [...] For all barbarians, however, beauty in itself is not good enough. Lacking a sense for the unconditioned purposefulness of its purpose-less play, they required assistance and advice from outside sources. With uncouth as well as sophisticated non-Greeks, art is simply a slave of either sensibility or reason. [...] Already during the initial stage of culturation [Bildung] and while still under the tutelage of nature, Greek poetry encompasses the whole of human nature in uniform completion. [...] Its golden age reaches the highest peak of ideality (the complete self-determination of art) that is possible in natural culturation [Bildung] of any sort. What is peculiar to it is that it is the [...] complete copy of human nature in general. The his-tory of Greek poetic arts is a general, natural history of the poetic arts." *Study of Greek Poetry*, 48.

keit duch die willkürlichen Scheidungen und Mischungen des lenkenden Verstandes unwiderbringlich verloren. [...] Der Gipfel der natürlichen Bildung
der schönen Kunst bleibt daher für alle Zeiten des hohe Urbild der künstlichen Fortschreitung. (*Studium*, 293)[71]

Although this natural perfection of art will never be regained, because
humanity is no longer in the state of nature, Greek cultural history provides, through its completeness of rise and fall, an idea of the structure
of human progress. Schlegel takes Herder's notion of the structural
ideal, the structural prototype of ideal art, and combines it, like Schiller,
with the demand for reachievement on a higher reflexive level, which
can be, if not achieved, then certainly approximated.[72]

Das Übermaß des Individuellen [which was the result of reflexive philosophical abstraction] führt also von selbst zum Objektiven, das Interessante [the
product of philosophical modernity] ist die Vorbereitung des Schönen, und
das letzte Ziel der modenen Poesie kann kein andres sein als das höchste
Schöne, ein Maximum von objektiver ästhetischer Vollkommenheit. (*Studium*, 253)[73]

Although Schlegel's attachment to the ancient original initially appears
even stronger than Schiller's, and produces the same unevenness of argument in his essay, he too makes the leap of faith regarding modernity,
with the aid of dialectics. The previously blind and frantic striving has
become constructive and directed through internal dialectical productivity. The maximum of aesthetic perfection is a concept Schlegel had
previously applied to the ancients only. Under modern conditions "a
relative maximum", like Schiller's ideal, can be achieved in the shape of
an "unsurpassable fixed approximation".[74] Herder's simple difference of

---

71 "Only where all elements of art and taste evolve, form and complete themselves in
   equal proportion is the greatest beauty possible – that is in natural culturation [Bil-
   dung]. In artificial culturation [Bildung] this symmetry is irrevocably lost by the arbitrary division and mixture undertaken by the regulative understanding. [...] The pinnacle of the natural culturation [Bildung] of fine art remains thus for all times the great
   prototype of artistic progress." *Study of Greek Poetry*, 58.
72 H.R. Jauss clearly recognised this historicising of the ideal, but he relates Schlegel's efforts to Hegel's *Ästhetik*, not to Herder's historicist ideas. Cf. *Provokation*, 91.
73 "The predominance of the individual leads of its own accord to the objective; the interesting is the propaedeutic for the beautiful, and the ultimate goal of modern poetry
   can be nothing else than the *ne plus ultra* of beauty, a maximum of objective aesthetic
   perfection." *Study of Greek Poetry*, 35.
74 "ein relatives Maximum" and "ein unübersteigliches fixes Proximum" *Studium*, 288;
   Study of Greek Poetry, 55.

a "more" of history between the ancient and the modern condition has developed into a theory of historical progress that connects modernity to antiquity. This connection is made possible through the dialectical dynamic. From the historical perspective, antiquity is the origin from which its other, i.e. modernity, has derived, which in turn will develop a new identity that combines features of the origin and its other. From a cultural perspective (in an anthropological sense), the "natural" experiences the same dynamic development: from a pre-rational origin it develops into its oppositional other, the artificial or rational, which in turn will provide the basis for re-achieving the new, synthesised natural on a higher level. By presenting ancient culture and the concept of the natural in their historical dialectical processes, Schlegel describes a grand historical dialectic of art and the human intellect.

Both Schiller and Schlegel struggle with the problems of history and historicity, with the destabilising "more" of history that had created the complex multiplicity of the qualitatively transformed, the different modern condition. Both identify the need for a theory that is based on historical analysis. Taking their cue from Herder, they suggest that their awareness of historicity requires an entirely new kind of ideal: the structural equivalent in the historical process. Surveying the course of the historical process, different successive equivalents can then be related to each other by antithetical dialectical successions, which makes it possible to accommodate the genuinely new without fully losing the old, combining progress and impermanence with achievement and validity. Schiller and Schlegel have different foci for the historical process. Schiller's focus is humanity, and his concept of art for the improvement and realisation of humanity has a social dimension. Schlegel's focus, on the other hand, is the concept of poetry and of the beautiful *per se*. Art is to deliver the spiritual salvation of humanity. Herder investigates history primarily to reach a clearer understanding of each individual phase, Schiller and Schlegel investigate history to draw conclusions for a universal theory (of humanity and art respectively). The historicist principle of change over time is employed to produce (universal) theories of purposeful development. The aim is historical completeness, which is the basis for the new theory of eventual perfection, replacing the notion of achieved, imitable perfection. The universal ideal is replaced by the consummate ideal. The dialectic dynamic that powers this process of purposeful change makes it possible to synthesise the mutually exclusive positions of the French *Querelle*, which again preoccupied the thinkers of the late 18th century, because, as a consequence of their historicist awareness, they felt drawn to both extremes. Worried by the destructive and arrogant aspects of Enlightenment thinking, they turned to admire an ideal of original perfection, which they nevertheless recognised as historically lost due to progress, because, as the children of the Enlightenment, they equally subscribed, for better or for worse, to the very notion of progress. Modernity, initially seen as an inferior deterioration of the old ideal of the natural, is fully redeemed by being a stepping-stone to the re-achievement of the new consummate natural that integrates the reflexive condition. The position of the *anciens*, or the concept of an old ideal of perfection, is of course in principle a *pre*-Enlightenment notion. But it could easily be accommodated in Enlightenment thought, because it did not challenge the Enlightenment prerequisite of the constancy of parameters. (Perfection could be calculated and could then be attempted.) What makes the historically informed notion of progress, so crucial to Schiller and Schlegel, different from the Enlightenment concept of perfectibility is the assumed qualitative difference between the different phases of the historical process, which are nevertheless equal in intrinsic value, because human knowledge and experience of the world undergo transformations, rather than statistical augmentation from one phase to the next. Through their engagement in historical dialectics, moving from cultural analogy towards the productivity of cultural dialectics, the writers discussed here are able to emancipate modernity from its inferior position without having to denigrate the ancient ideal. The transience of the historical process makes this possible.

Herder deconstructed the ideality of Greek art into its structural elements, to establish its function and identify its relevance within Greek culture, with the intention to identify cultural products that had the same relevance and could assume the same function within modern culture. He did this by relating cultural products to their tradition, a procedure that inevitably made him focus on cultural origins. Schiller, although deeply attached to the original in culture through his attraction to the natural, focused on the opposite direction, i.e. the aim of culture, which inevitably generated the task of relating past and future to each other through a theoretical relationship. This theoretical relationship found expression as historical dialectics. Schlegel, similarly attached to the natural-original, and equally driven to re-introduce it in an appropriate manner into advanced modernity, combined the two approaches; his theoretical endeavour was to uncover the coherence, i.e. the theory, of modern poetry (and culture) by embracing the entire dynamics of its history, investigating both "Ursprung" and "Ziel".

Wir müssen also nach einer doppelten Richtung nach ihrer Einheit [der modernen Poesie] forschen; rückwärts nach dem ersten Ursprunge ihrer Entstehung und Entwicklung; vorwärts nach dem letzten Ziele ihrer Fortschreitung. Vielleicht gelingt es uns auf diesem Wege, ihre Geschichte vollständig zu erklären, und nicht nur den Grund, sondern auch den Zweck ihres Charakters befriedigend zu deduzieren." (*Studium*, 229)[75]

It is clear that all three are dealing with the same problems: Their awareness of historicity complicated the (re-)definition of universal ideals and theories. Their deep-rooted attachment to a "lost origin", be this the genuinely overcome past of a different culture such as ancient Greece or the forgotten origin of their own modern culture that lay buried in medieval and early modern art, made them search for ways in which the lost original-natural could be meaningfully re-introduced into an advanced culture defined by historical impermanence. Their search is equally driven by the (related) desire to emancipate modernity, their own culture, from cultural inferiority.

In terms of the *Querelle*, they are *modernes* who wish they could be *anciens* too. And they set about utilising their awareness of historicity to fulfil their wish. Their answers all tend in the same direction: towards discovering and integrating features first identified and admired in ancient culture within its modern successor-culture and -identity, and position ancient and modern (their own) culture within a purposeful historical process that would eventually approach a consummate perfection that mirrored, but surpassed the lost (and now overcome) original perfection. These tendencies find clear expression in the new concepts of literature that each formulates respectively.

Responding to Historicity with New Literary Theories: Herder's *Volkspoesie*, Schiller's *Aesthetic Education* and Friedrich Schlegel's *Universalpoesie*

Defining the differences and relations between ancient and modern culture and positioning modern culture within the historical process inevitably made these thinkers consider what kind of (new) concepts of lit-

---

[75] "Thus we must search after [its] unity in a twofold manner; we must turn backward toward the initial origin of its genesis and evolution and forward toward the ultimate objective of its progression. Perhaps in this way we will succeed in completely explaining its history and satisfactorily deducing not only the basis, but also the purpose of its character." *Study of Greek Poetry*, 24.

erature would be viable for contemporary literature and could point the way towards a new and improved modern culture. Herder, Schiller and Schlegel all produced their essays on literary theory discussed below within a few years of their contributions to the *Querelle*-issues. All three were convinced that literature had a special role to play in the successful and meaningful progression of modern culture: it was to be instrumental in (re-)directing the modern cultural process towards achieving its full potential. At first sight this seems to differ little from the Enlightenment concept of the usefulness of literature. What is different, however, is that for all three the same dialectical structures, which also organise the relationship between ancient and modern culture, underlie their descriptions of literary development and progress. This dialectics is based on differentiating the areas of the natural, the original and the synthetic from areas of the rational, the abstract, the utilitarian and the analytical, which, in analogy to the relationship between ancient and modern culture, are first opposed and then synthesised in the new concepts of literature.

The new literature was to address and remedy what they considered the key contemporary intellectual, cultural and social problems. All three thought that literature needed to be reconnected to something natural and original which predated pure conceptual thought, i.e. which was untouched by the problems of (especially contemporary) modernity. This proposition is closely linked to their preoccupation with a "lost natural origin", which resulted from their endeavours to solve the *Querelle* and achieve a historical synthesis of ancient and modern characteristics. It is part of the general framework within which Enlightenment ideas are critically assessed. This reconnection to the natural and original was to make possible the creation of something concrete in literature that provided a specific and particular, a *real*, experience. This "real" stands in close connection to the notion of the natural. It is, so to speak, its realisation in the here and now, which can be experienced by the senses (as well as the mind), while the "original" is the realisation of the natural in time, it points out the place of the natural in temporal development.

All three thought that the natural and original entity, which was currently forgotten, obscured or ignored, was closely linked to what each considered the essence of humanity, that which was essential if human beings were to experience and understand their humanity fully, and hence know their purpose. For Herder this essence was the national or local, for Schiller the beautiful, and for Schlegel it was the resurrection and reappreciation of the (original) all-inclusiveness of true poetry.

Again, the very impermanence of cultural achievement, which had initially created and then exacerbated the contemporary problems, becomes part of the solution of these problems by offering the prospect of a better future, i.e. a future that is profoundly different from the present. Not surprisingly, all three present structural blueprints of literature that are derived from examples which to them represent certain culturally successful points in human cultural development. None of the concepts *prescribe* literary form or content in a concrete manner, which would have been customary in the time of universal literary ideals. Instead they *describe* ways in which dialectical cultural concepts can be meaningfully linked in literature. This is their (new) way of achieving concretisation under the conditions of historical impermanence and (re-)integrating the ignored entities of the natural, original and synthetic, which are necessary for productive progress.

Herder: *Volkspoesie* in *Briefwechsel über Ossian* and
"Würkung der Dichtkunst auf die Sitten der Völker"

Herder is credited with the creation of the concept of *Volkspoesie*, although it has for a long time been widely acknowledged that he never offered a precise definition. It encompasses *Naturpoesie* and *Nationalpoesie* and represents the essence of a national group as well as the "natural" product of the poetic activities of those unaffected by social and educational refinement. This may, however, be less of a hazy imprecision on Herder's part than a deliberate attempt to closely associate the concepts of nature, *Volk* and nation and suggest that social groups and their cultures are natural and original entities. This upgrades the image of the ignorant and unrefined who, in *Sturm-und-Drang* thinking, had retained many of the positive qualities of naturalness and, by the same token, democratises the idea of the nation. Herder makes clear that to him this kind of poetry is the only true and real poetry, i.e. his blueprint for any poetic ideal. Through its propagation, Herder wished to restore to poetry its original power, importance and influence, its moving, unifying, inspiring and communicative force, which he believed his contemporaries were ignoring, to the detriment of themselves, of literature, and their nation. He first presents his notion of *Volkspoesie* at the beginning of the 1770s in the *Briefwechsel über Ossian*, and remains preoccupied with the beneficial example of early poetry throughout the *Sturm-und-Drang* decade, by the end of which he published several key publications that consolidated his views. His collections of *Volkslieder*, the evidence and illustration of his theory, eventually emerged from the printing press at the end of this decade,[76] when he was also working on the essay entitled "Über die Würkung der Dichtkunst auf die Sitten der Völker in alten und neuen Zeiten" (1778, written 1777),[77] which provides the literary history to prove his points.

As a key element in his *Sturm-und-Drang* theory, the concept of *Volkspoesie* is, as a reconnection to the "natural" and "original", immediately set against notions of artifice, intellectualism and decadence. In the *Briefwechsel* it is associated with an immediate, sensuous vitality: it expresses itself in realistic, life-like concreteness that appeals directly to the senses, the heart and the soul. It is powerful and confident in its images, which display what Herder repeatedly terms "Festigkeit", a rootedness and strength. It adheres to no rules other than the dictates of genius, i.e. the inspired soul, or of the situation, i.e. the requirements of the inspired moment. It faithfully projects emotions into images that can be easily understood and readily experienced. In its vibrant vitality it has a powerful impact on the imagination, which easily retains and delights in these images. Hence it is effective poetry. It is the opposite of poetry subject to an externally determined catalogue of rules and preoccupied with either philosophising abstraction or premeditated commercial or critical success, or both. Characterised by weakness and insecurity, the latter is a mere shadow of real poetry, because it fails to be effective, since it does not address the whole human being, and is hence only partially intelligible, or even insincere. The difference can be summed up as *nature* versus *artifice* and defines a dialectical opposition between older poetry and contemporary literature.

---

[76] The publication history of Herder's collections was troubled. The first was completed in 1773, in close temporal proximity to the *Ossianbriefe* and the Shakespeare-essay, but withdrawn from the printers in 1775 before printing was completed. It now features as *Alte Volkslieder* in vol. 25 of Suphan's *Sämmtliche Werke*, pp. 1–126. The second dates from 1777–78, contemporaneous with the "Würkung"-essay, and was published in two parts in 1778 and 1779 under the title of *Volkslieder*. A third was planned for decades, but its material only reached the printers posthumously as a collection edited by Herder's wife Caroline in 1807, entitled *Stimmen der Völker in Liedern*, which was the most successful collection financially and in terms of editions, although it enjoyed little academic acclaim throughout the 19th century. Cf. Carl Redlich, "Einleitung", *Herders Sämmtliche Werke*, vol. 25 (Volksliederband), ed. by C. Redlich, Berlin: Weidmannsche Buchhandlung, 1885, pp. vii-xx.

[77] The essay was written in the first few months following his move to Weimar, and published in 1781. Cf. Carl Redlich's "Vorbericht", *Herders Sämmtliche Werke*, vol. 8, p. v.

Volkspoesie always flourishes at the beginning of any specific cultural development. Herder finds it in Homer (and Ossian!), and in the poetry of "wilde Völker" (barbaric peoples), and still in Sophocles, Shakespeare and the songs of medieval minstrels. It is no longer present in the poetry of his time, when poets, critics and audience alike have forgotten how to imagine, to feel and to experience with heart and soul, i.e. to empathise, because the intellectual pretensions and the polite conduct of civilised society have made such behaviour outmoded. So the development from nature to artifice appears as a one-way historical deterioration. But Herder is keen to make clear that he is no primitivist. Although he champions old models (and there are plenty of primitivist-sounding passages), he rather wishes to re-introduce their cultural structures, not their content or the culture they represent, into contemporary literary development. He despises primitivist imitations, as he points out in the epilogue to the *Volkslieder* of 1778, "um schiefen Urteilen vorzubauen":

> Noch weniger kann es sein [des Sammlers, i.e Herders] Zweck seyn, regelmä-
> ßigere Gedichte, oder die künstlichere nachahmende Poesie gebildeter Völker
> zu verdrängen: denn dies wäre Thorheit, oder gar Unsinn; vielmehr, wenn
> [ich] etwas zu verdrängen Lust hätte, wärs die neuen Romanzenmacher und
> Volksdichterei, die mit der alten meistens so viel Gleichheit hat, als der Affe
> mit dem Menschen. Das Leben, die Seele ihres Urbildes fehlt ihr ja, nemlich
> [sic]: Wahrheit, treue Zeichnung der Leidenschaft, der Zeit, der Sitten; sie ist
> ein müßiger Stutzer in einen ehrwürdigen Barden, oder einen zerrissenen
> blinden Bettler verkleidet.[78]

By the time he had been dealing with "real" early literature for a decade, he was also keenly aware that recourse to historically distant models harbours its own serious problems. If the historical situation is too different and the language used no longer comprehensible, it is difficult, even impossible, to establish a meaningful connection.

> Man darf nur die Schilterschen Sammlungen aus den spätern Zeiten der Ka-
> rolinger ansehen; und über die Sprache wenigstens, bleibt kein Zweifel. Selbst
> die Deutsche Grammatik hat sich in dem Ablauf von Jahrhunderten so ver-

---

[78] Herder, *Sämmtliche Werke*, vol. 25, 308–309. "It can be even less the purpose [of the collector] to replace the more regular poems or the more artificial imitating poetry of civilised nations. This would be foolish, or even nonsense. If I wanted to replace something, it would be those new romance writers and that new folk poetry, which in most cases have as much in common with the originals as the monkey with the human. They lack life, the soul of their original, i.e. truth, faithful representation of passion, of the time, of the customs, they are pointless fops dressed up as venerable bards, or ragged blind beggars."

ändert, daß es immer beinah gleich viel wäre, ob wir Altfranzösische Romanische Dichter läsen oder sie. Also immer nur Zaubergestalt voriger Zeiten im
Spiegel der Gloßatoren, Alterthumsforscher und Paraphrasten – nicht Volkslieder für unsere Zeit.[79]

Herder is very much concerned with the value of the past for the present, not with the past for its own sake. Even early on Herder insists in
the *Ossianbriefe* that humanity is meant to progress. This does not
contradict his historicist beliefs, Herder insists that in the (progressive)
course of history all epochs of human development are of equal and
necessary value.

Glauben Sie nicht, daß ich deswegen unsre sittlichen und gesitteten Vorzüge
[…] verachte. Das Menschliche Geschlecht ist zu einem Fortgange von
Scenen, von Bildung, von Sitten bestimmt: wehe dem Menschen, dem die
Scene mißfällt, in der er auftreten, handeln und sich verleben soll! Wehe aber
auch dem Philosophen über Menschheit und Sitten, dem Seine Scene die
Einzige ist, und der die Erste immer, auch als die Schlechteste, verkennet!
Wenn alle mit zum Ganzen des fortgehenden Schauspiels gehören: so zeigt
sich in jeder eine neue, sehr merkwürdige Seite des Menschheit.[80]

There is no need for contemporary literary and cultural development to
regress to show signs of improvement, intellectuals and artists only need
to remember and take into account the two-sided nature of the human
mind, of which one side flourished earlier in cultural development than
the other. For Herder, rational understanding and sensuous experience

---

[79] "Vorrede" to *Alte Volkslieder, Sämmtliche Werke*, vol. 25, 5–13, 5/6. Unintentionally
Herder proves his own historicist point (that cultural products are bound by their historical time), when he wishes that the Germanic peoples had had an Ossian (ibid., 392),
because despite the (imagined!) temporal distance he feels deeply moved by his songs.
This clearly demonstrates how much John Macpherson's fakes were in tune with the
needs and knowledge of their age. "One only needs to look at Schilter's collections
from the later Carolingian period, and there can be no doubt regarding the language at
least. Even German grammar has changed so much over the centuries that it almost
makes no difference whether one reads Old French poets or these. So it always remains
a nebulous spectre of times past reflected by glossary-writers, historians and para-
phasers – no folk poetry for our time."

[80] "Auszug aus einem Briefwechsel über Oßian und die Lieder alter Völker", *Sämmtliche
Werke*, vol. 5, 159–207, 168. Forthwith "Oßian". "Do not think that because of this I des-
pise our moral and civilised advantages. The human race is destined to progress through
(different) scenes of education and customs. Woe to him who dislikes the scene in
which he is to appear, to act and to live! But also woe to the philosopher of morals who
only considers his own scene, and who misreads the first scene as the worst! All scenes
are part of the ongoing drama: each presents a new and particular side of humanity."

("Erkenntnis" and "Empfindung", "Oßian", 185) are both equal elements of the human make-up, and it is the contemporary one-sided preference for the abstract and analytical which Herder considers wrongheaded. It evinces to him an astonishing lack of knowledge about the human soul, "wie trocken und dürre stellen sich doch manche Leute die Menschliche Seele [...] vor" ("Oßian", 201).[81] By ignoring the true heterogeneous nature of humanity, which is capable of analysis as well as imaginative creativity, his contemporaries do not only promote inferior art, but also stunt human development and forego – despite the best intentions of the Enlightenment – the potential for the moral and spiritual improvement of humanity inherent in the inspirational power of poetry. To regain these lost powers, older models, which still address the emotional, imaginative, non-rational side (without, incidentally, being unrational), need to be consulted. "Oßian, die Lieder der Wilden, der Skalden, Romanzen, Provinzialgedichte könnten uns auf beßern Weg bringen, wenn wir aber auch hier nur mehr als Form, als Einkleidung, als Sprache lernen wolten [sic]." ("Oßian", 203)[82] Again, it is clear that Herder is interested in their cultural structure, not their culture *per se*. It is becoming equally clear that the bifocal relationship between the concepts of the original-natural and the advanced rational-reflexive, which was being employed to relate ancient to modern, was also applied in literary theory and used to define to the make-up of the human mind.

Herder aimed to reform literary theory and practice. Such a reform was to be part of an (unsystematic) programme to change the general direction of social and cultural development, away from its one-sided preoccupation with analytical abstraction and the static rules of reason towards an inclusive appreciation of all faculties of the human mind and soul. This included the recognition of the human need for the religious,

---

[81] "how dry and barren some people imagine the human soul to be".

[82] "Ossian, the songs of the barbarians, the scalds, romances, poems from Provence could teach us to improve if we were prepared to learn more than just the form, the external trappings and the language."

But such examples of traditional folk poetry, especially *Volkslieder*, which have so far mainly remained beneath contempt for civilised and educated minds, are in danger of being lost forever. Herder remarks, grimly ironic: "Der Rest der ältern, der wahren Volksstücke, mag mit der sogenannten täglich verbreitetern Kultur ganz untergehen, wie schon solche Schätze untergegangen sind – wir haben ja Metaphysik und Dogmatiken und Akten." ("Oßian", 190) "What is left of the older, true folk poetry may perish along with the so-called everyday culture, as such treasures have already perish – we have metaphysics and dogmatics and files."

which has its seat in the emotional, spiritual and imaginative realm. It is concerned with the soul.

> Meistens nennen wir diesen Zustand Wachstum der Philosophie: er seis; aber diese Philosophie dient der Dichtkunst und dem menschlichen Herzen wenig. Streicht alles Wunderbare, Göttliche und Große aus der Welt aus, und setzt lauter Namen an die Stelle; des wird sich kein Geschöpf auf Gottes Erdboden, als etwa der Wortgelehrte freuen. Die Dichtkunst kann nie entspringen und nie würken, als wo man Kraft fühlt, lebendige Kraft selbst siehet, aufnimmt und fortpflanzt. Bayle's atheistischer Staat wird wahrlich keine oder elende Dichter haben.[83]

The recurring theme in Herder's diagnosis of what is at fault in contemporary poetry (and culture and society) is the disappearance of any sort of grounding, of what he refers to with terms such as *Natur, Materie, Substanz, Nahrung*, in short the concrete basis of life. This is detrimental because the particular power of poetry lies in its concrete symbolism. It can name the mysterious without destroying it and convey the essential without complicating or profaning it, which purely rational-analytic reason cannot.

> Wahrlich Poesie kann würken, was Philosophie, Geschwätz und Abstraktionen nie würken können. Sie schildert, beschreibt, oder umschreibt nicht Wahrheit: sondern gibt sie, stellet sie dar – stellet sie nicht dürftig, nackt und lieblos dar, sondern flößt süße Neigung zu ihr ein, wie der Dichter selbst süße Neigung fühlte.[84]

---

[83] "Über die Würkung der Dichtkunst auf die Sitten der Völker in alten und neuen Zeiten", *Sämmtliche Werke*, vol. 8, ed. by Bernhard Suphan, Berlin: Weidmannsche Buchhandlung, 18, pp. 334–436, 410. Forthwith "Würkung". "Generally we call this condition the growth of philosophy. Very well, but this philosophy does little for poetry and the human heart. If you cut all that is wondrous, divine and great out of the world, and put names in their places, no creature in God's world, other than academics, will take any pleasure in them. Poetry can only spring up, only affect where vitality is felt, where living vitality can be seen, absorbed and reproduced. Bayle's atheistic state will have no or only poor poets."
For Herder religion and poetry are linked through their concern for what is sacred to the human mind and in human culture. "Nun wird mit der Religion des Volks der Dichtkunst Herz und Seele genommen; ein Volk, das keine Religion hat, oder sie als Burleske braucht: für das ist keine würkende Poesie möglich." (ibid.)

[84] "Würkung", 434, footnote version of unpublished original. "Truly, poetry can effect what philosophy, verbiage and abstractions can never effect. Poetry does not describe or circumscribe the truth, it gives truth, represents truth, but not in a pinched, naked and loveless manner, instead it produces a sweet inclination towards truth, just as the poet himself felt sweetly inclined towards it."

This capability typifies the ideal structure of poetry, which is presently disturbed. It is obvious that Herder is contrasting an earlier cultural condition of humanity with a later one. The concrete metaphorical language of early poetry predates the abstract and philosophical discourse that informs 18th-century literary criticism. The latter developed out of the former. But Herder argues that the human capacity for the former exists undiminished and that, if utilised, it offers the priceless advantage of effective and direct communication. Ignoring it is just another facet of his society's tendency to be a-historical, to focus on the future without understanding their past. Poetry offers a connection with this older part of human nature, with its original expression. With religion, another original remnant of early human expression, it shares immediacy; the immediacy of faith is akin to the immediacy of poetic expression. But unlike the antiquated language of early medieval literature and the much changed cultural background, which limit the direct access to and the immediate usefulness of *actual* old poetry, this *type* of poetry is in itself not dated or superannuated. As a structural type of poetry it has remained valid because it is an aspect of humanity itself. Its actual form and content, however, are shaped by the particulars and history of any given community, because poetry is also a true indicator of a group's identity and disposition, it is "Nachbild der Sitten" ("Würkung", 408).

All of European literature is in need of such reform, but German poetry is in an especially difficult situation: because not only does it follow the contemporary one-sidedness, it also lacks a tradition of suitable old models, which might help to redirect cultural development.

> Unsre Barden sind verloren, die Minnesinger lagen auf der Pariser Bibliothek ruhig; die mittlere Zeit hindurch ward Deutschland immer ausser Deutschland geschleppt oder mit andern Völkern überschwemmet; bekam also nicht Zeit, sich zu sammeln, und auf die Stimme seiner eignen Dichtkunst zu merken. ("Würkung", 428)[85]

In the early 1770s Herder was chiefly concerned with defining the problems besetting modern poetry (and society) in general and finding solutions for them. The German national dimension is always present, but it remains one aspect of a generally modern problem. In Herder's reform programme, the national is crucially important, but universally. Its im-

---

[85] "Our bards are lost, the minstrels lay silent in the Paris Library; during the Middle Ages Germany has always been dragged out of Germany, or has been flooded with other peoples, and thus never had the time to collect itself, to listen to the voice of its indigenous poetry."

portance lies in the function it fulfils in the process of human cognition. In his essay "Über die Würkung der Dichtkunst auf die Sitten der Völker", Herder suggests that the beautiful, the sublime, and the ethical can only be effectively expressed for a human individual in this individual's particular, i.e. national context.

> Aber warum mußten so erhabne Lehren und Triebfedern zur Sittlichkeit der Menschen in eine so enge, übertriebene, dunkle Nationaldichtkunst Eines Volkes verhüllet werden? [...] Für *dies* Volk waren sie ja eigentlich, und so mußten sie in der Sprache, den Sitten, der Denkart des Volkes und keines andern in keiner andern Zeit seyn. ("Würkung", 359–60)[86]

Only the particular has a concrete reality. And the concrete always precedes the abstract. Abstraction in itself is not wrong or inhuman, but it is emotionally unintelligible, if it has not developed directly from particular concreteness. Such coherently progressive development is only possible within one particular national context. It is evident how much these ideas set the scene for Fichte's and August Wilhelm Schlegel's pronouncements on living and dead languages. Effective poetry can never be academic, neither can it be international.

In his *Würkung*-essay Herder gives a detailed account of the historical factors responsible for the development that has gradually turned once vibrant and vital European poetries into the contemporary literature he despises. With great precision he pinpoints a complex combination of economic, social, geographical and political factors, which later became defined as the preconditions of modernity (in the post-medieval sense), as the causes of the process of modernisation. For one, European expansion has led to a globalisation of culture.

> Je mehr die Länder zusammen rückten, die Kultur der Wissenschaften, die Gemeinschaft der Stände, Provinzen, Königreiche und Welttheile zunahm; je mehr also, wie alle Litteratur, so auch Poesie an Raum und Oberfläche die Würkung gewann, desto mehr verlohr sie an Eindrang, Tiefe und Bestimmtheit. In engen Staaten, bei kleinen Völkern, ihren einförmigen Sitten, engem und jedem einzelnen Gliede anschaulichem Interesse, bei Thaten, wo jeder Richter und Zeuge seyn konnte, hatte sie gewürkt und geblühet. ("Würkung", 413)[87]

---

[86] "But why did such noble teachings and such spurs to human morality have to be cloaked into such a narrow, exaggerated and dark national poetry of one people? [...] But they were really intended for this people, thus they had to be in *their* language, according to *their* customs and way of thinking and no other in no other era."

[87] "The closer the countries moved together, the more the culture of science, the closeness of the classes, provinces, kingdoms and empires increased; the more, as a consequence,

Also, modern statecraft is unheroic:

> Der Rittergeist fiel allmählich; das Land kam […] in politische Ordnung. […]
> Monarchie im Staate erhob ihr Haupt. […] Die neuern Sitten, […] vom Ge-
> setze und Rechte und ganz veränderten Umständen der Welt giengen sie aus.
> Den Regenten schmeicheln, einförmige Kriegszüge, politische Rechtshän-
> del, machiavellische Negotiationen besingen, war das Zweck der Dichtkunst?
> ("Würkung", 409)[88]

While this is partly a sentimental lament about the prosaic, unheroic
and generally boring nature of modern social and political conditions,
when compared to an (idealised) vision of the flamboyant heroism in
medieval warfare and politics, it is equally a shrewd assessment of the
impact of the damage a one-dimensional unaccountable centralised government can do to local individualities. But even more detrimental to
poetic activities has been the rise of international commerce and capitalism.

> Zween Weltheile wurden erfunden [sic] – man denkt vielleicht beim ersten
> Anblicke: ei, wie neuer, reicher Stof zur Dichtkunst! Der Erfolg zeigt, daß die-
> ser Stof nichts zu bedeuten hatte, gegen die Würkung, die im Ganzen die
> Dichtkunst durch diese Entdeckungen verlohr. Gold und Silber, Gewürze
> und Bequemlichkeit mögen viel Gutes hervorbringen, nur nicht neues Leben
> für die Poesie. ("Würkung", 411)[89]

It is not the extension of the European horizon Herder objects to, but
the secularisation of existence, which is becoming entirely focused on
material needs (money and power) in this world.[90] Political and econ-

---

poetry, as all literature, gained influence in terms of space and surface, the more it lost
in terms of depth, certainty and its power to move. In narrow nations, among small
peoples, among their simple customs, their narrow interests obvious to each of their
number, among deeds which everybody witnessed and judged, poetry had flourished
and had influence."

88 "The chivalric spirit slowly decayed. A political order […] established itself in the
country. The monarchy raised its head. […] The newer customs […] were based on laws
and rights and very different conditions of the world. Was it the purpose of poetry to
flatter rulers, to sing about boring military campaigns, political legal disputes, or Mach-
iavellian negotiations?"

89 "Two continents were discovered, at first sight one might think what new rich material
for poetry! But the outcome shows that this material meant nothing compared to the influence that poetry as a whole lost due to these discoveries. Gold and silver, spices and
convenience may indeed have brought benefits, but no new lease of life for poetry."

90 Somewhat amusingly, Herder also blames, and this is possibly his most primitivist argument, the demise of what he considers real poetry on the invention of the printing

omic changes and conditions gravely affect, in fact create, the situation in which poetry exists. But it was a cultural trend which emerged with the Renaissance that damaged the development of poetry most severely. In Herder's view, the dogmatic preference for all things classical, i.e. Greek and Roman, fundamentally affected the purpose of poetry: "Daraus mußten Nachtheile entstehen, die einem gewissen Theile der Menschen das ganze Ziel der Dichtkunst verrückt haben." ("Würkung", 406)[91] The introduction of arbitrarily chosen forms and models alien to the national context led to an adoption of universal, but irrelevant norms and forms that have to be learnt, as they are not part of the local tradition. This means poetry becomes a segregated province of the educated.

> Das Volk verstand diese Sprache nicht, und aufs Volk konnte die Dichtkunst also nicht würken; der beste lebendige Zweck und Prüfstein der Güte gieng also verlohren. Gelehrte schrieben für Gelehrte, Pedanten für Pedanten. [...] Ein Schreiber klatschte dem andern zu: "du bist klassisch, ich bins auch! Jene, das Volk, sind Barbaren, Pöbel der lieben Frau Muttersprache, sind verflucht!" ("Würkung", 407)[92]

While the lower classes may still hang on to local, even old national poetic traditions, as these traditions are despised and neglected by the educated and ruling classes, they will deteriorate and decay. This is exactly how in Herder's analysis the particularly bad literary situation in Germany had come about. If traditions are severed, the resulting unintelligibility can become damaging. Such poetry can no longer influence a national group's ethics and identity. "Und so ward Dichtkunst nun das laue Ding, das Niemand zu haben und zu geniessen wußte." ("Würkung", 407)[93] Neither does it encourage the development of a rounded human being, as its analytical one-sidedness, necessary to write and understand the cerebral and civilised literature of the educated, stunts

---

press, which changed a communal experience of sound and vision into a (potentially) solitary pursuit conducted in silence. Cf. "Würkung", 411.

[91] "Disadvantages stemmed from this, which for some people have entirely changed the aim of poetry."

[92] "The ordinary people did not understand this language, consequently this poetry could not influence them. Thus the true purpose and test of poetry was lost. Scholars wrote for scholars, pedants for pedants. [...] One scribbler shouted to the next: 'you are classical, so am I!' Those, the people, are barbarians, the mob of the mother tongue, are cursed!"

[93] "And thus poetry became this lukewarm thing which nobody understood or knew how to enjoy!"

the emotional and intuitive side of humanity. So, "das laue Ding" disturbs the mental and cultural balance of the human being as well as the national group. Here the link between Herder's concern for the universal and the particular overlap. He considers the human being as having universal features, which prescribe the need for grounding in the particular.

Herder's *Würkung*-essay gives an historical over-view of the effective or ineffective usage of poetry throughout ancient and modern history. In didactic terms it applies the same formula as his *Shakespear*-essay: by outlining a historical development, which invariably springs from a promising and uncorrupted origin, he presents good and bad examples along the line of progress. In his grand picture of European cultural development Herder identifies four original ancient cultures: Hebrew and Germanic culture are presented alongside the two traditional representatives of (classical) antiquity, Greece and Rome. Hebrew, Greek, Roman and Germanic antiquity are all considered as eras in which, at least for extended periods, proper poetry flourished and national tradition was the source of national development. (In the case of the un-poetic and practical Romans, however, this source of national identity was expressed, not in poetry, but in the equally language-based treasure-trove of legal and political rhetoric. ("Würkung", 387)) In post-ancient times the picture changes. Of the Middle Ages, Herder presents an ambivalent picture: It is the time of a universal European culture, based on the Christian religion, feudalism and chivalry mixed with oriental influences. Its poetry is supra-national ("Würkung", 400), i.e. potentially ineffective. But Herder sees this international poetry as being redeemed by a genuinely uniform European culture, which means that poetry and society correspond to each other in relevant and meaningful fashion. And the nature of medieval culture as the "early" culture of modernity makes it genuine, vibrant and vital. But Herder remains cautious as to the possible model function of medieval literature. Not only is the culture it represents too distant in time, it is also too much of a mix.[94]

---

[94] "Schade nur, daß ihre Sprachen für uns so veraltet sind, und wie es der Geist der Sache war, auch die Mundart ein Gemisch von Sprachen seyn mußte! Dadurch ist für uns die Würkung, auch wenn die Zeit sich nicht so verändert hätte, grossentheils verloren." ("Würkung", 400–401) "It is a shame that their languages are so removed from us temporally. Just as the spirit of the matter, so did the dialect also have to be a mix of languages! Due to this their effect is largely lost on us, even if times had not changed so much."

Herder then proceeds to assess Italian, French, English, Spanish and German post-medieval poetry in terms of effectiveness as *Volkspoesie*. They all display the problems of modernity, but at least the Italians, English and Spanish can boast some evidence of *volks*-poetic qualities in their literature: they have Dante, Shakespeare and Cervantes respectively (who will remain familiar favourites ever after their rediscovery in the later 18th century). Only the French and the Germans have little to boast about. The French, in familiar fashion, have simply got it very wrong, and the Germans have not got going yet.

Herder's notion of *Volkspoesie* as the natural material substance, which represents and engages with the particular in an individual's cultural background and nourishes his humanity through a particular identity, is the essence that connects the present to the past, because it carries on through the ages. It was the first and original manner in which the human mind expressed concepts.

> In Bildern konnte gesagt werden, was sich durch mutternackte Abstraktionen nimmer oder äusserst matt und elend sagen läßt. Die Sprache der Leidenschaft und der Gesichte konnte unsichtbare oder zukünftige Welten umfassen, Dinge zur Aufmunterung, zum Trost darstellen, die erst eine späte Folgezeit entwickelte, ohne daß durch eine zu lichte Vorspiegelung eben die Erfüllung des Geweissagten verhindert wurde. Es waren Träume […] der geistigen und vesten Zukunft, in Nebel gehüllt, aber eben in einen erquickenden, gesunden Himmelsthau-triefenden Nebel. ("Würkung", 360–1)[95]

As a poetics, *Volkspoesie* is a developing essence, a historicised ideal that has historical continuity. As it possesses concrete historical reality it undergoes the inevitable changes of cultural and intellectual development, but remains true and relevant (within its cultural context). Severing the later growth from its root is perilous. In Herder's historical survey, the historical development of modernity has nearly completely obscured these roots of Europe's different national communities. It was the course of modernity in its most extended guise including everything post-classical (i.e. everything from the rise of Christianity onwards) that put an end to "die enge Nationaldichtkunst, sowie die enge National-

---

[95] "In pictures one could say what naked abstraction can never or only very feebly and miserably express. The language of passion and of second sight could embrace invisible or future worlds, could depict things to raise flagging spirits or to comfort, which only a later era would produce, without preventing the fulfilment of the prophecy by too much clarity. They were dreams […] of the spiritual and firm future, clad in mist, in a revitalising healthy mist that dripped with heavenly dew."

würkung derselben" (394).⁹⁶ The Middle Ages, although in many respects culturally uniform, were folksy, vibrant, and, most importantly,
religious enough to ensure a connection between poetry and the people.
But through the great cultural and social changes that developed from
the Renaissance onwards, Europe becomes ever more homogenous and
alienated from any cultural rootedness through an anti-culture of soph-
istic education, ungermaine models, international commerce, emerging
capitalism and political absolutism. Herder concludes:

> So lang unsere Dichtkunst Meßgut ist und Karmen an den Geburtstagen der
> Grossen, so wird jeder Chiron in den Fels gehen und einen jungen Achilles
> etwa allein die Leyer lehren. Kein Tyrtäus wird vor unsern nach Amerika ver-
> kauften Brüdern einherziehen und kein Homerus diesen traurigen Feldzug
> singen. Sind Religion, Volk und Vaterland unterdrückte, neblichte Namen; so
> wird auch jede edle Harfe dumpf und im Nebel tönen […], wird nie eine
> Leyer erschallen, die Sitten schaffe, die Sitten bilde. ("Würkung", 434)⁹⁷

However, in the longer, unpublished version of his essay,⁹⁸ Herder is not
without hope. Even German poetry can be effective and moving and
there are encouraging signs on the German literary firmament: in particular the appearance of Goethe ("Würkung", 432–3).

Schiller: The Beautiful in *Über die ästhetische Erziehung des Menschen in einer Reihe von Briefen*

Herder presents a difference between earlier and contemporary forms
of human cognition and expression, the latter based on subject-centred
reason, the mainstay of Western post-Renaissance thought, and the
former based on those cognitive forces that are ignored, suppressed and
excluded by traditional rationalism. He argues for the re-balancing of
these two forms in a synthetic equilibrium, because they represent the
structural cornerstones of human understanding and experience.

---

[96] "the narrow national poetry and its narrow national effect".

[97] "As long as our poetry can be weighed and measured and is used to celebrate the birth-
days of dignitaries, any Cheiron will go into the mountain and teach the young Achilles
the lyre alone. No Tyrtaeus will head the train of our brothers that have been sold to
America and no Homer will sing about this sad campaign. If religion, the nation and
the fatherland are suppressed vague words, any noble harp will sound dull in the fog, no
lyre will ring out that can create and shape morals."

[98] The probably original version was edited and cut for its eventual publication. Cf. Carl
Redlich's "Vorbericht": "Ältere Niederschrift aus Herders Nachlass", *Sämmtliche Werke*,
vol. 8, p. vii.

Herder's critique of Enlightenment ideas is taken up by Schiller in his *Ästhetische Erziehung* twenty years later. Schiller gives a similar diagnosis of the current state of culture and humanity: a debilitating one-sided outlook (and resulting social condition) can only be refocused and amended by re-connecting culture and society to real and comprehensive human culture. For Schiller humanity is two-sided, characterised by a duality between reason and the senses, between the rational and the natural, the realm of abstraction and ideality and that of material reality. Currently, under the cultural conditions of modernity, the relationship between these two elements is disturbed. Like Herder, Schiller believes that reason on its own is helpless and mute when confronted with the binary constitution of the human mind as "sinnlich-vernünftig". The one-sided dominance of reason in the advanced state of civilisation is primarily to blame for the current cultural, philosophical and social ills.

> Damals [in ancient Greece] bei jenem schönen Erwachen der Geisteskräfte, hatten die Sinne und der Geist noch kein strenge geschiedenes Eigenthum. [...] So hoch die Vernunft auch stieg, so zog sie doch immer die Materie liebend nach, und so fein und scharf sie auch trennte, so verstümmelte sie doch nie. [...] Bey uns [moderns] möchte man fast versucht werden zu behaupten, äußern sich die Gemüthskräfte auch in der Erfahrung so getrennt, wie der Psychologe sie in der Vorstellung scheidet, und wir sehen [...] ganze Klassen von Menschen nur einen Theil ihrer Anlagen entfalten, während die übrigen, wie bey verkrüppelten Gewächsen, kaum mit matter Spur angedeutet sind. [...] Die Kultur selbst war es, welche der neuern Menschheit diese Wunde schlug. Sobald auf der einen Seite die erweiterte Erfahrung und das bestimmtere Denken eine schärfere Scheidung der Wissenschaften, auf der andern das verwickeltere Uhrwerk der Staaten eine strengere Absonderung der Stände und Geschäfte nothwendig machte, so zerriß auch der innere Bund der menschlichen Natur.[99]

---

[99] *Über die ästhetische Erziehung des Menschen in einer Reihe von Briefen*, *Schillers Werke*, *Nationalausgabe*, vol. 20, Weimar: Böhlau Nachfolger, 1962, pp. 309–412, 321–24. Forthwith *ÄE*. "At the first fair awakening of the powers of the mind, sense and intellect did not yet rule over strictly separate domains. [...] However high the mind might soar, it always drew matter lovingly along with it; and however fine and sharp the distinctions it might make, it never proceeded to mutilate. [...] With us, one might almost be tempted to assert the various faculties appear as separate in practice as they are distinguished by the psychologist in theory, and we see [...] whole classes of men, developing but one part of their potentialities, while of the rest, as in stunted growths, only vestigial traces remain. [...] It was civilisation itself which inflicted this wound upon modern man. Once the increase of empirical knowledge, and the more exact modes of thought, made sharper divisions between the sciences inevitable, and once the increasingly complex machinery of State necessitated a more rigorous separation of ranks and occupations,

Although, for Schiller, the dominance of reason over nature is as fruitless as the dominance of nature over reason, he remains favourably disposed towards this key concept of the Enlightenment. In his view the
realisation of reason is still the aim of human history. He is more confident regarding progress than Herder, because he believes the development of reason is a purposeful historical process. So far, however, true
reason is yet unrealised, because cultural and social attempts to bring
this about have been flawed. Reason can never replace nature, but has to
find a harmonious accommodation with it. To Schiller, the increase in
knowledge and understanding is laudable, in fact necessary for the overall progress of humanity, but its beneficial effects have so far been prevented from materialising, because the new insights have not yet been
successfully communicated. Their communication has not been addressed to the human being in its entirety.

> Die Vernunft hat geleistet, was sie leisten kann, wenn sie das Gesetz findet
> und es aufstellt; vollstrecken muß es der muthige Wille und das lebendige Ge-
> fühl. [...] Der Weg zu dem Kopf [muß] durch das Herz geöffnet werden. Aus-
> bildung des Empfindungsvermögens ist also das dringendere Bedürfnis der
> Zeit, nicht bloß weil sie ein Mittel wird, die verbesserte Einsicht für das Leben
> wirksam zu machen, sondern selbst darum, weil sie zu Verbesserung der Ein-
> sicht erweckt. (*ÄE*, 330–32)[100]

Schiller's critique of the Enlightenment is that although it has liberated
the intellect and society from various forms of exploitation through the
irrational and unjust,[101] it has failed to effectively implement its achievements to improve society. Its one-sided focus on reason and rationality
has merely managed to further barbarism and skepticim.

---

then the inner unity of human nature was severed, too." *Friedrich Schiller. On the Aesthetic Education of Man. In a Series of Letters*. Edited and translated by Elizabeth M. Wilkinson and L.A. Willoughby, Oxford: Clarendon, 1967, pp. 31, 33. Forthwith AE.
[100] "Reason has accomplished all that she can accomplish by discovering the law and establishing it. Its execution demands a resolute will and ardour of feeling. [...] The way
to the head must be opened through the heart. The development of man's capacity for
feeling is, therefore, the more urgent need of our age, not merely because it can be a
means of making better insights effective for living, but precisely because it provides
the impulse for bettering our insights." AE, 49, 53.
[101] "Der Geist der freien Untersuchung hat die Wahnbegriffe zerstreut, die lange Zeit den
Zugang zu der Wahrheit verwehrten, und den Grund unterwühlt, auf welchem Fana-
tismus und Betrug ihren Thron erbauten." *ÄE*, 331. "The spirit of free enquiry has dissipated those false conceptions which for so long barred the approach to truth, and
undermined the foundations upon which fanaticism and deception had raised their
throne." AE, 49.

Die Aufklärung des Verstandes, [...] zeigt im ganzen so wenig einen veredeln-
den Einfluß auf die Gesinnungen, daß sie vielmehr die Verderbniß durch Maximen befestigt. Wir verläugnen die Natur auf ihrem rechtmäßigen Felde, um
auf dem moralischen ihre Tyranney zu erfahren. [...] Nur in einer völligen
Abschwörung der Empfindsamkeit glaubt man gegen ihre Verwirrungen
Schutz zu finden, und der Spott, der den Schwärmer oft heilsam züchtigt, lä-
stert mit gleich wenig Schonung das edelste Gefühl. [...] So sieht man den
Geist der Zeit zwischen Verkehrtheit und Rohigkeit, zwischen Unnatur und
bloßer Natur, zwischen Superstititon und moralischem Unglauben schwan-
ken. (*ÄE*, 320–321)[102]

Schiller considers the failure of the French Revolution, as he sees it, as
proof that the sudden introduction of a political system based purely on
rational ethics cannot survive the translation from theory into practice.
By aspiring to make the abstract laws of reason the cornerstones of the
new society, one courts failure because human nature will not honour
these new laws and theoretically advanced and beneficial social innovations because they address only one side of the human make-up.[103]
The Enlightenment has so far failed in its objectives, because it has
tended to deny the natural-sensual aspect of humanity, and by suppressing it, set it free underground, so to speak, to undermine moral aspirations, which, to secure their existence, have under such conditions to

---

[102] "That Enlightenment of the mind [...] has had on the whole so little of an ennobling
     influence on feeling and character that it has tended rather to bolster up depravity by
     providing it with the support of precepts. We disown nature in her rightful sphere only
     to submit to her tyranny in the moral. [...] Only by completely abjuring sensibility can
     we, so it is thought, be safe from its aberrations; and the ridicule which often acts as a
     salutary chastener of the enthusiast is equally unsparing in its desecration of the
     noblest feeling. [...] Thus do we see the spirit of the age wavering between perversity
     and brutality, between unnaturalness and mere nature, between superstition and moral
     unbelief." AE, 27, 29.
[103] "Das Gebäude des Naturstaates wankt, seine mürben Fundamente weichen, und eine
     physische Möglichkeit scheint gegeben, das Gesetz auf den Thron zu stellen, den Men-
     schen endlich als Selbstzweck zu ehren, wahre Freiheit zur Grundlage der politischen
     Verbindung zu machen. Vergebliche Hoffnung! Die *moralische* Möglichkeit fehlt, und
     der freygebige Augenblick findet ein unempfängliches Geschlecht." *ÄE*, 319. "The fab-
     ric of the natural State is tottering, its rotten foundations are yielding, and there seems
     to be a physical possibility of setting Law upon the throne, of honouring Man at last as
     an end in himself and making true freedom the basis of political association. Vain
     hope! The moral possibility is wanting, and the favourable moment finds an apathetic
     generation." *On the Aesthetic Education of Man in a series of Letters by Friedrich Schiller*,
     translated with an introduction by Reginald Snell, London: Routledge & Kegan Paul,
     1954, p. 35. Forthwith AE by Snell.

be enforced. External coercion, however, does not represent progress towards humanity existing in reason and freedom.

Enlightened insights are valuable and worth rescuing. They have to be communicated in a way better suited to human understanding, i.e. by addressing the complete human being. The most direct, and oldest, path of human cognition, which is through the beautiful and through art, needs to be reinstated. Only the experience of beauty makes thorough human cognition possible, because it is the very bridge between the senses and reason, between passive perception (Empfindung) and active thought. Aesthetic experience needs to be re-appreciated.

> Indem ich bloß einen Ausgang aus der materiellen Welt und einen Übergang in die Geisterwelt suchte, hat mich der freie Lauf meiner Einbildungskraft schon mitten in die letztere hineingeführt. Die Schönheit, die wir suchen, liegt bereits hinter uns, und wir haben sie übersprungen, indem wir von dem bloßen Leben zu der reinen Gestalt und zu dem reinen Objekt übergiengen. Ein solcher Sprung ist nicht in der menschlichen Natur, und um gleichen Schritt mit dieser zu halten, werden wir zu der Sinnenwelt wieder umkehren müssen. Die Schönheit ist allerdings das Werk der freyen Betrachtung, und wir treten mit ihr in die Welt der Ideen – aber [...] ohne darum die sinnliche Welt zu verlassen, wie bey Erkenntnis der Wahrheit geschieht. (*ÄE*, 395–96)[104]

As the connection between reason and the senses, beauty is also the origin of rational cognition. "[Die Schönheit] wird erstlich, als ruhige Form, das wilde Leben besänftigen und von Empfindungen zu Gedanken den Übergang bahnen. [...] Diesen [...] Dienst leistet sie dem Naturmenschen." (*ÄE*, 365)[105] The experience of the aesthetic allows the peaceful and integrated co-existence of the two opposing "drives" of humanity, "the sensual drive" and the "formal drive", as Schiller calls them, which characterise the duality of human nature as "sinnlich-vernünftig"

---

[104] "Whilst I was merely seeking a way out from the material world and a transition to the world of spirit, my imagination has run away with me and carried me into the very heart of this latter. Beauty, which is what we were out to seek, already lies behind us; we have o'erleapt it completely in passing from mere life directly to pure form and pure object. But a sudden leap of this kind is contrary to human nature, and in order to keep step with this latter we shall have to turn back once more to the world of sense. Beauty is, admittedly, the work of free contemplation, and with it we do enter upon the world of ideas – but [...] without therefore leaving behind the world of sense." AE, 185, 187.

[105] "[Beauty] first, as tranquil form, [...] will assuage the violence of life, and pave the way that leads from sensation to thought. [...] [This service] she renders to natural man." AE, 119, 121.

and represent the intellectual and cultural tension between the sensually and materially concrete and the universally abstract and ideal in human culture.[106] The "Stofftrieb" precedes the "Formtrieb". Schiller defines the former as follows:

> Der erste dieser Triebe, den ich den sinnlichen nennen will, geht aus von dem physischen Daseyn des Menschen oder von seiner sinnlichen Natur, und ist beschäftigt, ihn in die Schranken der Zeit zu setzen und zur Materie zu machen. [...] Materie aber heißt hier nichts als Veränderung oder Realität, die die Zeit erfüllt; mithin fodert dieser Trieb, daß Veränderung sey, daß die Zeit einen Inhalt habe. (*ÄE*, 344)[107]

The formal drive is its opposite.

> Der zweyte jener Triebe, den man den Formtrieb nennen kann, geht aus von dem absoluten Daseyn des Menschen oder von seiner vernünftigen Natur, und ist bestrebt, ihn in Freyheit zu setzen, Harmonie in die Verschiedenheit seines Erscheinens zu bringen und bey allem Wechsel des Zustands seine Person zu behaupten. [...] Er entscheidet also für immer wie er für jetzt entscheidet, und er gebietet für jetzt was er für immer gebietet. Er umfaßt mithin die ganze Folge der Zeit [...]: er hebt die Zeit, er hebt die Veränderung auf, er will, daß das Wirkliche nothwendig und ewig, und daß das Ewige und Nothwendige wirklich sei. (*ÄE*, 345–46)[108]

Clearly the two drives also represent the opposition between the condition of historicity and the human desire for permanence. Their diametrically opposed pull, towards the ever-changing diversity of matter on the one hand, and towards the eternal abstract ideal on the other, dominates the human condition, human history and human culture, dividing humankind between its sensual-physical origin and condition and its aspir-

---

[106] Cf. *ÄE*, 374. In fact, only once the latter is present has the human being fully risen above the animal.

[107] "The first of these, which I will call the sensuous drive, proceeds from the physical existence of man, or his sensuous nature. Its business is to set him within the limits of time, and turn him into matter. [...] By matter in this context we understand nothing more than change, or reality which occupies time. Consequently this drive demands that there shall be change, that time shall have a content." AE, 79.

[108] "The second of the two drives, which we may call the formal drive, proceeds from the absolute existence of man, or from his rational nature, and is intent on giving him the freedom to bring harmony into the diversity of his manifestations, and to affirm his Person among his changes of Condition. [...] Hence it decides for ever as it decides for this moment, and commands for this moment what it commands for ever. Consequently it embraces the whole sequence of time [...]: it annuls time and annuls change. It wants the real to be necessary and eternal, and the eternal and the necessary to be real." AE, 81.

ation towards metaphysical divinity. Only the aesthetic condition can remedy this split.

> In unserm Wohlgefallen an der Schönheit [...] läßt sich keine solche Succession zwischen der Thätigkeit und dem Leiden unterscheiden, und die Reflexion zerfließt hier so vollkommen mit dem Gefühle, daß wir die Form unmittelbar zu empfinden glauben. Die Schönheit ist also zwar Gegenstand für uns, weil die Reflexion die Bedingung ist, unter der wir eine Empfindung von ihr haben; zugleich aber ist sie ein Zustand unsers Subjekts, weil das Gefühl die Bedingung ist, unter der wir eine Vorstellung von ihr haben. Sie ist also zwar Form, weil wir sie betrachten; zugleich aber ist sie Leben, weil wir sie fühlen. Mit einem Wort: sie ist zugleich unser Zustand und unsere That. (*ÄE*, 396)[109]

The beautiful is the connecting link between temporal existence and universal ideal as well as the precondition for developing rational thought. But it also provides the path towards re-connecting abstract rationality to the sensual world once this link was been lost or severely damaged by an over-powerful reason. As it helped to make the "Naturmensch" think, it reintroduces the "geistige Mensch" to the realm of the senses.

> Sie [die Schönheit] wird [...] als lebendes Bild die abgezogene Form mit sinnlicher Kraft ausrüsten, den Begriff zur Anschauung und das Gesetz zum Gefühl zurückführen. [...] Durch die Schönheit wird der geistige Mensch zur Materie zurück geführt und der Sinnenwelt wieder gegeben. (*ÄE*, 365)[110]

So the experience of the beautiful stands at the beginning and the end of the history of the dominance of human reason, enabling reason to develop, which lifts the human being above the animal, and curbing its power, once it threatens to cancel out the natural. The beautiful performs this balancing act between reason and the senses throughout cultural history. Always countering the dominant power in order to approach an equilibrium, the beautiful appears in guises that vary accord-

---

[109] "In the delight we take in beauty [...] no such succession of activity and passivity can be discerned; reflection is here so completely interfused with feeling that we imagine that the form is directly apprehended by sense. Beauty, then, is indeed an object for us, because reflection is the condition of our having any sensation of it; but it is at the same time a state of the perceiving subject, because feeling is a condition of our having any perception of it. Thus beauty is indeed form, because we contemplate it; but it is at the same time life, because we feel it. In a word: it is at once a state of our being and an activity we perform." AE, 187.

[110] "[Beauty] [...] as living image, will arm abstract form with sensuous power, lead concept back to intuition, and law back to feeling. [...] By means of beauty spiritual [intellectual] man is brought back to matter and restored to the world of sense." AE, 121, 123. Brackets my suggestion.

ing to the needs of different historical and intellectual conditions. It is always a humanising force, due to the intricate relationship that true freedom enjoys with the aesthetic state of mind. If the two drives both pull the human being into opposite directions by the coercion (Nöti-gung) typical of a drive, in their harmonious co-existence in the aesthetic they cancel each other out, setting the will free. (*ÄE*, 372–74)

> Das Gemüth geht also von der Empfindung zum Gedanken durch eine mittlere Stimmung über, in welcher Sinnlichkeit und Vernunft zugleich thätig sind, eben deswegen aber ihre bestimmende Gewalt gegenseitig aufheben, und durch eine Entgegensetzung eine Negation bewirken. Die mittlere Stimmung, in welcher das Gemüth weder physisch noch moralisch genöthigt und doch auf beyde Art thätig ist, verdient vorzugsweise eine freie Stimmung zu heißen, und wenn man den Zustand sinnlicher Bestimmung den physischen, den Zustand vernünftiger Bestimmung aber den logischen und moralischen nennt, so muß man diesen Zustand der realen und aktiven Bestimmbarkeit den ästhetischen heißen. (*ÄE*, 375)[111]

Thus liberated, the previously coerced individual only now becomes fully human. Schiller continues:

> Sobald wir uns erinnern, daß ihm durch die einseitige Nöthigung der Natur beym Empfinden und durch die ausschließende Gesetzgebung der Vernunft beym Denken gerade diese Freyheit entzogen wurde, so müssen wir das Vermögen, welches ihm in der ästhetischen Stimmung zurückgegeben wird, als die höchste aller Schenkungen, als die Schenkung der Menschheit selbst betrachten. (*ÄE*, 378)[112]

The experience of the aesthetic, like the activity of playing, which Schiller sees linked to it,[113] is a symbol of human perfection and a taster of the

---

[111] "Our psyche passes, then, from sensation to thought via a middle disposition in which sense and reason are both active at the same time. Precisely for this reason, however, they cancel each other out as determining forces, and bring about a negation by means of an opposition. This middle disposition, in which the psyche is subject neither to physical or moral constraint, and yet is active in both these ways, pre-eminently deserves to be called a free disposition; and if we are to call the condition of sensuous determination the physical, and the condition of rational determination the logical or moral, then we must call this condition of real and active determinability the aesthetic." AE, 141.

[112] "As soon as we recall that it was precisely of this freedom that he was deprived by the one-sided constraint of nature in the field of sensation and by the exclusive authority of reason in the realm of thought, then we are bound to consider the power which is restored to him in the aesthetic mode as the highest of all bounties, as the gift of humanity itself." AE, 147.

[113] This aesthetic state of mind is experienceable in the reality of time and space in play. True aesthetics is play. Only at play can the human being be truly human. "Der

destination of human development, its "accomplished destiny", which
will only be achieved in the "totality of time".[114] In the present state, it
can only exist as aesthetic semblance, as "Schein".[115] In the realm of this
aesthetic semblance the human being can experience perfection, and experience acting in complete freedom, because here he is autonomous
and liberated, free from the dictates of reality and from coercing reason.

By extension, the "ästhetische Staat" is the culmination of all human
social organisations for Schiller. It suffers from none of the deficiencies
of its one-dimensional cousins.

> Wenn in dem dynamischen Staat der Rechte der Mensch dem Menschen
> als Kraft begegnet und sein Wirken beschränkt – wenn er sich ihm in dem
> ethischen Staat der Pflichten mit der Majestät des Gesetzes entgegenstellt
> und sein Wollen fesselt, so darf er ihm im Kreise des schönen Umgangs, in
> dem ästhetischen Staat, nur als Gestalt erscheinen, nur als Objekt des freyen
> Spiels gegenüber stehen. Freyheit zu geben durch Freyheit ist das Grundge-
> setz dieses Reichs. Der dynamische Staat kann die Gesellschaft bloß möglich
> machen [...]; der ethische Staat kann sie bloß (moralisch) nothwendig ma-
> chen, [...]; der ästhetische Staat allein kann sie wirklich machen, weil er den
> Willen des Ganzen durch die Natur des Individuums vollzieht. [because]
> Das Schöne allein genießen wir als Individuen und als Gattung zugleich.
> (*ÄE*, 410–11)[116]

Mensch spielt nur, wo er in voller Bedeutung des Wortes Mensch ist, und er ist nur da
ganz Mensch, wo er spielt." *ÄE*, 359. "Man only plays when he is in the fullest sense a
human being, and he is only fully a human being when he plays." AE, 107. This is because here too the two opposing drives are both active, i.e. cancel each other out,
which leads to physical as well as moral liberation. Cf. *ÄE*, 354. This aesthetic tendency has always been present in human nature and is a mark of man's humanity. Cf.
ÄE, 405.

[114] "ausgeführte Bestimmung" and "Allheit der Zeit", *ÄE*, 353.

[115] For an illuminating discussion of the contemporary meaning of the word *Schein* and
Schiller's use of it cf. Wilkinson/Willoughby, *Friedrich Schiller. On the Aesthetic Education
of Man* (AE), pp. 327–29.

[116] "If in the dynamic State of rights, it is as a force that one man encounters another, and
imposes limits on his activities; if in the ethical State of duties Man sets himself over
against man with the majesty of the law, and puts a curb on his desires: in those circles
where conduct is governed by beauty, in the aesthetic State, none may appear to the
other except as form, or confront him except as an object of free play. To bestow freedom by means of freedom is the fundamental law of this kingdom. The dynamic State
merely makes society possible [...]; the ethical State can merely make it (morally)
necessary [...]; the aesthetic State alone can make it real, because it consummates the
will of the whole through the nature of the individual. [...] Beauty alone do we enjoy
at once as individual and as genus." AE, 215, 217.

Like Herder, Schiller sees artistic and aesthetic activity as closely related to the successful and happy functioning of human social organisations, such as a state, society, or community. It is necessary to satisfy human beings spiritually, emotionally and intellectually as well as to make them useful and integrated members of their community.

The experience of the beautiful, play, and the aesthetic semblance are all variants of the synthesis Schiller seeks to establish between reality and abstraction, between matter and reason, between those entities that, if left unchecked, become tyrannical and deprive humans of their humanity and of freedom. While these entities exist in unrelated co-existence, they are experienced as a painful and dissatisfying split. Their successful interrelation makes available in space and time, albeit in a pretend fashion, the synthesis that is for all aspects of human existence achieved only in the fullness of time. The interrelations Schiller endeavours to establish are all based on a link between value and time: the absolute idea is joined to matter, the universal ideal is joined to changeability, it transforms.[117] The ideal can only appear as process in the reality of time and place. It must be historicised. Schiller is keen to convince his readers that such historicising of the ideal is no profaning, and will not damage its purity, but rather enhance its viability.

> Wir dürfen also nicht mehr verlegen seyn, einen Übergang von der sinnlichen Abhängigkeit zu der moralischen Freyheit zu finden, nachdem durch die Schönheit der Fall gegeben ist, daß die letztere mit der erstern vollkommen zusammen bestehen könne, und daß der Mensch, um sich als Geist zu erweisen, der Materie nicht zu entfliehen brauche. (*ÄE*, 397)[118]

Both Herder and Schiller are concerned with the inefficacy of reason on its own. Both are convinced that the abstract and the timeless have no

---

[117] "Das Ideal-Schöne, obgleich unteilbar und einfach, zeigt in verschiedener Beziehung sowohl eine schmelzende als energische Eigenschaft; in der Erfahrung *gibt* es eine schmelzende und energische Schönheit. So ist es, und so wird es in allen Fällen sein, wo das Absolute in die Schranken der Zeit gesetzt ist und Ideen der Venunft in der Menschheit realisiert werden sollen." *ÄE*, 361. "Beauty, though one and indivisible, exhibits under different aspects a melting as well as an energizing attribute; but in experience there actually *is* an energizing and a melting type of beauty. So it is, and so it always will be, in all those cases where the Absolute is set within the limitations of time, and the ideas of Reason have to be realized in and through human action." AE, 113.

[118] "We need, then, no longer feel at a loss for a way which might lead us from our dependence upon sense towards moral freedom, since beauty affords us an instance of the latter being perfectly compatible with the former, an instance of man not needing to flee matter in order to manifest himself as spirit." AE, 189.

proper bearing on the heterogeneous reality of a "sinnlich-vernünftig" humanity. Divorcing the human being from his roots in the sensual is to ignore his true nature. Both seek a concretisation of the abstract ideal in human reality. Both regard art as the medium that spans both the abstract and the concrete. Herder saw the national or local element in poetry as the link between abstract thought and concrete matter. It communicated the idea to the mind through the shared tradition that was evident, understood and real, yet ephemeral in its distant temporal origin. A tradition has concrete results in the present, but it is based on a chain of links that no longer exist in the temporal present, that are themselves ideas. For Schiller, the realm of aesthetics was the middle ground where the abstract and the concrete sides of humanity can co-exist and interact in such a way that the idea acquires reality. The national and the aesthetic make the abstract able to be experienced by placing it in the realm of matter, from which it grew and has become separate.[119] The linking entity is itself closely aligned with the concrete. Historically, it occupies a place, or emerges at a point in time, at which human beings first employed the most basic abstractions, i.e. revealed themselves as different from the rest of nature. The linking entity has a *historical* definition that qualifies it to be employed to remedy *conceptual* problems. The realm of matter is governed by time and subject to change. The abstract idea, previously thought absolute, must now undergo a process of development to make any sense. Schiller is precise about the process: the dominance of reason is not so much a deviation from the right course as a necessary stage in an all-over progression.

> Die mannichfaltigen Anlagen im Menschen zu entwickeln, war kein anderes Mittel, als sie einander entgegen zu setzen. Dieser Antagonism der Kräfte ist das große Instrument der Kultur, aber auch nur das Instrument; denn solange derselbe dauert, ist man erst auf dem Wege zu dieser. [...] Einseitigkeit in Übung der Kräfte führt zwar das Individuum unausbleiblich zum Irrtum, aber die Gattung zu Wahrheit. (*ÄE*, 326–27)[120]

---

[119] "So wird denn allmählich das einzelne konkrete Leben vertilgt, damit das Abstrakt des Ganzen sein dürftiges Daseyn friste, und ewig bleibt der Staat [der vernünftigen Ethik und Moral] seinen Bürgern fremd, weil ihn das Gefühl nirgends findet." *ÄE*, 324. "And so gradually individual concrete life is extinguished, in order that the abstract life of the whole may prolong its sorry existence, and the State remains eternally alien to its citizens because nowhere does feeling discover it." AE by Snell, 41.

[120] "If the manifold potentialities in man were ever to be developed, there was no other way but to pit them one against the other. This antagonism of faculties and functions is the great instrument of civilisation – but it is only the instrument; for as long as it per-

Dialectics is again the engine of progress. The certainty with which Schiller defines the current (deficient) state as a necessary stage grows from his clearly developed idea of the progressive nature of the world-historical process, which progresses dialectically, so that each stage has its own clear purpose. While Schiller owes this seminal idea of the intrinsic value of every era to Herder's new historicist thinking, he adds the functional element. Herder himself, as we have seen, gives no clear indication of how the historical progress necessarily proceeds. This is the reason why he does not attach a progressive significance to the ills he defines in his present. The dominance of reason is simply detrimental. This has made it easy to tar him with the brush of irrationalism and primitivism. But Herder, in a truly historicist act, merely leaves the specifics of the historical process open. Despite this key difference between Herder and Schiller, they are in agreement about the assessment of the present and the means of its improvement.

Both Herder and Schiller want to facilitate an understanding of art that can make art an instrument of social, or in their terms, of human progress. Both realise that while this process may be governed by reason, reason, if it is to have any bearing on humanity, cannot be external to time, and to space. So both hold on to a notion of an ideal, but in both cases this ideal is historicised, i.e. placed in direct contact with the effects of time. It thus becomes a developing ideal that evolves through manifestations in time. The developing essence is the historicised remnant of the classicist and enlightened notions of abstract ideals. The essence in Herder's concept of *Volkspoesie* is the national tradition which remains always the essence of one particular group, but as a tradition is alive, adapting to and reflecting the changes brought about by time. In Schiller's theory, the essence is the beautiful, which in its abstract form is indivisible and uniform, but in the reality of human experience appears in different guises, reflecting the needs of the times. Given that reason cannot be external to space if it is to affect humanity, both link the mediation of reason to a communal experience. The art they have in mind does not only connect the individual to the spiritual and sensual sides of his existence, it also connects him to the fellow-humans who share his existence. Art communicates complete human understanding. This can only be guaranteed through a medium that is accessible: the

---

sists, we are only on the way to becoming civilized. [...] One-sidedness in the exercise of his powers must, it is true, inevitably lead the individual into error, but the species as a whole to truth." AE, 41.

national tradition and the beautiful. The two are linked: the national tradition will produce the beautiful in art, a beauty that the particular individual can grasp in his specific particularity, just as the beautiful will appear in specific guises fitting the requirement of the particular moment. National particularity and a beautiful universal are not pitted against each other in mutual exclusion. In fact, Herder's approach takes the form of a historicised literary classicism, in which the "norm" can only exist as the origin that develops in time. On the other hand, Schiller's concept of art has strong elements of the *volks*-poetic, albeit in a universal sense, because it seeks to address its audience through the channel of a shared human tradition, the development of human reason from the senses. Schiller's concept *appears* as more universal, more "classicised", because it considers humanity as a whole, theoretically. In practice, however, Schiller is quite clear that art has to be particular: beauty wears the guise of the (historical) moment. At the very end of Schiller's *Briefe,* the aesthetic state and the national-communal tradition are indeed closely linked, linked through exactly the qualities of the concrete and the real that nevertheless have one foot in the realm of the abstract.

> Der Staat des schönen Scheins [...] [existiert], wo nicht die geistlose Nachahmung fremder Sitten, sondern eigne schöne Natur das Betragen lenkt, wo der Mensch durch die verwickeltsten Verhältnisse mit kühner Einfalt und ruhiger Unschuld geht und weder nöthig hat, fremde Freyheit zu kränken, um die seinige zu behaupten, noch seine Würde wegzuwerfen, um Anmut zu zeigen. (*ÄE,* 412)[121]

Evidently, the over-arching problem behind both Herder's and Schiller's efforts is that posed by the new awareness of historicity, which turned out to be the key problem of modernity, and of the identity of modernity. How can identity and any kind of normativity be sustained in a situation of temporal fluidity? With this question, the Pandora's Box of European rationalism springs open: rationalism was becoming seen as increasingly problematic. This understanding inaugurates a critical tradi-

---

[121] Incidentally, Schiller's description of the thus rounded "Mensch" echoes Herder's description of the natural genius. "The State of Aesthetic Semblance [exists] [...] where conduct is governed, not by some soulless imitation of the manners and morals of others [foreign manners and morals], but by the aesthetic nature we have made our own [our own aesthetic nature], where men make their way, with undismayed simplicity and tranquil innocence, through even the most involved and complex situations, free alike of the compulsion to infringe the freedom of others in order to assert their own, as of the necessity to shed their Dignity in order to manifest Grace." AE, 219. Brackets my suggestions.

tion that continues to this day in various attempts to revise, demask or abolish the subject-centred rationalist core of modern European culture, and finally launches the post-modern endeavour. Standing at the beginning of this phase of questioning a deeply rooted paradigm, Herder and Schiller were in the main revisionists. They still believed that the "right" sort of reason was progressive, beneficial, and most of all *itself*, rather than a mask for power or desire. In addressing the problem of modernity, Herder focuses on the origin of humanity, Schiller on its aim in finding solutions. They hold on to the reality of an ideal, which can and must be modified by time and (part-) realised in (a cultural-artistic) space. This position is not dissimilar to that of Jürgen Habermas, who places himself directly in the tradition of what might be called a constructive criticism of reason inaugurated by Schiller, Fichte and Hegel.[122] Habermas, to whom all post-enlightenment criticism is necessarily counter-enlightenment critique, argues for a "reconstructed dialectic of enlightenment" because "the defects of the Enlightenment can only be made good by further enlightenment. The totalized critique of reason undercuts the capacity of reason to be critical".[123] He, too, sees the path towards a solution in concretisation, which he calls "communicative reason" (and the resulting communicative action).

> The reason operating in communicative action not only stands under [...] external, situational constraints; its own conditions of possibility necessitate its branching out into the dimension of historical time, social space, and body-centred experiences. That is to say, the rational potential of speech is interwoven with the resources of any particular given lifeworld. [...] Concrete forms of life replace transcendental consciousness in its function of creating unity. In culturally embodied self-understandings, intuitively present group solidarities, and the competences of socialized individuals that are brought into play as know-how, the reason expressed in communicative action is mediated with the traditions, social practices and body-centred complexes of experience that coalesce into particular totalities.[124]

After two hundred years of critical efforts Habermas has little faith in the mediating powers of "consciousness", but he clearly recognises that any "neo"-Enlightenment paradigm, i.e. a universally acknowledged conceptual structure to explain and understand ourselves and the world,

---

[122] J. Habermas, *The Philosophical Discourse of Modernity*, (1985) trans. by Frederick Lawrence, Cambridge: Polity Press, 1987, repr. 1994, p. 295.
[123] Ibid., p. xvii.
[124] Ibid., 325–6.

must assimilate the awareness of historicity. His suggestion is the following:

> These particular forms of life [...] exhibit structures common to lifeworld in
> general. But these universal structures are only stamped on particular life
> forms through the medium of action oriented to mutual understanding by
> which they have to be reproduced. This explains why the importance of these
> universal structures can increase in the course of historical processes of differ-
> entiation. This is also the key to the rationalization of the lifeworld and to the
> successive release of the rational potential contained in communicative ac-
> tion. This historical tendency can account for the normative content of a mo-
> dernity threatened by self-destruction without drawing upon the construc-
> tions of the philosophy of history.[125]

Friedrich Schlegel: Progressive Universal Poetry in the *Athenäum*

Essential to both Herder's and Schiller's concepts of poetry was the need
for concretisation. Only concretisation could, in their view, assure successful communication, on which the successful functioning of poetry
ultimately relied. Through this notion of functionality, they retained an
obvious link with the Enlightenment concept of poetry, which they
sought to modify and improve. The early Romantic concept of poetry,
for which Friedrich Schlegel's pronouncements in the *Athenäum*
(1798–1800) may serve as a representative example, equally demands specific concretisation to allow successful communication,[126] but consider-

---

[125] Ibid., 326.

[126] "Das Spiel der Mitteilung und der Annäherung ist das Geschäft und die Kraft des
Lebens. [...] Darum darf es auch dem Dichter nicht genügen, den Ausdruck seiner
eigentümlichen Poesie, wie sie ihm angeboren und angebildet wurde, in bleibenden
Werken zu hinterlassen. Er muß streben, seine Poesie ewig zu erweitern, und sie der
höchsten zu nähern die überhaupt auf der Erde möglich ist; dadurch, daß er seinen Teil
an das große Ganze auf die bestimmteste Weise anzuschließen strebt: denn die tötende
Verallgemeinerung wirkt gerade das Gegenteil. Er kann es, wenn er den Mittelpunkt gefunden hat, durch Mitteilung mit denen, die ihn gleichfalls von einer andern Seite auf
eine andre Weise gefunden haben." (Friedrich Schlegel, *Gespräch über die Poesie, Kritische
Friedrich-Schlegel-Ausgabe*, vol. 2, ed. by Hans Eichner, Munich/Paderborn/Vienna:
Schönigh/Thomas Verlag, 1967, p. 286). Forthwith KFSA. "The play of communicating
and approaching is the business and the force of life. [...] Therefore, the poet cannot
be satisfied with leaving behind in lasting works the expression of his unique poetry as
it was native to him and which he acquired by education. He must strive continually to
expand his poetry and his view of poetry, and to approximate the loftiest possibility of
it on earth by endeavouring in the most specific way to integrate his part with the en-

ably reduces the notion of functionality. In Schlegel's theory of poetic art there is no trace of the "pretend"-aspect of Schiller's aesthetics. Schlegel attempts to transport what Schiller defined as only possible in play into historical reality.

Poetry, Romantic poetry as Schlegel understands it, is not a means to any end, but is itself the end beyond which humanity cannot go conceptually. Art has not a social function, it is an ontological reality, the most complete representation, and hence understanding of life that the human mind is capable of, which yet always remains an approximation. He declares in the seminal 116th *Athenäum Fragment*, (which contains much of early Romantic poetic theory *in nuce*):

> [Romantische Poesie] kann auch […] am meisten zwischen dem Dargestellten und dem Darstellenden, frei von allem realen und idealen Interesse auf den Flügeln der poetischen Reflexion in der Mitte schweben, diese Reflexion immer wieder potenzieren und in einer endlosen Reihe von Spiegeln vervielfachen. Sie ist der höchsten und allseitigsten Bildung fähig. (KFSA, II, 182–3)[127]

This idea shares Herder's insistence on the supreme power and importance of poetry and takes up Schiller's notion of the aesthetic as the only place where the antinomies of the human condition, the dialectics of humanity, can interact meaningfully. Poetry does not only need to be concrete itself, it is also the place where the results of thought, of philosophy, can become concrete and real through a productive dialectics. Schlegel lets Ludoviko argue in the *Gespräch über die Poesie*:

> Der Idealismus in jeder Form muß auf ein oder die andre Art aus sich herausgehn, um in sich zurückkehren zu können, und zu bleiben, was er ist. Deswegen muß und wird sich aus seinem Schoß ein neuer ebenso großer Realismus erheben. […] Dieser neue Realismus [wird], weil er doch idealischen Ursprungs sein, und gleichsam auf idealischem Grund und Boden schweben

---

tire body of poetry: deadening generalizations result in just the opposite. He can do this when he has found the centre point through communication with those who have found theirs from a different side, in a different way." *Friedrich Schlegel. Dialogue on Poetry and Literary Aphorisms*, translated, introduced and annotated by Ernst Behler and Roman Struc, University Park & London: Pennsylvania State University Press, 1968, pp. 54–55. Forthwith *Dialogue on Poetry*.

[127] "[Romantic Poetry] […] too can soar, free from all real and ideal interests, on the wings of poetic reflection, midway between the work and the artist. It can even exponentiate this reflection and multiply it as in an endless series of mirrors. It is capable of the highest and the most universal education." *Dialogue on Poetry*, 140–41.

muß, als Poesie erscheinen, die ja auf der Harmonie des Ideellen und Reellen
beruhen soll. (KFSA, II, 314–5)[128]

Schlegel works out his ideas in connection with concepts developed in
contemporaneous idealist-transcendental philosophy, especially by
Fichte. As philosophy has begun to think seriously about thinking,
Schegel maintains that by the same token – or the same dialectical reciprocity – poetry should incorporate in its presentations a critique of its
own creation, should include a poetry of poetry.

> Es gibt eine Poesie, deren eins und alles das Verhältnis des Idealen und des
> Realen ist, und die [...] Transzendentalpoesie heißen müßte. [...] So wie man
> aber wenig Wert auf eine Transzendentalphilosophie legen würde, die nicht
> kritisch wäre, nicht auch das Produzierende mit dem Produkt darstellte, und
> im System der transzendentalen Gedanken zugleich eine Charakteristik des
> transzendentalen Denkens enthielte: so sollte wohl auch jene Poesie die in
> modernen Dichtern nicht seltnen transzendentalen Materialien und Vor-
> übungen zu einer poetischen Theorie des Dichtungsvermögens mit der künst-
> lerischen Reflexion und schönen Selbstbespiegelung [...] vereinigen, und in
> jeder ihrer Darstellungen sich selbst mit darstellen, und überall zugleich Poe-
> sie und Poesie der Poesie sein. (Athenäum Fragment 238, KFSA, II, 204)[129]

The new poetry will develop in tandem with contemporary philosophy.
Schlegel repeatedly argues for the fusion of philosophy and poetry.[130]
But it is already clear from the new poetry's ability to "hover"
(schweben) "between the real and the ideal" that poetry occupies a meta-

---

[128] "Idealism in any form must transcend itself in one way or another, in order to be able
to return to itself and remain what it is. Therefore, there must and will arise from the
matrix of idealism a new and equally infinite realism. [...] This new realism, since it
must be of idealistic origin and must hover as it were over an idealistic ground, will
emerge as poetry which indeed is to be based on the harmony of the ideal and the real."
Dialogue on Poetry, 83–4.

[129] "There is a poetry whose One and All is the relationship of the ideal and the real: it
should [...] be called transcendental poetry. [...]. But we should not care for a transcendental philosophy unless it were critical, unless it portrayed the producer along
with the product, unless it embraced in its system of transcendental thoughts a characterisation of transcendental thinking: in the same way, that poetry which is not infrequently encountered in modern poets should combine those transcendental materials and preliminary exercises for a poetic theory of the creative power with the artistic
reflection and beautiful self-mirroring. [...] Thus this poetry should portray itself with
each of its portrayals; everywhere and at the same time, it should be poetry and the
poetry of poetry." *Dialogue on Poetry*, 145.

[130] Cf. Athenäum Fragment 451 (KFSA II, 255) and of course also Athenäum Fragment
116 (KFSA II, 182): "die Poesie mit der Philosophie und Rhetorik in Berührung setzen";
i.e. "put poetry in touch with philosophy and rhetorics." *Dialogue on Poetry*, 140.

level to philosophy. This makes poetry, rather than philosophy, the supreme medium of human understanding. Philosophy is a theoretical preparation that enables the poet to rise above his individual self and work and take up, at various times, a creative distance to his creation.[131] This enhanced self-understanding on the part of the poet-thinker enables the critique to become part of that which is being criticised, linking subject and object. For Schlegel, the aesthetic condition of the mind is no longer a form of play, a potential, make-believe situation outside reality that symbolises an ideal state as it was for Schiller. It *is* a symbolic condensation of reality. That Schlegel considers this configuration of thought in poetry as the only way to achieve a complete view of reality, not a playful option in a space of extra-reality, is evident from the 116th Fragment, where he sets the destined task (*Bestimmung*) of romantic poetry as "[to] make poetry full of life and sociable and make life and society poetic".[132]

Poetry is capable of this ultimate achievement because it can represent human existence in its dynamics. Schlegel's concept shares its dialectically dynamic character with Schiller's. But while Schiller's is only nominally open-ended (the ideal may not be fully attainable, but it exists), Schlegel's has genuine open-endedness as its key virtue. Schiller's dialectics is predicated on the neutralising capabilities of the dialectic: Schiller, as did Hegel, sought an eventual solution to the dynamically warring counter-forces, albeit that this solution was conceived of as existing beyond current human reality. Schlegel, on the other hand, does not focus on the neutralising resolution, he instead makes the dynamic process supreme. The 116th Athenäum Fragment proclaims:

> Die romantische Poesie ist eine progressive Universalpoesie. [...] Andere Dichtarten sind fertig, und können nun vollständig zergliedert werden. Die romantische Dichtart ist noch im Werden; ja, das ist ihr eigentliches Wesen, daß sie ewig nur werden, nie vollendet sein kann. Sie kann durch keine Theo-

---

[131] Ernst Behler argued that Schlegel joined philosophy and poetry (as he claims needs to be done in Athenäum Fragment 451) by abolishing the "distinction between poetry and philosophy" because both Idealist philosophy and transcendental poetry partake of the (same) reflective activity. (Behler, *German Romantic Literary Theory*, Cambridge: Cambridge University Press, 1993, p. 139). In my view Guido Naschert's description that Schlegel "[vollzieht] eine Detranszentalisierung der Wissenschaftslehre" ("Friedrich Schlegel über Wechselerweis und Ironie (Teil 2)", *Athenäum. Jahrbuch für Romantik* 1997, 11–36, 31) is more to the point.

[132] "die Poesie lebendig und gesellig, und das Leben und die Gesellschaft poetisch [zu] machen", KFSA II, 182.

rie erschöpft werden, und nur eine divinatorische Kritik dürfte es wagen, ihr Ideal charakterisieren zu wollen. Sie allein ist unendlich, wie sie allein frei ist. (Athenäum Fragment 116, KFSA II, 183)[133]

The dynamic dialectical process is not so much the path to the eventual solution, but the main event itself. The means through which the dynamic dialectic is achieved is Romantic irony, the concept that Friedrich Schlegel invented, more or less single-handedly, by going far beyond the basis of the ancient idea of rhetorical irony, (although he sees himself as part of the ancient tradition).[134] In the *Critical Fragments* (1797) he defines irony as follows:

> Sie entspringt aus der Vereinigung von Lebenskunstsinn und wissenschaftlichem Geist, aus dem Zusammentreffen vollendeter Naturphilosophie und vollendeter Kunstphilosophie. Sie enthält und erregt ein Gefühl von dem unauflöslichen Widerstreit des Unbedingten und des Bedingten, der Unmöglichkeit und Notwendigkeit einer vollständigen Mitteilung. Sie ist die freieste aller Lizenzen, denn durch sie setzt man sich über sich selbst weg; und doch auch die gesetzlichste, denn sie ist unbedingt notwendig. (Kritisches Fragment 108, KFSA II, 160)[135]

This sort of irony, when employed by a writer-speaker who is equipped with the critical self-understanding afforded by transcendental philosophy, is capable of completely presenting, and communicating, human reality.

Schlegel fully subscribes to the heterogeneity of humanity, the split between mind and senses, which has come about by the advances of reason, whose dominance has in turn become questionable by the new awareness of historicity. In terms of the working poet, this split is mani-

---

133 "Romantic poetry is a progressive universal poetry. [...] Other types of poetry are completed and can now be entirely analyzed. The Romantic type of poetry is still becoming; indeed its particular essence is that it is always becoming and that it can never be completed. It cannot be exhausted by any theory, and only a divinatory criticism might dare to characterize its ideal. It alone is infinite, as it alone is free." *Dialogue on Poetry*, 141.

134 Cf. Behler, *German Romantic Literary Theory*, 134–53.

135 "It originates in a sense of an art of living and a scientific intellect, in the meeting of accomplished natural philosophy and accomplished philosophy of art. It contains and excites a feeling of the insoluble conflict of the absolute and the relative, of the impossibility and necessity of total communication. It is the freest of all liberties, for it enables us to rise above our own self; and still the most legitimate [the liberty most governed by laws], for it is absolutely necessary." *Dialogue on Poetry*, 131. In brackets my suggestion.

fest in the state of heightened intellectual sophistication that has dissociated him from a common source of inspirational nourishment, which Schlegel describes in images of vitalising nature.

> Ihr müßt es oft im Dichten gefühlt haben, daß es Euch an einem festen Halt für Euer Wirken gebrach, an einem mütterlichen Boden, einem [umwölbenden Sternen-]Himmel, einer lebendigen [erfrischenden Lebens-]Luft [um frei aufzuatmen].[136]

That he, too, expects poetry to play the key role in sorting out the problems created by this split is evident from the notion of Idealism bringing forth a new realism, i.e. poetry. It is also evident from his definition of the intellectual mythology (*Mythologie des Geistes*) in the *Gespräch*. If Romantic irony is the means to be used by an individual writer to present the whole of reality in an individual work, then this new mythology is the general result of such efforts. It could be, once it has been created, a kind of meta-poetry common to all modern poets.

> Einen Vorzug hat die Mythologie. Was sonst das Bewußtsein ewig flieht, ist hier dennoch sinnlich-geistig zu schauen, und festgehalten, wie die Seele in dem umgebenden Leibe, durch den sie in unser Auge schimmert, zu unserm Ohre spricht. [...] Die Mythologie ist ein solches *Kunst*werk der *Natur*. In ihrem Gewebe ist das *Höchste wirklich* gebildet. (KFSA II, 318, my italics)[137]

The added italics make the deeply synthetic nature of mythology, in terms of the human constitution and human experience, quite clear. It links the immaterial-abstract and the physically concrete in a reciprocal animation. It is natural and (artificially) created at the same time. It gives the intangible reality. By calling it mythology, he deliberately connects this new poetry to the first and original artistic-intellectual form of human expression, suggesting that this form, or rather its structures, need to be resurrected and adapted. Always mindful of the complex relationship between the ancient and the modern, Schlegel is happy to

---

136 KFSA II, 312. The brackets give the variant readings according to Friedrich Schlegel. *Sämtliche Werke*, V, 1823, which are given as footnotes in KFSA II. "While [writing poetry] you must often have felt the absence of a firm basis for your activity, a matrix, a sky, a living atmosphere." *Dialogue on Poetry*, 81.

137 "Mythology has one great advantage. What usually escapes our consciousness can here be perceived and held fast through the senses and spirit like the soul in the body surrounding it, through which it shines into our eye and speaks to our ear. [...] Mythology is such a work of art created by nature. In its texture the sublime is really formed." *Dialogue on Poetry*, 85–86.

point out that neither irony nor mythology are specific to modernity,[138] both in fact originate in antiquity. But, in reconditioned form, both have a crucial function to perform for modern culture.[139]

But for all the upbeat, hopeful optimism which suggests that solutions are possible and within reach, as expressed in the "Rede über die Mythologie" and in his assessment of Goethe's genius, Schlegel equally expresses doubts as to what extent these problems of modern humanity are really capable of a lasting solution. (This is, no doubt, also the result of the transcendentalist poet-thinker's ironic self-understanding.) The very infinity of the Romantic project belies the possibility of any settlement. A nominal infinity is also present in Schiller's educational project – and in Fichte's philosophical one, as we shall see – but for these two the logical inevitability of the final solution, which they can already grasp in theory, remains the focus. And herein lies the difference: Schlegel takes the notion of infinity more seriously, this "Bewußtsein der ewigen Agilität",[140] which fixes his focus on the process itself, because it is all that is likely to ever really exist. For him, poetry can never fully provide lasting solutions, but it can *present* the status quo in such a manner that the human mind is afforded a glimpse of the totality of its situation. And this glimpse affords no more than the momentary experience of an individual totality by means of an artistic creation: "Gebildet ist ein Werk, wenn es überall scharf begrenzt, innerhalb der Grenzen aber grenzenlos und unerschöpflich ist, wenn es sich selbst ganz treu, überall

---

[138] Cf. Kritisches Fragment 42, KFSA II, 152.

[139] Schlegel also perceives precedents for his concepts of irony and mythology in the literature of modernity, which is only newly being defined as "romantic" by himself and his brother August Wilhelm: "Da finde ich nun eine große Ähnlichkeit mit jenem großen Witz der romantischen Poesie, der [...] in der Konstruktion des Ganzen sich zeigt, und den unser Freund uns schon so oft an den Werken des Cervantes und des Shakespeare entwickelt hat. Ja diese künstlich geordnete Verwirrung, diese reizende Symmetrie von Widersprüchen, dieser wunderbare ewige Wechsel von Enthusiasmus und Ironie, der selbst im kleinsten des Ganzen lebt, scheinen mir schon eine indirekte Mythologie zu sein." (KFSA II, 318–9) "Here I find a great similarity with the marvellous wit of romantic poetry which [...] manifests itself [...] in the structure of the whole and which was so often pointed out by our friend for the works of Cervantes and Shakespeare. Indeed, this artfully ordered confusion, this charming symmetry of contradictions, this wonderfully perennial alteration of enthusiasm and irony which lives even in the smallest parts of the whole, seem to me to be an indirect mythology themselves." *Dialogue on Poetry*, 86.

[140] *Ideen* 69, KFSA II, 263; "consciousness of an eternal agility".

gleich, und doch über sich selbst erhaben ist." (Athenäum Fragment 297, KFSA II, 215)[141]

Schlegel's thought of this period is marked by two tendencies running counter to each other, his own dialectic so to speak, which he is trying to grasp within one framework: the optimistic "solutionist" tendency is expressed in the imminence of the new intellectual mythology, the limiting tendency finds expression in his insistence on the essential presence of irony. Schlegel's Romantic irony offers the writer the means to capture and present, but not neutralise, the antinomies of human existence. The "prospect of an endlessly developing classicism"[142] which the "progressive Universalpoesie" provides pinpoints this dual approach; it is meant to be a classicism, but one that is in the continuous process of becoming.[143]

---

[141] "A work is formed when it is clearly delimited everywhere, but limitless and inexhaustible within these limits, when it is true to itself and the same everywhere, and yet rises above itself."

[142] "Aussicht auf eine grenzenlos wachsende Klassizität" (Athenäum Fragment 116).

[143] It needs no reiteration that Schlegel was deeply influenced by Fichte's *Wissenschaftslehre* of 1794/5. Both Schelling and Hegel sought in their own philosophical endeavours to complete what they thought Fichte had left undone: a thorough grounding of the Fichtean consciousness in the world. They sought to define a direct and meaningful relationship between subject and object, a relationship that bridges the two Kantian worlds, and yet allows the world of objects a distinct existence outside the subject's consciousness (which Fichte's theory does not). Friedrich Schlegel set out to accomplish exactly this, too. Here the intellectual unity of the Jena circle comprising thinkers preoccupied with philosophy and the arts becomes most palpable. Schlegel thought that this grounding of reflexion could only occur through the submergence of philosophy within poetry. He criticises Fichte not just for his ignoring of the world of objects, of nature, of history, and his own historicity (cf. Behler, *German Romantic Literary Theory*, 190), but for what Schlegel sees as an inconsequential treatment of the dialectical dynamic. His quarrel is with Fichte's "first principle, which he criticises for not being dynamic in itself, which in turn makes the beginning of the dynamic process problematic. He contrasts Fichte's "Grundsatz" with his own "Wechselerweis" or "Wechselgrundsatz": "In meinem System ist der letzte Grund ein Wechselerweis. In Fichte's ein Postulat und ein unbedingter Satz." (KFSA vol. 18, 521–2). Cf. G. Naschert, "Friedrich Schlegel über den Wechselerweis und Ironie" *Athenäum: Jahrbuch für Romantik* 1996, 47–90 and 1997, 11–34. In Schlegel's view, Fichte devalues the world of objects; as nonego they only function as stimulant to the ego, which will gradually assimilate them. He wishes to make them equal elements in a fruitful oppositional reciprocation. So Schlegel places dialectic heterogeneity at the very beginning (of consciousness), which highlights again his preoccupation with the dynamic process and his doubts about any static entities, about stable solutions. He appears to acknowledge the relation between subject and object in Kantian fashion as a split between two worlds, while asserting, in

Schlegel's theory of criticism is a theory of human understanding, of how the mind processes and expresses impressions, not just of works of art, but of experiences in general, hence his "Poesie der Poesie" corresponds to the "Philosophie der Philosophie". Reflection has reached the level of self-reflection. Both are capable of the all-important ironic reflexivity. But his theory, like the others discussed here, exists on the basis of history. The notion of ongoing processes informs this theory and shapes its dialectical dynamics and open-endedness. The need for a connection between theory and history, and the sequential nature of this connection, is very clearly expressed in his *Gespräch über die Poesie*, four short lectures that are given and discussed in a circle of friends. The dialectical dynamic is presented formally in the advancing discussion, which at the same time avoids presenting any one view as the only or the right one. The need for a connection between theory and history is voiced directly by the participants,[144] and also finds expression in the way the four lectures are related to each other: "Epochen der Dichtkunst" gives a very concise, but most innovative overview of literary his-

---

Fichtean fashion, the existence of a meaningful interaction between the two, while yet again, in post-Fichtean fashion, wishing to leave the right of the world (non-ego, nature) to an independent existence intact. From Schlegel's point of view, Fichte, rather than Kant, could be seen as providing the final culmination of Cartesian subject-centred rationalism, rather than its first thorough critique. Once the dynamic process is set in motion, though, Schlegel has few problems with Fichte's principles. In fact he employs Fichtean processes to explain historical processurality: the way in which Fichte's ego gradually absorbs the non-ego is decidedly similar to the way in which Schlegel's evolving universal poetry gradually absorbs all historical phenomena of poetry. And, it should be added as an ironic footnote, that Schlegel himself seems at one point to suggest that human mental activity sprang from one unique and unitary origin. In the "Rede über die Mythologie", that most Idealist of sections in the *Athenäum*, he asserts that "weder dieser Witz [der alt-romantischen Poesie] noch eine Mythologie können bestehn ohne ein erstes Urspüngliches und Unnachahmliches, was schlechthin unauflöslich ist, was nach allen Umbildungen noch die alte Natur und Kraft durchschimmern läßt". (KFSA II, 319) It should not be overlooked that there is always a polemical element in Schlegel's treatment of Fichte. Initially enthralled by the older man's theories, Schlegel found it a struggle to break free from Fichte's mesmerising influence, as did Novalis. His relationship with Fichte was complicated by their personal acquaintance in Jena, which was beset with tensions – Fichte is acknowledged as a "difficult" person, opinionated and blunt, who intimidated by exuding self-assurance – and in which Fichte always remained the senior partner. When Schlegel for example criticises Fichte's effectiveness as a public speaker (cf. Behler, *German Romantic Literary Theory*, 188), his assessment runs counter to virtually all extant reports on this topic, which acknowledge Fichte as an exceptionally engaging speaker.

144 KFSA II, 307 (Andrea).

tory, while "Rede über die Mythologie" provides a theory of poetry as the supreme communicative medium of human expression. The "Brief über den Roman" then links history and theory by deducing from (literary) history that the novel, Schlegel's definition of which is notoriously wide enough to include Shakespeare's plays, is the quintessential literary form of modernity. Schlegel's theory of the novel relies on historical analysis. Finally, in the piece about "Goethe's Styl", he proceeds to present a successful example of modern literature: Goethe points the way to the future.

In his rhapsodic appraisal of Goethe, Schlegel comes very close to propagating the achievability of the ideal of his progressive universal poetry.

> Drei Eigenschaften scheinen mir daran [Goethes *Wilhelm Meisters Lehrjahre*] die wunderbarsten und die größten. Erstlich, daß die Individualität, welche darin erscheint, in verschiedne Strahlen gebrochen, unter mehrere Personen verteilt ist. Dann der antike Geist, den man bei näherer Bekanntschaft unter der modernen Hülle überall wiedererkennt. Diese große Kombination eröffnet eine ganz neue endlose Aussicht auf das, was die höchste Aufgabe aller Dichtkunst zu sein scheint, die Harmonie des Klassischen und des Romantischen. Das dritte ist, daß das unteilbare Werk in gewissem Sinne doch zugleich ein zweifaches, doppeltes ist. [...] Goethe hat sich [...] zu einer Höhe der Kunst heraufgearbeitet, welche zum erstenmal die ganze Poesie der Alten und der Modernen umfaßt, und den Keim eines ewigen Fortschreitens enthält. (KFSA II, 346–7)[145]

The notion of joining the classical, i.e. that which is typical of antiquity, and the romantic, i.e. the best of modernity, occupies Schlegel throughout the 1790s[146] and is evidence that Schlegel, too, clings, if only in residual fashion, to a progressive and cumulative ideal in the Schillerian sense, the realisation of which will constitute the resolution of the human condition.

---

[145] "Three of its qualities seem to me most wonderful and great. First, that the individuality which appears in it is refracted into various rays, distributed among several persons; then, the spirit of antiquity which at closer acquaintance one recognises everywhere under modern cloak. This great combination opens an entirely new and unlimited perspective on what seems to be the ultimate goal of all literature, the harmony of the classical with the romantic. The third is that the one indivisible work is at the same time twofold and double. [...] Goethe has worked himself up [...] to a height of art which for the first time encompasses the entire poetry of the ancients and the moderns and contains the seed of eternal progression." *Dialogue on Poetry*, 112–13.

[146] Cf. for example, the letter to his brother August Wilhelm of 27 February 1794, quoted in "Einleitung", KFSA II, p. XCVII.

In order to cope with the absence, at least in practice, of an ideal in the present, Schlegel develops the idea of an "individual ideal", which is inherent, but never fully realised in each work of art, against which the critic must measure the artistic creation.[147] Again, the notion of the ideal is particularised and historicised. This notion puts the critic in the elevated position of meta-artist. Hans Eichner pointed out that such an individual ideal still does not fully succeed in solving the problem of creating (or having) any norms in a historicised world where everything is relative.[148] Pushing back the validity of rules as far as possible, but stopping just short of abandoning them altogether, always leaves the spectre of an ideal on the horizon: the developing essence achieves realisation only at the final frontier of historical reality. Schlegel's concept of irony moves furthest away from this ideal on the horizon, by condensing the dialectic process into a mental experience that is devised by the writer and experienced by the reader. It is Friedrich Schlegel's most modern, not to say post-modern achievement.[149]

It is evident that in this intellectually active and poetically fertile period between 1770 and 1800 different concepts of literature emerge, which despite their different foci share crucial features. Herder's *Volkspoesie*, Schiller's aesthetic education, and Friedrich Schlegel's progressive universal poetry are each marked by a clear awareness of historicity. Each endeavours to make sense of historicity by relating value to time. Each has at its core the concept of a developing essence that is to provide a concrete and particular experience, which is only possible by making art appeal not just to the intellect, but equally to the senses. To achieve this, all three suggest that the reconnection to or rediscovery of an obscured original entity (tradition, aesthetic experience of the

---

[147] Cf. Hans Eichner, "Friedrich Schlegels Theorie der Literaturkritik", *Zeitschrift für deutsche Philologie* 88 (1969) Sonderheft, 2–19, 7.

[148] H. Eichner, "Friedrich Schlegels Theorie der Literaturkritik", 6–8.

[149] As one can draw a line, denoting an increasing belief in the viability (and necessity) of a direct connectedness between consciousness and world, from Kant via Fichte to Friedrich Schlegel, one can similarly draw a line from Kant via Fichte to Schelling and Hegel. Both Hegel and Schlegel suspect that any kind of solution to the problems of modern humanity will only be found in a clear understanding of this connectedness. The difference between Hegel and Schlegel is that Hegel was convinced that this connection could be effected in the medium of thought alone, the last truth could be understood as "absolutes Wissen", while Schlegel thought that the connection could only acquire existence in the medium of the symbol, the last truth could only be intuited.

beautiful, structures of mythology), which takes account of the pre-rational(ist) imaginative human capacities, was necessary. In this preoccupation with intellectual and artistic origin and originality, both Schiller and Schlegel take up Herder's ideas. Such reconnection or rediscovery, which is not conceived as a return or regression, but as a merging of the cultural and intellectual advances achieved over time with original and effective modes of expression and representation, is to produce an historicised ideal, of literature in this case, which can accommodate rather than negate the historical conditions of impermanence.

All three are united by their desire to understand the way in which human understanding understands itself and the world, has understood these matters in the past, and under which circumstances this understanding will be accurate and possibly complete. Their ideas develop in the general intellectual context that also produced the cognitive theories of German Idealism, the relation of which with historicity will be discussed in the next chapter. But in brief, the problem these thinkers, writers as well as philosophers, face is twofold. They are confronted with the difference between self and world, which results from the fact that rationalism and empiricism are no longer integrated into one framework of theology (explicating the ubiquitous and constant godhead), nor can they rely on a system of ubiquitous and constant reason. These frameworks based on ubiquitousness and constancy had been shattered by the increasing awareness of the altering effect of time. To create any kind of new framework that could connect self and world in a changing environment, which was necessary to establish any form of meaning and certainty, they needed to find a way of accommodating these altering effects.

The *Sturm-und-Drang* historicist, the Weimar classicist and the Jena romanticist do this in accordance with their own intellectual tendencies. Herder focuses on the origin of human intellectual development, which for him already contained *in nuce* all aspects of real and complete humanity. His historicist appreciation of the process itself – all stages are intrinsically of equal value – deals a deadly blow to the notion of an immutable ideal and opens up the arena for a discussion about the primacy of developmental processes. Herder's steadfast conviction of the equality of periods makes him less inclined to focus on the eventual result of the process, or its precise dynamics, because this tends to imply the superiority of the final outcome. This conviction is responsible for Herder's focus on the origin to anchor the process. The origin is the fixed point in the flow of time, from which we must begin our investigation into human nature and human understanding. Schiller functionalises the nature of the origin for his focus on the aim of this process, which is a fully realised perfect and complete humanity. Understanding the cultural and intellectual history of humanity will enable the artist to contribute towards the acceleration of this process. Schiller's aim-oriented focus amounts to a position closest to any form of classicism, because it keeps an eventually immutable ideal clearly within sight. But Schiller's ideal is also firmly out of reach, which positions him outside any "classical" classicist doctrine. Schlegel, finally, shares an aim-oriented outlook with Schiller and an intense interest in the process with Herder. He situates his focus primarily *on*, or even *within* this process by closely investigating the possibility of achieving a glimpse of complete reality within time, which, to a large extent, abandons the pre-occupation with the problem of how an eventually immutable ideal can realistically be worked towards in history. In general outline these *differences* between Herder on the one hand and Schiller and Schlegel on the other[150] and between Herder and Schlegel[151] have been long established. Focusing on historicity when going over their ideas and concepts, however, illuminates the fundamental springboard-like importance of Herder's work for the later two. It makes it possible to test the assumed differences between Classical and Romantic outlook of the later two writers in the context of a wider, yet dominant intellectual framework, which reveals these differences as tendencies within generally similar structures of response to the intellectual, cultural and historical situation. All three accept the process of temporal flux and its resulting impermanence and endeavour to find a way of integrating the two opposing concepts of the original-natural and the rational-reflexive in order to achieve an approximation of a full poetic and intellectual experience and with it an approximation of completely successful communication. Herder establishes parity between the two opposing concepts and wishes to bring back the older one to improve a presently one-sided culture and communication. Schiller presents the grand historical sweep from cultural-intellectual origin through to projected aim, during which the two concepts vie for dominance, and focuses on the joints within the process at which change occurs. To him, these provide models of integration and synthesis, which help to understand the

---

[150] Cf. Jauß, *Provokation*, 74–75.
[151] Cf. Mennemeier, *Friedrich Schlegels Poesiebegriff*, 52.

means through which the process can be accelerated towards its aim. Schlegel prioritises the self-dynamising process in which the opposing concepts constantly and perpetually dislocate each other and concludes that through the structures of mythology a new poetry can provide the experience of the antagonism and the complementariness between the two concepts, i.e. between ideality and reality, emotion and intellect and creation and analysis. The similar structures of their responses point to the general coherence of the whole period.

Implicitly or explicitly, all three believe that the intellectual and literary constellation in Germany is particularly promising for the realisation of these new concepts of literature. Herder in the 1770s is still cautious, but confident:

> Da also so viele Hinderniße der Deutschen Muse und ihrer Würkung in den Weg treten; soll man den Muth sinken lassen? [...] Nichts minder! Wir gehen langsam aber nur desto sicherer: wir kommen spät, aber vielleicht desto gerader ans Ziel. Haben einige neue Stücke zweier oder dreier Dichter [...] nicht gezeigt, was auch in Deutschland Natur, wenn sie simpel, treu, gerade, stark geschildert ist, für Würkung tun könne? Wie Feuer zünden sie umher. [...] Fast sind wir durch alle Nachahmungen durch: alle Fehler sind erschöpft, und das Gute wird folgen. ("Würkung", 432–3, original manuscript version)[152]

Schlegel comes to the same conclusion. Andrea remarks in "Epochen der Dichtkunst": "Man müsse zu den Alten und zu der Natur zurückkehren, und dieser Funken zündete bei den Deutschen, nachdem sie sich durch alle Vorbilder allmählig durchgearbeitet hatten." (KFSA II, 302)[153] Schlegel pinpoints the present conjunction of intellectual and literary endeavour in Germany as follows:

> Die Philosophie gelangte in wenigen kühnen Schritten dahin, sich selbst und den Geist des Menschen zu verstehen, in dessen Tiefe sie den Urquell der Fantasie und das Ideal der Schönheit entdecken, und so die Poesie deutlich anerkennen mußte. [...] Philosophie und Poesie, die höchsten Kräfte des Menschen, die selbst zu Athen jede für sich in der höchsten Blüte doch nur

---

[152] "Should we lose courage, as there are so many hurdles in the path of the German muse and its influence? [...] Not at all! We progress slowly, but all the more surely: we arrive late at the finish line, but possibly on a straighter course. Have a few new pieces by two or three poets [...] not shown us what kind of effect nature, if it is presented simple, true, straight and strong, can have in Germany, too? Like wildfire they spread around. [...] We are nearly through with all those imitations: all mistakes have been made, the good will out."

[153] "To return to the ancients and to nature, and this spark caught fire with the Germans after they had gone through almost all their models." *Dialogue on Poetry*, 73.

einzeln wirkten, greifen nun ineinander, um sich in ewiger Wechselwirkung
gegenseitig zu beleben und zu bilden. (KFSA II, 302–303)[154]

The Germans' strength is their lateness, they can avoid the mistake of
one-sided developments that others made before them and profit from
their achievements, an option that is made available to them by their
modern understanding of history. Their historical situation already pre-
destines them to attain a universality, which has clear culminatory aspects and is to benefit humanity as a whole.

Just like Schiller at the very end of his *Ästhetische Briefe*, Schlegel, too,
suggests that a concept of *Volkspoesie* as a developing essence has its merits.[155]

Es fehlt nichts, als daß die Deutschen [...] dem Vorbilde folgen, daß Goethe
aufgestellt hat, die Formen der Kunst überall bis auf den Ursprung erfor-
schen, um sie neu beleben oder verbinden zu können, und daß sie auf die
Quellen ihrer eignen Sprache und Dichtung zurückgehn, und die alte Kraft,
den hohen Geist wieder frei machen, der noch in den Urkunden der vater-
ländischen Vorzeit vom Liede der *Nibelungen* bis zum Flemming und Weckherlin bis jetzt verkannt schlummert: so wird die Poesie, die bei keiner modernen Nation so ursprünglich ausgearbeitet und vortrefflich erst eine Sage
der Helden, dann ein Spiel der Ritter, und endlich ein Handwerk der Bürger
war, nun auch bei eben derselben eine gründliche Wissenschaft wahrer Ge-
lehrten und eine tüchtige Kunst erfindsamer Dichter sein und bleiben.
(KFSA II, 303)[156]

---

[154] "Philosophy arrived in a few daring steps to the point where it could comprehend itself
and the spirit of man, in whose depths it was bound to discover the primordial source
of the imagination and the ideal of beauty, and thus was compelled to recognise
poetry. [...] Philosophy and poetry, the two most sublime powers in man, which even
in Athens in the period of their highest fruition were effective only in isolation, now
intermingle in perpetual interaction in order to stimulate and develop each other."
Dialogue on Poetry, 74.

[155] Schlegel also indulges in the familiar negative evaluation of French classicism. "Aus
oberflächlichen Abstraktionen und Räsonnements, aus dem mißverstandenen Alter-
tum und dem mittelmäßigen Talent entstand in Frankreich ein umfassendes und zu-
sammenhängendes System von falscher Poesie, welches auf einer gleich falschen Theorie der Dichtkunst ruhete; und von hieraus verbreitete sich diese schwächliche
Geisteskrankheit des sogenannten guten Geschmacks fast über alle Länder Europas."
KFSA II, 302.

[156] "Nothing further is required but that the Germans [...] follow the example set by
Goethe, explore the forms of art back to their sources in order to be able to revive or
combine them, and that they go back to the origins of their own language and poetry,
and release the old power, the sublime spirit which lies dormant, unrecognised, in the
documents of the fatherland's prehistory, from the song of the Nibelungs, to Fleming

There is one other aspect to the German literary scene that makes Herder, Schlegel and Schiller feel justified in their great expectations: the appearance of Goethe. In *Naïve und Sentimentalische Dichtung*, Schiller uses his new friend as an example of the rarest of creatures, a largely naïve poet in a sentimental period who can successfully deal with sentimental themes.[157] Herder's description of the new and moving literature in "Würkung" in 1777 quoted above actually alludes to Goethe's *Werther* first published three years earlier. And Schlegel used Goethe as the shining example of a poetic trendsetter throughout the *Athenäum*-period. The literature section will examine how Goethe's *Wilhelm Meisters Lehrjahre* and, finally, his *Faust I* relate to these new concepts of literature, the problems associated with historicity, and the newly defined German identity.

---

and Weckherlin. Thus poetry – which in no nation was so excellent and originally developed – beginning as a heroic legend, then becoming a pastime of the knights, and finally a trade of the citizens – will be and will remain in this nation a basic discipline [thorough science] of true scholars and an effective art of ingenious poets." *Dialogue on Poetry*, 74–75, my suggestion in brackets.

[157] Cf. *NSD*, 459.

Chapter 2

The Historicity of Modern Knowledge and Consciousness: German Idealism

The striving to link history and theory, which marked German writing on culture in the late 18th century, was also central to German Idealism, the dominant philosophical movement at the time. Here too efforts focus on, in theoretical terms, (re-)connecting and synthesising the real (that which exists) and the ideal (that which is thought to exist generally) or, in historical terms, reconnecting rational activity and that which pre-dates human rationality yet still exists alongside it. The latter is closely related to notions of the natural and original, i.e. what was thought to have been superseded by rational activity – either lost or believed over-come – but what could no longer be ignored now that rational activity was reaching its own limits and limitations. Now it needed to be taken into account and investigated in order to approximate to a comprehensive view of human understanding, experience and existence.

Since the decline of medieval – theological – metaphysics, the natural sciences had steadily grown in importance and scope. Rationalism, with its focus on the rational operations of mind and world, could exist alongside an emerging empiricism, which prioritised the experience of the world as source of understanding, because both mind, i.e. the subject, and world, i.e. the object of experience, were thought to be governed by reason. But when the (empiricist) investigation of the world began to extend beyond the natural physical world to include the past, the empiricist analysis of the data suggested that things had been very different then, thus preparing the "discovery" of historicity. This began to threaten not just the symbiotic co-existence of rationalism and empiricism, but the validity of their supreme category, reason. Historical empiricism suggested that reason was not constant after all, and that thus the trust in the universality of reason might be unfounded.

The crisis of reason in the later 18th century is a much discussed subject, then as now, but in critical treatments little attention has been given
to how much the emerging awareness of historicity has contributed to
this crisis.[1] Frederic Beiser has dedicated a most valuable study to the
problems faced by the authority and autonomy of reason during the second half of the 18th century. And although he deals with the emerging
notion of the cultural conditioning of reason, which implies its historicity, and recognises the potential of organic vitalism as a solution, his
analysis focuses on the destructiveness of reason's own rational critique
when applied to itself as the major cause of its crisis.[2] In the main, the
problem of the autonomy and authority of reason is also the premise on
which Manfred Frank had rested his discussion of the re-activation of
myth a few years earlier.

> Daß es Vernunft gibt und warum sie gerade so und nicht anders eingerichtet
> ist, ferner: welchem Zweck sie dient, das sind Fragen, die die Vernunft – be-
> trachtet als ein funktionales System von Gedanken – nicht beantworten kann:
> Es wären in einem transzendentalen System synthetische Urteile, deren der
> Rationalismus sich zu enthalten hat; obwohl er selbst ohne vorgängige Syn-
> thesen buchstäblich nichts zu beißen hätte.[3]

While Beiser and Frank focused on the unfolding awareness of the deficiency of reason, which so alarmed the last generation of enlightened
thinkers, Christoph Jamme's analysis centred on the tyranny and exploitation that reason imposed on nature and the natural.

> Die Zeit um 1800 ist für uns Heutige deshalb so interessant, weil wir hier die
> Genese einer Aufklärungs- und Vernunftkritik beobachten können, die die
> Vernunft als Form von Herrschaft entlarvte und die rationalistische – wie öko-
> nimische – Verkrustung nur für aufbrechbar hielt durch eine Öffnung zur
> Ganzheit des Lebens. [...] So wird unter dem Einfluß des Rationalitätsbe-
> griffs der Aufklärung auch die Natur zum Objekt. Der Leib wird diszipliniert
> und unterworfen, der Verstand gewinnt eine alles beherrschende Macht. Der

---

[1] Particularly, if one disregards the early 20th-century studies that deal with the rise of historicism (e.g. Meinecke's *Entstehung des Historismus*) and with the consolidation of the
uniquely German intellectual tradition (e.g. Nohl's *Deutsche Bewegung* or Korff's *Geist der
Goethezeit*), which chiefly aimed at establishing a non-Enlightenment origin for modern
German culture.

[2] Cf. F. Beiser, *The Fate of Reason. German Philosophy from Kant to Fichte*, Cambridge MA:
Harvard University Press, 1987.

[3] M. Frank, *Der kommende Gott: Vorlesungen über die neue Mythologie*, Frankfurt aM: Suhrkamp, 1982, p. 112.

Tod der Natur ist ein Ereignis, der im Inneren des Subjektes tiefe Wunden schlägt. Die jungen Idealisten treten dagegen mit dem Anspruch auf, das Andere der Vernunft (die Natur) als Subjekt eigenen Rechts zu erweisen.[4]

That such criticism by the Idealists at the turn of the 19th century anticipates the mid-20th-century "discovery of the dialectics of the enlightenment" has been repeatedly pointed out since the 1980s.[5] Jamme's analysis, like Beiser's, Frank's and Adorno/Horkheimer's, also rests on a perceived deficiency: reason is tyrannical, because it is one-sided, it needs to suppress "nature" to safeguard itself from the latter's insurrection. Although all of them are aware that a particular theory of history lies behind any sustained critique of universal reason, none of them deals at any length with the role that the awareness of historicity plays in the discovery of the deficiency of reason. This gap is to be filled in the following.

With the benefit of hindsight it is easy to see that, if reason is to be salvaged, rationalism and empiricism need to be integrated into a framework that addresses the problem of historicity and accommodates the effects of change. German Idealism attempted exactly this, rescuing reason in some form to prevent the breakdown of an entire intellectual tradition. Since the 16th century, in a process of gradually increasing intensity, not just the natural sciences, but also philosophy and political and moral thought had come to rely on the existence and value of reason. To salvage reason German Idealism set out to integrate empiricism and rationalism into a historically grounded framework. This was to be achieved through creating a new metaphysics, a new rationalism, which would be a fully scientific theory, i.e. would rely on empiricist data for building its theory, but draw this data from history, from development in time rather than the physical world or the world of pure concepts. Such a science of reason would ground reason securely under the new conditions of impermanence. The object of such a science would necessarily be the mind and its relation to the world of objects external to it.

---

4 C. Jamme, "Aufklärung via Mythologie. Zum Zusammenhang von Naturbeherrschung und Naturfrömmigkeit um 1800", C. Jamme/Gerhart Kurz, ed.s, *Idealismus und Aufklärung: Kontinuität und Kritik der Aufklärung in Philosophie und Poesie um 1800*, Stuttgart: Klett-Cotta, 1988, pp. 35–58, 38 and 47.
5 Cf. Jürgen Habermas, *Der philosophische Diskurs der Moderne*, Frankfurt aM: Suhrkamp, 1985; Rolf Grimminger, *Die Ordnung, das Chaos und die Kunst. Die neue Dialektik der Aufklärung*, (1st 1986) Frankfurt aM: Suhrkamp, 1990, p. 23.

In his *Critiques*, Immanuel Kant began to produce such a science. Kant limited rationalism by making reason a human faculty only, which, through its categories, constructed, out of its experiences, which are specific to the rational species of humanity, its world. The world is only knowable through experience, which is the empiricist claim, but one must be aware that these experiences are conditioned by the human rational apparatus that has them, a qualification that holds on to the rationalist claim that the human being brings prior equipment to experience. This avoids the question of whether we *are* reasonable or *made* reasonable, because it removes the quarrel over the primacy of reason or experience through the suggestion of constructivist behaviour: the rational human being experiences the world in his own specific way and constructs his own world out of these specific experiences. (Thus reason is safe from empiricism because the rational humans can only experience according to their nature, which means the world will be constructed to fit it.) The price of this reconciliation is that reason is no longer supreme, but human, and that the world as it really is cannot be known by the human mind. While the gap between rationalism and empiricism closes, a new gap between mind and world opens.

Kant's scientific explication of the mechanics of the mind does not address the question of historicity. Yet any successful self-critical grounding of reason needed to take account of the changing conditions of the newly defined specifically human reason and reconnect mind and world. Post-Kantian German Idealist thought endeavours to do just that. Through the introduction of a temporal framework to knowledge and experience, Kant's rigid division between the world as the human mind constructs it and the world as it really is in itself, recedes. The static categories of the mind are turned into the dynamics of consciousness. Post-Kantian philosophical thought is based on the occurrence and experience of a temporal process that will eventually lead to a revelatory consummation, an eventually perfect understanding of the world. (Whether this can be achieved or only approximated to is not entirely clear.) Perfectibility is achieved through evolution, it does not yet exist, has never before existed and will only come into existence at the conclusion of the (historical) process. This trend is latently evident is Kant's work already, but becomes integral to Idealist philosophy from Fichte onwards. It reflects the need for reason to become adapted to historicity.

Defining the Process and Purpose of Modern Thinking:
Fichte's *Wissenschaftslehre* (1794/5),
Schelling's *System des Transzendentalen Idealismus*
and Hegel's *Phänomenologie des Geistes*

Fichte's *Wissenschaftslehre* of the mid-1790s is the first step in this endeavour. It sets out to explain the dynamics of human knowledge and consciousness, which ultimately aim at self-knowledge and self-consciousness. His starting-point is the I, or ego, whose distinguishing features are freedom and reason, although it exists in a world of necessity. He endeavours to present a system of deduction that demonstrates the process of knowing. This process is made up of actions of positings, beginning with "I am I", moving on to a finite ego, the subject, positing the non-ego (the world), which it is gradually getting to know and assimilate. Through this gradual assimilation the finite ego approximates towards the infinite ego, the total assimilation of the external world by the subject, but complete identity between subject and world is never achieved.

Fichte presents a purely theoretical system, often illustrated by algebraic equations, which makes no mention of anything historical. And yet it is a most thorough account of the historicity of the human self, human thought, knowledge and experience. This is evident in his focus on the dialectical process of knowing, which is conceived of as striving, and on action itself: the ego goes from the initial act of positing itself through a series of dialectical processes which move it closer to the ideal of the infinite ego.[6] In 1793 Fichte even considered "philosophy of striving" (*Strebungsphilosophie*) as a title for his work. It is not entirely clear whether this process applies to the individual ego only, which would amount to a theory of individual human consciousness, or to the human self in general, i.e. whether Fichte presents a teleology of human knowledge. But what is clear is that the striving and the process of knowing are organicist historicist processes in that they occur in distinct successive stages of growth that produce irreversible changes and are designed to lead up to an unprecedented state of completion (which can however only be approximated to).

---

[6] Concerning problems regarding the aspect of striving in Fichte, see Wayne Martin, *Idealism and Objectivity: Understanding Fichte's Jena Project*, Stanford, CA: Stanford University Press, 1997, pp. 118 ff. However, this is not a discussion of the internal problems of Fichte's philosophy. I am concerned with its distinctive features in relation to the intellectual and cultural climate.

The Idealist endeavour is driven by the desire to establish a theory that could incorporate the awareness of change and of the scattered fragments of knowledge that empiricism kept producing. The identity of subject (individual mind) and object (world) was sought through reason, which may have been the superannuated principle of traditional rationalism, but which was to be revived in a new guise: the new reason unfolds in a gradual process of becoming aware of its historically imposed limitations and overcoming them historically.

Fichte's focus on the striving self is Faustian in more senses than one: not only is the painful and illuminating process of digesting experience, which Fichte describes, very similar to that which Goethe makes his hero undergo, the process of creating the *Wissenschaftslehre* was also every bit as protracted and difficult as the writing of Goethe's major drama. It occupied Fichte from the early stages of his professional career up to his death. He re-wrote the *Wissenschaftslehre* at almost every stage of his own intellectual journey. The notion of the process of productive development did not just determine the content of thought, it also dominated its form.

Schelling's *System des transzendentalen Idealismus*

Schelling's *System* (1800)[7], the next milestone publication in German Idealist thought after Fichte's *Wissenschaftslehre*, is similarly searching for a theory that could explain, grasp, the identity of subject and object. Schelling, too, was convinced that such a theory can only be found through the close examination of the development of self-consciousness. Like Fichte, Schelling conceives of this developmental process as productively dialectic. Through a series of limitations and their overcoming the two opposites are brought into relation to each other. But Schelling considers the dynamics not only of individual consciousness, but also of the development of human consciousness in general, of the conscious species as a whole, which leads him necessarily to a more direct treatment of history. Fichte was interested in analysing how (individual) consciousness works, how its dynamic mechanisms produce and process knowledge. His starting-point was the individual mind, which is

[7] Schelling, *Das System des Transzendentalen Idealismus*, *Schellings Werke*, vol. 2, nach der Originalausgabe in neuer Anordnung von Manfred Schröter, Munich: Beck, 1927, pp. 327–634. Forthwith *System*.

the representative of mind in general. Understanding its processes and objectives would inevitably reveal the aim of consciousness in general. Schelling, on the other hand, approaches the analysis of the processes of consciousness from a different premise. Displaying a decidedly Herderian tendency, he is certain that it is its history and origin that hold the clue to understanding the workings and purpose of human consciousness. Believing the origin of consciousness will give pointers, Schelling investigates the frontier between nature and mind, the point where – and more crucially *when* – mind must have emerged from nature. Schelling reckons that consciousness developed from an unconscious natural state, or, in other words, that subjectivity grew from objectivity and tends back towards it. This process, to him, encompasses the complete scope of all human history. The structure of Schelling's process is the same as that which Fichte's world-assimilating ego undergoes. The difference lies in the scale and the importance accorded to the temporal nature of the process. For Fichte, it is simply a development, not a history, whereas for Schelling the developmental unfolding is the history of human consciousness.[8] Schelling crucially differs from Fichte in his inclusion in his considerations of nature (*das Objektive*) as an independent entity. While objectivity was a result of Fichte's process achieved by the subject, the world was only significant in its direct relation to the ego that was gradually assimilating it. Fichte's perspective focuses exclusively on the ego and its consciousness. (Hence he could be called the final flower of Cartesian subjective rationalism.) Schelling's perspective is bifocal: consciousness and nature are equal spheres of existence, between which he seeks to establish a relational link, nature being not only the world of objects perceived by consciousness but an independent force. By focusing on nature and consciousness, and the temporal point of their separation from one another, Schelling is closer than Fichte to thinkers interested in the original and natural, that which has been left behind (and needs to be understood and reintegrated on a higher level) when consciousness leaves behind nature.

Investigating the frontier between nature (world) and mind, which does not only exist on the historical level, i.e. at the beginning and end of mind, but also in the present, in the immediate relationship between

---

[8] Again, the self is actively and productively engaged, on the one hand, in activity directed at the world, at the things-in-themselves, *das Objektive*, aiming at "producing infinity". On the other hand, it is engaged in activity directed inwards, towards *das Subjektive*, wishing to contemplate itself in infinity.

mind and world, Schelling wrestled, like Fichte before and Hegel after him, with the connection between the two realms that Kant disconnected from one another. In his own transcendental endeavour Schelling proposes that the mind shapes the world as much as the world shapes the mind. The relationship is reciprocal and based on a fundamental identity between the productive activities that generate world and mind. In nature this activity is primarily unconscious – unconscious activity brings forth nature, or the objective world (*System*, 349) –, in the mind it gradually achieves consciousness. This identity is, however, no longer obvious and can only be traced at the original emergence of the conscious mind. The identity exists only originally ("ursprünglich").

> Wie zugleich die objektive Welt nach Vorstellungen in uns, und Vorstellungen in uns nach der objektiven Welt sich bequemen, ist nicht zu begreifen, wenn nicht zwischen den beiden Welten, der ideellen und der reellen, eine vorherbestimmte Harmonie existiert. Diese vorherbestimmte Harmonie aber ist selbst nicht denkbar, wenn nicht die Thätigkeit, durch welche die objektive Welt producirt ist, ursprünglich identisch ist mit der, welche im Wollen sich äußert, und umgekehrt. Nun ist es allerdings eine produktive Thätigkeit, welche im Wollen sich äußert; alles freie Handeln ist produktiv, nur mit Bewußtseyn produktiv. Setzt man nun, da beide Thätigkeiten doch nur im Princip Eine seyn sollen, daß dieselbe Thätigkeit, welche im freien Handeln mit Bewußtseyn produktiv ist, im Produciren der Welt ohne Bewußtseyn produktiv sey, so ist jene vorausbestimmte Harmonie wirklich, und der Widerspruch gelöst. (*System*, 348)⁹

So, while on the universal level, i.e. appertaining to the human being and the world, the activities of freely acting consciousness and unconscious nature are in principle one and the same, practical knowledge of this on the individual level would prohibit the existence of self-consciousness. For self-consciousness to exist in the subject, these activities

---

9   "How both the objective world accommodates to presentations in us, and presentations in us to the objective world, is unintelligible unless between the two worlds, the ideal and the real, there exists a pre-determined harmony. But this latter is itself unthinkable unless the activity, whereby the objective world is produced, is at bottom identical with that which expresses itself in volition, and vice versa. Now there is certainly a productive activity that finds expression in willing; all free action is productive, albeit consciously productive. If we now suppose, since the two activities have only to be one in principle, that the same activity which is consciously productive in free action, is productive without consciousness in bringing about the world, then our predetermined harmony is real and the contradiction resolved." *System of Transcendental Idealism (1800) by F.W.J. Schelling*, translated by Peter Heath, with an introduction by Michael Vater, Charlottesville: University of Virginia Press, 1978, pp. 11–12. Forthwith *Transcendental Idealism*.

need to be dialectically separate within consciousness, in order to inter-act productively (*streiten*) in a perpetual struggle of expansion and limi-tation. The identity of the two activities remains obscure to conscious-ness, because the limiting activity remains unconscious. This obscure nature of the original identity is the pre-condition for the development of individual self-consciousness. To deduce this proposition, Schelling turns to the origin of consciousness, the (historical) moment of its emergence from nature as self-consciousness.

> Der ursprüngliche Akt des Selbstbewußtseyns ist zugleich ideell und reell. Das Selbstbewußtseyn ist in seinem Princip bloß ideell, aber durch dasselbe ent-steht uns das Ich als bloß reell. Durch den Akt der Selbstanschauung wird das Ich unmittelbar auch begrenzt. [...] Durch das Selbstbewußtseyn allein wird die Schranke gesetzt, sie hat also keine andere Realität, als sie durch das Selbstbewußtseyn erlangt. [...] Die Schranke, um Schranke des Ichs zu seyn, muß zugleich abhängig und unabhängig vom Ich seyn. Dies läßt sich nur da-durch denken, daß das Ich gleich ist einer Handlung, in welcher zwei ent-gegengesetzte Thätigkeiten sind, eine, die begrenzt wird, von welcher eben deßwegen die Schranke unabhängig ist, und eine, die begrenzend, eben deß-wegen unbegrenzbar ist. Diese Handlung ist eben das Selbstbewußtseyn. [...] Die begrenzende Thätigkeit kommt nicht zum Bewußtseyn, wird nicht Ob-jekt, sie ist also die Thätigkeit des reinen Subjekts. Aber das Ich des Selbstbe-wußtseyns ist nicht reines Subjekt, sondern Subjekt und Objekt zugleich. Die begrenzte Thätigkeit ist nur die, die zum Objekt wird, das bloß Objektive im Selbstbewußtseyn. Aber das Ich des Selbstbewußtseyns ist weder reines Sub-jekt noch reines Objekt, sondern beides zugleich. Weder durch die be-grenzende noch durch die begrenzte Thätigkeit für sich kommt es also zum Selbstbewußtseyn. Es ist sonach eine dritte, aus beiden zusammengesetzte Thätigkeit, durch welche das Ich des Selbstbewußtseyns entsteht. [...] Das Ich ist also selbst eine zusammengesetzte Thätigkeit, das Selbstbewußtseyn ein synthetischer Akt. (*System*, 390–1)[10]

---

10 "The original act of self-consciousness is at once ideal and real. Self-consciousness is in principle purely ideal, but through it the self arises for us as purely real. Through the act of self-intuition the self also immediately becomes limited. [...] The boundary, to be a boundary of the self, must be simultaneously dependent on, and independent of, the self. This is conceivable only if the self is equivalent to an action in which there are two opposite activities, one which undergoes limitation, and of which the boundary is therefore independent, and one which limits, and is for that very reason illimitable. This action is, of course, self-consciousness. [...] The limiting activity does not come to consciousness, or become an object, and is therefore the activity of the pure subject. But the self of self-consciousness is not the pure subject, but subject and object to-gether. The limited activity is merely that which becomes an object, the purely objective element in self-consciousness. But the self of self-consciousness is neither pure subject nor pure object, but both of these at once. Thus neither through the limiting nor the

So consciousness is not only part of the dialectical difference between mind and world, or consciousness and nature, it also has its own inner dialectic (of limited and limiting activities), which mirrors the opposition between mind and nature. Within consciousness, this dialectic produces self-consciousness. Self-consciousness is a dynamic action that is constantly expanding through its drive towards objectivity and constantly limited by its connection to pure unconscious subjectivity. Nature, on the other hand, being subject to parallel generative activities, equally has its own inner dialectic. Within nature, this dialectic produces the world of objects. "Die Natur [...] wird als ein mit Bewußtseyn hervorgebrachtes Werk, und doch zugleich als Produkt des blindesten Mechanismus erscheinen müssen; sie ist zweckmäßig, ohne zweckmäßig erklärbar zu sein." (*System*, 349)[11]

These parallels are the basis for Schelling's system of identity. The inclusion of pre-self-conscious states and activities of the self make Schelling focus on the origin of self-consciousness and enable him to deal with a layer of questions implicitly underlying Fichte's analysis. The inclusion of nature in the development of consciousness, and the dialectical relationship between nature and consciousness, leads Schelling to a direct treatment of human history, which to him is "to practical philosophy what nature is to theoretical philosophy", because his panorama of intellectual development includes pre- and post-intellectual phases of consciousness. The existence of nature is a monument to the pre-self-conscious past of consciousness, "die objektive Welt ist nur die ursprüngliche, noch bewußtlose Poesie des Geistes" (*System*, 349),[12] and as such a vital part of its history.

History is the domain of the subject and characterised by freedom of action and the impossibility of being *a priori* theoretically determined. (*System*, 589) But as the sum of all individual self-consciousnesses, history is generated, like self-consciousness on the individual level, by a productive dialectic. History's chief characteristic is, after all, "dass sie

---

limited activities, by themselves, do we arrive at self-consciousness. There is, accordingly, a third activity, compounded of these two, whereby the self of self-consciousness is engendered. [...] The self is thus itself a compound activity, and self-consciousness itself a synthetic act." *Transcendental Idealism*, 43–44.

[11] "Nature [...] will have to appear as a work both consciously engendered, and yet simultaneously a product of the blindest mechanism; nature is purposive, without being purposively explicable." *Transcendental Idealism*, 12.

[12] "The objective world is simply the original, as yet unconscious, poetry of the spirit." *Transcendental Idealism*, 12.

Freiheit und Nothwendigkeit in Vereinigung darstellen und nur durch diese Vereinigung möglich seyn soll" (*System*, 593).[13] History's own dialectic must be parallel to the relation between necessity and freedom that Schelling perceives in nature. In nature, their co-existence has already achieved harmonious unity.

> Die vollständige Erscheinung der vereinigten Freiheit und Nothwendigkeit in der Außenwelt gibt mir also allein die organische Natur. [...] Sie [ist] [...] ein objektiv gewordenes Produciren, insofern also an das freie Handeln grenzend, jedoch ein bewußtloses Anschauen des Producirens, insofern also wieder wieder ein blindes Produciren. (*System*, 608)[14]

But how can, in history, the freedom of human action be reconciled to necessity without turning freedom into a sham? In the same way, in which subjective and objective activity were related and reconciled to each other in the subject: through the existence of a higher identity. History, too, partakes of the (hidden) identity of subject and object.

> Eine solche prästabilirte Harmonie des Objektiven (Gesetzmäßigen) und des Bestimmenden (Freien) ist allein denkbar durch etwas Höheres. [...] Wenn nun jenes Höhere nichts anderes ist als der Grund der Identität zwischen dem absolut Subjektiven und dem absolut Objektiven, dem Bewußten und dem Bewußtlosen, welche eben zum Behuf der Erscheinung im freien Handeln sich trennen, so kann jenes Höhere selbst weder Subjekt noch Objekt, auch nicht beides zugleich, sondern nur absolute Identität seyn. [...] Dieses ewig Unbewußte [...] ist zugleich dasselbe für alle Intelligenzen, die unsichtbare Wurzel [...] und das ewig Vermittelnde des sich selbst bestimmenden Subjektiven in uns und des Objektiven oder Anschauenden, zugleich der Grund der Gesetzmäßigkeit in der Freiheit und der Freiheit in der Gesetzmäßigkeit des Objektiven. (*System*, 600)[15]

---

[13] "That it should exhibit a union of freedom and necessity, and be possible through this union alone." *Transcendental Idealism*, 203.

[14] "The complete appearance of freedom and necessity unified in the external world therefore yields me organic nature only. [...] Nature itself is already a producing become objective, and to that extent therefore approximates to free action, but is nevertheless an unconscious intuiting of producing, and hence to that extent is itself again a blind producing." *Transcendental Idealism*, 216.

[15] "Such a preestablished harmony of the objective (or law-governed) and the determined (or free) is conceivable only through some higher thing. [...] Now if this higher thing be nothing else but the ground of identity between the absolutely subjective and the absolutely objective, the conscious and the unconscious, which part company precisely in order to appear in the free act, then this higher thing itself can be neither subject no object, nor both at once, but only the absolute identity. [...] This eternal unknown [...] is simultaneously the same for all intelligences, the invisible root [...] and the eternal

Again, this identity was only obvious originally, "ursprünglich". And again Schelling turns to the historical moment when consciousness emerged from unconsciousness to make his point. He holds that freedom and necessity separated at the first moment of consciousness. This is why they appear as separate to the subject. The individual self acts freely and consciously, yet the sum of all free acts amounts to the unconscious *Objektive*. Every free act is at the same time an unconscious necessity. (This foreshadows Hegel's cunning of reason.)

> Aber wenn nun die Intelligenz aus dem absoluten Zustand, d.h. aus der allgemeinen Identität, in welcher sich nichts unterscheiden läßt, heraustritt, und sich ihrer bewußt wird (sich selbst unterscheidet), welches dadurch geschieht, daß ihr Handeln ihr objektiv wird, übergeht in die objektive Welt, so trennt sich das Freie und Nothwendige in demselben. Frei ist es nur als innere Erscheinung, und darum sind wir, und glauben wir innerlich immer frei zu sein, obgleich die Erscheinung unserer Freiheit, oder unsere Freiheit, insofern sie übergeht in die objektive Welt, ebenso unter Naturgesetze tritt wie jede andere Begebenheit. (*System*, 602–3)[16]

So both the self-consciousness of the individual and the phenomenology of history are heterogeneous, characterised by rivalling, inter-acting subjective (conscious) and objective (unconscious) activities, which are nevertheless identical on a higher level. They are identical not only with each other, but also with the twin forces of nature which create the world of objects. Theoretical comprehension of this identity is Schelling's aim. The existence of this identity is guaranteed by the emergence of consciousness (which otherwise would not have occurred) and should be traceable in the activities and manifestation of human consciousness in general, i.e. in history.

> Wenn nun aber jenes Absolute der eigentliche Grund der Harmonie zwischen dem Objektiven und dem Subjektiven im freien Handeln, nicht nur des In-

---

mediator between the self-determining subjective within us, and the objective or intuitant; at once the ground of lawfulness in freedom, and of freedom in the lawfulness of the object." *Transcendental Idealism*, 208–209.

[16] "But if now the intelligence steps out from the absolute point of view, that is, steps out of the universal identity in which nothing can be distinguished, and becomes conscious of (distinguishes) itself, which comes about in that its act becomes objective to it, or passes over into the objective world, the free and the necessary are then separated therein. It is free only as an inner appearance, and that is why we are and believe ourselves to be always inwardly free, although insofar as it passes into the objective world the appearance of our freedom, or our freedom itself, falls just as much under laws of nature as any other occurrence." *Transcendental Idealism*, 210–211.

dividuums, sondern der ganzen Gattung ist, so werden wir die Spur dieser ewigen und unveränderlichen Identität am ehesten in der Gesetzmäßigkeit finden, welche als das Gewebe einer unbekannten Hand durch das freie Spiel der Willkür in der Geschichte sich hindurchzieht. (*System*, 601)[17]

Freedom is not negated by necessity, because the identity between freedom and necessity only exists on the higher level. In human consciousness, they are, as the activities of self-consciousness, infinitely dialectical, which means the historical process continues in human perpetuity.

Der Gegensatz zwischen der bewußten und der bewußtlosen Thätigkeit ist nothwendig ein unendlicher, denn wäre er je aufgehoben, so wäre auch die Erscheinung der Freiheit aufgehoben, welche einzig und allein auf ihm beruht. [...] Ist nun die Erscheinung der Freiheit nothwendig unendlich, so ist auch die vollständige Entwicklung der absoluten Synthesis eine unendliche, und die Geschichte selbst eine nie ganz geschehene Offenbarung jenes Absoluten, das zum Behuf des Bewußtseyns, also auch nur zum Behuf der Erscheinung, in das Bewußte und Bewußtlose, Freie und Anschauende sich trennt, selbst aber in dem unzugänglichen Lichte, in welchem es wohnt, die ewige Identität und der ewige Grund der Harmonie zwischen beiden ist. (*System*, 602–3)[18]

Human freedom is guaranteed because the final synthesis is endlessly deferred. The practical experience of this identity must remain prospective. Its occurrence would terminate the existence of the subject in freedom and alter intellectual conditions unrecognisably.[19] Like Friedrich

---

17 "But now if this absolute is the true ground of harmony between objective and subjective in the free action, not only of the individual, but of the entire species, we shall be likeliest to find traces of this eternal and unalterable identity in the lawfulness which runs, like the weaving of an unknown hand, through the free play of choice in history." *Transcendental Idealism*, 209.

18 "The opposition between conscious and unconscious activity is necessarily an unending one, for were it ever to be done away with, the appearance of freedom, which rests entirely upon it, would be done away with too. [...] Now if the appearance of freedom is necessarily infinite, the total evolution of the absolute synthesis is also an infinite process, and history itself a never wholly completed revelation of that absolute which, for the sake of consciousness, and thus merely for the sake of appearance, separates itself into conscious and unconscious, the free and intuitant; but which itself however, in the light inaccessible wherein it dwells, is eternal identity and the everlasting ground of harmony between the two." *Transcendental Idealism*, 210–211.

19 "Diese vollkommene Offenbarung würde erfolgen, wenn das freie Handeln mit der Prädetermination vollständig zusammenträfe. Wäre aber je ein solches Zusammentreffen, d.h. wäre die absolute Synthesis je vollständig entwickelt, so würden wir einsehen, daß alles, was durch Freiheit im Verlauf der Geschichte geschehen ist, in diesem Ganzen gesetzmäßig war, und daß alle Handlungen, obgleich sie frei zu seyn schienen, doch nothwendig waren. [...] Wir können uns also keine Zeit denken, in welcher sich

Schlegel, with whom he was in close contact at this time, Schelling only considers the *process* of becoming to acquire reality in human experience. Because history is characterised by freedom and unpredictability in the present (as opposed to the higher level "in unzugänglichem Lichte"), history generates novelty, the new. The dialectical relationship between subjective and objective activities described by Schelling only appears, i.e. is productive, during the process of history, when the original identity of unconscious and conscious activity is obscured. Freedom and necessity are only antithetically dialectical in the historical state of subjectively perceived non-identity (which is all that matters to the individual, because it is all the individual can ever experience). On the universal level, history, too, follows laws. But these are imperceptible to the acting subject who hence has no reason to assume it is not acting freely. Freedom is only *in the end* revealed as necessity. So history reveals itself not as an arbitrary collection of independent acts, although it appears thus in the state of non-identity, but as striving for an ideal, for the re-achievement of identity. This, however, cannot be realised by the individual who cannot comprehend the totality of the absolute, which guarantees his freedom. It applies only to the species as a whole.

> Geschichte [besteht] weder mit absoluter Gesetzmäßigkeit noch auch mit absoluter Freiheit, sondern [ist] nur da, wo Ein Ideal unter unendlich vielen Abweichungen so realisirt wird, daß zwar nicht das Einzelne, wohl aber das Ganze mit ihm congruirt. Nun kann aber ferner ein solches successives Realisiren eines Ideals, wo nur der Progressus als Ganzes [...] dem Ideal Genüge thut, nur durch solche Wesen als möglich gedacht werden, welchen der Charakter einer Gattung zukommt, weil nämlich das Individuum eben dadurch, daß es dieß ist, das Ideal zu erreichen unfähig ist, das Ideal aber, welches nothwendig ein bestimmtes ist, doch realisirt werden muß. (*System*, 588–9)[20]

---

die absolute Synthesis, d.h. wenn wir uns empirisch ausdrücken, der Plan der Vorsehung vollständig entwickelt hätte." *System*, 601–2. "This perfect revelation would come about if free action were to coincide completely with determination. But if there ever were such a coincidence, if the absolute synthesis, that is, were ever completely evolved, we should recognise that everything which has come about through freedom in the course of history, was governed in the whole by law, and that all actions, although they seemed to be free, were in fact necessary. [...] We can therefore conceive of no point in time at which the absolute synthesis – or to put it in empirical terms, the design of providence – should have brought its development to completion." *Transcendental Idealism*, 209–210.

[20] "History comes about neither with absolute lawfulness nor with absolute freedom, but exists only where a single ideal is realised under an infinity of deviations, in such a way that, not the particular detail indeed, but assuredly the whole, is in conformity thereto.

So theory is not really abandoned in history, it is merely relocated behind the historical experience of the individual. It can be deduced, but not experienced. In practical experience history and theory are themselves antithetical, "Theorie und Geschichte sind völlig Entgegengesetzte" (*System*, 589).[21] Schelling constructs a system, within which rational theory (the immutability of the laws of nature) can be accommodated by history, i.e. within a temporal framework of impermanence. History is the general development of self-consciousness and must thus include the study of the dynamics of consciousness, Fichte's endeavour. The history of consciousness must include the study of nature, as the latter is not only characterised by parallel activities, but represents an earlier form of them, which is structurally identical. Consciousness and nature are related to each other within the grand process of existence in time.

The unconscious entity, be it the unlimitably limiting activity within the subject or the hidden necessity of history, always appears "bigger" than its conscious counterpart. They do necessarily so, because they remain unconscious as they are not limited or limitable objects that can be consciously grasped. This is in turn necessary for the dialectical process to remain infinite, infinitely productive: the outer limits are never quite reached, which means the interaction carries on. The dynamic nature of the dialectical process is a vital aspect of the solution of the contemporary intellectual problem: the relation between time and value, the historicity of theory and ideals, which is to be newly defined. Dialectics is the engine of a productive process that produces partial solutions along the way and promises a final solution that it never quite reaches practically. This productive process, due to its very productivity also easily accommodates the principle of change and its results, novelty. Change and novelty are in fact part of its structure, which means change does not destabilise the structure. This structure makes possible the reintegration of the natural and unconscious into achieved structures of rational consciousness.

The unsatisfying aspect of Schelling's system is the practical obscurity of its crux, the concept of the ultimate identity. While Fichte's system

---

But now such a progressive realizing of an ideal, where only the progress as a whole [...] does justice to the ideal, can moreover be thought of as possible only through such beings as have the character of a species; for the individual, in fact, precisely because he is so, is incapable of attaining to the ideal, though the latter, which is necessarily determinate, has still got to be realized." *Transcendental Idealism*, 199–200.

[21] "Theory and history are totally opposed." *Transcendental Idealism*, 200.

thoroughly deferred its conclusive result, it promised the satisfying work on the progress towards it, the Idealist version of Enlightened perfectibility. Unlike Fichte, Schelling is convinced of the *actual existence* of an absolute harmony and unity, which he terms the Absolute. While for Schelling, too, the complete revelation of the absolute is only a future potential, he nevertheless clearly felt, because of his conviction in its actual and permanent existence, the need to suggest a way of some sort of direct access to it. He argues that it is possible to reveal glimpses of it in art. Art can already reveal what theory can not yet grasp. This is Schelling's answer to the unsatisfactory unfinished nature of the dialectical process in relation to reaching absolute identity and synthesis, to the rationally unsatisfactory idea that something exists that the human mind, as it is, cannot know or experience. Artistic creativity is both conscious and unconscious, both nature and consciousness, and thus re-attains the original unity of activity which was lost at the moment when the individual achieved consciousness. "Es wird also postulirt, daß im Subjektiven, im Bewußtseyn selbst, jene zugleich bewußte und bewußtlose Thätigkeit aufgezeigt werde. Eine solche Thätigkeit ist allein die ästhetische, und jedes Kunstwerk ist nur zu begreifen als Produkt einer solchen." (*System*, 349)[22] Hence:

> Das Kunstwerk reflektiert uns die Identität der bewußten und der bewußtlosen Thätigkeit. Aber der Gegensatz dieser beiden ist ein unendlicher, und er wird aufgehoben ohne alles Zuthun der Freiheit. Dieser Grundcharakter des Kunstwerks ist also eine bewußtlose Unendlichkeit [Synthesis von Natur und Freiheit]. Der Künstler scheint in seinem Werk außer dem, was er mit offenbarer Absicht dareingelegt hat, instinktmäßig gleichsam eine Unendlichkeit dargestellt zu haben, welche ganz zu entwickeln kein endlicher Verstand fähig ist. (*System*, 619)[23]

---

[22] "It is therefore postulated that this simultaneously conscious and unconscious activity will be exhibited in the subjective, in consciousness itself. There is but one such activity, namely the aesthetic, and every work of art can be conceived only as a product of such activity." *Transcendental Idealism*, 12.

[23] "The work of art reflects to us the identity of the conscious and unconscious activities. But the opposition between them is an infinite one, and its removal is effected without any assistance from freedom. Hence the basic character of the work of art is that of an unconscious infinity [synthesis of nature and freedom]. Besides what he has put into his work with manifest intention, the artist seems instinctively, as it were, to have depicted therein an infinity, which no finite understanding is capable of developing to the full." *Transcendental Idealism*, 225.

Here the Idealists' reflections on consciousness meet with the writers' discussions on the nature and purpose of art. Schelling's definition of art shares several key features with Schiller's definition of the beautiful and Schlegel's universal poetry. Like Schlegel's poetry, Schelling's artwork is a progressive universal project that captures totality. The parallels with Schiller are perhaps more surprising. Schelling's concept of the aesthetic in art, like Schiller's concept of the beautiful, is based on a synthesis between on the one hand the realm of rational thought and freedom and on the other the non-rational sensual-natural realm. Schelling prefers to juxtapose the terms conscious and unconscious in this context. For both this synthesis represents a symbol or a taster of a perfect and unified state. The difference between the two is that Schiller believed that true unconditional freedom and reason existed or at least could exist, whereas Schelling saw them as human capabilities that, while they existed in human experience, were beyond human experience subsumed into a greater design in which they had no independent existence. In both Schiller and Schelling one finds the notion that in history only a "pretend" freedom exists for the human being. "Really" the human being is subject to necessity, is coerced. The difference is that according to Schelling we do not, and cannot, experience this coercion in practice, while according to Schiller we do and we can only escape this experience through play or the appreciation of the beautiful. Schiller still believes in the need for liberation, whereas Schelling considers the human being as already free in his historical existence, but feels the need to enclose this freedom by a protective superstructure of providence. This pinpoints the difference between one thinker leaning towards Enlightenment thought and the other tending towards Romantic mysticism. Despite this difference, the parallels suggest that these concepts of art, whether produced by a "Classicist" or a Romantic philosopher share crucial concerns.

Schelling developed further his theory of art in his *Philosophie der Kunst* two years later. In the *System*, Schelling also briefly deals with history directly, when he associates different levels of consciousness, i.e. to what extent and in what way consciousness conceives of a relation between itself and the world around it, with different eras in human history. Until the heyday of ancient Greece, consciousness is faced with a blind power: fate dominates, cold, unconscious and unpredictable. From the Roman republic onwards, consciousness experiences the world as a more predictable place when it establishes that the forces which dominate it are based on natural laws. And finally, some time in the future consciousness will conceive of providence in the world, which recognises the gradual appearance of a design in history. (*System*, 603–4) Fichte did not apply the dynamics of the I to the species as a whole in the *Wissenschaftslehre*. He only turns to history in this respect in 1803 when he comes to write his *Grundzüge des gegenwärtigen Zeitalters*, sequelled by the *Reden an die deutsche Nation* in 1807. Here, too, history, which is European and Oriental history, evinces and represents the intellectual progress of humanity.

Hegel's *Phänomenologie des Geistes*

In the same year as Fichte began to write his *Reden an die deutsche Nation*, Friedrich Hegel published his first larger work, the *Phänomenologie*, the next milestone in the development of German Idealism. Like Fichte and Schelling before him, Hegel takes Kant's philosophy as his starting-point. While Fichte intended to produce clarifying additions and extensions to Kant's system, which were to provide a link between pure reason and practical reason, and Schelling set out to do the same to Fichte's theory of the self-positing ego, Hegel contended that Kant's division between the world as the rational human sees it, the world-for-itself, and the world as it actually is, the world-in-itself, is wrong. All three were of course concerned with the nature of this division, and Hegel's efforts build very much on Fichte's and Schelling's contributions, which makes him, out of the three, the one most removed from Kant. If one can summarise Fichte's contribution as investigating the relation between ego and world within consciousness, and Schelling's as situating this self-positing consciousness within its own history as a product of nature, then Hegel's contribution must be seen as making the process of self-positing, self-determining, self-realising, the very process of increasing (self-)consciousness, not only supreme, but also actual. Because he is interested in the general nature and progress of this process, he focuses, like Schelling, on the species, on humanity as a whole, and on the summary of its actions, which is history. This focus on history is still somewhat implicit in the *Phänomenologie* and only becomes explicit in the last phase of his work, when he presents his analysis of history in his *Vorlesungen über die Philosophie der Geschichte* in the 1820s. Nevertheless, his thinking is deeply historical from the start.

Hegel rejects Kant's split between consciousness and world, because he is convinced that, as we are part of the world, our rational concepts can only be shaped in such a way that makes them identical with the conceptual structures of the world. Hence they are predestined to grasp the world as it is. Schelling had suggested that consciousness rises from un-consciousness at a particular juncture, which means consciousness has its origin in and is produced by unconsciousness. This historical link be-tween the conscious rational self and unconscious nature makes it pos-sible for Hegel to assert that humanity's origin in nature guarantees its ultimate compatibility with it: the origin of consciousness is uncon-sciousness, as the origin of the subject is a world of objects, of which it gradually becomes conscious. However, Hegel rejects Schelling's theory of identity as an explanation of the link between consciousness and na-ture. In fact he is particularly scathing about his school friend's notion of a permanent, but extra-conscious existence of such absolute identity in his famously sarcastic description of this identity as the "night in which all cows are black", which appears in the "Vorwort" of the *Phänomeno-logie*.[24] For Hegel, Schelling's solution to the problem of connecting world and consciousness smacked too much of an abdication of the in-tellect in favour of non-analytical mysticism. His own solution, by contrast, was to locate the absolute (that in which world and conscious-ness are one) within in the historical process. There it does not appear so much split as developing. The absolute is not an eternal presence which philosophy comes closer and closer to understanding, but it is itself a pro-cess, an unfolding: it is actuating itself not just throughout, but through history. The link between experience and conceptual thought is this: not only does thought become increasingly better able to explain experience, (which was the Enlightenment position), but advancing thought grad-ually creates a world that edges ever closer to the experience of (absolute) reality. His focus on the productive power of conceptual theory in history makes Hegel not just the most historical, but also the most practically oriented of the Idealists, and his philosophy the most thorough appli-cation of historicity to conceptual theory. The ideal, i.e. the universal ab-solute, is constantly becoming. The intellect progresses only in the pro-cess, which ensures that any approach to the absolute is on a cognitive route, and not on a regressive one back towards blind faith and vacuity.

Die lebendige Substanz [...] ist als Subjekt die reine einfache Negativität, eben dadurch die Entzweiung des Einfachen, oder die entgegensetzende Ver-doppelung, welche wieder die Negation dieser gleichgültigen Verschiedenheit

---

[24] *Phänomenologie des Geistes. Georg Wilhelm Friedrich Hegel's [sic] Werke*. Vollständige Aus-gabe durch einen Verein von Freunden des Verewigten, vol. 2, 2nd edn, ed. by D. Johann Schulze, Berlin, Dunker und Humblot, 1841, p. 13. Forthwith *Phänomenologie*.

und ihres Gegensatzes ist: nur diese sich wiederherstellende Gleichheit oder
die Reflexion im Andersseyn in sich selbst – nicht eine ursprüngliche Einheit
als solche, oder unmittelbare als solche, ist das Wahre. Es ist das Werden seiner selbst, der Kreis, der sein Ende als seinen Zweck voraussetzt, und zum An-
fange hat, und nur durch die Ausführung und sein Ende wirklich ist. (*Phänomenologie*, 14–5)[25]

The actuation of the absolute, which is the gradual self-realisation of reason, is the process of unfolding the perfect knowledge of the world, and
self, as it is. History is the record of ever improving forms of consciousness. Every era has its own version of the absolute truth and its own
intrinsic value. Hegel applies Herder's notions. But some versions are
hazier than others, and Hegel conceives of the process as a gradual clari-
fication over time. The engine of this process is again dialectics, a
method that was to become synonymous with Hegelian thought, and
which Hegel perfected, but which, as we have seen, he picked up from
thinkers who published before him. The dialectical process is the way in
which the absolute actuates itself.

Das Wissen [ist] nur als Wissenschaft oder als System wirklich, und [kann]
nur [als solches] dargestellt werden, ferner [ist] ein sogenannter Grundsatz
oder Princip der Philosophie, wenn er wahr ist, schon darum auch falsch, insofern er nur als Grundsatz oder Princip ist. – Es ist deswegen leicht, ihn zu
widerlegen. Die Widerlegung besteht darin, daß sein Mangel aufgezeigt wird;
mangelhaft aber ist er, weil er nur das Allgemeine oder Princip, der Anfang ist.
Ist die Widerlegung gründlich, so ist sie aus ihm selbst genommen und entwickelt, […]. Sie würde also eigentlich seine Entwicklung und somit die Er-
gänzung seiner Mangelhaftigkeit seyn, wenn sie sich nicht darin verkennte,
daß sie ihr negatives Thun allein beachtet, und sich ihres Fortgangs und Re-
sultates nicht auch nach seiner positiven Seite bewußt wird [which still needs
to occur]. (*Phänomenologie*, 18)[26]

---

[25] "The living Substance […] is, as Subject, pure simple negativity, and is for this very reason the bifurcation of the simple; it is the doubling which sets up opposition, and then
again the negation of this indifferent diversity and of its anti-thesis [the immediate sim-
plicity]. Only this self-restoring sameness, or this reflection in otherness within itself –
not an original or immediate unity as such – is the True. It is the process of its own becoming, the circle that presupposes its end as its goal, having its end also as its beginning; and only by being worked out to its end, is it actual." *Hegel's Phenomenology of
Spirit.* Translated by. A.V. Miller with Analysis of the Text and Foreword by J.N. Findlay, Oxford: Oxford University Press, 1977, p. 10. Forthwith *Phenomenology.*

[26] "Knowledge is only actual, and can only be expounded, as Science or as system; and
furthermore, that a so-called basic proposition or principle of philosophy, if true, is also
false, just because it is only a principle. It is, therefore, easy to refute it. The refutation

In the *Phänomenologie* Hegel outlines what is perhaps best described as the history of consciousness as it manifests itself in history. The succeeding forms of consciousness are gaining ever greater levels of accuracy and inclusiveness. This is always a movement from substance to subject, from being via consciousness to self-consciousness. Being becomes conscious of its other – what it is not, which it studies as object – and through this process discovers itself, becomes self-conscious. So far Hegel repeats the activities of the Fichtean I. Going beyond Fichte, Hegel suggests that this dynamic is also at work in the intellectual life of human communities, and of the species at large. In this collective medium, reason can acquire self-consciousness and reach the level of spirit, or *Geist*. *Geist* is the key concept in Hegel's entire system. It describes self-conscious reason which knows itself to such an extent that it is aware it can only realise itself through action. In Hegel's distinction between reason and (human) action Schelling's difference between necessity and freedom, which he endeavoured to link in his transcendental identity, is re-addressed. It is also the distinction between theoretical and practical reason, the connection between which had preoccupied every post-Kantian thinker. Hegel links the two in the self-realisation process of increasing consciousness in history. The theoretical nature of reason actuates itself by becoming conscious of itself, an object to itself, so it can appear in history as spirit.

> Die Vernunft ist Geist, indem die Gewißheit, alle Realität zu seyn, zur Wahrheit erhoben, und sie sich ihrer selbst als ihrer Welt, und der Welt als ihrer selbst bewußt ist. [...] Das an- und fürsichseyende Wesen aber, welches sich zugleich als Bewußtseyn wirklich und sich sich selbst vorstellt, ist der Geist. (*Phänomenologie*, 317–8)[27]

Spirit is inherently dynamic.

---

consists in pointing out its defect; and it is defective because it is only the universal or principle, is only the beginning. If the refutation is thorough, it is derived and developed from the principle itself [...]. The refutation would, therefore, properly consist in the further development of the principle, and in thus remedying the defectiveness, if it did not mistakenly pay attention solely to its negative action, without awareness of its progress and result on their positive side too." *Phenomenology*, 13.

27 "Reason is Spirit when its certainty of being all reality has been raised to truth, and it is conscious of itself as its own world, and of the world as itself. [...] But essence that is in and for itself, and which is at the same time actual as consciousness and aware of itself, this is Spirit." *Phenomenology*, 263.

Er [Geist] ist an sich die Bewegung, die das Erkennen ist, – die Verwandlung jenes Ansichs in das Fürsich, der Substanz in das Subject, des Gegenstandes des Bewußtseyns in Gegenstand des Selbstbewußtseyns, d. h. in ebensosehr aufgehobenen Gegenstand oder in den Begriff. Sie ist der in sich zurückgehende Kreis, der seinen Anfang voraussetzt und ihn nur im Ende erreicht. (*Phänomenologie*, 585)[28]

Spirit is the animating principle of humanity, of the individual as well as of communities. It is knowledge of one's own identity and purpose, which is expressed in one's actions. It is still particular. Once particular spirit acquires full consciousness of itself, through an encounter with its other, it becomes universal, and spirit is fully realised. This constitutes absolute knowing (*absolutes Wissen*). At the end of the *Phänomenologie* Hegel introduces his notion of the *Weltgeist*,[29] which realises itself in the course of human history through succeeding *Volksgeister*, the conception that he will detail in his later work on his philosophy of history.

Das Geisterreich, das auf diese Weise sich in dem Daseyn [der Geschichte] bildet, macht eine Aufeinanderfolge aus, worauf einer den andern ablöste, und jeder das Reich der Welt von dem vorhergehenden übernahm. Ihr Ziel ist die Offenbarung der Tiefe und diese ist der absolute Begriff; [...]. Das Ziel, das absolute Wissen, oder der sich als Geist wissende Geist hat zu seinem Wege die Erinnerung der Geister, wie sie an ihnen selbst sind und die Organisation ihres Reiches vollbringen. Ihre Aufbewahrung nach der Seite ihres freien in der Form der Zufälligkeit erscheinenden Daseyns, ist die Geschichte, nach der Seite ihrer begriffenen Organisation aber die Wissenschaft des erscheinenden Wissens; beide zusammen, die begriffene Geschichte, bilden die Erinnerung und Schädelstätte des absoluten Geistes. (*Phänomenologie*, 591)[30]

---

[28] "It is in itself the movement which is cognition – the transformation of that in-itself into that which is for-itself, of Substance into Subject, of the object of consciousness into an object of self-consciousness, i.e. into an object that is just as much superseded, or into the Notion. The movement is the circle that returns into itself, the circle that presupposes its beginning and reaches it only at the end." *Phenomenology*, 488.

[29] "Ehe daher der Geist nicht an sich, nicht als Weltgeist sich vollendet, kann er nicht als selbstbewußter Geist seine Vollendung erreichen." *Phänomenologie*, 585.

[30] "The realm of Spirits which is formed in this way in the outer world constitutes a succession in Time in which one Spirit relieved another of its charge and each took over the empire of the world from its predecessor. The goal is the revelation of the depth of Spirit, and this is the absolute Notion. [...] The goal, Absolute Knowing, or Spirit that knows itself as Spirit, has for its path the recollection of the Spirits as they are in themselves and as they accomplish the organization of their realm. The preservation, regarded from the side of their free existence appearing in the form of contingency, is History; but regarded from the side of their [philosophically] comprehended organization, it is the Science of Knowing in the sphere of appearance: the two together, com-

Hegel's crucial points in this context are his insistence that the synthesis of the theoretical and practical occurs in self-consciousness, which has its phenomenology in human history. In the pursuit of knowledge thinkers used to research nature, or the world, i.e. space, for the truth of facts. Hegel suggests that this will result in getting stuck with a static concept of reason, which has been questioned by the increasing awareness of historicity. So this kind of pursuit of knowledge is no longer in tandem with human intellectual development. It has been left behind by advancing self-consciousness, which now considers itself to be historical. The pursuit of knowledge now needs to research time, where it will find the truth as process.

> Dieß Ich gleich Ich ist aber die sich in sich selbst reflectirende Bewegung; denn indem diese Gleichheit als absolute Negativität der absolute Unterschied ist, so steht die Sichselbstgleichheit des Ichs diesem reinen Unterschiede gegenüber, der als der reine und zugleich dem sich wissenden Selbst gegenständliche, als die Zeit auszusprechen ist, so daß, wie vorhin das Wesen als Einheit des Denkens und der Ausdehnung ausgesprochen wurde, es als Einheit des Denkens und der Zeit zu fassen wäre. (*Phänomenologie*, 586)[31]

This extends the Fichtean productivity of the self, the self as act, to the realm of pure thought, and of truth, which must have given Hegel the sense of really having effected a reconciliation between pure reason and practical reason, without having resorted to an inexplicable entity. But this apparent solution is also what has been recognised as most problematic about Hegel's thought.[32] If the definition of absolute knowledge, and Hegel's philosophy, were the answer, then the historical process

---

prehended History, form alike the inwardizing and the Calvary of absolute Spirit." *Phenomenology*, 492–3.

[31] "But this 'I' = 'I' is the movement which reflects itself into itself; for since this identity, being absolute negativity, is absolute difference, the self-identity of the 'I' stands over against this pure difference which, as pure and at the same time objective to the self-knowing Self, has to be expressed as Time. So that, just as previously essence was declared to be the unity of Thought and Extension, it would now have be grasped as the unity of Thought and Time." *Phenomenology*, 489.

[32] Cf. J. Habermas, *The Philosophical Discourse of Modernity*, (1985) trans. by Frederick Lawrence, Cambridge: Polity Press, 1987, repr. 1994, pp. 43, 22. Also W. Schneider, "Vom Weltweisen zum Gottverdammten. Über Hegel und sein Philosophieverständnis", Jamme/Kurz ed.s, *Idealismus und Aufklärung. Kontinuität und Kritik der Aufklärung in Philosophie und Poesie um 1800*, pp. 201–16, 215/16 and 210. Schneider focuses on the dialectics of Hegel's achievement theoretically and practically for Hegel personally. And also cf. *Oxford Companion to Philosophy*, ed. by Ted Honderich, Oxford/New York: Oxford University Press, 1995, Hegel-entry, p. 342.

would be about to come a halt, would have reached its destination, which would make Hegel himself god-like in terms of understanding. The position Hegel himself takes up within his system does not allow for its own historicity, its own preliminariness.

The up-shot of Idealist thought from Fichte to Hegel is the following: in a gradual process the human mind becomes conscious of who it is and initiates actions in accordance with this knowledge, which generates identity. This is identity in the philosophical sense of complete congruence between theory and practice, subject and object, and thought and experience, which is lastly identity in the common sense of the answer to the question who am I (which is I am I). The knowledge of any identity is achieved through difference, through the experience, investigation and overcoming (assimilation) of difference. Dialectics is the engine of this process. Absolute knowledge, which is the experience and understanding of absolute reality, is only possible once all differences have been assimilated. Only Hegel traces this process consequently through its historical appearances: the different forms of consciousness appear in different social communities and organisations, which through their different limitations keep the dialectical process going. The Hegelian Idealist process in history is explicitly worked out in his *Geschichte der Philosophie*, but underlies his entire work. History has replaced nature as the paradigm on which theory is based.

The awareness of historicity has led to a conceptual focus on history. History is defined as the record of how things change and become. Things change because of the existence and development of difference. Difference is the basis on which the newly discovered inconstancy of human nature and human experience rests. Although absolute identity is the overall aim, particularity and difference are vital during the process of reaching this absolute identity. So to know myself, to become fully self-conscious, I must know what is external to me, not just spatially, the world, but equally temporally, the past. The Idealist effort consisted of making difference meaningful by making it a tool of knowledge.

The German *Querelle* is one aspect of this process of achieving identity. Schiller's and Schlegel's struggles with the ancient ideal follow the same pattern: the ancients are profoundly different, and yet are they vital to the moderns. The fundamental difference between ancient and modern, or between "naive" and "sentimental", is the basis for the historical dialectic. In the theory of modernity that Schiller and Schlegel propose, the ancients are the *other* that needs to be assimilated and overcome. Insisting on the natural features of antiquity, whereas modernity is characterised by consciousness, Schiller and Schlegel suggest that antiquity represents simple consciousness, an awareness of the world as object that is other and interesting, whereas modernity represents self-consciousness, which relates the other to the self in order to make sense of the latter.

The theory of modernity that Schiller and Schlegel develop shares structure and direction with Idealist theory: the dialectical process and a potential resolution in the fullness of time. Both are based on the notion that existence and knowledge are a dialectical process in time. Both define modernity (or the present state of affairs) as based on the principle of striving, and its historical phenomena, the products of striving, form the basis for the consummation of striving. This restless and dissatisfied striving makes modernity initially seem inferior to the self-assured serenity of antiquity, but equally produces the basis of superiority. It places modernity on the road towards achieving a new and ultimate serenity. Modernity has the makings of consummateness, *because* it is based on striving. It carries the "ancient" condition within it, as increasingly conscious memory, which it strives to reconcile with its new and different condition. This makes modernity dialectical itself and gives it its dynamic nature, which is required for further development. The fundamental difference between ancient and modern is mirrored in the distinction between Kant's world for human reason and the world-in-itself, in the difference between Fichte's I and non-I, and in the Idealist difference between subject and object. With their focus on the dynamics of the modern condition Schiller and Schlegel go, like Fichte, beyond Kant and point towards the historicist dynamics of Schelling and Hegel. The new cultural and philosophical thought establishes the following: historical flux generates difference and novelty (which might be termed new otherness). The dialectical process makes difference dynamic. Static dichotomous structures become dialectical structures and hence dynamic. Knowledge and identity can only be the result of a dialectical process. Conceptual theory, pure thought, is thus inextricably connected to the passage of time, which unfolds theory in history.

Chapter 3

Historicity, Modernity and German Identity: "Stammvolk Europas" and Modern *Kulturnation*

The growing awareness of historicity has been identified as the impetus for the reflections on the nature of cultural and intellectual development and identity discussed in the previous chapters. As "Historismus", aspects of this awareness have had a long and varied career as an element of German self-definition. For the intellectual historians of the later 19th and early 20th centuries the historicist outlook was the key achievement of German thought, which made it distinct from the "Western" tradition of natural law that informed Enlightenment thinking and from which they wished to distinguish an independent German tradition. The historical approach is indeed the distinguishing feature of modern German thought. But rather than the concept of historicism that emerged in academic thinking in the later 19th century, it was the new awareness of the historical nature of the human existence and human understanding – which is an awareness of a problematic – that played a crucial role in the definition of the modern German self-definition. And it did so already at the end of the 18th century. When Friedrich Meinecke in his *Entstehung des Historismus* denies true historicist credentials to those late 18th-century thinkers, such a Lessing, Schiller or Hegel, who still subscribe to some form of ideal, even a constantly developing one, because in his view this is evidence of their inability to grasp the mystery of historical individuality, i.e. leaves them intellectually too attached to the Enlightenment, he merely rehearses the *Sturm-und-Drang* quarrel with the Enlightenment, which demanded a historical approach in favour of the static doctrines of natural law. The discussions around 1800 in which a modern German identity took shape, and to which Schiller and Hegel contributed immensely, are premised on the notion of historicity and the desire to integrate what was considered natural and original with advancing understanding. The awareness of historicity initially led to a close investigation of "natural origins" and was then functionalised to aid the integration of the natural and the original with self-conscious understanding.

A. W. Schlegel's *Berliner* and *Wiener Vorlesungen*: The Cultural Content of the Internal Dialectic of Modernity – Christianity and the Germanic

The theory which sees modernity as embedded in a dialectical historical process of self-realisation, generates a distinctive new understanding of the purpose of individual and historical, including national, particularity. The word *Romantic* came to cover both the essence of modernity and its historical manifestation. The Romantic was defined as a theoretical concept, as well as a phase in the historical process. The term Romantic comes into use, almost as a synonym for modern, when the identity of modernity is given a specific cultural content. Conceptually the Romantic is, like the modern, based on the principle of striving which is possibly infinite. This principle becomes historically manifest and dominant for the first time in the culture of the Middle Ages. That the Middle Ages represent the early culture of modernity had been spelt out by Herder. But the precise cultural specification of the modern in the shape of the Romantic originates in the thinking of the Schlegel brothers, especially August Wilhelm, whose definitions have held sway well into the 20th century.[1] Friedrich's brother Wilhelm formulates his theory of modernity as a theory of the Romantic in several series of lectures: the *Jenaer Vorlesungen* of 1798–99 (the *Kunstlehre*), the *Berliner Vorlesungen* of 1801–04 (*Schöne Literatur und Kunst*) and the *Wiener Vorlesungen* of 1808 (*Dramatische Kunst und Literatur*). Apart from his fame as a gifted translator of Shakespeare, Wilhelm Schlegel is best known as a critic of literature and culture. In his lectures he formulates a theory of critique which addresses the contemporary problem of the relation of theory to historicity and clearly exhibits Idealist influences. In fact Schlegel works very much at the cutting edge of contemporary critical thinking.

---

[1] Cf. the influential 20th-century study by Fritz Strich, *Klassik und Romantik oder Vollendung und Unendlichkeit* of 1922.

Not surprisingly, Schlegel's lectures are in the main *histories* of literature, because for him, too, history is the basis of any theory of art.

Man möchte denken, wenn der Theorie einmal das allgemeine Factum der
vorhandenen Kunst gegeben wäre, so könnte sie nachher der Geschichte den
Abschied geben, und unbekümmert um sie fortfahren zu demonstriren, was
in der Kunst geleistet werden soll. Allein dieß darf sie nicht aus doppeltem
Grunde: weil ihre Gegenstände nicht von der Art sind, daß sie nach dem blo-
ßen Begriff erkannt werden könnten, sie muß also immerfort auf die Gegenstände selbst hinweisen; und weil die Aufgaben der schönen Kunst sämtlich
von der Art sind, daß ihre Möglichkeit nur durch die wirkliche Lösung eingesehen wird. Sie muß mithin, sowohl ihrer Verständlichkeit als ihrer Beglaubigung wegen ihren Begriffen eine Reihe entsprechender Anschauungen unter-
legen, welche ihr die Geschichte darbietet. Diese bleibt für sie der ewige
Codex, dessen Offenbarungen sie nur immer vollkommener zu deuten und
zu enthüllen bemüht ist. [...] Die Kunstgeschichte [ist] das unentbehrliche
Correlat der Kunsttheorie.[2]

Again, history is the new empirical data, replacing nature as the material
for theory, which had been the basis for 17th- and 18th-century empiricism. According to Schlegel, history and theory need to be related to
each other by means of "Kritik". "[Es] wird sich bey [der] Erörterung
[des Begriffs der Kritik] zeigen, daß Kritik sowohl für Theorie als Kunstgeschichte das unentbehrliche Organ, und das verbindende Mittelglied beyder ist." (BV, 196).[3] "Kritik" is the ability to "judge" (beurteilen)
works of art. A critique is a thorough (rational) investigation of the nature of an object, which synthesises the realms of theory and history.

---

2 A.W. Schlegel, *Vorlesungen über Schöne Literatur und Kunst* (Berliner Vorlesungen) in *Vorlesungen über Ästhetik I*, ed. by Ernst Behler (*August Wilhelm Schlegel. Kritische Ausgabe der
Vorlesungen* vol. 1) Paderborn: Schönigh, 1989, pp. 190–91. Forthwith BV. "One might
think that, once theory has taken account of the general fact of existing art, it could dis-
miss history and proceed, without heeding history further, to demonstrate what ought
to be accomplished in art. But theory cannot be allowed to do this for two reasons: its
objects are not of the kind that can be comprehended through mere concepts, thus theory perpetually has to point to those objects themselves. Furthermore the tasks of art are
without exception such that their achievability is only recognised through their real fulfilment. Thus theory must, in order to be understood as well as legitimised, provide a
series of corresponding objects for its concepts, which are provided by history. For any
theory, history remains the eternal codex, the revelations of which it endeavours to interpret and uncover with increasing clarity. [...] The history of art is the indispensable
correlate to the theory of art."
3 "The discussion [of the concept of critique] will demonstrate that critique is the indis-
pensible organ for both the theory and history of art as well as the link between them."

Objectiv, über unsere Person hinaus gültig, kann es [das Urteil] nur dadurch werden, daß die Vergleichung mit solchen Gegenständen angestellt worden, die wirklich dazu gehören. [...] Zu einer gründlichen Kritik [wird] historisches Studium, Kenntniß der Kunstgeschichte, wesentlich erfodert. [...] Ferner liegt in ihr [der Kunstgeschichte] eine beständige Beziehung auf die Theorie. Denn das Urteil kann nur durch Begriffe klar gemacht und ausgesprochen werden, die erst durch ihre Stelle in einem vorausgesetzten Systeme [...] ihre volle Bestimmung erhalten. Die kritische Reflexion ist eigentlich ein beständiges Experimentiren, um auf theoretische Sätze zu kommen. Auf der anderen Seite wird durch sie das, was in einer Kunst vorhanden ist, erst zum Objekte für die Kunstgeschichte und dadurch mittelbar auch für die Theorie verarbeitet, denn beyde haben es ja nicht mit den Kunstwerken zu thun, [...] sondern mit ihrem Geiste. (BV, 199–200)[4]

No doubt by assigning such an important function to criticism – without it theory cannot engage with history, while history is meaningless chaos without theory – Schlegel also justifies his own job as an art critic. It is unlikely to be a coincidence that Schlegel's three areas (of theory, history, and *Kritik*) echo the three subjects of Kant's *Critiques* (i.e. pure reason, practical reason, and judgement). Like Schlegel's "Kritik", Kant's *Critique of Judgement* was supposed to provide the link between pure and practical reason. It was a link that occupied all post-Kantian Idealists, first Fichte, then Schelling, and finally Hegel to the extent that it is fair to say that the weakness they perceived in Kant's link was the spur for their own endeavours. Schlegel, it seems, was no exception. He reiterates these intentions in the Vienna Lectures on dramatic literature and art (1808):

Ich werde mich in den folgenden Vorträgen bemühen, die Theorie der dramatischen Kunst mit ihrer Geschichte zu verbinden. [...] Die Geschiche der schönen Künste lehrt uns, was geleistet worden, die Theorie, was geleistet werden soll. Ohne ein verbindendes Mittelglied würden beide abgesondert und unzulänglich bleiben. Die Kritik ist es, welche die Geschichte der Künste auf-

---

4   "An objective verdict, i.e. a verdict beyond individual notions, can only be achieved when a comparsion has taken place between objects which can be compared. [...] Thorough critique essentially requires historical study, knowledge of art history. [...] Furthermore art history bears a constant relation to the theory of art. This is because the verdict can only be made clear and voiced through concepts, which only receive their full definition through their place [...] within an assumed system. Critical reflection is a permanent experimenting in order to arrive at theoretical maxims. On the other hand only critique turns that which forms the catalogue of any art form into the objects of art history, and thus makes them accessible for theory, since neither deal with the art works themselves, [...] but with their spirit."

klärt, und ihre Theorie fruchtbar macht. Die Vergleichung und Beurtheilung der vorhandenen Hervorbringungen des menschlichen Geistes muß uns die Bedingungen an die Hand geben, die zur Bildung eigenthümlicher und gehaltvoller Kunstwerke erforderlich sind.[5]

Schlegel envisages this synthesis through "Vermittlung", the Idealist term for mediation, also crucial in Schelling's *System*, and in Hegel's *Phänomenologie*. Theory and history are to be mediated at all times through critique, which partakes of both and is necessarily reflective on a higher level.[6] Schlegel conceives of the nature of history in a manner similar to Schelling and later Hegel: it represents the identity of necessity and freedom, it is the interlocking of theory and practice. And it must always be the basis for theory.

Indem ich eine historische Darstellung der Poesie ankündige, habe ich ihr schon die gebührende Stelle anzuweisen gesucht; denn in meinem Sinne gibt es nur davon eine Geschichte, was dem Menschen kraft seiner höheren Natur aufgegeben ist, und wobei er, als Individuum, jedoch mit gesetzmäßiger Freiheit wirkend erscheint.[7]

---

5 A.W. Schlegel, *Vorlesungen über dramatische Kunst und Literatur*, ed. by G.V. Amoretti, 2 vols in 1, Bonn/Leipzig: Kurt Schröder Verlag, 1923, I, pp. 3–4. Forthwith *Dramatische Kunst*. "The object of the present series of Lectures will be to combine the theory of Dramatic Art with its history. […] Now, the history of the fine arts informs us what has been, and the theory teaches what ought to be accomplished by them. But without some intermediate and connecting link, both would remain independent and separate from one and other, and each by itself, inadequate and defective. This connecting link is furnished by criticism, which both elucidates the history of the arts, and makes the theory fruitful. The comparing together, and judging of the existing productions of the human mind, necessarily throws light upon the conditions which are indispensable to the creation of original and masterly works of art." *Lectures on Dramatic Art and Literature by August Wilhelm Schlegel*, trans. by John Black, 3rd edn, rev. by A.J.M Morrison, London: Bell & Sons, 1894, pp. 17–18. Forthwith *Dramatic Art*.
6 It is not the case, as Anneke Grosse-Brockhoff suggested, that one is to be rescued by the other when it has got stuck in a dead-end. Cf. Anneke Grosse-Brockhoff, *Das Konzept des Klassischen bei Friedrich Schlegel und August Wilhelm Schlegel*, Cologne/Vienna: Böhlau, 1981, p. 204.
7 A.W. Schlegel, *Geschichte der Romantischen Literatur* in *August Wilhelm Schlegel. Kritische Schriften und Briefe* vol. 4, ed. by Edgar Lohner, Stuttgart: Kohlhammer, 1965, p. 12. Forthwith *Romantische Literatur*. The *Romantische Literatur* forms part of the *Berliner Vorlesungen*. "By promising a historical description of poetry I have already endeavoured to give history its due place. Because according to my understanding there can only be a history of those things that humanity is meant to achieve due to its higher nature and in the course of which the human being appears, as individual, to act with freedom governed by laws."

Schlegel's reflections on the relation between theory and history place him at the forefront of contemporary thought, irrespective of whether he was able to effect a thorough synthesis or not.[8]

In the decade between 1798 and 1808 Schlegel continued the investigations conducted by his brother and Schiller in the 1790s and worked on the historical dialectic exemplified in the difference between ancient and modern, and on the related immanent dialectic of modernity, which finds expression in modern striving and longing, and which was the engine of progress in general and the basis of the superiority of modernity in particular. In the Berlin and Vienna Lectures Schlegel strove to integrate the ancient and the modern into a preliminarily complete history of literature.[9] Taking the conceptual and historical structures of the two cultures which Friedrich and Schiller had analysed as his starting point Wilhelm Schlegel moved on to investigate their specific cultural content. As always, the dialectic of history is based on the notion that antiquity was followed by an era that was profoundly different in character. Wilhelm Schlegel put this difference down to the religion that informed modernity.

> Die Religion ist die Wurzel des menschlichen Daseyns. Wäre es dem Menschen möglich, alle Religion, auch die unbewußte und unwillkürliche zu verläugnen, so würde er ganz Oberfläche werden, und kein Inneres wäre dabei. Wenn dieses Centrum verrückt wird, so muß sich folglich danach die gesamte Wirksamkeit der Gemüths- und Geisteskräfte anders bestimmen. Und dieß ist denn auch im neuern Europa durch die Einführung des Christenthums geschehen. (*Dramatische Kunst* I, 10–11)[10]

---

[8] Grosse-Brockhoff is very doubtful regarding Schlegel's success on this point, and also quotes other critical voices. Cf. Grosse-Brockhoff, *Das Konzept des Klassischen*, 195 ff. But in view of the general difficulty regarding this experienced by all post-Kantians, recognising the problem and dealing with it is clearly a considerable achievement.

[9] His brother Friedrich was of course making his own attempts in this direction. In his mercurial, ingenious and somewhat erratic manner, he had already reached this position of a double dialectic by 1800. In fact, the young Friedrich himself serves well as an example of the Fichtean 'I'. Casting himself as a single-minded admirer of the ancients, he begins by defining the moderns as different and inadequate in his *Studium-Aufsatz*, but, having defined them exhaustively, realises that they truly represent his own identity, for better or for worse, which leads him to define the ancients as the other instead, which now needs to be assimilated into the modern identity to make it complete.

[10] "Religion is the root of human existence. Were it possible for man to renounce all religion, including that which is unconscious, independent of the will, he would become a mere surface without any internal substance. When this centre is disturbed, the whole system of mental faculties and feelings becomes redefined. And this is what has actually

By making the new era dependent on a spiritual basis that is oriental in origin and came to the fore under ancient conditions, he underlined the dialectical nature of the world-historical development: the thesis generates its antithesis.

> Bey den Griechen war die menschliche Natur selbstgenügsam, sie ahndete keinen Mangel, und strebte nach keiner anderen Vollkommenheit, als die sie wirklich durch ihre Kräfte erreichen konnte. […] In der christlichen Anicht hat […] die Anschauung des Unendlichen das Endliche vernichtet; das Leben ist zur Schattenwelt und zur Nacht geworden, und erst jenseits geht der ewige Tag des wesentlichen Daseyns auf. Eine solche Religion muß die Ahndung, die in allen gefühlvollen Herzen schlummert, zum deutlichen Bewußseyn wecken, daß wir nach einer hier unerreichbaren Glückseligkeit trachten. […] Die Poesie der Alten war die des Besitzes, die unsrige ist die der Sehnsucht; jene steht fest auf dem Boden der Gegenwart, diese wiegt sich zwischen Erinnerung und Ahndung. […] Das griechische Ideal der Menschheit war vollkommene Eintracht und Ebenmaaß aller Kräfte, natürliche Harmonie. Die Neueren hingegen sind zum Bewußtseyn der inneren Entzweiung gekommen, […] daher ist das Streben ihrer Poesie, diese beiden Welten, zwischen denen wir uns getheilt fühlen, die geistige und die sinnliche, miteinander auszusöhnen. (*Dramatische Kunst* I, 12–3)[11]

Broadly following the distinctions made by Schiller and his brother, negative, antithetical modernity is irresistibly drawn towards what it is not, an harmonious existence, and beyond its antithetical nature, aware of its own internal dialectic, which it strives to resolve. So, again, the modern mindset represents not just the other side of happiness, on which the temporal dialectic of ancient and modern history is based,

---

occurred in modern Europe through the introduction of Christianity." (*Dramatic Art*, 24).

[11] "Among the Greeks human nature was itself all-sufficient; it was conscious of no defects, and aspired to no higher perfection than that which it could actually attain by the exercise of its own energies. […] In the Christian view […] every thing finite and mortal is lost in the contemplation of infinity; life has become shadow and darkness, and the first day of our real existence dawns in the world beyond the grave. Such a religion must waken the vague foreboding, which slumbers in every feeling heart, into a distinct consciousness that the happiness after which we are here striving is unattainable. […] The poetry of the ancients was the poetry of enjoyment [possession], and ours is that of desire, the former has its foundation in the scene which is present, while the latter hovers betwixt recollection and hope. […] The Greek ideal of human nature was perfect unison and proportion between all the powers, – a natural harmony. The moderns, on the contrary, have arrived at the consiousness of an internal discord […] and hence the endeavour of their poetry is to reconcile these two worlds between which we find ourselves divided. *Dramatic Art*, 26–27. My suggestion in brackets.

modern consciousness is also split within itself, "entzweit in zwei Welten" between the sensual-physical and the spiritual in its nature, between which it finds it difficult to build a bridge. In this dividedness of the modern human mind the sensual-physical side, in familiar fashion, represents an earlier form of existence, while the spiritual side represents a later development. Schlegel proceeds to fill these two opposing concepts of the spiritual and the physical with cultural content. They are Christianity and what Schlegel called "deutsche Stammesart".[12] The latter is an inclusive ethnic and cultural essence shared by most Central and Western European peoples, excluding, however, the Slavs, on grounds of world-historical unimportance, and the Asiatic Turks, on grounds of religion.[13] Schlegel here uses the term *deutsch* in its late 18th-century meaning of Germanic.[14]

At first sight the Christian and the Germanic seem to combine harmoniously to create the new modern identity. Their fruitful fusion is evinced in the culture of the European Middle Ages, with its signature cultural achievement of chivalry and its breathtaking architecture, which was being reappreciated at the time. This, Schlegel argues, is the original culture (in the Herderian sense) of post-classical Europe, its first and truly its own. He goes to great lengths to set up and define this cultural root of modernity. In the Berlin Lectures he establishes the medieval, from which modernity in its distinctiveness has developed, as the

---

[12] *Romantische Literatur*, 82.

[13] "Wenn wir also wie billig diese östlicher wohnenden slavischen Völkerschaften [...] und die asiatischen, immer noch nicht recht einheimisch gewordenen Fremdlinge abrechnen: so behalten wir für unser Europa, die kleineren Ausnahmen abgerechnet, nur eine einzige, durch Sprache und Abstammung durchgängig verwandte, große Völkermasse übrig. Deutsche Stämme waren es, welche durch den Umsturz des abendländischen Römischen Reichs im Süden, dann durch Ausbreitung im Norden das neuere Europa gründeten und erfüllten." *Romantische Literatur*, 21.

[14] The term "Germanic" is only just coming into use and will be employed by Schlegel five years later in his Vienna lectures on dramatic art in exactly the same context: "Nächst dem Christenthum ist die Bildung Europa's seit dem Anfang des Mittelalters durch die germanische Stammart der nordischen Eroberer [...] entschieden worden." *Dramatische Kunst*, 11. "After Christianity, the character of Europe has, since the commencement of the Middle Ages, been chiefly influenced by the Germanic race of northern conquerers [...]." *Dramatic Art*, 25. No doubt Schlegel also plays on the original meaning of "deutsch", well known at the time, which, unlike the words denoting other European nationalities, meant "folkish" or "of the people", i.e. referred to a conceptual generality rather than named a particular nationality, which suited Schlegel's purposes well, as we shall see.

true opposition to ancient. This is Schlegel's contribution to a discussion which started in the mid-18th century and aimed at emancipating modern culture from classicist ideals, when parallels were first drawn between early ancient (Greek) culture and medieval culture, in which the latter is seen as an expression of modernity in its infancy.[15]

On closer inspection, however, Schlegel's medieval culture turns out to remain internally heterogeneous. Its key elements, the Germanic and the Christian religion, are conceptually and culturally antithetical. Christianity is characterised as "religiöser orientalischer Idealismus" whereas the original ethnic disposition of the Germanic Europeans was towards realism: "Im Okzident war der Realismus heimisch" (*Romantische Literatur*, 85).[16] Schegel concludes, with one eye on antiquity: "Die klassische Bildung ist durchgehends gleichartig und einfach; hingegen Heterogeneität der Mischungen bezeichnet die moderne urspünglich, und so suchte sich auch in ihrem Fortschritte immer das Entgegengesetzte zu verbinden." (*Romantische Literatur*, 83)[17] But this joining of opposites was, in Schlegel's view, rarely perfect and often produced results that were weighted one way or the other. The old tribal legacy based on the warrior virtues of courage and honour, although ameliorated by the civilising influence of the new religion, lived on.

> Überhaupt sind manche Gesetze der Ehre eine unschätzbare Überlieferung der Vorzeit, die uns in weit mehr Stücken lenkt und bestimmt, als wir anzuerkennen geneigt sind. Auf die Entwicklung dieser großen Idee, welche damals die ganze Sittlichkeit umfaßte, hatte unstreitig das Christentum viel Einfluß, zum Teil aber hat sie ihre Unabhängigkeit neben der Religion behauptet. […] Weil das Christentum nicht wie die alten Religionen sich mit äußerlichen Leistungen begnügte, so [hat] sich das Bewußtsein der Freiheit in ein neben der Frömmigkeit bestehendes, zuweilen mit ihr im Widerspruch begriffenens weltliches Sittengesetz hinübergerettet, und die Ehre gleichsam als eine ritterliche Religion gestiftet. (*Romantische Literatur*, 96–7)[18]

---

[15] Cf. Curne de la Sainte-Palaye op. cit., Richard Hurd, op. cit., Johann Jacob Bodmer, *Von den vortrefflichen Umständen für die Poesie unter den Kaisern aus dem schwäbischen Hause* (1743).

[16] "The West was the home of realism."

[17] "Classical culture is thoroughly uniform and simple, modern culture, on the other hand, is originally characterised by a heterogeneity of mixtures. Thus, as it progressed, opposites always endeavoured to become linked."

[18] "Some codes of honour are an invaluable legacy from earlier times, which determine and direct us far more than we are inclined to recognise. Undoubtedly Christianity deeply influenced the development of this great idea which comprised morality in its entirety in those days, but in part it successfully defended its independence alongside

Alongside this secular code of honourable conduct a religious code of conduct developed, which was drawn entirely from the oriental-ancient origin of the Christian religion. This led to the co-existence of two intrinsically antithetical moral codes, one secular, one religious. Chivalry is set against monasticism.

> Aus der Kombination der kernigen und redlichen Tapferkeit des deutschen Nordens mit dem Christentum [...] ging der ritterliche Geist hervor, eine mehr als glänzende, wahrhaft entzückende, und bisher in der Geschichte eine beispiellose Erscheinung. Dem Rittertum stand das Mönchtum symmetrisch gegenüber, [...] dieses [hatte] aus der Bereinigung desselben [Christentums] mit etwas Altem, ja Veraltetem, nämlich der nicht mehr verstandenen, nur in Bruchstücken bekannten dennoch unbedingt verehrten Autorität des klassischen Altertums seinen Geist als Scholastik fixiert. (*Romantische Literatur*, 83)[19]

Brought up in the tradition of enlightened Protestantism, Schlegel was naturally suspicious of Catholic monasticism. To him it represented an unproductive dialectic of ancient and modern, where an ancient tradition (early Christianity with its strong classical connections) is imported without organic integration into a new (modern) environment. This is a "bad" example of cultural practice after the fashion of Herder's French classicism in his Shakespeare-essay. Although chivalric culture produces a harsh and scarring intellectual and emotional experience for the individual, it results, in Schlegel's view, in a more productive dialectic. Here the sensual, practical, realistic nature of the Germanic is in constant interactive opposition with the demands of an idealistic, theoretical and spiritual religion.

> Ganz andere Begriffe über den Wert strenger Zucht und Sittsamkeit machte eine durchaus geistige Religion zu den herrschenden, es wurde für verdienstlich erklärt, dem Triebe der Natur zu entsagen, [...]. In der ritterlichen Zeit versuchte die Liebe nun gleichsam, sich mit diesen Gesinnungen zu vereini-

---

religion. [...] Because Christianity is not, like those older religions, content with external achievements, the consciousness of freedom escaped into a secular morality, which existed alongside piety and which occasionally stood in opposition to the latter. It thus created through the concept of honour a chivalric religion."

[19] "The chivalric spirit [...] developed out of the combination of the strong and honest valour of the German(ic) North with Christianity. It was a splendid, truly delightful phenomenon, unrivalled in history. Chivalry and monasticism faced each other symmetrically, [...] the latter had fixed its spirit as scholasticsm, which developed out of the adjustment of the same Christianity to something ancient, something superannuated even, which was no longer understood, but still unconditionally revered, i.e. the authority of classical antiquity."

gen. Wenn man die klassische Bildung mit einem Worte schildern will, so war sie vollendete Naturerziehung. Jetzt, da aus den Trümmern jener und einem Chaos verschiedenenartiger Elemente eine neue Welt hervorging, konnte Freiheit mehr das herrschende Prinzip werden, welche denn auch nicht unterließ, die Natur zu unterdrücken, und sich so als Barbarei kundzugeben. Die Natur machte aber ihre Rechte geltend, und dieser Zwist bestimmte den Charakter der modernen Bildung, in welcher die unauflöslichen Widersprüche unseres Daseins, des Endlichen und des Unendlichen in uns, mehr hervortreten, aber wieder verschmolzen werden. (*Romantische Literatur*, 99)[20]

This "quarrel" is of course the mark of modernity; it is what Schlegel calls Romantic. In familiar fashion, the problematic nature of the Romantic is at the same time its glory. "Und dieses finden wir durchaus das Verhältnis der modernen Bildung zur antiken, daß in jener höhere Anforderung liegt, die aber eben deswegen unvollkommner zu Darstellung gebracht ist." (*Romantische Literatur*, 100)[21] Its higher aim and its innate striving productivity make it superior.

The inner dialectic of Romantic modernity makes it more than simply an opposite to antiquity. It is antiquity's progress. Here the historical dialectic of antiquity and modernity links with the internal dialectic of modernity itself. Modernity contains antiquity within it. The modern world is built on the ruins of its ancient predecessor. But modernity cannot, and did not, inherit any of antiquity's distinctive features of original naturalness and simplicity. At the earliest, pre-dialectical, stage of its existence, one of the founding elements, the Germanic, possessed its own version of these qualities. Before the advent of the antithetical force of Christianity, modernity's own "ancient" tribal culture comes across in Schlegel's description as "Naturerziehung", the term with which he de-

---

[20] "A thoroughly spiritual religion made very different values of strict discipline and virtuousness dominant. It became commendable to renounce all sexual inclinations. […] Thus during the chivalric era love endeavoured to incorporate these attitudes. If one wants to sum up classical culture in one word, it was a perfect education under the tutelage of nature. Now that a new world was being born out of a chaos of disparate elements on the rubble of the ancient world, freedom could become the more dominant principle, which did not refrain from suppressing nature, and thus expressed itself as barbarism. But nature demanded its rights, and this division determined the character of modern culture, in which the irreducible contradictions of our existence, of the finite and the infinite within us, become more prominent, but again dissolve into one another."

[21] "And this describes the relationship between modern and ancient culture: the former makes greater demands, which, because of their difficulty, can only be represented less perfectly."

fined ancient culture,[22] but it obviously remained far beneath the cultural level that their natural Greek brothers had achieved. Nevertheless, the ancient Germans had a structurally similar polytheistic mythological religion and little abstract concept of an eternal beyond. Their preoccupation with war, freedom, and individualism lies this side of reality. But they were undistinguished in their "ancient" and "natural" state, *their* time came with the new religion. While the ancient state of humanity was realised in perfection by Greece (and Rome), the Germanic peoples rose to significance when natural humanity clashed with its own spiritual progress, which created modern culture and identity. Schlegel does not expatiate on why the Germanic Europeans made such a fertile match with Christianity. Hegel would turn to that question in the 1820s when working on his *Philosophy of History*. But Schlegel hints that the Germanic essence, which is distinct from the Greek essence, not in its natural form but in content, is the key. It provided the antithetical context, in which productive dialectics could flourish. In Schlegel's view, post-classical, i.e. post-natural religions only flourish in a soil that is profoundly different form the values they propagate. He believes that the "Unwirksamkeit [des Christentums im Orient] scheint eben von der Gleichartigkeit mit dem Boden, welchem es dort eingepflanzt ward, herzurühren." (*Romantische Literatur,* 84)[23] He explains:

> Der Mohamedanismus war insofern gleichartig mit dem Christentum, als beide gegen das Heidentum, d. h. nationale Mythologie und symbolische Naturreligion gerichtet waren. Innerhalb dieser Gleichartigkeit bildeten sie aber wieder den vollkommensten Gegensatz: das Christentum ist der idealistische, der Mohamedanismus der realistische Monotheismus. [...] Aus eben dem Grunde, warum das Christentum nur im Abendlande, war [...] der Mohamedanismus nur im Morgenlande vorzugsweise wirksam: nämlich wegen der ihm innewohnenden Fremdartigkeit. Von jeher war nämlich im Orient der Idealismus, im Okzident der Realismus einheimisch. (*Romantische Literatur,* 84–5)[24]

---

[22] Cf. a repetition of this definition in the Vienna Lectures: "Die Bildung der Griechen war vollendete Naturerziehung." *Dramatische Kunst,* 10. "The mental culture of the Greeks was a finished education in the school of Nature." *Dramatic Art,* 24.

[23] "The ineffectiveness [of Christianity in the Orient] seems to be caused by the sameness of the soil, into which it was planted there."

[24] "Islam is insofar of the same kind as Christianity as both are directed against paganism, i.e. national mythology and symbolic natural religion. But within their sameness they form a perfect opposition: Christianity is idealistic monotheism, while Islam is realistic monotheism. [...] For the same reason that Christianity was only effective in the West,

Schlegel's characterisation of modernity unfolds around a dialectical spiral, a kind of Russian doll of dialectics. It develops out of the historical dialectic between antiquity and modernity. But Romantic modernity is dialectical itself. As such it is not only the antithesis of antiquity, but already contains, in its own productive dialectics, the synthesis of both. Here the difficulty Peter Szondi diagnosed for Schiller's definitions of naive and sentimental returns: not only is the naïve – still and again – already the sentimental, the modern is also the ancient.[25] It is self-evident that Schlegel was defining a generally *European* modernity, rather than just a German one. Already in his introduction he insists that medieval Europe had been "one country", bound together by closely related languages, a universally valid feudalism, a common religion, and the code of chivalry, all of which combined to create a "truly European patriotism" (*Romantische Literatur*, 22). But in the same introduction Schlegel makes clear that some Europeans are more fruitfully modern than others. From his juxtaposition of chivalry and monasticism quoted above, it is already obvious that in Schlegel's view ancient influence, if direct and unmediated, can stifle modernity, in which case a fruitless dialectic results. Schlegel illustrates his view of a fruitless modern dialectic at greater length through another example: what he calls the neo-Latin languages. This takes up Herder's *Sturm-und-Drang* criticism of French classicism, as put forward in his Shakespeare-essay, against the sophisticated background of the Idealist and early Romantic investigations into the development of human consciousness and cognition.

These neo-Latin languages are made up from a mixture of Latin and forms of German and evolved from the early Middle Ages onwards as the Germanic invaders learnt the language of the Romanised peoples they had conquered in what later became France, Spain, Portugal and Italy.[26] Although Schlegel calls them the "beautiful languages", their close dependence on an ancient cultural context impedes their organic growth under modern cultural conditions on two counts: the Latin-trained intelligensia of the late Middle Ages and the early modern period regarded these new mixtures as vulgarised Latin beneath their contempt and ignored them. Conversely, when poetry began to blossom

[...] Islam was preferably effective in the Orient. Because of their respective foreignness. The Orient has always been the home of idealism, while the West has been the home realism."

[25] Cf. "Das Naïve ist das Sentimentalische", 174–206.
[26] Cf. *Romantische Literatur*, 32–3.

in these "Low Latin" languages around the same time, it was proudly
preserved, which only served to fix the new languages at the stage of earliest poetic achievement and cultural development. But worst of all, cut
off from their own original linguistic roots, it was very difficult to create
new words when the need for them arose as culture developed. All these
circumstances are retarding.

> Auf diese Weise wurden alle [neulateinischen Sprachen] frühzeitig fixiert,
> und das immer nicht sehr umfassende Prinzip der Progression gehemmt.
> Denn in der Abteilung neuer Wörter mußten sie ihrer Natur nach sehr be-
> schränkt sein, sie konnten sich fast nur durch die Rückkehr zu ihrer Wurzel,
> dem Lateinischen, bereichern. Man sieht leicht ein, welch ein Nachteil es für
> die freie Sprachbildung ist, nur als eingeimpfer Zweig auf einem großenteils
> abgestorbenen Stamm zu existieren und den fruchtbaren Boden nicht unmit-
> telbar zu berühren, sondern nur durch diesen weiten Umweg Nahrungssäfte
> einsaugen zu können. (*Romantische Literatur*, 33)[27]

Due to this lack of productive creativity Schlegel pronounced them
"partially dead" (*Romantische Literatur*, 34). German, which to Schlegel
includes all non-Romance, Germanic European languages, on the other
hand is a living language, and particularly inventive in the area of word
creation, which puts the German-speaking peoples at a distinct advantage in the present. But Schlegel was careful to present this superiority as
a potential, mindful of the relative lack of German poetic achievement
in post-medieval centuries compared to Italian, Spanish, French and
English poetry. The day of the German language has yet to come, but is
possibly about to dawn. Its genius can, as far as he can see, only come
into its own in a climate of intense intellectual exchanges.[28]

---

[27] "In this way all [neo-Latin languages] became fixed early on, and the often not very
comprehensive principle of progression was impaired. These languages were, due to
their nature, most limited in the development of new words, for they could only extend
their vocabulary by returning to their original root, i.e. Latin. It is easy to see that it is a
great disadvantage for the free development of language to be a graft on a mainly dead
trunk and never to touch directly the fertile ground, but have access to nourishment
only by this long detour."

[28] It is worth pointing out that Schlegel does not (entirely) come across as a bigoted xe-
nophobe; he pours scorn on the linguistic purists who refuse to tolerate any borrowing.
All languages are hybrids to some extent, and this is no bad thing. " ... die so einge-
fleischte Puristen sind, daß sie nicht das geringste fremde Tüttelchen in der Sprache
dulden wollen, und sich darüber mit seltsamen Erfindungen von Wörtern den Kopf
zerbrechen, ohne zu bedenken, daß sie etwas Unmögliches wollen, daß der allgemeine
Völkerverkehr in allen Sprachen einzelne Einmischungen veranlaßt hat. [...] Das Deutsche ist zwar im Verhältnis gegen die gemischten neulateinischen Sprachen und das

Unsere Sprache ist allerdings etwas, worauf wir nicht gerade stolz, aber doch des reichhaltigen Besitzes uns bewußt sein sollen. Dazu kommt eine Eigenschaft [...], die sich erst in einer Periode künstlerischer Ausbildung recht entwickeln konnte. Ich meine die vielfache Biegsamkeit unserer Sprache, wodurch sie geschickt wird, sich den verschiedensten fremden anzuschmiegen, ihren Wendungen zu folgen, ihre Silbenmaße nachzubilden, ihnen beinahe ihre Töne abzustehlen. [...] Was aber die Sprachen des neueren, nach meinem Begriff bestimmten Europas betrifft, so kann das Deutsche aus allen mit Glück übertragen. (*Romantische Literatur*, 34–5)[29]

The priceless advantage of German is its adaptability to all that is excellent in other languages and literatures. German thus acquires the makings of the culminatory medium, becomes the quintessential language of modernity. As such it is the only language that can be on a par with the quintessential language of antiquity, Greek, which is as always the covert point of reference: "Das Deutsche ist seinem ganzen Bau nach weit mehr dem Griechischen verwandt und kann sich absichtlich dieser unübertrefflichen Sprache nähern." (*Romantische Literatur*, 34)[30] Bearing in mind the culminatory nature of modernity in relation to antiquity, German might even aspire to becoming the quintessential language of humanity. These key characteristics of the German language, adaptability and vitality, in contrast particularly to French rigidity, were already put forward by Herder in 1796. But Herder did not place these differences in a dialectical context.[31] In many respects Schlegel's ideas pave the way for Hegel's later assertion that "der germanische Geist ist der Geist der neuen Welt", which is the key idea in the last part of his *Philosophy of History*.

Englische eine reine und ursprüngliche, aber keineswegs so absolut. Die Anzahl der lateinischen Wörter [...] ist [...] weit größer, als man gewöhnlich denkt. Ja es läßt sich nachweisen, daß auch die lateinische Grammatik [...] einen bedeutenden Einfluß auf unsere Wortfügung gehabt hat. Dies ist nun freilich zu einem Ganzen verschmolzen." *Romantische Literatur*, 31–2.

[29] "We should perhaps not be proud of our language, but we should be aware of what a rich possession it is, nevertheless. It has one quality [...], which could only properly develop in a period of artistic development. I refer to the agility of our language, which allows it to closely follow foreign languages, to follow their turns, to recreate their metres, almost steal their sounds. [...] As far as the languages of modern Europe, according to my definition, are concerned, German can translate happily from all of them."

[30] "In its entire formation German is far closer to Greek, and thus can intentionally approach this unsurpassable language."

[31] Cf. Herder, *Humanitätsbriefe. Achte Sammlung, Herders Sämmtliche Werke*, vol. 18, ed. by Bernhard Suphan, Berlin: Weidmannsche Buchhandlung, 1883, p. 114.

Nationalising the Modern
and Internationalising the German:
Fichte's *Reden an die deutsche Nation*

The idea of an unproductive dialectic, which affects the "Neo-Latin" nations of Southern Europe in contrast to the productive dialectic inherent in the purely Germanic Europeans is taken up more aggressively shortly afterwards by Johann Gottlieb Fichte in his *Reden an die deutsche Nation* (1807–8). Written in the desperate aftermath of the crushing Prussian defeats at Jena and Auerstedt, when most of the German territories had come under French occupation and Napoleon had reached the zenith of his power, Fichte's *Reden* outline a programme of national education that would make the Germans recognise their potential, which, in Fichte's view, it was their duty to realise. Fichte argues that the Germans are so special that, if were they to fail to make their contribution to the development of human history, which to Fichte is, in Idealist terms, the realisation of reason in freedom, humanity would not attain its philosophical goal. To define this special nature, Fichte employs the contemporary definition of superior modernity and focuses on the suggestions of a specifically German superiority already intrinsic within it. Only the Germans can bring the modern dialectic to fruition because they possess in their language an entity that partakes of an original (potentially premodern) condition, which is required to overcome the modern problems of division and striving.

Initially Fichte sets up a blueprint for an inclusive modern European identity. But this inclusive Euro-Germanic identity was soon divided into "Romanische Germanen" and "Germanische Germanen",[32] and the German language is the key divider. Again the distinction is one between living and dead. For Fichte, language expresses humanity in its general nature in a way of which the individual speaker may be unaware. "Nicht eigentlich redet der Mensch, sondern in ihm redet die menschliche Natur."[33] National language does the same for the national genius.

---

[32] Fichte uses the term Germanic in the same context as Schlegel used the older inclusive form of *deutsch*. Cf. note 14.

[33] Fichte, *Reden an die deutsche Nation, Fichtes Werke* vol. 7, ed. by Immanuel H. Fichte, Berlin: Veit, 1845–46, repr. Berlin: De Gruyter, 1971, 257–501, 4. Rede, pp. 311–327, 314–15. "It is not really man that speaks, but human nature speaks in him." *Johann Gottlieb Fichte. Addresses to the German Nation*, ed. by George Armstrong Kelly, originally trans.

This is particularly applicable to the representation of concepts (die sinnbildliche Bezeichnung des Übersinnlichen) in language.

> Im allgemeinen erhellet, dass diese sinnbildliche Bezeichnung des Übersinnlichen jedesmal nach der Stufe der Entwicklung des sinnlichen Erkenntnisvermögens unter dem gegebenen Volke sich richten müsse; dass daher der Anfang und Fortgang dieser sinnbildlichen Bezeichnung in verschiedenen Sprachen sehr verschieden ausfallen werde, nach der Verschiedenheit des Verhältnisses, das zwischen der sinnlichen und geistigen Ausbildung des Volkes, das eine Sprache redet, stattgefunden, und fortwährend stattfindet. (4. Rede, 317)[34]

In this respect Fichte's definition of language is not dissimilar to that of Hegel's *Geist*, in its general and national manifestations, which, presented in Hegel's *Phänomenologie*, enters the public arena in the same year.[35] Linguistic development works in tandem with the grasp of the abstract, it faithfully reflects the intellectual development of a human collective. When this is the case, which to Fichte is the original and natural state of affairs, the language in question can be defined as an "Ursprache", which stresses the organic link to the past. Language is interactive, it is shaped by the people as an expression of their culture and equally influences this culture in explaining and maintaining to the individual and the group their identity as reflected in their understanding. But this development is negatively affected if a community takes over the language of another historically distinct community and expresses its conceptual world through a linguistic medium that was not shaped by the same history.

> Wenn ein Volk, mit Aufgebung seiner eigenen Sprache eine fremde, für übersinnliche Bezeichnung schon sehr gebildete annimmt; [...] also dass es seinen eigenen Anschauungskreis der Sprache aufdringe, und diese, von dem Stand-

---

by R. F Jones and G.H. Turnbull, New York: Harper & Row, 1968, p. 48. Forthwith *Addresses*.

[34] "Speaking generally, it is evident that this designation of the supersensuous by means of sensuous images must in every case be conditioned by the stage of development which the power of sensuous perception has reached in the people under consideration. Hence, the origin and progress of this designation by sensuous images will be very different in different languages and will depend on the difference in the relation that existed and continues to exist between the senuous and intellectual development of the people speaking a language." *Addresses*, 50–51.

[35] Fichte's "Weltplan" is defined along the same lines as the purpose of Hegel's *Weltgeist*: "Der göttliche Weltplan bei der Erschaffung des Menschengeschlechts, ... [ist] ja nur da, um von Menschen gedacht, und durch Menschen in die Wirklichkeit eingeführt zu werden." 14. Rede, 498.

puncte aus, wo sie dieselbe fanden, von nun an in diesem Anschauungskreise sich fortbewegen müsse. [...] Diese Veränderung [ist] von den bedeutendsten Folgen in Rücksicht des übersinnlichen Theils der Sprache. (4. Rede, 320)[36]

This incongruity of concept and representation reduces, according to Fichte, the inspiring influence language has on human life, because it reduces the clarity and independence of thought. This may not necessarily occur through subjugation, but voluntarily, as it did when Germanic tribes conquered territories inhabited by Romanised peoples in Western and Southern Europe after the decline of the Roman Empire.

Für die späteren Eroberer derselben aber enthält das Sinnbild [der angenommenen Sprache] eine Vergleichung mit einer sinnlichen Anschauung, die sie entweder schon längst [...] übersprungen haben, oder die sie dermalen noch nicht gehabt haben, auch wohl niemals haben können. Das höchste, was sie hierbei thun können, ist, dass sie das Sinnbild und die geistige Bedeutung desselben sich erklären lassen, wodurch sie die flache und todte Geschichte einer fremden Bildung, keinesweges aber eigene Bildung erhalten, und Bilder bekommen, die für sie weder unmittelbar klar, noch auch lebenanregend sind, sondern völlig also willkürlich erscheinen müssen. [...] So muß er [der Eroberer] sich diese Bedeutung [...] erklären lassen, und kann diese Erklärung eben nur blind glauben, und wird so stillschweigend gewöhnt, etwas für wirklich daseyend und würdig anzuerkennen, das er, sich selbst überlassen, vielleicht niemals des Erwähnens werthgefunden hätte. (4. Rede, 320–22)[37]

---

[36] "When a people gives up its own language and adopts a foreign one which is already highly developed as regards the designation of supersenuous things, [...] when it forces its own circle of observation on the adopted language, which, when it develops from the position in which they found it, must thenceforward proceed in this circle of observation. [...] This change has consequences of the greatest importance in respect of the supersensuous part of the language." *Addresses*, 53–54.

[37] "For those who acquire the language later [i.e. the conquerers of later times], the verbal image contains a comparison with an observation of the senses, which they have either passed over long ago [...], or else have not yet had, and perhaps never can have. The most that they can do in such a case is to let the verbal image and its mental significance explain each other [have the verbal image and its mental significance explained to them!]; in this way they receive the flat and dead history of a foreign culture, but not in any way a culture of their own. They get symbols which for them are neither immediately clear nor able to stimulate life, but which must seem to them entirely as arbitrary as the sensuous part of the language. [...] He [the conquerer] must have this meaning explained to him [...], and he can only accept this explanation blindly. So he becomes tacitly accustomed to acknowledge as really existing and valuable something which he, if left to himself, would perhaps never have found worth mentioning." *Addresses*, 54–55; the brackets contain my versions.

Here the natural and original reciprocity between language and community is disturbed or even cancelled. This condition fosters social division and despotism.

> In einer Nation von der ersten Art [mit Ursprache] ist das grosse Volk bildsam, und die Bildner einer solchen erproben ihre Entdeckungen an dem Volke, und wollen auf dieses einfliessen; dagegen in einer Nation der zweiten Art [ohne Ursprache] die gebildeten Stände vom Volke sich scheiden, und des letztern nicht weiter, denn als eines blinden Werkzeugs ihrer Pläne achten. (4. Rede, 327)[38]

This also makes productive free thought, and hence true philosophy, difficult to achieve, because the speaker's understanding of the "übersinnlich" layer of existence lacks thoroughness and clarity. In the Romance world, philosophical thought, although unfettered and excellent, has in fact remained in the grip of sensual understanding and never reached the level of pure philosophical truth.

> Im Auslande […] erhob das […] freie Denken sich leichter und höher, ohne die Fessel eines Glaubens an Übersinnliches; aber es blieb in der Fessel des Glaubens an den natürlichen, ohne Bildung und Sitte aufgewachsenen Verstand; und weit entfernt, dass es in der Vernunft die Quelle auf sich selbst beruhender Wahrheit entdeckt hätte.[39]

Fichte sees the German ability, stimulated by their original language, to think thoroughly and freely, coupled with an innately German seriousness of mind, as the reasons why the enlightening influence of the Renaissance inspired the Germans to rethink the spiritual ("übersinnlich") basis of their existence and start the Reformation.

> Die neue Klarheit ging aus von den Alten, sie fiel zuerst in den Mittelpunct der neurömischen Bildung, sie wurde daselbst nur zu einer Verstandeseinsicht ausgebildet, ohne das Leben zu ergreifen und anders zu gestalten. Nicht länger aber konnte der bisherige Zustand der Dinge bestehen, sobald dieses Licht

---

[38] "In a nation of the former kind [possessing an original language] the mass of people is capable of education, and the educators of such a nation test their discoveries on the people and wish to influence it; whereas in a nation of the latter kind [without an original language] the educated classes separate themselves from the people and regard it as nothing more than a blind instrument of their plans." *Addresses*, 61.

[39] Fichte, *Reden an die deutsche Nation, Fichtes Werke* vol. 7, 6. Rede, pp. 344–358, 352. "[Outside Germany] this free-thinking […] rose higher and more easily, unfettered by a belief in the supersensuous. It remained fettered, however, by a belief of the senses in the natural understanding that develops without mental or moral training. [It was] Far from discovering in reason the source of truth which rests upon itself." *Addresses*, 85; first brackets contain my version.

in ein in wahrem Ernste und bis auf das Leben herab religiöses Gemüth fiel [Luther], und wenn dieses Gemüth von einem Volke umgeben war, dem es seine ernstere Ansicht der Sache leicht mitteilen konnte. [...] So tief auch das Christentum herabsinken mochte, so bleibt doch immer in ihm ein Grund-bestandtheil, in dem Wahrheit ist, und der ein Leben, das nur wirkliches und selbständiges Leben ist, sicher anregt: die Frage: was sollen wir thun, damit wir selig werden? (6. Rede, 346)[40]

The term *Gemüt* becomes intricately bound up with German self-defini-tion at this time. It is crucial in Fichte's *Reden*. For him, it summarises such qualities as earnestness, honesty, and faithfulness. It goes beyond a notion of intellectual spirit by adding a depth of earnest feeling and con-cern. "Einem Volke der ersten Art [mit Ursprache] ist es mit aller Gei-stesbildung rechter eigentlicher Ernst [...], dagegen eines von der letzten Art diese vielmehr ein genialische Spiel ist [...]. Die letztern haben Geist, die erstern haben zum Geist auch noch Gemüth." (4. Rede, 327)[41] These qualites are part of the Germanic heritage: "Die im Mutterlande zurückgebliebenen Deutschen hatten alle Tugenden, die ehemals auf ihrem Boden zu Hause waren, beibehalten: Treue, Biederkeit, Ehre, Ein-falt." (6. Rede, 355).[42] The originally Germanic seriousness of mind is kept alive by an original language, which encourages and enables the speaker to think things through thoroughly. The German earnestness as a contrast to Southern light-heartedness, not to say frivolity, was not a new idea. Herder had drawn a similar picture in 1796. Comparing Ger-man *Minnesinger* with Provençal troubadours, he summarised the "gut-müthige und biedere Charakter der Nation" as follows:

---

[40] "The new light proceeded from the ancients and, falling first upon the central point of neo-Latin culture, was there developed into nothing more than an intellectual view of things, without taking hold of life and shaping it differently. But it was impossible for the existing state of things to continue once this light had fallen upon a soul whose re-ligion was truly earnest and concerned about life, when this soul was surrounded by a people to whom it could easily impart its more earnest view. [...] However low Chris-tianity may fall, there always remains in it an essential part which contains truth and which is sure to stimulate life, if only it is real and independent life. That part is the question: What shall we do to be saved?" *Addresses*, 79–80.

[41] "A people of the former kind is really and truly in earnest about all mental culture [...], whereas a people of the latter kind [without an original language] looks upon mental culture as an ingenious game. [...] [The latter have *Geist*, the former also have *Gemüth* in addition to *Geist*.] *Addresses*, 61; curiously, perhaps tellingly, the contents of the brackets is missing in the translation.

[42] "The Germans who remained in the motherland had retained all the virtues of which their country had formerly been the home – loyalty, uprightness, honor and simplic-ity." *Addresses*, 88.

Nicht nur von Seiten der Sitte gewinnen die unsern, sondern oft auch in Rücksicht der innigen Empfindung. In Süden, wenn ihr wollt, ist mehr Lustigkeit und Frechheit; hier mehr Liebe und Ehre, Bescheidenheit und Tugend, Verstand und Herz. Rechtliche Ehrlichkeit also, Richtigkeit in Gedanken, Stärke im Willen und Ausdruck, dabei Gutmüthigkeit, Bereitschaft zu helfen und zu dienen, dies ist die Gemüthsart unseres Volkes.[43]

August Wilhelm Schlegel, too, identified "alte[n] Biedersinn, Einfalt der Sitten und kräftigen Freiheitssinn" as ancient German(ic) qualities in his lectures on Romantic Literature (38).[44] Quoting his brother Friedrich, he insists that the "strength of virtue" inspires German art and science. "Rechtlich, treuherzig, gründlich, genau und tiefsinnig ist dieser Charakter, dabei unschuldig und etwas ungeschickt." (*Romantische Literatur*, 39)[45] The same picture emerges in Schiller's (unpublished) "Deutsche Größe": the German is "redlich aus dem tiefsten Herzen"[46], an image that is contrasted with the grasping materialism of the British and the violent military prowess and clever wit of the French.

In every case, these qualities are part of the ancient Germanic heritage that has survived uncontaminated only in the Germans, but in whom it has so far frequently only come across as retarded naivety. Their serious thoroughness is responsible for the tendency to detailed imitation, which has made them look characterless, but which now equips them for the new historic tasks of the Spirit (*Geist*). One such task they have already achieved in the Reformation. That the Reformation was only successful in the Germanic parts of Europe serves Fichte as evidence that the "romanische Germanen" were incapable of it. In more recent times, the (eventual) failure of the Revolution in France, this inspired attempt at a liberation from absolutist shackles, political and spiritual, is another example for Fichte of the incapability of the "Ausland" to achieve true philosophical progress. The French ideas, which Fichte initially fer-

---

[43] Herder, *Humanitätsbriefe. Achte Sammlung, Herders Sämmtliche Werke*, vol. 8, 115–16. "Our ancestors do not only win out in terms of morality, but often also in terms of deep emotion. In the South there is, if you like, more merry-making and cheekiness, up here more love and honour, modesty and virtue, understanding and heart. So, righteous honesty, a rightness in thought, strength of the will and of expression, also good-naturedness, a readiness to help and serve, this is the nature of our people."

[44] "old sense of simple honesty, simplicity of morals and a strong sense of freedom".

[45] "This character is righteous, trusting, thorough, exact and deep, also innocent and a little clumsy."

[46] Schiller, "Deutsche Größe", *Schillers Werke. Nationalausgabe*. Vol. 2.1 (1983) 431–36, 436; "honest from the bottom of their hearts".

vently welcomed, did not fall on the ears, or minds, of a properly educated, thinking population.

> Unter den Augen der Zeitgenossen hat das Ausland eine andere Aufgabe
> der Vernunft und der Philosophie an die neue Welt, die Errichtung des voll-
> kommenen Staates, leicht und mit feuriger Kühnheit ergriffen, und kurz
> darauf also fallen lassen, dass es durch seinen jetzigen Zustand genöthigt ist,
> den blossen Gedanken der Aufgabe als ein Verbrechen zu verdammen. [...]
> Der Grund dieses Erfolges liegt am Tage: der vernunftgemäße Staat lässt
> sich nicht durch künstliche Vorkehrungen aus jedem vorhandenen Stoffe
> aufbauen, sondern die Nation muss zu demselben erst gebildet und herauf-
> erzogen werden. Nur diejenige Nation, welche zuvörderst die Aufgabe der
> Erziehung zum vollkommenen Menschen durch die wirkliche Ausübung
> gelöst haben wird, wird sodann auch jene des vollkommenen Staates lösen.
> (6. Rede, 353–4)[47]

He is clearly in agreement with the points Schiller had put forward on
this topic earlier in his *Ästhetische Erziehung*. The Germans are already
well on the way to achieving this perfect state of culture that precedes
perfect statehood. It is to be a wholly new type of state, based on the
German qualities Fichte exalts in his *Reden*. A new state is now the aim
for Fichte. It was not the main aim for the other thinkers treated here (although Schiller comes close), which shows the change in attitude brought
about by the Napoleonic occupation, by the direct intrusion of political
and military reality into philosophical and cultural thinking.[48] When the

---

[47] "We, their contemporaries, have seen how the inhabitants of a foreign country took up
lightly, and with fervent daring, another problem of reason and philosophy for the
modern world – the establishment of the perfect state. But, shortly afterward, they
abandoned this task so completely that they are compelled by their present condition
to condemn the very thought of the problem as a crime. [...] The reason for this result
is as clear as day; the state in accordance with reason cannot be build up by artificial
measures from whatever material may be at hand; on the contrary, the nation must first
be educated and trained up to it. Only the nation which has first solved in actual practice the problem of educating perfect men will then also solve the problem of the perfect state." *Addresses*, 87.

[48] From 1806, the general low point after the defeats at Jena and Auerstedt and the dissolution of the (albeit in all but name already defunct) Holy Roman Empire, the de-
liberations about the German nation acquire a decidedly political dimension, which
increases again from 1813 onwards, when the end of Napoleon's rule over Europe becomes a viable political and military possibility, a development that may clear the way
for fresh attempts to achieve national self-determination. The wish to create a unified
German state forms the background to increasingly vociferous calls for constitutional
reform, which seemed to find sympathetic ears among the princes, who were in need

French Revolution disappointed his hopes for a new state of reason and freedom, Fichte sought other avenues along which it could be brought about. His growing preoccupation with the course of world-history made him receptive for historically developed definitions of national genius, such as inform the *Reden*. Now only an independent nation could be the home of thinking, independent individuals. It had become difficult to believe that a nation could achieve freedom and independence through its culture alone, the latter must be linked to a real political entity.

> Setze man den Fall, daß unsre Sprache lebendig und eine Schriftstellersprache bleibe, und so ihre Literatur behalte; was kann denn das für eine Literatur sein, die Literatur eines Volkes ohne politische Selbständigkeit? Was will denn der vernünftige Schriftsteller [...]? Nichts anderes, denn eingreifen in das allgemeine und öffentliche Leben. [...] Er will urspünglich und aus der Wurzel des geistigen Lebens heraus denken, für diejenigen, die ebenso ursprünglich wirken, d.i. regieren. Er kann deswegen nur in einer solchen Sprache schrei-

---

of popular support if they entertained any realistic hopes of throwing off French control. In concrete form, such constitutional reforms – often in the shape of *introducing* a constitution into previously absolutist regimes – were initially supposed to be carried out at the level of individual principalities. But the national-political movement soon found itself up against powers it could not vanquish. The inspiration for such political reforms drew on the early (the "bourgeois") stage of the French Revolution. And it was this link between revolutionary democracy and nationalism that made any ideas of the nation state so suspect to the aristocratic elites and prevented any serious form of national and constitutional consolidation after the Congress of Vienna in 1815. An anecdote illustrates this matter poignantly: When during the Congress of Vienna the moderate Prussian reformer Freiherr vom Stein approached Emperor Francis of Austria about an audience, he asked the Emperor: "Would his Majesty not like to take up a place at the head of the German nation?" To which the Francis replied, alarmed and horrified: "Nation – that has a Jacobin ring!" (Quoted by Walter Grab in "Burschenschaften im Kontext national-revolutionärer Emanzipationsbewegungen anderer Länder 1815–1825" in Burghard Dedner, ed., *Das Wartburgfest und die oppositionelle Bewegung in Hessen*, Marburg: Hitzeroth, 1994, pp. 11–29, 11.) The reactionary forces began to work towards re-establishing the status quo ante, i.e. the Ancien Régime. And they used the radical actions of the most left-wing elements in the national-democratic movement, such as the book-burning at the *Wartburgfest* in 1817 and the political assassination of the writer August von Kotzebue in 1819, as justification to clamp down on any reform movement with the draconian *Karlsbader Beschlüsse* in the same year. For a more detailed analysis of radical early 19th-century notions of how to bring about a German constitutional nation state see Maike Oergel, "Revolutionaries, Traditionalists, Terrorists? The *Burschenschaften* and the German Counter-cultural Tradition" in *Counter-Cultures in Germany and Central Europe: From Sturm und Drang to Baader-Meinhof*, ed. by Steve Giles and Maike Oergel, Bern/Berlin: Peter Lang, 2003, pp. 61–86.

ben, in der auch die Regierenden denken, [...] in der eines Volkes, das einen selbständigen Staat ausmacht. (12. Rede, 452–3)[49]

Being the original stock of the moderns, the Germans are in fact the "Urvolk der neuen Welt" (13. Rede, 359)[50], who brought Christianity and the Germanic essence together on the ruins of antiquity. Equipped with an inspiring, democratising and representative language, defined by Fichte as the basis of all spiritual, intellectual and political progress, they are also the hope on which the future of modern humanity rests. They have already accomplished the Reformation. They are predestined to take on the task of first educating themselves further, then the rest of their European brethren and finally to set up the state of reason which will sort out the social and spiritual problems of humanity once and for all. And this is, according to Fichte, their historic task. The final *Rede* is one long impassioned appeal to the thus defined Germans to wake up and work towards the fulfilment of their world-historical task of making the German nation the "Wiedergebährerin und Wiederherstellerin der Welt" (14. Rede, 486).[51] If they will not, nobody else can. "Ist in dem, was in diesen Reden dargelegt worden, Wahrheit, so seid unter allen neuern Völkern ihr es, in denen der Keim der menschlichen Vervollkommnung am entschiedensten liegt [...]. Gehet Ihr in dieser eurer Wesensart zu Grunde, so gehet mit euch zugleich alle Hoffnung des gesamten Menschengeschlechts auf Rettung aus der Tiefe seiner Übel zugrunde." (14. Rede, 499)[52] The choice is theirs.

> Es hängt davon ab, ob ihr das Ende sein wollt, und die letzten eines nicht achtungswürdigen [...] Geschlechtes, bei dessen Geschichte die Nachkommen, falls es nämlich in der Barbarei, die da beginnen wird, zu einer Geschichte kommen kann, sich freuen werden, wenn es mit ihnen zu Ende ist [...]; oder,

---

[49] "But let us suppose that our language remains a living and a literary language and so preserves its literature; what sort of literature can that be, the literature of a people without political independence? What does a sensible writer want [...]? Nothing else but to influence public life and the life of all. [...] He wants to think originally, and from the root of spiritual life for those who act just as originally, i.e. govern. He can, therefore, only write in a language in which the governors think, [...] in the language of a people that forms an independent state." *Addresses*, 183.

[50] "Original people of the modern world". Also "Stammvolk" (6. Rede, 356).

[51] "Through the German nation the world will be *reborn* and *restored*."

[52] "If there is truth in what has been expounded in these addresses, then you are of all modern peoples the one in whom the seed of human perfection most unmistakably lies. [...] If you perish in this your essential nature, then there perishes together with you every hope of the whole human race for salvation from the depths of its miseries." *Addresses*, 228.

ob ihr der Anfang sein wollt und der Entwicklungspunkt, einer neuen, über alle eure Vorstellungen herrlichen Zeit. (14. Rede, 486)[53]

The last quotations from Fichte's *Reden*, as the *Reden* themselves, have since the mid-20th century been taken to represent (and pave the way for) the worst excesses of German hubris: The notion of the German *Übermensch* born in reaction to a feeling of inferiority, lateness and frustration. Fichte himself hints that he knows his words are extreme and over the top. He tries to pre-empt attacks on the nationalist content of his *Addresses*, which in Fichte's political context amounted to left-wing extremism, by suggesting, in his defence, that his extremism is linked to the extremity of the situation: "Wir ringen ums Leben; wollen sie, daß wir unsre Schritte abmessen, damit nicht etwa durch den erregten Staub irgendein Staatskleid bestäubt werde? Wir gehen unter in den Fluten; sollen wir nicht um Hilfe rufen, damit nicht irgendein schwachnerviger Nachbar erschreckt werde?" (12. Rede, 455)[54] Fichte expected attacks from princely rulers and their obedient governments, who would no doubt view his ideas as encouraging Jacobinist sedition against the (international) order of princely rule, for whose supporters nationalism went hand in hand with democracy as a left-wing conspiracy. Fichte seemed to anticipate the reactionary clamp-down of the 1819 Karlbad Decrees and the resulting "Demagogenverfolgungen" initiated by the defenders of the Ancien Régime,[55] who certainly would have targeted him, if he had still been alive.[56]

---

[53] "It depends on you whether you want to be the end, and to be the last of a generation [race] unworthy of respect [...] a generation [race] of whose history (if indeed there can be any history in the barbarism that will then begin) your descendants will read the end with gladness [...]; or whether you want to be the beginning and the point of development for a new age glorious beyond all your coneptions." *Addresses*, 215–16; my suggestion in square brackets.

[54] "We are fighting for life; do they want us to walk delicately, lest some robe of state be covered with the dust we may raise? We are sinking beneath the torrent; are we to refrain from calling for help, lest some weak-nerved neighbor may be alarmed?" *Addresses*, 186.

[55] "Sollte es sich [...] etwa zeigen, daß schon jetzo Diener besonderer Staaten von Angst, Furcht und Schrecken so eingenommen wären, daß sie solchen, eine Nation eben noch als daseiend voraussetzenden, und an dieselbe sich wendenden Stimmen zuerst das Lautwerden, oder durch Verbote die Verbreitung versagten." 12. Rede, 454–55. "If it should [...] be evident that state officials in the separate states were already so obsessed by anxiety, fear, and terror, that they first forbade such voices to make themselves heard or prohibited the spreading of the message, voices which assumed that a nation was still in existence and addressed themselves to it." *Addresses*, 185.

[56] Aged 51, Fichte died unexpectedly of typhus in January 1814.

Fichte clearly felt the weight of history upon him. Having established the likely course of world history in his *Grundzüge*, it seemed to him in 1806 that the "gegenwärtige Zeitalter" of 1803 had come to a close. The *Reden* were inspired by what Fichte perceived as the possible dawn of the fourth age of the *Grundzüge*, the "Zeitalter der anhebenden Vernunft", which promised the chance of setting up a new and better social and political framework. And he felt called upon to point this out.[57] If with hindsight this seems arrogant and myopic in equal measure, it is useful to remember that ever since the (European) world had begun to quake in 1789, the historical and political process seemed to have accelerated far beyond expectations, opening windows of opportunity that suggested the previously impossible might be within reach.

To sum up, the Germans stand in a special relationship to modernity because they represent the productive version of the modern dialectic. Accoring to A.W. Schlegel they have successfully integrated the two key cultural elements of Christianity and the Germanic heritage into a new identity. This identity is predisposed towards striving, which is driven by yearning, the somewhat negative, and torturous, side of modernity, but which equally produces progress, its positive potential. As such the Germans represent modernity. But they also are the lynchpin in the dialectical process of modern identity, because they possess, through their original language, a link with their (lost) original and natural state, which will give them the opportunity to achieve a perfect communal organisation and philosophical understanding. This equals the synthetic solution of the modern dialectic. The German identity holds the key to solving the problems of European modernity. In a sense, the Germans are Europe. Fichte certainly sees them as the gauge of European well-being: "Wie aber Deutschland herabsinkt, sieht man das übrige Europa eben also sinken, in Rücksicht dessen, was das Wesen betrifft, und nicht den blossen äußeren Schein." (6. Rede, 356)[58] The Germans appear *beyond* the national. They are, as Fichte is quick to remind his audience, the *Volk* schlechthin, which is, after all, what *deutsch* means (ibid., 359).

---

[57] Otto W. Johnston traces some direct political involvement on Fichte's part. Cf. O. Johnston, *The Myth of a Nation. Literature and Politics in Prussia under Napoleon*, Columbia NC: Camden House, 1989, pp. 15–28.

[58] "But, as Germany sinks, the rest of Europe is seen to sink with it, if we regard, not the mere external appearance, but the soul." *Addresses*, 90.

Although Fichte's *Reden* voice in an extreme form ideas about the culminatory and consummate nature of the German character, these ideas were never far from the surface of the German *Querelle* and German Idealism. We have see in chapter 1 how suggestions of this nature found expression in Herder's, Schiller's and Friedrich Schlegel's confident predictions about the imminent emergence of German literary and cultural excellence. In the present context the consummate nature of the German character is seen to be expressed in the German trait of universality. August Wilhelm Schlegel asserted:

> Das höhere künstlerische Nachbilden [...] ist auf nichts Geringeres angelegt, als die Vorzüge der verschiedenen Nationalitäten zu vereinigen, sich in alle hineinzudenken und hineinzufühlen, und so einen kosmopolitischen Mittelpunkt für den menschlichen Geist zu stiften. Universalität, Kosmopolitismus ist die wahre deutsche Eigentümlichkeit." (*Romantische Literatur*, 36)[59]

When he spoke of translating as the key activity of the human mind, rather than a loss-making activity that turns an original in a shadow of its former self, he no doubt had this German quality in mind.[60] In the *Studiumaufsatz*, Friedrich Schlegel considered the German tendency towards slavish imitation of other nations (the French), and their resulting lack of character, as the prerequisite and harbinger of the new universality, which was the high aim of his grand project, the new, the consummate poetry.

> Die berüchtigte Deutsche Nachahmungssucht mag hie und da wirklich den Spott verdienen [...]. Im Ganzen aber ist Vielseitigkeit ein echter Fortschritt der ästhetischen Bildung, und ein naher Vorbote der Allgemeingültigkeit. Die sogenannte Charakterlosigkeit der Deutschen ist also dem manirierten Charakter andrer Nationen weit vorzuziehen, und erst, wenn die nationale Einseitigkeit ihrer ästhetischen Bildung mehr verwischt, und berichtigt sein wird, können sie sich zu der höhern Stufe jener Vielseitigkeit erheben. (*Studium*, 259)[61]

---

[59] "The higher artistic imitation [...] aims at nothing less than to unite the advantages of the different nationalities, to empathise with them in thought and feeling, and to create a cosmopolitian centre for the human spirit. Universality and cosmopolitanism are the true German particularity."

[60] "Der menschliche Geist [kann] eigentlich nichts als Übersetzen, alle seine Tätigkeit bestehe darin." *Romantische Literatur*, 35.

[61] "The notorious German obsession to imitate may now and then deserve [to be mocked] [...] On the whole, however, versatility indicates a genuine progression of aesthetic development [Bildung] and is near harbinger of universality. The so-called characterlessness of the Germans is far preferable to the maneristic character of other nations. Only

The idea that the so far lamentable German tendency to imitate rather than to create characteristic originals could be a useful preparation for impending greatness, is also put forward by – and this may come as a surprise – Herder at exactly the same time. In the eighth collection of his *Humanitätsbriefe* (1797) he writes that as long as the imitating is not done blindly and slavishly (which he castigated in his Shakespeare-essay nearly 25 years earlier) it may well lead to the Germans reaching the highest level of culture:

> Wäre also auch Nachahmung der Charakter unsrer Nation, und wir ahmten nur mit Besonnenheit nach: so gereichte dieses Wort uns zur Ehre. Wenn wir von allen Völkern ihr Bestes uns eigen machten: so wären wir unter ihnen das, was der Mensch gegen die Neben- und Mitgeschöpfe ist, von denen er Künste gelernt hat. Er kam zuletzt, sah Jedem seine Art ab, und übertrift und regiert sie alle.[62]

Herder believes that imitation is a general, and necessary, human trait, that it makes an important contribution to historical progress. Each nation builds on the achievements of the preceding ones.[63]

---

when the national bias of their aesthetic development [Bildung] is more attenuated and rectified will they be able to elevate themselves to a higher level of that versatility." *Study of Greek Poetry*, 39. Evidence for the Germans' greater advancement in their aesthetic culture lies, according to Schlegel, in the appearance a new poetic genius in their midst: Goethe, whose work proves that the last great turning-point in artistic and moral history is about to be reached. "Seine Werke sind eine unwiderlegliche Beglaubigung, daß das Objektive möglich, und die Hoffnung des Schönen kein leerer Wahn der Vernunft sei. [...] So wird das Objektive auch bald allgemeiner, es wird öffentlich anerkannt, und durchgängig herrschend werden. Dann hat die ästhetische Bildung den entscheidenden Punkt erreicht, wo sie sich selbst überlassen nicht mehr sinken [...] kann. Ich meine die große, moralische Revolution, durch welche die Freiheit in ihrem Kampfe mit dem Schicksal (in der Bildung) endlich ein entscheidendes Übergewicht über die Natur bekommt." *Studium*, 262. "His works are an irrefutable attestation that the objective is possible and that the hope for the beautiful is not an empty delusion of reason. [...] The objective soon becomes more general; it is publicly acknowledged, and becomes all-prevailing. The aesthetic development [Bildung] has attained the decisive point, where, left to itself, it can never wane. [...] I mean the great moral revolution, by means of which freedom in its struggle with fate (within culture [Bildung]) finally achieves a decisive advantage over nature." *Study of Greek Poetry*, 40–41.

[62] *Humanitätsbriefe, Achte Sammlung, Herders Sämmtliche Werke* vol. 18, 113. "Even if imitation were the character of our nation, if we only imitated with care and thought, this would do us honour. If we made the best of all nations our own, we would be among them what man is within the Creation, from whose creatures he has learnt his skills. He came last, copied everybody and now excels, and rules them all."

[63] Cf. ibid.

While Schiller's *Naive und Sentimentalische Dichtung*, unlike Friedrich Schlegel's essay, does not mention the Germans as such, there is evidence that Schiller shared the view of the culminatory and consummate nature of his nation, which finds expression in their universality. He clearly expressed these ideas, although he never published them, in the fragment now called "Deutsche Größe" (probably 1801)[64], which deserves a closer look to illustrate to what extent Schiller was in tune with the current idea of German national identity. The notion of the culminatory nature of the German identity runs through the entire fragment. The Germans are the "golden fruit"[65] ripening towards its harvest, which is "die Aernte der ganzen Zeit" (433).[66] The task of the Gemans, who are the "core of humanity", is to play a pivotal role in bringing about true humanity: "Er ist erwählt von dem Weltgeist, während des Zeitkampfs / an dem ewgen Bau der Menschenbildung zu arbeiten." (433)[67] Again, their ability to assimilate guarantees their universality: "Alles was schätzbares bei andern Zeiten u: Völkern aufkam, mit der Zeit / entstand und schwand, hat er aufbewahrt / es ist ihm unverloren" (433).[68] They have even assimilated the ancient genius: "Wir kennen [sic] das jugendlich / griechische und das modern ideelle ausdrücken." (432)[69] This universal, potentially consummate nature is capable of achieving an all-inclusive level, "Nach dem höchsten soll er streben, / Die Natur und das Ideal" (433),[70] which takes up the concerns, and the antimomies of Schiller's *Naive und Sentimentalische Dichtung*-essay. Again, the German language, "which expresses everything" (432) is singled out for special praise. It will, due to its superior qualities, which are not elaborated further than that they give a faithful image of the Germans, "rule the world" (432). And they have already provided evidence of their special spiritual nature: they decisively contributed to the progress of world history when they initiated the Reformation, which is characterised as follows:

---

[64] This name, now commonly accepted, was given to the fragment by Bernhard Suphan when he edited and published it in 1902. The dating of the fragment is still not conclusively settled. Cf. *Schillers Werke. Nationalausgabe*, Bd. 2 II B, pp. 257–8.

[65] Schiller, "Deutsche Größe", *Schillers Werke. Nationalausgabe*, vol. 2 I, pp. 431–36, 432.

[66] "time's harvest".

[67] "He has been chosen by the world spirit to work on the eternal construction of forming and educating humanity while history's struggles take place."

[68] "Everything valuable from other peoples and other times, which was created and has disappeared, he has preserved, he cannot lose it."

[69] "We can express that which is youthfully Greek as well as that which is ideal and modern."

[70] "He is to strive for the highest, towards nature and towards the ideal."

Der der Wahrheit Blitz geschwungen,
Der die Geister selbst befreit,
Freiheit der Vernunft erfechten,
Heißt für alle Völker rechten,
Gilt für alle Ewigkeit. (435)[71]

In spirit and intensity this comes close to Fichte's *Reden*, and makes equally disturbing reading for any post-1945 reader. But when phrased differently Schiller might come across as a "guter Weltbürger", who famously wrote together with Goethe in the *Xenien*: "Zur Nation euch zu bilden, ihr hofft es, Deutsche, vergebens; / Bildet euch, ihr könnt es, dafür freyer zu Menschen euch aus."(Xenion 96)[72] The culminatory identity is beyond the (nationally) particular.[73]

What is striking in all passages dealing with the culminatory nature of the German character is the belief in the impending reality of a decisive turning-point. The (spiritual) revolution is quite possibly about to happen. In the wake of the Revolution in France, it seems the climate had remained fluid enough to entertain the hope that sudden great changes may be brought about, by the Germans. The German particularity is universality, which is a dialectical synthesis in itself and puts them in a position to survey the other nations' contributions and go beyond them (but ultimately with them) into a universal future of humanity. This is their historical advantage which combines well with their inherited nature: the thoroughness of thought, the depth of *Gemüt*, the seriousness of mind, all of which are facilitated by their singular language. Their dialectically synthetic nature is also evident in their historical existence in time. They are not only the guarantors of the future, and characterised as youthful in the sense that their day has not yet fully dawned,[74] they are also the original people of the European nations,

---

[71] "He who has wielded the lightning [sword] of truth, Who has liberated the spirit itself, To win victory for the freedom of reason means to fight for the rights of all nations, and this victory has validity forever."

[72] "You Germans hope in vain to form a nation, rather you should, because you can, become free human beings."

[73] For a detailed analysis of "Deutsche Größe" including its relation to the Schiller's published (theoretical) works and its parallels to Fichte's *Reden* cf. Maike Oergel, "The German Identity, the German *Querelle*, and the Ideal State. A Fresh Look at Schiller's "Deutsche Größe" in *Schiller. National Poet – Poet of Nations*, ed. by Nicholas Martin, Amsterdam: Rodopi, forthcoming.

[74] When Fichte draws a parallel between the Germanic tribes, who appeared on the horizon of the declining ancient world and were recognised as young, fresh and powerful

who have preserved the original characteristics of European modernity, which allow the historical dialectic to progress along its most productive course. They are the alpha and the omega of Europe, its *Stammvolk* as well as its most forward-looking *Kulturnation*. The increasing awareness of historicity, and the dialectic dynamic developed to deal with the problems of its implied relativism, is directly related to the notion of the culminatory identity. It is the outcome of striving towards completeness through the assimilation of difference.[75]

In these discussions around 1800, the relation between the cultural and the political remained unclear and shifting. It is clear, and well recognised, that the first decade of the 19th century marks a change in favour of more political conceptions, which could, however, not assert themselves for over sixty years, by which time they had fundamentally changed in nature. Before 1800 the cultural dimension dominated: in Herder, Friedrich Schlegel, and Schiller there is little or no mention of *exclusively political* unity. Goethe famously rejected the idea in his thoughts on what he called *Literarischer Sansculottismus* in 1795. This changed with the advent of Napoleon and his successful expanisonist campaigns and policies in Europe. Fichte began to speak of the need for a unified state in a direct reaction to Napoleonic occupation. It is equally clear that the German "particular universality" is essentially cultural. But alongside the widely professed conviction that German *cultural* identity can facilitate the beneficial progress of human history, there always remained doubt over whether this potentially universal identity can actually be effective without going through a national stage. Hence there were continuous, sometimes covert efforts to argue for a national solution, to catch up with the national stage that all other European nations that interested the German thinkers had gone through. But crucially, the over-riding concern remained that any political and national identity needed to be preceded by a cultural and spiritual identity, if the political identity was to be fair and successful. In other words, there can be no successful revolution without Reformation. Schiller believed that the cultural sphere dominated the political to such an extent that cultural domination would inevitably lead to-

---

(cf. 14. Rede), and his German contemporaries in relation to the rest of the European nations, he echoes Herder's charactisation of the Germans as "very young". Cf. *Humanitätsbriefe, Achte Sammlung, Sämmtliche Werke* vol. 18, p. 111).

[75] But it can be argued that the culminatory identity is as parasitic as it is redemptive, as hubris-ridden as it is well-intentioned.

wards political rule.[76] In the present case an intellectually and spiritually mature cultural identity was to be the content of the new political organisation.

In the light of the material presented here, the question arises whether the German identity constructed around 1800 is not so much a *pre-political* or *non-political* expression of nationalism (and hence either retarded or deviant), but an identity that deliberately seeks to be post-national in its political aspirations, because it considers the national as a (soon to be superseded) stage on the road of human development. From the cosmopolitan notion of the Enlightenment that the national is merely window-dressing by an eternally constant human nature, and human reason, it moves through an appreciation of all nations being equal parts of humanity to the notion that assigns each nation a specific role in the process of humanity, which creates the possibility of a culminatory human identity.

---

[76] "Dem, der den Geist bildet, beherrscht, / muß zulezt die Herrschaft werden, denn / endlich an dem Ziel der Zeit, wenn anders die / Welt einen Plan, wenn des Menschen / Leben irgend nur Bedeutung hat, endlich / muß die Sitte und die Vernunft siegen." "Deutsche Größe", 432. "He who forms, and rules, the spirit, will rule everything in the end, for, at the end of time, morals and reason must eventually prevail, if there is a world plan, if human life has a point at all."

Chapter 4

Grasping the Historical Dialectic of the Modern German Existence: Goethe's *Wilhelm Meisters Lehrjahre*

It is clear from the preceding chapters how profoundly the shifting terms of debate on the notions of ancient and modern underpinned and indeed defined late 18th-century thinking about historicity, identity and the purpose of culture in Germany. The concepts of ancient and modern formed the background to the endeavour to integrate history with theory, which aimed at making productive the problematic relationship between conceptual thought, which tends towards universals, and the newly perceived temporal impermanence of such universals. Dialectical processes came to be seen as the way to achieve such integration, to relate conceptual opposites to each other and, more importantly, to the condition of temporal motion. Goethe's work has always been regarded as representative of the period, which is the *Goethezeit* after all. But the following two chapters will show just how thoroughly he engaged with the complex intellectual and artistic challenges of his time: how he investigated the relationship between Enlightenment ideas and their critical assessment in post-Enlightenment thinking from *Sturm und Drang* to (German) Romanticism and presented these relationships by employing intellectual and artistic techniques that served as models for the new literary concepts premised on the historicity of culture.

I approach the novel as presenting a dialectical dynamic rather than a solid programme or the failure of such a programme. Over the last 50 years criticism of *Wilhelm Meister* has hotly debated whether the view that the novel presents educational progress on Wilhelm's part can, should or must be upheld.[1] The starting point for this discussion was

---

[1] In the last decade the view of a synthesising openness of the work has dominated. Gerhart Mayer claimed: "Die Forschung hat im allgemeinen die Ansicht vertreten, Wil-

Karl Schlechta's assertion in 1953 that the *Lehrjahre* is not a successful
"Bildungsroman" at all because Wilhelm's development, far from being
a process of maturing, is actually a decline (Abstieg).[2] As a consequence
of such critical wrangling over the nature and value of its most famous
model, the concept of the *Bildungsroman* has suffered a fate similar to
that of German *Klassik*. Both critical deconstructions occur in the context of the inquest into the historical conditions of the German character in the wake of the Nazi-period. But in this context it is useful to
remember that discrepancies regarding what is being achieved educationally in Goethe's novel go right back to the earliest interpretations.
While both Schiller and Schlegel clearly took the novel to be the tale
of individual learning and development,[3] of an individual arranging
himself with the world, they very much disagreed regarding the content
and the point of this education. Schlegel's conclusion that not much
has been learnt seems to stand halfway between Schlechta's claim of failure, Wilhelm's famous "Abstieg", and Schiller's confident assertion of
achievement, with which Hegel later concurred. But Schlegel nevertheless interpreted the conclusion as a positive achievement: Goethe, rather
than Wilhelm, has grasped, and masterfully depicted, a true poetic and
intellectual reality. Understanding this reality is for Schlegel the only
path towards a better humanity, i.e. it clearly represents an "Aufstieg".

---

helms Bildungsgang stelle das Thema des Romans dar [...]. Andererseits hat man be-
hauptet, dieser Roman kenne keinen eigentlichen Helden, [...] das Werk solle daher
weniger als Figuren- denn als Raumroman begriffen werden, [...]. Dieser Widerspruch
dürfte durch die im folgenden anzuwendende Betrachtungsweise insofern relativiert
werden, als die Prinzipien des Bildungsprozesses in den *Lehrjahren* ja nur mittels des
Vergleichs einer Reihe von Lebensläufen erschlossen werden können." *Der deutsche Bildungsroman. Von der Aufklärung bis zur Gegenwart*, 2nd edn, Stuttgart: Metzler, 1992, p. 43.
Rolf Selbmann argued that the novel depicts an open and changeable plurality of approaches to *Bildung*. Cf. *Der deutsche Bildungsroman*, 2nd edn, Stuttgart: Metzler, 1994,
p. 74. And in 1997 M. Minden concluded: "Despite the *Lehrjahre*'s evident anthropo-
centric optimism, a trend of interpretation has [...] persisted which either rejects that
optimism as unpoetic, facile or reactionary (Novalis, Schmidt, Baioni), or else reads the
text with a kind of reverent perversity against itself (Schlechta, the Schlaffers, Hörisch).
These divergent lines of interpretation correspond to the energies held in synthesis
within the novel." *The German Bildungsroman. Incest and Inheritance*, Cambridge: Cambridge University Press, 1997, p. 54.

[2]   Karl Schlechta, *Goethes "Wilhelm Meister"*, Frankfurt: V. Klostermann, 1953.

[3]   As did Karl Morgenstern, the academic credited with the invention of the technical term
     Bildungsroman in 1803. Cf. Jürgen Jacobs, *Wilhelm Meister und seine Brüder. Untersu-
     chungen zum deutschen Bildungsroman*, Munich: Fink, 1972, p. 10 and Selbmann, 9.

The above approach of taking the novel as representing a dialectical dynamic reveals the *Lehrjahre* not as evincing social and political conservatism (or downright avoidance of the political),[4] but as exploring wide-ranging intellectual, social and political developments, German as well as generally European. While in the short term German thought on the improvement of the human lot in the two decades following the French Revolution certainly prioritised the cultural approach, it would be short-sighted to interpret this as un-political in its general intentions. Rather than simply challenging the (already much challenged) traditional notions of the *Bildungsroman* and ideals of *Klassik*, my reading proposes to take a step beyond the frequently partisan debates about the merits and evils of these two concepts and integrate the novel first and foremost into its contemporary framework rather than into the history that followed. This approach is not to deny that the novel contains crucial pointers to national preoccupations. On the contrary, it will highlight these, and in so doing seek to challenge both the tacit avoidance of national issues in dealing with Goethe and the obsessive desire to make the 20th-century "German catastrophe" the only reference point for approaches to a modern German identity. And in this interpretation, too, Goethe's text will emerge as an intricate presentation, and analysis, of the German intellectual, cultural and political situation that makes visible a cultural tradition and projects a cultural and political future. The historical dimension within which Goethe conceives this development is that of modernity. And its approach to it is decidedly German.

The publication of *Wilhelm Meisters Lehrjahre* in 1795–6 occurred at exactly the same time as Schiller and Schlegel were reflecting on the problem of modernity. The novel crucially influenced Schlegel's ideas on modern poetics expressed in the *Athenäum*. And indeed in Goethe's novel one finds the German subject existing in the conditions of modernity (Wilhelm) and the German subject self-consciously writing in and about them (Goethe).

Through its characters the novel alludes to the different stages of the development of modernity from its emergence out of historical un-self-consciousness, which Goethe suggests occurred around the end of the

---

4   As T.J. Reed argued in "Revolution und Rücknahme: *Wilhelm Meisters Lehrjahre* im Kontext der Französischen Revolution" *GJB* 107 (1990) 27–43. Also H. Pyritz, *Goethe-Studien*, ed. by I. Pyritz, Cologne: Böhlau, 1962, 125ff and G. Baioni, *"Märchen – Wilhelm Meisters Lehrjahre – Hermann und Dorothea*. Zur Gesellschaftsidee der deutschen Klassik" *GJB* 92 (1975) 73–127, 80.

medieval period,[5] to the contemporary crisis of reason and rationality. Through its structural integration of the characters into oppositional yet mirroring relations within the plot the novel prepares a dialectical dynamic. Through similarities and congruences between opposites the structure transcends dichotomous constellations and becomes dialectically self-reflexive. The inner dynamic of modernity is shown to hinge on the secularisation, or rationalisation, of an originally religious-mythic consciousness into a rational one. Such secularised rational consciousness in turn faces a rational, and destructive, enquiry into its legitimising foundations, which allows its original natural dimension to re-emerge, albeit problematically. This crisis of rationality is the philosophical pivot of the novel. It results, on the surface, from the inner dialectic of the Enlightenment, which becomes visible in the *Sturm-und-Drang* rebellion. In this respect, the novel provides a differentiated investigation into the complex relationship between *Sturm und Drang* and Enlightenment ideas. But, set against the background of the intellectual and aesthetic history of modernity, the differences between *Sturm und Drang* and Enlightenment are presented to appear as the constitutive dialectic of modernity, where an insuppressable memory of original unconscious oneness spurs an ever increasingly self-conscious striving towards regaining this harmonious oneness on a self-conscious level. Beyond the historical confines of modernity this dialectic then appears as the universal dialectic of humanity, in which nature and consciousness, the senses and reason, form the antithetical pairs. The blending of these interlocking dialectical constellations produces a widening scope of reference and suggests universality, without detaching the issue from its concrete historical position in contemporary intellectual and aesthetic debates.

The formal and intellectual techniques Goethe employs to tackle the conceptualisation and presentation of such complex issues and relations are thoroughly post-Enlightened, are, for want of a better term, Romantic. They partake of the intellectual context, in which Schiller reflects on the purpose and nature of art and in which Friedrich Schlegel defines the need for the self-reflexivity of poetry and in which contemporary philosophy explores the activities of the self-conscious mind.

Against the background of the development of modernity, the novel treats three distinct, but related dialectics. The first is the philosophical

---

[5] Previously modernity existed, of course, in its original un-self-conscious form.

dialectic concerned with the nature of (modern) humanity and the aim of human (intellectual) development, which finds expression in the interaction between the mythic mindset of the Harper and Mignon on the one hand, and the rational world-picture of the Tower Society on the other.[6] This is the contrast between art and science, the difference between synthesis and analysis, between forms of the natural-original and the rational-conceptual. The second is the dialectic of education concerned with the way in which human development should be influenced, which is expressed in the opposition between Wilhelm's views on unsystematic learning through experience and the Tower Society's systematic and premeditated approach to learning through being taught. This opposition unfolds around the definition of the theatre as a valuable instrument of learning, which is approached dialectically. And finally there is the social dialectic concerned with the concrete conditions under which modern human development takes place. It is expressed in the opposition between aristocracy and bourgeoisie. The bourgeoisie is presented as questioning its confined and limiting social position and seeking an extension of aristocratic privileges to members of its own class, a demand that is welcomed by the forward-looking parts of the aristocracy. All three dialectics have a historical as well as an individual dimension: the historical dimension relates to the philosophical and social history of modernity, the individual dimension to Wilhelm's psychological and social development as a modern individual.

All three oppositions are presented as dialectically dynamic, i.e. as historical constellations in the process of changing. In this the novel reflects contemporary intellectual concerns and contemporary social conditions. The social dialectic refers to a pre-Revolution situation of bourgeois dissatisfaction and an aristocratic division between intransigence and the acquiescence to reform. The educational dialectic refers to the contemporary challenge to those concepts of education focused on uniform teaching by new ideas that focus on learning tailored to individual needs. And the philosophical dialectic refers to the increasingly unsustainable Enlightenment belief in the knowable rationality of world and mind, which was being questioned on two fronts. On the one hand,

---

[6] Already Friedrich Schlegel suggested that there is an intrinsic equality between these two spheres when in his famous review of the novel he referred to Mignon and the Harper as the "heilige Familie der Naturpoesie" and "klagende Gottheit" vis à vis the Abbé who hovers over the whole novel like the "Geist Gottes". "Über Goethes Meister", *Kritische Friedrich-Schlegel-Ausgabe* vol. 2, 146.

there were the doubts about whether reason could be metaphysically grounded, which culminated in Kant's *Critiques*. On the other hand, from *Sturm und Drang* on new aesthetic theory suggested that pure rationality unmediated by a concrete experience is incomplete, hence unreliable and worthless.

Mignon and the Harper: The Function of the Ancient Form in the History of Modernity

Mignon and the Harper are generally described as the irrational element, lyrical in expression, enigmatic in nature, awesome in their unreflected suffering. Reminiscent of the Ossianic figures in *Werther*, they are essentially mythic: they are alien and fantastic strangers in the world of the civilised and enlightened 18th century, because they belong to a symbolic sphere beyond the social, the rational, or the decorous. They are mythic constructs that represent the violent and the naked, a still untamed and unsocialised humanity, helplessly and uncomprehendingly at the mercy of its demonic desires and fears, but well able to express their emotions and experiences metaphorically. These mythic qualities make them, historically speaking, *pre*-rational rather than *ir*rational.

Philosophically Mignon represents the human intellect in its passive state, immediately after its emergence from unconsciousness – after the expulsion from the Garden of Eden, so to speak – bereft of unconscious happiness, but yet unable to reflect on its situation and profit from consciousness. Individually she is overwhelmed by the world around her, of which she has no rational understanding, because it stands in no constructive relation to her. She represents the Fichtean ego before it starts positing anything. She is the radically subjective that knows no objective order, and hence has no freedom. So she is inescapably and irredeemably subject to forces beyond her control, to her fate, which she equally fears and accepts. "Ich möchte dir mein ganzes Innre zeigen, / Allein das Schicksal will es nicht."[7] The Harper represents the same intellectual

---

[7] Johann Wolfgang Goethe, *Sämtliche Werke in 18 Bänden*, Zürich: Artemis Verlag, 1977, (unveränderter Nachdruck der Artemis-Ausgabe, ed. by Ernst Beutler et al., Munich: dtv, 1949) vol. 7 *Wilhelm Meisters Lehrjahre*, p. 383. This edition is used throughout the chapter. To facilitate cross referencing to other editions, references will forthwith be given in the following manner: first the number of the book, then the chapter number, and lastly the page number, e.g. in this case (5, 16; 383). "How gladly would my tongue obey thee / Did not the voice of Fate forbid." *Wilhelm Meister. Apprenticeship and Travels.*

state, but he has been reduced to this after he has run the entire gauntlet of the philosophical options of modernity from religious mysticism to an existentialist despair occasioned by the loss of all metaphysical parameters.

> Ich habe gelitten wie keiner, von der höchsten süßesten Fülle der Schwärmerei bis zu den fürchterlichen Wüsten der Ohnmacht, der Leerheit, der Vernichtung und Verzweiflung, von den höchsten Ahnungen überirdischer Wesen bis zu dem völligsten Unglauben, dem Unglauben an mir selbst. (8, 9; 624)[8]

When he discovers a way out of his unhappy loneliness through the love of a young woman only to find this escape barred by both religious and secular law, because the woman turns out to be his half-sister, he rebels against the constrictions of religion and society. He rebels in the name of nature, with which he identifies love and the heart.

> Fragt nicht den Widerhall eurer Kreuzgänge, nicht euer vermodertes Pergament, nicht eure verschränkten Grillen und Verordnungen, fragt die Natur und euer Herz, sie wird euch lehren, vor was ihr zu schaudern habt, sie wird euch mit dem strengsten Finger zeigen, worüber sie ewig und unwiderruflich ihren Fluch ausspricht. Seht die Lilien an: entspringt nicht Gatte und Gattin auf einem Stengel? [...] In der Stille des Klosters und im Geräusche der Welt sind tausend Handlungen geheiligt und geehrt, auf denen ihr Fluch ruht. Auf bequemen Müßiggang so gut als überstrengte Arbeit, auf Willkür und Überfluß, wie auf Not und Mangel sieht sie mit traurigen Augen nieder, zur Mäßigkeit ruft sie, wahr sind alle ihre Verhältnisse, und ruhig alle ihre Wirkungen. (8, 9; 625–6)[9]

Translated from the German by R.O. Moon, 2 vols, London: Foulis & Co., 1947, I, p. 307. Forthwith Moon. Only volume 1 will be referred to. Moon here quotes Thomas Carlyle's translation.

[8] "I have suffered like no one from the loftiest, sweetest fullness of enthusiasm to the most perfect wastes of weakness, emptiness, destruction and despair; from the loftiest premonitions of life beyond this earth to the most complete disbelief – disbelief in myself." Moon, 499.

[9] "Do not enquire about the echoes of your cloisters, nor your moth-eaten parchment, nor your limited fancies and regulations! Enquire of Nature and your own heart! They will teach you what you have to fear; they will point to you with strictest finger about what they pronounce eternally and irrevocably their curse. Behold the lilies! Do not husband and wife arise from the same stem? [...] In the tranquillity of the monastery and in the turmoil of the world, a thousand transactions are hallowed and honoured, on which her curse rests. She looks down with sorrowful eyes on comfortable leisure as well as on overstrained work, on what is arbitrary and superfluous as well as on need and want; she calls to moderation; all her relations are true, and all her actions peaceful." Moon, 500.

This "nature" stands for his intense individual desires. He claims the priority of the "freie Welt seiner Gedanken und Vorstellungen" (8, 9; 626).[10] This is the rebellious subjective individualism of *Sturm und Drang*. Augustin passionately attacks social and religious constraints as unnatural in much the same way in which Herder set civilisation against nature when he assessed the ills of contemporary literature in his *Briefwechsel über Ossian* in 1773.

> In der alten Zeit aber waren es Dichter, Skalden, Gelehrte, die eben diese Sicherheit und Vestigkeit des Ausdrucks am meisten mit Würde, mit Wohlklang, mit Schönheit zu paaren wußten; [...] so entstanden daher für uns halbe Wunderwerke von Sängern, Barden, Minstrels, wie die größten Dichter der ältesten Zeiten waren. [...] Bis endlich die Kunst kam und die Natur auslöschte. [...] man quälte sich von Jugend auf, [...] nach Regeln zu arbeiten, deren wenigste ein Genie als Naturregeln anerkennet; [...] Leidenschaften zu erkünsteln, die wir nicht haben. [...] Wenn das der Begriff unsrer Zeit ist, so wollen wir auch in den alten Stücken [...] selten [finden], was in ihnen singt, den Geist der Natur.[11]

Augustin claims that his love is subject to the same disfiguring conditions which the young Herder identified as plaguing literature. To escape these constraints, he chooses to make a complete break from society and becomes a wandering minstrel, the "Harper", a choice that links in with Herder's admiration for the "poets of the long gone past". The Harper is a version of the bard-figure, which came to the fore as the original ideal of the poet from the mid-18th century onwards and is closely associated with *Sturm-und-Drang* notions of natural poetry, as the quotation from Herder makes plain. As Harper, Augustin becomes a force of nature like the bard of his own song, "Ich singe, wie der Vogel singt, / Der in den Zweigen wohnet." (2, 11; 139)[12] In keeping with the high value that *Sturm-und-Drang* thinkers placed on such naturalness, he is the anony-

---

[10] "the free world of his thoughts and ideas", ibid.

[11] *Herders Sämmtliche Werke* vol. 5, 182–83. "In ancient times it was poets, scalds, wise men who knew how to best unite this certainty and firmness of expression with dignity, with beauty and with sweet sounds. [...] It was thus that what to us appears almost as miraculous works were created by singers, bards, minstrels, who were the greatest poets in ancient times. [...] Until in the end, art came along and extinguished nature. [...] From a young age writers struggled painfully to work according to rules, the fewest of which a genius would recognise as natural rules, to manufacture passions, which we do not possess. [...] If this is the concept [of art] of our time, we will rarely discover in those old texts their true voice, which is the spirit of nature."

[12] "I sing but as the linnet sings, / That on the green bough dwelleth." Moon, 112, quoting Thomas Carlyle's translation.

mous seer who is in touch with a healing wholeness that resurrects the emotional and imaginative capacities which have been obscured by the dominance of the rational. Wilhelm experiences the old man's words and songs as edifying, and reviving.

> Auf alles, was der Jüngling zu ihm sagte, antwortete der Alte mit der reinsten Übereinstimmung durch Anklänge, die alle verwandten Empfindungen rege machten und der Einbildungskraft ein weites Feld eröffneten. […] So erbaute der Alte seinen Gast, indem er, durch bekannte und unbekannte Lieder und Stellen, nahe und ferne Gefühle, wachende und schlummernde, angenehme und schmerzliche Empfindungen in eine Zirkulation brachte, von der in dem gegenwärtigen Zustande unders Freundes das Beste zu hoffen war. (2, 13; 147–8)[13]

After his decision to break the stranglehold of society, Augustin re-assumes an original natural state of consciousness and existence. But his sanctification as a resurrected bard is ambiguous, it is only achieved through regression, which finds expression in his handling of language. As Harper Augustin develops a difficulty in expressing himself verbally, through rational discourse (which he clearly did not have before). Wilhelm notices that "der Mann ungern sprach." (2, 13; 146)[14] On the other hand, he expresses himself harmoniously, if cryptically, in song. It is exactly that kind of song that since the mid-18th century was considered "Naturpoesie" and that Herder celebrated as "halbe Wunderwerke". The Harper communicates through what since Johann Georg Hamann, the mentor of the *Sturm und Drang* who insisted on the value of the other side of rationality, had been known as the "Muttersprache der Menschheit", the original and imaginative language of humanity. Goethe deliberately muddied the waters as to how the authorship of the Harper's songs is to be understood. While Herder, at least in the passage quoted above, suggests that the ancient bards created their material – although authorship clearly is not important, only the product counts – Goethe implies that the Harper uses "traditional" materials, he plays "well-known and unknown" songs, which in the ballad-mania of the second

---

[13] "To everything which the young man said to him the old man answered with the clearest agreement by means of concord which stirred all kindred feelings and opened a wide field for the imagination. […] Thus did the old man edify his guest, while from songs and passages known and unknown he brought into circulation feelings near and distant, awake and slumbering, pleasant and painful emotions from which in the present condition of our friend the best was to be hoped." Moon, 118–119.

[14] "The old man spoke unwillingly." Moon, 118.

half of the 18th century would have been considered the common property of humanity. This feature, anonymous and diachronically communal authorship, became a commonplace in the definition of original
natural poetry from Herder to Uhland. But it was, nevertheless, identified as an archaic method that could – however sadly – no longer be
practised by contemporary artists (although much could be learnt from
studying such poetry). The Harper, however, comes across as actually
being *like* those ancient rhapsodists or medieval minstrels, who may not
have written their own songs, but present them with such conviction
that their activities go beyond mere copying and suggest a form of
ownership. "Er trug das Lied mit so viel Leben und Wahrheit vor, daß es
schien, als hätte er es in diesem Augenblicke und bei diesem Anlasse ge-
dichtet." (2, 11, 137)[15] This makes him an anachronistically archaic figure
in the 18th century: the Harper is the contemporary fantasy of a natural
poet-singer. That, despite his historical displacement, he has such a
strong and beneficial effect on Wilhelm illustrates that Goethe continued to attach some credence to the *Sturm-und-Drang* notion that the
natural and pre-critical were still valuable forms of expression and
understanding.

The post-*Sturm-und-Drang* Goethe, however, is aware of the perils of
Augustin's social self-exclusion and intellectual regression. Augustin remains unable to reconcile his new-found anarchic conviction of the
priority of "natural" desire over law with the moral side of his former
self. "Der ungebundene freie Verstand sprach ihn los; sein Gefühl, seine
Religion, alle gewohnten Begriffe erklärten ihn für einen Verbrecher."
(8, 9; 626)[16] Augustin makes no further attempt to solve his existential
problems intellectually. Instead he spends his life on the run from the
shadow of inescapable doom, which he fears and accepts. "Die Rache,
die mich verfolgt, ist nicht des irdischen Richters; ich gehöre einem un-
erbittlichen Schicksale." (4, 1; 223)[17] He has no hope of redemption.

Mignon has the same difficulty in expressing herself through rational
discourse. "Nur mit Worten konnte es [das Kind Mignon] sich nicht

---

[15] "He delivered the song with so much life and truth that it seemed as though he had
composed it at this moment and on this occasion." Moon, 110–111.

[16] "His free, unbridled reason released him, his religion, all his accustomed conceptions
proclaimed his as a criminal." Moon, 500–501.

[17] "The vengeance which pursues me is not of the early judge; I belong to an inexorable
destiny." Moon, 178–179. Cf. also the Harper's song: "Denn alle Schuld rächt sich auf
Erden." (2, 13; 146) "On earth all guilt will be avenged."

ausdrücken, und es schien das Hindernis mehr in seiner Denkungsart als in den Sprachwerkzeugen zu liegen." (8, 9; 628)[18] And she shows the same talent at expressing herself in the same kind of song. Mignon learnt to sing and play the sitar without being taught (ibid.), i.e. naturally, following her instincts and inclinations. The Harper and Mignon are capable of rendering their natural songs so authentically because their individual intellectual circumstances are congruent with a particular phase in human development, which it was thought civilisation had long superseded. Mignon never progresses beyond a prerational state, while the Harper regresses into it. She exists on the level of natural or original aesthetic ambitions, the Harper successfully re-attains them.

But for all their exalting qualities, mythic, oracular, tragic, which connect them to the earliest stages of human intellectual and artistic development and make them awe-inspiring figures of tragic greatness, Goethe is careful to make them the realistic products of their society. They are the victims of social and religious bigotry, which has made them social outcasts. Deprived of her father by social convention, abandoned by her mother due to an abuse of institutionalised religion, the orphaned Mignon grew up wild and unsocialised. The realistic explanation for Augustin's problems seems to lie in his mental disposition. Described by his brother, the Marchese, as intense, artistic and intellectual, yet unbalanced the over-excited monk Augustin exhibits, before his transformation into the Harper, the violent mood-swings of what in psychoanalytical terminology is classed as manic depression.

> Indessen hatte Bruder Augustin im Kloster seine Jahre in dem sonderbarsten Zustande zugebracht; er überließ sich ganz dem Genuß einer heiligen Schwärmerei, jenen halb geistigen, halb physischen Empfindungen, die, wie sie ihn eine Zeitlang in den dritten Himmel erhuben, bald darauf in einen Abgrund von Ohnmacht und leeres Elend versinken ließen. (8, 9; 622)[19]

Not simply anachronistic intruders into an advanced rational civilisation, the Harper and Mignon also represent the realm of the human

---

[18] "Only in words it [the child] could not express itself, and the obstacle seemed to lie more in its way of thinking than the mechanism of speech." Moon, 502.

[19] "Meanwhile, my brother Augustin had spent his years in the monastery in the most wonderful [peculiar] circumstances. He abandoned himself completely to the enjoyment of a holy enthusiasm, to those half-spiritual, half-physical sensations which, as they elevated him for a time to the seventh heaven, soon afterwards let him sink into an abyss of impotence and misery." Moon, 497; my suggestion in brackets.

subconscious, where the individual's needs, desires and fears operate in a sub-rational space, which surfaces when the controlling social context is stripped away by circumstance or mental illness. Thus the historical development of human civilisation is mirrored (and contained *in nuce*) in the psychological development of the individual who retains the different stages in his psychological and intellectual make-up.

By making the Harper and Mignon appear on the one hand as the retarded, stunted or self-stunting creatures of unfortunate circumstances, yet on the other as admirable remnants from a superior era of human expression, which could still point the way to better poetry in the future, Goethe presents both the forward- and backward-looking thrusts of contemporary aesthetic thinking. The Harper and Mignon represent the complex dialectic of the original-natural, which is temporal (the awe-inspiring original is no longer appropriate) as well as qualitative (a mythic consciousness clashes with its rational environment). The potential productiveness of this dialectic is suggested in the beneficial and educative effect the two figures have on Wilhelm.

The temporal dialectic they represent has a specific historical dimension: Mignon and the Harper stand in a special relation to the history of modernity. In them *ancient* elements have acquired a *modern* reincarnation. Their hybrid nature is already suggested in their origin: they are the "Romantic" figures who nevertheless come from Italy. They are associated with Catholicism.[20] This links them with the Christian religiosity of modernity, which the Schlegels were soon to define as the root of the modern disposition due to its focus on the immaterial realm of the beyond. But as the "Italian figures", they come from a place that for Goethe is, particularly after his Italian journey, not primarily the country of Catholicism, but the land of the Renaissance, which had partaken of classical antiquity, and revisited its heritage to bring forth new

---

[20] By implication this links them with Catholic mysticism and Catholic obscurantism, which discourage self-reliance and independence. Schiller had approvingly considered this religiosity as the key reason for their doom. "Die Katastrophe sowie die ganze Geschichte des Harfenspielers erregt das höchste Interesse; wie vortrefflich ich es finde, daß Sie diese ungeheuren Schicksale von frommen Fratzen ableiten, habe ich oben schon erwähnt." An Goethe, 2 July 1797, *Goethe-Schiller. Briefwechsel*, ed. by Walter Killy, Frankfurt aM/Hamburg: Fischer, 1961, p. 118. "The catastrophe, as well as the harper's entire history, creates the greatest interest. I have already mentioned above how excellent I find it that you trace these monstrous fates back to demons of piety." Catholicism is also relentlessly criticised through the sad story of Mignon's mother.

concepts of independent individuality and intellectual clarity.[21] *In them* the original-natural appears as ancient (original Greco-Roman) as well as modern (Romantic Christian influences of yearning), while *in their background* the progress of modernity is reflected in two dialectically related processes: on the one hand modernity acquires neo-classical characteristics when antiquity is rediscovered during the (modern) Renaissance. On the other hand original and simple Christianity gradually acquires complex organisation in the shape of (monastic) Catholicism. The historically complex Renaissance ideas and the highly developed Catholicism of historically advanced Christianity face each other as opposites at the end of the medieval period. In the representation of the Harper and Mignon the ancient-classical is original as well as advanced, and the modern-Romantic has a natural as well as developed side.

Modern Italy, which is marked by the absorption of antiquity into modernity, i.e. the Renaissance, is the homeland of the Harper and Mignon. The uncivilised wild-child Mignon remembers that she comes from a place of classical temples and marble statues. "Kennst du das Haus, auf Säulen ruht sein Dach, [...] und Marmorbilder stehn und sehn mich an." (3, 1; 155)[22] This building is later revealed as a neo-classical Italian country house near to where she grew up. "Wenn sie zurückkehrte, setzte sie sich unter die Säulen des Portals von einem Landhause in der Nachbarschaft; [...]. Dann lief sie in den großen Saal, besah die Statuen." (8, 9; 629).[23] (Modernised) Ancient and (archaic-ancient) modern overlap. As a modern natural, Mignon no doubt experiences

---

[21] In the novel, Italy is the land of art. "Der Italiener hat überhaupt ein tieferes Gefühl für die hohe Würde der Kunst als andere Nationen." (8, 7; 612) "The Italian, in general, has a deeper feeling for the high value of art than other nations." Moon, 489. Both Wilhelm's grandfather's and the *Oheim's* art collections, the latter exhibited in the *Oheim's* Italianate house, were imported from Italy.

[22] "Knowest thou the house? On pillars rest its beams / [...] And marble statues stand and look on me." Moon, 124, quoting T. Martin's translation.

[23] "When she came back, she sat among the pillars of the gateway in front [the columns of the portal] of a country house in the neighbourhood [...]. She ran into the great hall, looked at the statues." Moon, 503; my suggestion in brackets. Moon doubtlessly used "pillar" to make the connection to the earlier passage.
The house has been identified as the Villa Rotunda in Vicenza, which contains the works of the Renaissance artist Andrea Palladio. Cf. Karin Keppel-Kriems, *Mignon und Harfner in Goethes "Wilhelm Meister": Eine geschichtsphilosophische und kunsttheoretische Untersuchung zu Begriff und Gestaltung des Naiven*, Frankfurt aM/Bern/New York: Peter Lang, 1986, p. 127.

the ancient statues in a naturally un-self-conscious (ancient) manner, like the imagined original-natural Greek, although they are products of refined neo-classical sensibilities.[24] On the other hand, Augustin, the monk who represents the advances of modernity in both their aspects, fully developed Catholicism as well as neo-classical modernity, consciously slips out of his classicised Italian background into the identity of the Nordic bard when he disappears into Germany.[25] As the *bard*-figure he now represent the original-natural in both its ancient and modern variants. As a *Nordic* bard he conjures up a vision of Ossian, behind whom in the contemporary imagination of the *Goethezeit* always loomed the figure of Homer. The link that facilitates these overlappings is the Herderian assumption that stages of cultural and intellectual development are structurally similar.

But for the moderns the *original* harmony of a *natural* experience, whether in its ancient or modern guise, must remain an unachievable and fleeting dream. Not surprisingly both Mignon and Augustin dream of an *ancient* paradise. Modernity was, even at its natural origin, the inherently inharmonious successor to antiquity, which, in its configuration as the antithesis of antiquity, never possessed harmony. So Mignon famously turns the Italy of citrus fruits, laurel and myrtle with its blue skies and soft winds into the *classicised* paradise of her lost childhood, to which she longs to return and from which she is separated by the grey and misty mountains of the North, which harbour the mythic beasts of the Northern tradition, the dragons. Augustin fits his imagined paradise of love with similar trappings.[26] The singeing hell-fires of the Christian North are contrasted with a vision of a "natural" arcadia:

> Begegnet uns unter jenen Zypressen, die ihre ernsthaften Gipfel gen Himmel wenden, besucht uns an jenen Spalieren, wo die Zitronen und Pomeranzen neben uns blühn, wo die zierliche Myrte uns ihre zarten Blumen darreicht,

---

[24] Mignon represents the hybrid nature of modernity in one other way: linguistically. Her German is broken, infused with the Romance languages of French and Italian. Like the acquisition of her musical and artistic skills, Mignon's language acquisition is unconscious and unmethodical.

[25] The *Oheim's* Italianate house with its collection of classical art represents the opposite movement: he consciously brings the Renaissance north into Germany. His classicist concept of art contrasts with Mignon's and the Harper's Romanticist one.

[26] Giuliani Baioni pointed out the "mythical landscape of archetypal plants" of which this paradisical flora consists and which indicates their imagined qualities. G. Baioni, "'Märchen' – 'Wilhelm Meisters Lehrjahre' – 'Hermann und Dorothea'. Zur Gesellschaftsidee der deutschen Klassik", 89.

und dann wagt es, uns mit euren trüben grauen, von Menschen gesponnenen Netzen zu ängstigen! (8, 9; 625)[27]

Mignon and Augustin are moderns longing for their other, one consciously the other unconsciously. The fact that their yearning, to which they give expression in a duet,[28] is unfulfilled and never-ending makes them creatures of a post-classical modernity. They are not, as has been claimed, symbols of antiquity itself.[29] Even Mignon, who represents the unreflectively naïve, realises this feature under distinctly modern conditions. Thus Mignon and the Harper are sentimental and naïve, in Schiller's sense, at the same time. Precisely this circumstance is responsible for the Romantic-Ancient overlap in their presentation.[30] Their sentimentality makes their naivety problematic. And their naivety makes their sentimentality fruitless – unlike the sentimentality that Schiller and Friedrich Schlegel eventually define – because it remains intellectually unreflected, which deprives them of the progressive and eventually self-redemptive potential of the modern condition. They cannot (in the case of Mignon) and will not (in the case of Augustin) avail themselves of the ever increasing reflexiveness, which contemporary thinkers were identifying as the only road towards a new, a modern, happiness. In their one-sidedness they remain out of step with the process of intellectual

---

[27] Intriguingly though, the wording of Mignon's and Augustin's versions of their paradisical gardens is also reminiscent of Goethe's translation of the biblical Song of Songs, which adds Hebrew antiquity to Goethe's crucible of "antiquities". Cf. James Simpson, *Goethe and Patriarchy: Faust and the Fates of Desire*, Oxford: European Humanities Research Centre, 1998, p. 51. A fusion of Judaeo-Christian and classical allusions links the two key cultural imports into European culture. "Meet us beneath those cypresses which turn their solemn tops to the [towards] heaven, visit us at those espaliers where the lemons and oranges are blooming beside us, where the delicate myrtle stretches out to us her tender flowers, and then dare to plague us with your gloomy dark nets which men have spun." Moon, 499; my suggestion in brackets.

[28] "Nur wer die Sehnsucht kennt, weiß was ich leide!" (4, 11; 258) "Only he who knows yearning, understands how much I suffer!"

[29] Keppel-Kriems, *Mignon und Harfner in Goethes "Wilhelm Meister*, 126 ff.

[30] Karin Keppel-Kriems is correct in pointing out that the Harper does not appear in a "konkreten epochalen Gewand", but she is wrong to suggest that he is not "ideengeschichtlich-epochal" delineated, nor that such delineation is "unimportant" (ibid., 114). That the "naïve" makes its appearance in modernity is of course a direct result of the *Querelle*. As the battle for an independent modern identity intensified, modern thinkers bestowed this feature on the early phases of *all* cultures: Schiller spoke, in the wake of Herder, of the "Jugendwelt" of culture. Herder had equated Shakespeare with Sophocles, and equations of Homer and Celtic and Germanic bards soon followed.

history, which has left them behind. On the other hand, their one-sided-ness safeguards in them an artistic vitality that is natural and original. From the past of modernity erupt dark and demonic forces of unbridled emotion that revive the original spell-binding power of natural poetry. This is the past of modernity in a two-fold sense: antiquity that preceded modernity and the early culture of modernity itself. Both are imagined to share an original vitality. In a post-medieval, a post-Renaissance, an Enlightened world this eruption of untamed emotion was as shocking as it was affecting and fascinating. Goethe suggests, no doubt mindful of his *Sturm-und-Drang* convictions and experiences, that in this raw emotion lies the origin of modern art, and in its memory the original inspiration of the individual artist.

The associative background of Augustin's and Sperata's love, although essentially modern, incorporates similar ancient/Romantic-modern over-lappings. The incest between Augustin and his sister, the underlying reason for the unhappy conclusion of their story, is of course a motif from ancient myth, but Goethe has reconfigured it in modern terms. Their love is doubly forbidden, it offends against the (modern) Christian law of monastic celibacy as well as the secular prohibition of incest. By hinting at the story of Heloise and Abelard as well as at the incest-motif of ancient myth, it spans the entire European history of forbidden heterosexual love. But their relationship also has a narrower late 18th-century context. The incest between brother and sister has been identified as a symbol of the rebellion against bourgeois society and paternal law in later 18th-century and Romantic literature.[31] Thus their behaviour is linked to the *Sturm-und-Drang* rebellion. But first and foremost Augustin's and Sperata's *love* is a modern phenomenon. It is of the secret and unfulfillable kind, which is ubiquitous in the literature of Christian modernity and has its origin, most generally, in the early Christian view of love as the basis of existence and knowledge, and more particularly in the chivalric tradition of courtly love. It is a quintessentially modern concept[32] that in post-medieval times acquired the attribute of secular redemptiveness when the lovers consider each other as soul-mates,

---

[31] Cf. Leslie A. Fiedler, *Love and Death in the American Novel*, Cleveland, 1962, p. 90, quoted in Baioni, "Gesellschaftsidee", 89, cf. also Baioni, ibid., 101.

[32] The great value and importance that post-classical thinking attached to heterosexual love compared to classical antiquity was summarised by Paul Kluckhohn in *Die Auffassung der Liebe in der Literatur des 18. Jahrhunderts and in der Romantik*, (1922) 3rd unchanged edition, Tübingen: Niemeyer, 1966, pp. 1–17.

which is clearly hinted at with Augustus and Sperata. Early Romantic thought finally proclaimed the synthesis of the originally Christian contemplative and spiritual love with sexual love.[33] This must be seen as part of the general secularisation process as well as part of the contemporary philosophical endeavour to connect intellect and nature, body and soul, (sensual) world and mind. In the 18th-century sibling-incest came to symbolise the attempt to realise absolute identity. It is the attempt of the alienated and divided individual to reattain absolute harmony by uniting the two complementary halves of the same origin. Augustin illustrates this point with his example of the lily, a hermaphrodite plant. In this respect Augustin's and Sperata's inclinations are connected to the concerns that prompted Schelling's *Identitätsphilosophie*. As the product of such a union, Mignon must inevitably hint at completeness, which is expressed in her own indeterminate sex. But her equally subhuman (vegetative) as well as super-human (potentially self-sufficient) completeness deprives her of vital human aspects. She is disconnected from society, save for her relationship with her imagined father-lover Wilhelm, which is again an incestuous relationship that is an extension of herself, and she lacks reflexive capability, which, if she had it, would urge her to establish a relationship between herself and the world. Goethe presents the problematic of the absolute, be it absolutely original nature or reattained absolute completeness, when it is placed in reality rather than posited in the conceptual realm of thought.

Such an accommodation of antiquity within modernity, which A.W. Schlegel suggested and Goethe achieves here, is only possible once antiquity, and culture, had become defined as historically conditioned. The original basis for this view was laid during the Renaissance, when modern thinkers for the first time engaged consciously with "antiquity", which became seen not just as modern culture's predecessor, but predominantly its (superior) "other", the inimitable perfection, which in time was to form the original basis of the quarrel between ancients and moderns. But through the ensuing *Querelle* its perfection became revealed as limited, when compared to modern aspirations. Modernity had to produce its own ideals while being mindful of its origin and history, including its relation to antiquity. Once the *Querelle* had set in motion the process that generated the historical perspective, which afforded a differentiated view of both antiquity and modernity, prohibiting a

---

[33] Cf. Kluckhohn, *Auffassung der Liebe*, 606 ff.

simple binary opposition of nature versus art(ifice), or harmony against disharmony,[34] the Renaissance-perspective, the starting-point, itself became obsolete.

The Difficulty of Modern Progress: Shakespeare's *Hamlet*

In the novel Shakespeare appears as the Herderian modern ancient, who, as a poet, still has access to the original poetic power and is capable of depicting, rather than only analysing the conditions of his historical existence. The precarious condition of modernity is expressed in his *Hamlet*. Wilhelm reacts to Shakespeare's works in typical *Sturm-und-Drang* fashion, paraphrasing Herder's evaluation of 1773.

> [Shakespeares Stücke] scheinen ein Werk eines himmlischen Genius zu sein, der sich den Menschen nähert, um sie mit sich selbst auf die gelindeste Weise bekannt zu machen. Es sind keine Gedichte! Man glaubt vor den aufgeschlagenen ungeheuren Büchern des Schicksals zu stehen, in denen der Sturmwind des bewegtesten Lebens saust, und sie mit Gewalt rasch hin und wieder blättert. [...] Alle Vorgefühle, die ich jemals über Menschheit und ihre Schicksale gehabt, die mich von Jugend auf, mir selbst unbemerkt, begleiteten, finde ich in Shakespeares Stücken erfüllt und entwickelt. Es scheint, als wenn er uns alle Rätsel offenbarte, ohne daß man doch sagen kann: hier oder da ist das Wort der Auflösung. (3, 11; 205)[35]

Further propagating Herderian ideas, he suggests that Shakespeare's plays are suitable dramatic material for a new German national literature and theatre.[36] Beyond Herder, Wilhelm's assessment of *Hamlet* moves

---

[34] Here Schiller's relation between the naïve and the sentimental works both ways: not only is the sentimental capable of producing the new naïve in the end, the naïve, Goethe suggests, cannot be recognised without the sentimental spur.

[35] "They seem to be the work of some heavenly genius, who draws nigh to men in the gentlest of manners to make them acquainted with themselves. These are no fictions! You think you are standing before the open, awful books of fate, in which the whirlwind of the most animated life rushes, violently turning the leaves hither and thither. [...] All earlier feelings I have ever had regarding mankind and his destiny, which have accompanied me from youth upwards, though unobserved by myself, I find developed and fulfilled in Shakespeare's plays. It seemed as though he revealed to us enigmas, though we cannot say. Here or there is the word of solution. [though we cannot say for certain: here or there ...]" Moon, 165. My version in brackets. In Moon this passage appears towards the end of chapter 10, rather than at the beginning of chapter 11 as it does in the original.

[36] "Diese wenigen Blicke, die ich in Shakespeares Welt getan, reizen mich mehr als irgend etwas andres, in der wirklichen Welt schnellere Fortschritte vorwärts zu tun, mich in die

towards an appreciation similar to that of Friedrich Schlegel. Shakespeare created "natural poetry", but rather than presenting the condition or preoccupations of a pre-rational humanity, his poetry represents modern humanity struggling with their intellectuality. The figure of Hamlet defines a modern problem different from those of Mignon and Augustin. While they are trapped by their un-reflective approach – by their un-reflected sentimentality – Hamlet is paralysed by his intellectual and reflexive capacity in a state of (Schlegelian) "maximal despair", which prevents him from taking the action his less intellectually advanced surroundings ask of him.

> Hier wird ein Eichbaum [i.e. the archaic idea of physical revenge] in ein köstliches Gefäß gepflanzt, das nur liebliche Blumen in seinen Schoß hätte aufnehmen sollen; die Wurzeln dehnen sich aus, das Gefäß wird zernichtet. Ein schönes, reines, edles, höchst moralisches Wesen, ohne die sinnliche Stärke, die den Helden macht, geht unter einer Last zugrunde, die es weder tragen noch abwerfen kann. (4, 13; 263)[37]

According to Wilhelm's interpretation, Hamlet suffers a terrible loss. It is the loss that originally made modernity and created its sentimental nature.

> Er sieht sich nun durch seinen Oheim [...] vielleicht auf immer [von der Thronfolge] ausgeschlossen; er fühlt sich nun so arm an Gnade, an Gütern, und fremd in dem, was er von Jugend auf als sein Eigentum betrachten konnte. Hier nimmt sein Gemüt die erste traurige Richtung. [...] Der zweite Schlag, der ihn traf, verletzte tiefer. [...] Auch seine Mutter verliert er, und es ist schlimmer, als wenn sie ihm der Tod geraubt hätte. Das zuverlässige Bild, das sich ein wohlgeratenes Kind so gern von seinen Eltern macht, verschwindet. [...] Nun erst [fühlt er sich] recht verwaist, und kein Glück der Welt kann ihm wieder ersetzten was er verloren hat. Nicht traurig, nicht nach-

---

Flut der Schicksale zu mischen, die über sie verhängt sind, und dereinst, wenn es mir glücken sollte, aus dem großen Meere der wahren Natur wenige Becher zu schöpfen, und sie von der Schaubühne dem lechzenden Publikum meines Vaterlandes auszuspenden." (3, 11; 206) "These few glances which I have cast into Shakespearean world [Shakespeare's world, MO] spurs me more than anything else to quicken my steps forward in the actual world, to mingle in the flood of the destinies which overhang it [which have been decreed for it, MO], and some day, if I am fortunate, to draw a few cups from the great ocean of true nature and distribute them from the stage to the thirsting public of my fatherland." Moon, 165.

37 "Here is an oak tree planted in a costly vase which should only have borne pleasing flowers in its bosom, but the roots expand and the vase is shattered. A beautiful, pure, noble, highly moral nature without the sensuous strength which makes the hero, sinks beneath a burden which it can neither bear nor cast away." Moon, 211–212.

denklich von Natur, wird ihm Trauer und Nachdenken zur schweren Bürde.
(4, 13; 262)[38]

According to Wilhelm, Hamlet is caught on the borderline between two
contrasting approaches to society and metaphysics. Prepared by a higher
education for a more Enlightened world of reason and morality, he has
become unfit for the old world of physical violence and supernatural
guidance. But his new intellectual approach has not yet provided him
with the ability to transform that world. So he is destroyed by the forces
of the old world. Despite being on the verge of identifying the historical
dynamic that creates Hamlet's problems, Wilhelm does not recognise
Hamlet as the tragedy of modernity, but considers it as the tragedy of an
individual. This leaves Wilhelm lost in the impenetrable and unsatisfying chaos of modern existence, because he has not yet grasped that this
is not simply the human condition, but arises out of specific historically
determined intellectual conditions.

> Geschichtschreiber und Dichter möchten uns gerne überreden, daß ein so
> stolzes Los dem Menschen fallen könne. Hier werden wir anders belehrt; der
> Held hat keinen Plan, aber das Stück ist planvoll. Hier wird nicht etwa nach
> einer starr und eigensinnig durchgeführten Idee von Rache ein Bösewicht be-
> straft, nein, es geschieht eine ungeheure Tat, sie wälzt sich in ihren Folgen
> fort, reißt Unschuldige mit. [...] Denn das ist die Eigenschaft der Greueltat,
> daß sie auch Böses über den Unschuldigen, wie der guten Handlung, daß sie
> viele Vorteile auch über den Unverdienten ausbreitet, ohne daß der Urheber
> von beiden oft weder bestraft noch belohnt wird. [...] Weder Irdischen noch
> Unterirdischen kann gelingen, was dem Schicksal allein vorbehalten ist. Die
> Gerichtsstunde kommt. Der Böse fällt mit dem Guten. (4, 15; 272–73)[39]

---

[38] "He now sees himself excluded [from the succession] by his uncle [...] perhaps forever.
He is now poor in favour, in goods and a stranger in that which from his youth he could
regard as his property. Here his temper assumes its first mournful direction. [...] The
second blow that struck him wounded deeper. [...] His mother, too, he loses, and it is
worse than if death had robbed him of her. The trustworthy picture which a well-ad-
vised [well-bred or good! MO] child is so glad to make of its parents vanishes. [...] Now
for the first time he feels [...] orphaned, and no good fortune in the world can replace
what he has lost. Neither melancholy nor reflective by nature, melancholy and reflection have become for him a heavy burden." Moon, 210–211.

[39] "Historians and poets are glad to persuade us that so proud a lot may fall to man. Here
we are taught differently; the hero has no plan, but the play is full of plan. Here there is
no villain punished according to some rigid and self-willed idea of vengeance; no, a
monstrous deed occurs, it rolls itself along with its consequences, carrying along with it
the innocent. [...] For it is the property of crime to extend its evil over the innocent, as
it is that of good action to extend many advantages even over the undeserving, without
the originator of either being punished or rewarded. [...] Neither earthly nor unearthly

Friedrich Schlegel, independently of Goethe's novel or not, characterised Hamlet's problems shortly afterwards as representing "maximal despair", which he takes to be the quintessential condition of modernity.

> Es gibt vielleicht keine vollkommnere Darstellung der unauflöslichen Disharmonie, welche der eigentliche Gegenstand der philosophischen Tragödie ist, als ein so gränzenloses Mißverhältnis der denkenden und der tätigen Kraft, wie in Hamlets Charakter. Der Totaleindruck ist ein Maximum der Verzweiflung. Alle Eindrücke [...] verschwinden als trivial vor dem, was hier als das letzte, einzige Resultat alles Seins und Denkens erscheint; vor der ewigen Kolossalen Dissonanz, welche die Menschheit und das Schicksal ewig trennt.[40]

Schlegel concluded that "im ganzen Gebiete der modernen Poesie ist dieses Drama für den ästhetischen Geschichtschreiber eins der wichtigsten Dokumente" (ibid.).[41] Through the Harper and Hamlet Wilhelm experiences the tragic sides of the modern condition, when the wholesale rejection of reflexive intellectuality as well as its one-sided priority in an intellectually still unreflexive world only paralyse. Goethe pinpoints the condition of the Shakespearean period – or the historical constellation that Shakespeare depicts in *Hamlet* – as having only just left medieval religiosity behind, which opens the path to reflect consciously on the modern condition, determine its characteristics and find answers to its problems.[42] In fact the different philosophical traditions of post-

---

power can succeed in what is reserved for destiny alone. The hour of judgement comes; the wicked falls with the good." Moon, 219.

[40] Friedrich Schlegel, *Studium, Kritische Friedrich-Schlegel-Ausgabe*, vol. 1, 248. "There is perhaps no more perfect representation than the character of Hamlet of the indissoluble disharmony that is the actual object of philosophical tragedy – that is to say, a limitless disparity between the thinking and active force – as in Hamlet's character. The overall impression of this tragedy is that of a maximum of despair. All impressions [...] disappear nonetheless before that which discloses itself as the ultimate and solitary result of all being and thought, before the eternal colossal dissonance that ceaselessly separates humanity and fate." *Study of Greek Poetry*, 33.

[41] "In the whole of modern poetry this play is one of the most important documents for the writer of the history of aesthetics."

[42] For Goethe, Shakespeare's tragedies are hybrids regarding ancient and modern. Fifteen years after he finished *Wilhelm Meisters Lehrjahre* Goethe published a short piece on Shakespeare in which he characterises the despotic phase of modernity presented by Shakespeare as a mix of ancient and modern. Cf. "Shakespeare und kein Ende!" *Morgenblatt für gebildete Stände*, 12 May 1815, *Johann Wolfgang Goethe. Schriften zu Literatur und Theater*, ed. by Walter Rehm, (*Gesamtausgabe der Werke und Schriften in 22 Bdn*, Bd. 15) Stuttgart: Cotta, 1963, pp. 994–1008. According to Goethe the English dramatist, a modern poet, incorporated elements of the ancient world view into a modern framework (without becoming ancient). While the ancient individual's situation was characterised by the

medieval modernity offer different solutions for the building of the
missing defences. The two Goethe discusses are Protestant pietism and
Enlightened worldly reason. The post-*Hamlet* Wilhelm will be brought
into contact with both of them through the Tower Society.

The Tower Society: Conscious Responses
to the Challenge of Modernity

Diametrically opposite Mignon and the Harper (and Hamlet) in intellectual terms stands the Society of the Tower, made up of forward-think-
ing members of the aristocracy. Having dedicated their association to

---

insurmountable power of external necessity, Goethe maintains that the modern
individual is conditioned by internal free will. He argues that Shakespeare creates
the tragic (modern) excess of free will, which cannot find fulfilment, by stimulating
it through external influences. "Ein Wollen, das über die Kräfte eines Individuums
hinausgeht, ist modern. Daß es aber Shakespeare nicht von innen entspringen, sondern
durch äußere Veranlassung aufregen läßt, dadurch wird es zu einer Art von Sollen, und
nähert sich dem Antiken." Ibid., 1002. "The desire for something that is beyond the
powers of the individual is a modern phenomenon. But as Shakespeare originates it not
within the individual's being, but through external instigation, it turns from a form of
wanting into a form of coercion, which approaches ancient notions." His examples for
the external influences are the ghost in *Hamlet* and the witches in *Macbeth*. This represents an external domination of the individual's will and power and introduces the
element of uncompromising fate into the action, against which the protagonist cannot
win. Goethe, however, considers this an achievement. For him it amounts to overcoming ancient or modern one-sidedness, and provides a dialectical synthesis, which appears to Goethe as a "miracle", the holy grail of the modern artist. While this may be a
belated contribution to making Shakespeare a worthy equivalent to ancient dramatists,
it is interesting to note that Goethe holds the spiritual circumstances of Shakespeare's
period responsible for the achievement of the miraculous synthesis. "Freilich hat er den
Vorteil, daß er zur rechten Erntezeit kam, daß er in einem lebensreichen, protestan-
tischen Lande wirken durfte, wo der bigotte Wahn eine Zeitlang schwieg, so daß einem
wahren Naturfrommen wie Shakespeare die Freiheit blieb, sein reines Innere, ohne
Bezug auf irgendeine bestimmte Religion, religios [sic] zu entwickeln." Ibid., 1002–3.
"Certainly, he had the advantage to live in the right era for harvesting, that he was
allowed to work in a lively Protestant country, where bigoted madness was silent for a
while, which gave someone like Shakespeare, who worshipped the natural, the freedom
to develop his true inner being in a religious manner, without referring to a particular
religion." Again, the "Epochenschwelle" of the Renaissance is pinpointed. Shakespeare
is able to be a "rounded" rather than desperate modern, because the force of the religion of modernity, which was largely held responsible for creating the modern condition, had been mellowed. (It is not "irgendeine" religion, Goethe means Christianity,
which produced the yearning turn of the modern mind.)

the improvement of society through rational planning and restructuring, they represent the key tenet of the Enlightenment. Inspired by a trust in reason, they advocate interventionist action (education) based on analytical theory (rational philosophy), to improve the world. They believe that the wild uncompromising passion that plagues Mignon and the Harper should be transformed into calm and conscious balance and harmony, while Hamlet's unproductive intellectualising must be converted into purposeful activity. The Tower Society believe themselves in possession of answers to the problems caused by the condition of modern humanity: during the performance put on at Wilhelm's initiation the ghost of Hamlet's father appears in a happy frame of mind, "ich [...] scheide getrost, da meine Wünsche für dich [...] erfüllt sind" (7, 9; 532).[43] Wilhelm's story is supposed to become that of a happy sorted-out anti-*Hamlet*. The Tower Society's confidence expresses the serene feeling of superiority of Enlightenment thought, which believed the world to be rational, knowable, and perfectible. The Tower Society is characterised by a belief in clearly appreciated purpose, opposed to any aimless drifting, such as Wilhelm's (and Hamlet's) "schlendern". Their emissaries make these points. The Stranger lectures Wilhelm:

> Das Gewebe dieser Welt ist aus Notwendigkeit und Zufall gebildet; die Vernunft des Menschen stellt sich zwischen beide, und weiß sie zu beherrschen; sie behandelt das Notwendige als den Grund ihres Daseins; das Zufällige weiß sie zu lenken, zu leiten und zu nutzen. [...] Wehe dem, der [...] in dem Notwendigen etwas Willkürliches finden zu wollen, der dem Zufälligen eine Art von Vernunft zuschreiben möchte, welcher zu folgen sogar eine Religion sei. Heißt das etwas weiter, als seinem eigenen Verstande entsagen, und seinen Neigungen unbedingten Raum geben? Wir bilden uns sein, fromm zu sein, indem wir ohne Überlegung hinschlendern, uns durch angenehme Zufälle determinieren lassen, und endlich dem Resultate eines solchen schwankenden Lebens den Namen einer göttlichen Führung geben. [...] Jeder hat sein eigen Glück unter den Händen, [...]. Nur die Fähigkeit dazu wird uns angeboren, sie will gelernt und sorgfältig ausgeübt sein. (1, 17; 75–6)[44]

---

[43] "I [...] depart consoled as my wishes for you are fulfilled." Moon, 424.

[44] "The web of the world is formed out of necessity and chance; the reason of man is placed between the two and knows how to govern them; it treats the necessary as the basis of its being; chance it knows how to lead and guide. [...] Woe to him, who [...] has accustomed himself to wish to find something arbitrary in the necessary, and who may ascribe to chance a kind of reason, and to follow it is even a religion. Does that mean anything more than to renounce one's own understanding and to give unrestrained space to one's inclination? We imagine that we are pious when we meander along without reflection, allow ourselves to be determined by pleasant chances, and fin-

The Parson does not believe in the beneficial workings of fateful coincidences, either:

> Das Schicksal [...] ist ein vornehmer, aber teurer Hofmeister. Ich würde mich immer lieber an die Vernunft eines menschlichen Meisters halten. Das Schicksal, für dessen Weisheit ich alle Ehrfurcht trage, mag an dem Zufall, durch den es wirkt, ein sehr ungelenkes Organ haben. Denn selten scheint dieser genau und rein auszuführen, was jenes beschlossen hatte. (2, 9; 129)[45]

He also sets great store by education. "Anfang und Ende möchte es [ein glückliches Naturell] wohl sein und bleiben; aber in der Mitte dürfte dem Künstler manches fehlen, wenn nicht Bildung das erst aus ihm macht, was er sein soll, und zwar frühe Bildung." (2, 9; 128)[46] Jarno urges Wilhelm to a life of active service: "Lassen Sie den Vorsatz nicht fahren, in ein tätiges Leben überzugehen, und eilen Sie, die guten Jahre, die Ihnen gegönnt sind, wacker zu nutzen. [...] Mögen Sie Ihre Kräfte und Talente unserm Dienste widmen." (3, 11; 206)[47] All three wish to promote individual self-reliance and independence through education. So they select suitable individuals whom they intend to guide towards a clear understanding of their purpose.

Goethe associates the philosophical origins of the Tower Society with spiritual and intellectual movements that are traditionally regarded as the foundations of self-conscious (i.e. post-medieval) European modernity: the Reformation and the Enlightenment. These new religious and intellectual movements share a focus on the independence of the individual, free from the constraining reliance on priests, fate and nature. Individual conscience and individual rationality are the means of this independence. The establishment of spiritual independence

---

ally give to the result of such irresolute life the name of a divine guidance. [...] Everyone has his own happiness in his hands, [...] only the capacity for it is innate, it wants to be learnt and carefully practised." Moon, 62–63.

[45] "Fate [...] is a superior but expensive tutor. I would myself always rather keep to the reason of a human master. Fate, for whose wisdom I have every respect, may have on the chance by which it works a very unsuitable instrument [in chance, through which it works, MO]. For the latter seldom appears to carry out exactly and clearly what the former has commanded." Moon, 104.

[46] "The first and last, beginning and end it [a fortunate disposition] may well be and remain, but in the middle the artist is deficient in much, if the culture, and indeed the early culture, has not made him what he ought to be." Moon, 104.

[47] "Don't let go of your purpose of embarking on an active life and hasten on to employ vigorously the good years that are granted to you. [...] If you like to devote your powers and talents to one [our! MO] service." Moon, 165–166.

through the Reformation precedes the rational independence of the Enlightenment intellect. These two stages are represented by the *Stiftsdame* and the *Oheim* respectively. The *Stiftsdame* only achieves spiritual independence, which is based on the individual's reliance on conscience and communion with God. This represents a withdrawal from the world into an inner self. In her case, independence means a rejection of the world. The *Oheim* on the other hand wishes to see human independence made fruitful for society. He finds a pure spiritualism unhealthy and dangerous.

> Man [tut] nicht wohl, der sittlichen Bildung, einsam, in sich selbst verschlossen, nachzuhängen; vielmehr wird man finden, daß derjenige, dessen Geist nach einer moralischen Kultur strebt, alle Ursache hat, seine feinere Sinnlichkeit zugleich mit auszubilden, damit er nicht in Gefahr komme, von seiner moralischen Höhe herab zu gleiten, indem er sich den Lockungen einer regellosen Phantasie übergibt. (6, 439–40)[48]

Here the aspirations of the reformed religion and the Enlightenment clash. But the *Stiftsdame's* symbolic meaning is not limited to religiosity, she also has a directly philosophical dimension. She represents the extreme subjectivism of the Cartesian ego, which by relying entirely on itself, makes the surrounding world alien and untrustworthy.

> Es war als wenn meine Seele ohne Gesellschaft des Körpers dächte; sie sah den Körper selbst als ein ihr fremdes Wesen an, wie man etwa ein Kleid ansieht. [...] Alle diese Zeiten [die Vergangenheit] sind dahin; was folgt wird auch dahin gehen: der Körper wird wie ein Kleid zerreißen, aber Ich, das wohlbekannte Ich, Ich bin. (6, 447)[49]

Cartesian subjectivism was the philosophical response to the sudden loneliness of the individual in the post-medieval, post-religious world. It makes a virtue out of a necessity, and intensifies the alienation between subject and world. The *Oheim's* view of the nature and the task of the ego are geared towards establishing a relation between subject and world.

---

[48] "He does not act well who in solitary exclusion by himself follows after moral culture; much rather will it be found that he whose spirit strives after moral culture has every reason at the same time to cultivate his finer sensuous powers, so that he may not run the risk of sinking down from his moral height by giving himself over to the enticements of a lawless fancy." Moon, 349–350.

[49] "It was as if my soul were thinking apart from the body; it looked upon the body itself as something foreign to it, as one looks upon a piece of clothing. [...] All those times are past, the future will also pass away, the body will fall to pieces like a garment, but I, the well-known [familiar, MO] I, I am." Moon, 355.

Des Menschen größtes Verdienst bleibt wohl, wenn er die Umstände so viel als möglich bestimmt und sich so wenig als möglich von ihnen bestimmen läßt. Das ganze Weltwesen liegt vor uns, wie ein großer Steinbruch vor dem Baumeister, der nur dann den Namen verdient, wenn er aus diesen zufälligen Naturmassen ein in seinem Geiste entsprungenes Urbild mit der größten Ökonomie, Zweckmäßigkeit und Festigkeit zusammenstellt. Alles außer uns ist nur Element, ja ich darf wohl sagen, auch alles an uns; aber tief in uns liegt diese schöpferische Kraft, die das zu erschaffen vermag, was sein soll, und uns nicht ruhen und rasten läßt, bis wir es außer uns oder an uns […] dargestellt haben. (6, 436)[50]

His definition of the creative ego is similar to Fichte's.[51] Here Fichte's philosophy appears as the final stage in the modern project of rationality. He still prioritises the subject, which the later Idealists no longer do, but his aim was already the reconnection of subject and object.

Both *Stiftsdame* and *Oheim* are presented with a certain ambiguity, which suggests that Goethe viewed both Pietism and the Enlightenment as inherently problematic. In her confessions, the former comes across as self-centred and self-righteous, and is subtly criticised by her niece Natalie. "Eine sehr schwache Gesundheit, vielleicht zu viel Beschäftigung mit sich selbst, und dabei eine sittliche und religiöse Ängstlichkeit ließen sie das der Welt nicht sein, was sie unter andern Umständen hätte werden können" (8, 3; 556).[52] The *Oheim* clearly represents an advance in dealing with the problems of modernity – reaching the stage of contemporary philosophy –, but remains, by his own admission, unable to reconcile his reason and his senses adequately.

Und doch mußte er selbst gestehen, daß ihm gleichsam Leben und Atem ausgehen würden, wenn er sich nicht von Zeit zu Zeit nachsähe, und sich er-

---

[50] "Man's greatest merit is to determine his circumstances as much as possible, and as little as possible to be determined by them. The whole world lies before us as a great quarry before the architect, who only deserves the name when out of the fortuitous mass he can put together with the greatest economy, fitness and durability, a form which originated in his spirit. Everything without us, indeed, I may say, everything in us, is only an element, but deep within us lies this creative force which can create what it was meant to be, and does not let us rest until out of us, or in us […] that thing has been represented." Moon, 346–347.

[51] The *Oheim* is in my opinion a better object through which to assess Goethe's view of Fichte's philosophy of the *Wissenschaftslehre* than the scene in which the Graf encounters Wilhelm in his armchair, which Ill-Sun Joo has recently suggested. Cf. *Goethes Dilettantismus-Kritik*, Frankfurt aM: Peter Lang, 1999, pp. 160f.

[52] "Very poor health, perhaps too much occupation with herself, did not admit of her being to the world what, in different circumstances, she might have been." Moon, 443.

laube, das mit Leidenschaft zu genießen, was er eben nicht immer loben und entschuldigen konnte. Meine Schuld ist es nicht, sagte er, wenn ich meine Triebe und meine Vernunft nicht völlig habe in Einstimmung bringen können. (8, 5; 578–79)[53]

The *Stiftsdame* on the other hand achieves, it would appear, a complete identity of necessity and freedom, which moves her into the regions of the divine, but at the cost of a relation with the world.

Ich erinnere mich kaum eines Gebotes; nichts erscheint mir in Gestalt eines Gesetzes; es ist ein Trieb, der mich leitet und immer recht führet; ich folge mit Freiheit meinen Gesinnungen, und weiß so wenig von Einschränkungen als von Reue. (6, 452)[54]

The *Oheim* remains caught in what Schlegel was to call the dissonance of modernity, in which the ideal can only ever be approximated to because the human being is of this world while the ideal is not. While the *Stiftsdame* succeeds in overcoming the problem of modernity, she does this at the expense of her social humanity.

The *Oheim* and the *Stiftsdame* represent the history of the modern effort to find solutions to its problems. In the present the Tower Society revolves around the French Abbé, a richly ambiguous late Enlightenment figure, who also alludes to the Catholic past of European culture. He was originally engaged as a tutor for Lothario and his siblings by the *Oheim* after the deaths of their parents, and initially carries on the *Oheim's* intentions of reconnecting in a practical way the independent subject with the world or society he or she inhabits. Touched by the currents that fed *Sturm und Drang*, he believes in the concept of individual subjectivity, according to which every individual has his own specific make-up and needs to find his own purpose, which is not necessarily self-evident, and develop towards it in accordance with his innate disposition. Natalie reports:

Er war [...] überzeugt, daß die Erziehung sich nur an die Neigung anschließen müsse. [...] Er behauptete: [...] Nur unsere zweideutige Erziehung

---

53 "He had, however, himself to confess that he would, as it were, have to give up life and breath if he did not from time to time indulge himself and allow himself passionately to enjoy what he could not always praise and justify. 'My fault,' he said, 'it is not that I have been unable to bring into complete harmony my impulses [desires, MO] and my reason.'" Moon, 461–462.

54 "I scarcely remember a commandment; nothing appears to me under the aspect of law; it is an impulse that guides and leads me always aright; I follow my feelings and know as little of restraint as of repentance." Moon, 359.

macht die Menschen ungewiß; sie erregt Wünsche statt Triebe zu beleben, und anstatt den wirklichen Anlagen aufzuhelfen, richtet sie das Streben nach Gegenständen, die so oft mit der Natur, die sich nach ihnen bemüht, nicht übereinstimmen. Ein Kind, ein junger Mensch, die auf ihrem eigenen Wege irre gehen, sind mir lieber als manche, die auf fremden Wegen recht wandeln. Finden jene, entweder durch sich selbst oder durch Anleitung, den rechten Weg, das ist den, der ihrer Natur gemäß ist, so werden sie ihn nie verlassen, anstatt daß diese jeden Augenblick in Gefahr sind, ein fremdes Joch abzu-schütteln, und sich einer unbedingten Freiheit zu übergeben. (8, 3; 558–59)[55]

This notion of individuality and its organic unfolding places the Abbé in the intellectual orbit of Rousseau, whose educational notions are alluded to here, and who remained attached to Enlightenment notions, while inspiring novel ideas in his German readers, such as Herder.[56]

---

[55] "He was [...] conscious [convinced, MO] that education ought to be adapted to the in-clinations. [...] He maintained [...] it is only our ambiguous dissipating education which makes men uncertain; it awakens wishes instead of animating impulses; instead of animating our real capacities it turns them to strive after objects which are often quite out of harmony with the nature that is working at them. A child or youth who goes astray on a path of their own are, in my opinion, better than many who wander aright on a path that is foreign to them. If the former find the right way either by them-selves or through guidance, that is the path suited to their nature; they will never leave it, whereas the latter are every moment in danger of shaking off a foreign yoke and abandoning themselves to unrestricted licence." Moon, 445–446.

[56] Despite his late-Enlightened sensibilities, the Abbé has no understanding of Mignon. She may be allowed to rest in the Hall of the Past, but her body is treated like an inter-esting specimen that is conserved for a scientist's collection cabinet. He says at her ex-equies: "Diese zärtliche Neigung [zu Wilhelm], diese lebhafte Dankbarkeit schien die Flamme zu sein, die das Öl ihres Lebens aufzehrte; die Geschicklichkeit des Arztes konnte das schöne Leben nicht erhalten, die sorgfältigste Freundschaft vermochte nicht es zu fristen. Aber wenn die Kunst den scheidenden Geist nicht zu fesseln vermochte, so hat sie alle ihre Mittel angewandt, den Körper zu erhalten und ihn der Vergänglich-keit zu entziehen. Eine balsamische Masse ist durch alle Adern gedrungen, und färbt nun an der Stelle des Bluts die so früh verblichenen Wangen. Treten Sie näher, [...] sehen Sie das Wunder der Kunst und Sorgfalt." (8, 9; 617–18) "This tender affection [for Wilhelm], this lively gratitude, seemed to be the flame consuming the oil of her life; friendship, with the greatest care, was unable to prolong it. But if art was unable to bind the departing spirit, it had applied all its means to maintain her body and withdraw it from the past. A quantity of balsam is driven through the veins and now, in place of blood, colours the cheeks that had so early become pale. Come nearer [...], behold this miracle of art and care." Moon, 493–4. Tellingly, the Abbé makes no difference between art and science. What he here refers to as art is clearly a skill based on natural science. This is made possible by the etymological background of the German word *Kunst*, which is derived from "können". He alludes to the meaning of highest capability in *Kunst*, which links art and science as (limitless) human endeavour, a sign of Enlighten-

For the Abbé, education and guidance are still necessary to limit and counteract unfavourable conditions. But his firm belief in the benefit of errors expresses his emphasis on learning, rather than teaching.

For all their philosophical advances and their efforts to tackle the problems of the modern condition the Tower Society's activities, and their presentation, are interwoven with an internal dialectic. Despite the Society's Protestant descent, its key teacher is the Abbé, whose title associates him with the most Catholic of institutions, the monastery, and whose background suggests involvement with that most dedicated of counter-Reformation forces, the Jesuits (8, 5; 589). The building that functions as the Society's seat and has provided its name is the most medieval part of a castle that is a veritable Gothic pile, the opposite to the *Oheim's* Italianate villa.

> Ein altes unregelmäßiges Schloß, mit einigen Türmen und Giebeln, schien die erste Anlage dazu gewesen zu sein; allein noch unregelmäßiger waren die neuen Angebäude, die teils nah, teils in einiger Entfernung davon errichtet, mit dem Hauptgebäude durch Galerien und bedeckte Gänge zusammenhingen. (7, 1; 455)[57]

The Gothic castle links the Enlightened Society not just with its own medieval European past, but associates it with stock elements in contemporary Gothic horror and miracle stories.

Despite their championing of independent rational thought and self-reliance, the Society's interference appears in the novel, to Wilhelm at any rate, in the guise of fate (*Schicksal*), the very notion it professes to unmask as mystic mummery enslaving the rational independent mind. On one occasion they intervene as the epitome of the mystic messenger of fate, a ghost, when the Abbé, or his twin, mysteriously appears to play Hamlet's father, a role for which no actor could be found, and through his appearance makes the production such a success. The final element in their education of Wilhelm is not a disputation or discussion, but an initiation ritual that hovers between performance and oracle. And by the end Wilhelm has not even become convinced of the value of their

---

ment confidence. The Abbé's "Kunst" relies on scientific research, empirical understanding and a rational creativity, all of which are literally incomprehensible to Mignon.

[57] "An old, irregularly shaped castle with some towers and gables seemed to have been the first plan, but the newly adjoining buildings were still more irregular. They had been erected partly close by and partly at some distance, connected together by galleries and covered corridors." Moon, 361.

efforts. He says in the final chapter: "Wir sind elend und zum Elend bestimmt, und ist es nicht völlig einerlei, ob eigene Schuld, höherer Einfluß oder Zufall, Tugend oder Laster, Weisheit oder Wahnsinn uns ins
Verderben stürzen?" (8, 10; 650)[58]

From the Tower's point of view these practices are of course mere
means to an end. Jarno reports that the Abbé believed "es [making the
production of *Hamlet* a success] [sei] der einzige Weg, Sie zu heilen,
wenn Sie heilbar wären." (8, 5; 591)[59] Their methods have been chosen
to maximise their impact on Wilhelm, who after all understands best in
the language of the theatre, a trait the Tower cannot educate out of him.
Even after he has already been in their sphere some time, towards the
close of Book 8, he still translates abstract ideas into the "terminology of
the theatre" to facilitate his understanding them (8, 7; 613). For him the
sphere of the theatre remains an enabling space. By the same token, it
could be argued that the Tower Society has to take the route of fateful
coincidences because it is the only way to produce an effect on Wilhelm
who believes in the beneficial workings of providence. He tells the
Stranger early on:

> Waren Sie niemals in dem Falle, daß ein kleiner Umstand Sie veranlaßte,
> einen gewissen Weg einzuschlagen, auf welchem bald eine gefällige Gelegen-
> heit Ihnen entgegen kam, und eine Reihe von unerwarteten Vorfällen Sie end-
> lich ans Ziel brachte, das Sie selbst noch kaum ins Auge gefaßt hatten? Sollte
> das nicht Ergebenheit in das Schicksal, Zutrauen zu einer solchen Leitung
> einflößen? (1, 17; 76)[60]

The Tower's means are chosen with the recipient in mind. But regarding
the Abbé, his "directing" and theatrics are presented as actually part of
his personality, which is hinted at when Jarno, not entirely respectfully,
exclaims: "Der Schalk! [...] Ich wollte wetten, der denkt sich was aus.
So wie er überhaupt gern ein wenig das Schicksal spielt." (8, 5; 594)[61]

---

[58] "We are wretched and destined for wretchedness, and is it not completely all the same,
    whether our own fault, higher influence or chance, virtue or vice, wisdom or madness
    plunge us into ruin?" Moon, 520.

[59] "It was the only way to cure you, if you were to be cured." Moon, 472.

[60] "Were you never so situated that a small circumstance caused you to enter upon a cer-
    tain way, on which a pleasant opportunity came to meet you and a series of unexpected
    events at length brought you to the object which you had yourself scarcely fixed your
    gaze upon? Should that not inspire submission to destiny, trust in such guidance?"
    Moon, 62.

[61] "The rogue [joker, MO]! I bet he is thinking something out. As above all he likes to play
    a little part of Destiny [likes to play Destiny a little, MO]." Moon, 474.

This undermines the seriousness of the Tower's purpose. It also suggests the deeply problematic position of reason as a supreme category in the 1790s, or 1770s. It simply cannot do without mysterious and religious pre-rational structures if it is to be effective for the human being.

Progress or Equality? The Interaction between Mignon and the Harper and the Tower Society

Yet despite its inner contradictions and deliberately ambiguous presentation, the values that the Tower Society represents – rationality and self-reliance – are shown to be in charge. In the course of the plot Mignon and the Harper, the representatives of the "other" of the Tower Society, are taken over and destroyed by the Tower, which itself survives intact to the end of the novel. The mythic manner of dealing with the world, which presents rather than analyses, comes under scrutiny, supposedly for its own benefit. Both Mignon and the Harper are taken in by associates of the Tower Society and treated as patients for what is perceived as psychological and psycho-somatic disorders. The rational investigation of their mythic mindsets, to which both are subjected, is shown to be directly conducive to their deaths. When the Harper has, under the guidance of the Tower, left his mythic bard-persona behind, has once again become Augustin, and is confronted with his old fears of doom – being killed by a young boy –, he cannot cope and commits suicide. Mignon's gradual decline is occasioned as much by Natalie's inquisitive, pseudo-therapeutic prodding as Wilhelm's absence. The Tower Society's rational-analytic investigations into the origin of the Harper's and Mignon's conditions are not even presented as entirely successful: Not only can they not help Mignon and the Harper, they cannot even fully uncover their secrets. The rational-investigative practice is not shown to be *all*-powerful. Only a chance discovery, a coincidence of "real" fate intervening, leads to the answer to the perplexing problem which these figures present to the reasonable mind: the Harper's brother just happens to appear and inform everybody of their origin and history.

On one level, Mignon and the Harper represent nature overpowered by science, or the mythic scrutinised by reason. Science attempts to make them right, i.e. useful and conforming members of society, and in dealing with them destroys them. That nature and the unreflecting intellect would come to be dominated by increasing rational powers appears to lie in the nature of the historical process of human conscious-

ness as it was understood around 1800. The victory of the Tower over
Mignon and the Harper also reflects the cultural development of modernity as it was understood at the time: a dependent fatalistic (Catholic) human mind enthralled by myth and mysticism gradually throws
off its shackles through Renaissance and Reformation to reach an Enlightened stage. In the late 18th century this was widely regarded as a
beneficial process, but the increasing unease about the potentially tyrannical rule of reason that had come to the fore in the philosophical "crisis
of rationality" is clearly evident here, too. The tyrannical aspect of reason finds expression in the destruction of Mignon and the Harper,
which is mitigated only by the fact that both figures are presented as
deeply unhappy. This clearly was enough to assuage Schiller's conscience. But it was not enough for Novalis, whose ferocious criticism of
Goethe's novel as "eigentlich ein Candide, gegen die Poesie gerichtet"[62],
sustained by a "künstlerischer Atheismus", in which "das Romantische
[…] zugrunde geht, auch die Naturpoesie, das Wunderbare",[63] refers to
these circumstances.[64] The killing of Mignon and the Harper makes
plain that modernity had reached a stage of crisis regarding its guiding
principle, reason, and its suppressed "other". The Tower may win out
against Mignon, but in doing so deprives itself of balance.

That the Tower Society as against the Harper and Mignon represent
different aspects of the same humanity, as well as successive stages in
human intellectual development, is suggested by the intriguing connections between these counter-poles. The Abbé and the Harper share an
emblematic namelessness. All are members of the same late 18th-cen-
tury aristocracy. The Marchese, Mignon's uncle and the Harper's
brother, was a close friend of the enlightened, cultured *Oheim*, who
hovers in the background, and the past, of the Tower Society. The two
uncles, the reader is told, travelled Italy together and purchased works
of art. Their respective nephew (Lothario) and niece (Mignon) repre-

[62] Quoted by Jacobs, *Wilhelm Meister und seine Brüder,* 138.
[63] Novalis, "Schriften", 1802, quoted by Klaus F. Gilles, *Goethes "Wilhelm Meister": Zur Rezeptionsgeschichte der Lehr- und Wanderjahre,* Königstein/Ts: Athenäum, 1979, p. 56.
[64] A similar view, more historically focused, is put forward by Josef Görres a few years
later. "So verkünden die Zeichen der neuesten Zeit, daß die Poesie in die Ökonomie
und Industrie sich verlieren wird. Diesen Übergang in die kalte Zeit bezeichnet *Meister*
prophetisch. […] Die Prosa trägt den Sieg davon, und selbst der Held fristet seine Exi-
stenz nur, indem er sich an die prosaisch-ökonomische Gesellschaft anschließt."
Quoted by Klaus F. Gilles, *Goethes "Wilhelm Meister"*, p. XVI.

sent the diametrically opposed effects modernity can have on the individual.

The spheres of the Tower Society and of Mignon and the Harper represent the two different ways of ordering and comprehending human existence in the world as the late 18th century understood them, the mythic and the rational. The mythic mode had only recently been "rediscovered" in the wake of a changed appreciation of myth as original human conceptualisation, initiated by thinkers like the Göttingen classical philologist Christian Gottlieb Heyne and the philosopher Johann Georg Hamann, whose ideas crucially influenced Herder. While original myth was considered complete in itself as long as it fulfilled its function in a pre-rational environment, Mignon and the Harper represent the incompleteness the pre-rationally mythic acquires in a rational world if it remains closed to the rational. Within the novel Mignon and the Harper and the Tower Society each represent an incomplete aspect of humanity. Thus Mignon and the Harper suffer from severe psychological traumas, and the Tower Society has to report gruesome failures: Mignon, the Harper, and Aurelie. In their different orbits Wilhelm is exposed to the one-sided in humanity, to which he responds with fascination as well as hesitant reluctance. He is fascinated by Jarno, worships Lothario, and is drawn to the Harper and Mignon, but he repeatedly pushes Mignon aside and he remains critical of the Tower Society's efforts on his behalf.[65] Throughout Wilhelm retains an attachment to (many-sided) reality and a sense of his individual self by not following Mignon or the teachings of the Tower Society blindly.

The ambiguity concerning the relationship between these two approaches to conceptualisation – are they successive or equally valid approaches? – suggests an internal dialectic between them. It also prompted different interpretations right from the beginning. Is the novel an advertisement for the principles of the Tower Society or does it celebrate "Naturpoesie"? Schiller and Friedrich Schlegel, those perceptive early readers, differed regarding the assessment of Mignon and the Harper, but agreed that the Tower Society represents "Verstand" and that it is central to the meaning of the novel.[66] Schiller even perceived in the

---

[65] For example, at the initiation ritual (7, 9; 532), when he speaks to Natalie (8, 3; 559) and
      in his conversation with Jarno when the "Lehrbrief" resurfaces (8, 5; 587).
[66] Schlegel referred to it as the "geheime Gesellschaft des reinen Verstandes", a "secret society of pure understanding". "Über Goethes Meister", *Kritische Friedrich-Schlegel-Ausgabe* vol. 2, 145.

aims and maxims of the Society the central message of the novel.[67]
To him, the "Mächte des Turms" are the "Maschinen, die in gewissem
Sinne die Götter oder das regierende Schicksal darin vorstellen".[68] He
justified the capricious theatrical behaviour of the "higher understanding" which, although it is human, rules like inscrutable fate, as necessary
in the case of a hero who has not yet attained the level of understanding
of his betters. But Schiller was worried about the effect that the ambiguous presentation of the "machinery" might have on the readers and
urged Goethe to safeguard the integrity and seriousness of the Tower Society in his final version.

> Bei dem allen aber hätte ich doch gewünscht, daß Sie das Bedeutende dieser
> Maschinerie, die notwendige Beziehung derselben auf das Innere Wesen, dem
> Leser ein wenig näher gelegt hätten. [...] Viele Leser, fürchte ich, werden in je-
> nem geheimen Einfluß bloß ein theatralisches Spiel und einen Kunstgriff zu
> finden glauben, um die Verwicklungen zu vermehren, Überraschungen zu er-
> regen und dergleichen. [...] Mir deucht, daß Sie hier die freie Grazie der Be-
> wegung etwas weiter getrieben haben, als sich mit dem poetischen Ernste ver-
> trägt. (ibid., 127)[69]

Goethe refused to comply, famously referring to his "realistischer Tic"
in his prompt reply.[70] Schlegel, on the other hand, celebrated the ambiguous nature of the Tower Society. He saw it as the representation of
artistic "Willkür" that lies at the heart of Romantic literary theory and

---

[67] "Ein verborgen wirkender höherer Verstand, die Mächte des Turms, begleiten ihn mit
ihrer Aufmerksamkeit, und ohne die Natur in ihrem freien Gange zu stören, be-
obachten, leiten sie ihn von Ferne zu einem Zwecke, davon er selbst keine Ahnung hat,
noch haben darf. So leise und locker auch dieser Einfluß von außen ist, so ist er doch
wirklich da, und zur Erreichung des poetischen Zwecks war er unentbehrlich." An
Goethe, 8 July 1796, *Goethe-Schiller Briefwechsel*, 126–7. "A higher understanding, working secretly, the powers of the Tower accompany him attentively, but without interfer-
ing with nature on its free course, and watch, guide him from afar towards a purpose, of
which he himself is, and must remain, ignorant. As quietly and gentle as this external
influence may be, it is nevertheless real, and was indispensable for achieving the poetic
aim."

[68] Ibid., 126. "The powers of the Tower represent in a certain sense the machinery of the
gods or of ruling fate."

[69] "Despite all those things, though, I would have wished that you might have brought a
little closer to the reader the importance of this machinery, its necessary relation with
the inner being. [...] Many readers, I fear, will consider that secret influence a mere
game of theatrics and an artificial ploy to increase the complications, create surprises
and such like. [...] It seems to me that regarding artistic licence [literally: the free grace
of movement] you have gone beyond what agrees with poetic seriousness."

[70] Cf. An Schiller, 9 July 1796, *Goethe-Schiller Briefwechsel*, 130.

which "Wilhelm und sich selbst zum Besten hat".[71] While the ambiguity of the presentation interfered with Schiller's clearly defined educational objective for Wilhelm,[72] it worked well for Friedrich Schlegel, who did not consider Wilhelm's education as the central focus of the novel. Rather, it was the presentation of the art of living, and of education through living, which results in poetry that is concrete and conceptual at the same time.

> Wir sehen nun klar, daß es [das Werk] [...] die Kunst aller Künste, die Kunst zu leben, umfassen soll. Wir sehen auch, daß diese Lehrjahre eher jeden andern zum tüchtigen Künstler oder zum tüchtigen Mann bilden wollen und bilden können, als Wilhelmen selbst. Nicht dieser oder jener Mensch sollte erzogen, sondern die Natur, die Bildung selbst sollten in mannichfachen Beispielen dargestellt, und in einfache Grundsätze zusammengedrängt werden. [...] Für Wilhelmen wird wohl endlich auch gesorgt: aber sie haben ihn fast mehr als billig oder höflich ist, zum besten; selbst der kleine Felix hilft ihn erziehen und beschämen, indem er ihm seine vielfache Unwissenheit fühlbar macht. [...] Er resigniert förmlich darauf, einen eignen Willen zu haben. [...] Wie mögen sich die Leser dieses Romans beim Schluß desselben getäuscht fühlen, da aus allen diesen Erziehungsanstalten nichts herauskommt, als bescheidene Liebenswürdigkeit, da hinter allen diesen wunderbaren Zufällen, weissagenden Winken und geheimnisvollen Erscheinungen nichts steckt als die erhabenste Poesie, und da die letzten Fäden des Ganzen nur durch die Willkür eines bis zur Vollendung gebildeten Geistes gelenkt werden![73]

---

71 "makes fun of itself and Wilhelm". "Über Goethes Meister", *Kritische Friedrich-Schlegel-Ausgabe* vol. 2, 145.

72 Wilhelm was, according to Schiller, "von einem leeren und unbestimmten Ideal in ein bestimmtes tätiges Leben [zu treten], aber ohne die idealisierende Kraft dabei einzubüßen" (An Goethe, 8 July 1796, *Goethe-Schiller. Briefwechsel*, 128). "[to step] from an empty and undefined ideal into a clearly defined and active life, but without losing his ability to idealise in the process".

73 Friedrich Schlegel, "Über Goethes Meister", *Kritische Friedrich-Schlegel-Ausgabe* vol. 2, 143–44. "Now we see clearly that it [this work] is to comprise the art of all arts, the art of living. We also see that this apprenticeship would, or could, sooner make anyone other than Wilhelm into an efficient artist or an efficient person. Not this or that person is to be formed, but the nature of education itself is to be represented in manifold examples, and compressed into simple principles. [...] Wilhelm is taken care of eventually: but they make more fun of him than is right or polite, even Little Felix helps to educate and shame him by making him feel his ignorance of many things. [...] He gives up having a will of his own. [...] The readers of this novel may well feel cheated at the end, as all these educational efforts result in no more than modest politeness, as behind all these wondrous coincidences, prophetic hints and mysterious phenomena there is nothing but sublime poetry and as the last strings of the whole are pulled by the arbitrary spirit of a writer who is cultivated to perfection."

Schlegel's inclusive approach leaves room to include the "sacred family of natural poetry", and the theatre, among the agencies that influence Wilhelm's path through life.[74]

This divergence in interpretation regarding the objective of Wilhelm's education, and the agencies that effect it, illustrates the intrinsic ambiguity about them. The sacred family and the Tower must appear, conceptually, as equal antitheses, which, in their historical dimension, also form a dialectical succession, the synthesis of which is yet outstanding, is not achieved at the end of the novel.

The Dialectic of Education: The Challenges of Individuality and Historicity

Education is the process by which the individual is being equipped to exist, happy and purposeful, under the conditions of modernity. The Tower Society has ideas regarding how this can be achieved. But Wilhelm has his own. Both sides agree that the individual is capable of learning, of being formed. They have inherited this belief in the plasticity of the individual from the Enlightenment belief in perfectibility. The Abbé and Wilhelm agree on the individual's ability and need to develop his or her individuality and both sides are conscious of the Enlightenment problematic concerning the supremacy of reason. But they differ on how this learning should be achieved. Again Goethe investigates a facet of the contemporary interaction between Enlightenment ideas and their post-Enlightenment re-assessment from *Sturm und Drang* onwards. Again this interaction is presented in the wider context of the historical development of modernity, and eventually of humanity as a whole as it was understood at the time.

Wilhelm puts forward the idea of the organic unfolding of what is already present *in nuce*, the Herderian notion of the seed growing into a tree.[75] He outlines this notion in his letter of justification to Werner. He

---

[74] Schiller focuses on the profitable socialisation of the individual without (too much) loss of inspiration, while Schlegel, who also acknowledges that the art of living (happily) is the educational objective, is more pessimistic about a successful integration of socialisation and individuality. Any attempt at it leads to the compromise of aesthetic living, which must relinquish control to the arbitrariness of existence. Schlegel only has faith in the (aesthetic) achievement of the poets.

[75] This concept of the organic growth of individuality has its origin in *Sturm-und-Drang* thinking. It is under this motto of self-realisation, which is the *Sturm-und-Drang* de-

also defends the notion of an original and immutable "Naturell" in his discussion with the Parson in Book 2. According to this concept perfection is an immanent potential. Wilhelm claims for his true self the right not be curbed by externally imposed social or philosophical limitations, such as his bourgeois background or a prescribed educational discipline or the dictates of reason, all of which he mistrusts as authoritarian and disciplinarian schoolmasters. *Sturm-und-Drang* Wilhelm wants to be taught by nature, art, and life, by the quirky leaps of history, where chance may in time be revealed as fate. This notion of education, which is to safeguard the realisation of the individual as a self, focuses on individuation. It does not deny that external influences, such as the vagaries of birth and fate, may be crucial, and it allows for the project of *Bildung* to fail. Its success remains an unpredictable potential, and reflects the aspirations, and intellectual innovations, of *Sturm und Drang*. But Wilhelm's iconoclastic love of freedom is treated ironically within the novel. While he rebelliously demands liberation from the man-made constraints imposed on him, he happily submits to the guidance of fate, "Schicksal".[76] Unavoidably any attempt at free self-realisation is subject

---

mand for individuation, that Wilhelm prepares to leave his parental home and reject his father's plans for his son's career as a merchant, which he believes would be tantamount to self-alienation. Wilhelm believes his true self will only be realised through a relationship with the actress Mariane and a career on the theatre. Wilhelm identifies both Mariane and the theatre as his natural inclinations and purpose. His individuation also has a social component: with the creation of a national theatre Wilhelm hopes to help alleviate the cultural misery of his country. In typical *Sturm-und-Drang* fashion his social aspirations focus on the liberation of a nation alienated from itself, which is an extension of the alienated individual.

[76] Wilhelm's positive identification of his inclination is ordained by fate. "Er glaubte den hellen Wink des Schicksals zu verstehen, das ihm durch Marianen die Hand reichte, sich aus dem stockenden, schleppenden, bürgerlichen Leben heraus zu reißen, aus dem er schon so lange sich zu retten gewünscht hatte. [...] Seine Bestimmung zum Theater war ihm nunmehr klar; das hohe Ziel, das er sich vorgesteckt sah, schien ihm näher, indem er an Marianens Hand hinstrebte, und in selbstgefälliger Bescheidenheit erblickte er in sich den trefflichen Schauspieler, den Schöpfer eines künftigen National-Theaters, nach dem er so vielfältig hatte seufzen hören. Alles, was in dem innersten Winkel seiner Seele bisher geschlummert hatte, wurde rege." (1, 10; 37) "He thought he understood the clear intimation of destiny, which reached out a hand to him through Mariana, to tear him out of the dull and stupid bourgeois life, out of which he had long wished to rescue himself. [...] His destination for the theatre was now clear to him, the lofty aim, which he saw standing out before him, appeared to him nearer, as he strove for Mariana's hand [as he moved onwards hand in hand with Mariana, MO], and in self-complacent modesty saw in himself the splendid actor, the creator of a national

to chance, but Wilhelm invariably interprets the coincidences of life as
pointers towards destiny, which leaves him exposed to the tyranny of coincidence, unless he accepts the rule of a higher agency, which would ultimately make him unfree. This pinpoints the dialectic between freedom
and necessity, which so occupied the Idealist philosophers who tried to
find a conceptual framework that could contain the two. His experiences make Wilhelm uncertain. During the initiation ritual he wonders:
"Sollten zufällige Ereignisse einen Zusammenhang haben? Und das, was
wir Schicksal nennen, sollte es bloß Zufall sein?" (7, 9; 531)[77]

The Tower Society, on the other hand, favours the concept of the
individual being formed by wise external agencies, undergoing a programme of education to make him or her fit, happily and purposefully,
into the world. This notion prioritises the socialisation of the individual.
It does not deny the need for and possibility of individual happiness and
self-realisation, but assumes that this occurs within a social or communal framework. This approach relies on earlier 18th-century notions of
education along universal parameters. To a large extent it predates the
concept of fully-fledged individuality and the full awareness of historicity, and the increasing desire for freedom inherent within them.[78] But
the Tower Society's approach to teaching, and shaping, people according to their vision is not whole-heartedly endorsed within the novel.
Their efforts are dogged by failures: Mignon, the Harper, possibly the
Gräfin and Friedrich, and certainly Aurelie.[79] Most importantly, their
treatment of Wilhelm remains inconclusive.

---

theatre in the future for which he had heard people sighing so frequently. Everything
which had slumbered in the innermost recesses of his soul was now awake." Moon,
31–32.

[77] "Should chance events have a connection? And is that which we call Destiny but
Chance?" Moon, 423.

[78] Mayer pointed out that: "Die Aufklärung sah keinen prinzipiellen Konflikt zwischen
dem Anspruch des Individuums auf glückliche Entfaltung und der Forderung nach
dessen gesellschaftlicher Brauchbarkeit, denn nur durch deren Erfüllung glaubte sie die
persönliche Selbstverwirklichung gewährleistet." Mayer, *Der deutsche Bildungsroman*, 22.

[79] Aurelie is a *Sturm-und-Drang* character who shares significant features with Wilhelm.
Bearing in mind Aurelie's fate, this closeness in character indicates the precariousness
of the Tower Society's efforts regarding Wilhelm. As for Wilhelm, for her the theatre is a
space in which she feels she can fulfil herself in a way that is denied her elsewhere,
which in her case is reality. (In Wilhelm's it is society.) She imagines to commune
through her art with the true genius of her nation. "Ich war auch einmal in diesem
glücklichen Zustande, als ich mit dem höchsten Begriff von mir selbst und meiner
Nation die Bühne betrat. Was waren die Deutschen nicht in meiner Einbildung, was

This difference in focus – prioritising either individuation or socialisation – can be pinpointed in their partly overlapping, but crucially dif-

---

konnten sie nicht sein! [...] Wie ich wirkte, wirkte die Menge auf mich zurück, ich war
mit meinem Publikum im besten Vernehmen; ich glaubte, eine vollkommene Harmonie zu fühlen und jederzeit die Edelsten und Besten der Nation vor mir zu sehen."
(4, 16; 277) "I, too, was once in that happy condition when I entered on the stage with
the highest belief in myself and my nation. What were not the Germans in my imagination, what might they not become? [...] How I affected the multitude and was affected
by them in turn; I was in the best relationship with my public; I thought I felt a wel-
come harmony between us, and every time I saw before me the noblest and best of the
nation." Moon, 222–23. In this (imagined) condition she fulfils the highest standards
of Herderian *Volkspoesie*, or "Volkskunst" in this case, when artist and audience stand in
a reciprocal relationship of complete relevance. Aurelie also explicitly engages with the
Sturm-und-Drang idea of national revival: she is preoccupied with the "nation", and
shares Wilhelm's interest in the concept of a national theatre. But the purity of her imagined relationship with the audience cannot survive off-stage, where it becomes sullied
by the sexual advances the male members of the audience make towards the pretty
young actress, which disgust her (cf. 4, 16; 277–8). Like Wilhelm, Aurelie seeks self-rev-
elation in Shakespeare's *Hamlet*. Although she has some reservations about Ophelia,
she identifies with the character (cf. 4, 14; 265). Utterly disillusioned after her relationship with Lothario fails, Aurelie makes (Schiller's) aesthetic semblance her only reality.
Playing Countess Orsina in *Emilia Galotti*, "sie [zog] alle Schleusen ihres individuellen
Kummers auf, und es ward dadurch eine Darstellung, wie sie sich kein Dichter in dem
ersten Feuer der Erfindung hätte denken können." (5, 16; 380) "She [...] opened all the
sluices of her personal sorrow, and thus was a representation of a character such as no
poet in the first glow of his invention could have imagined." Moon, 305. Although
Aurelie is tragically misguided in her identification of the aesthetic experience with reality, her ideas and behaviour evince spiritual seriousness and moral purity. She does not
take lovers from among her admiring male fans, like Mariane. Aurelie is the only one
not to get drunk at the after-show party following the *Hamlet*-premiere (351) and she
fiercely disapproves of the frivolous Philine. No doubt it was this seriousness that had
earned her the attentions of the Tower, in the shape of Lothario. He gave her views of
the theatre and the nation a turn that is strikingly similar to the purpose of humanity
put forward in the "Lehrbrief", which says: "Nur alle Menschen machen die Menschheit aus, nur alle Kräfte zusammengenommen die Welt. [...] Alles das und weit mehr
liegt im Menschen, und muß ausgebildet werden; aber nicht in einem, sondern in
vielen. Jede Anlage ist wichtig und muß entwickelt werden." (8, 5; 592) "It is only all
men who complete mankind, and only all powers taken together which complete the
world. [...] All that, and still more, lies within man and has to be cultivated, not in one
person, however, but in many. Every disposition is important, and it has to be developed." Moon, 473. Lothario advised her: "Er machte mir's zur Pflicht, auch in meinem
Fache wahr, geistreich und belebend zu sein. Nun schien ich mir selbst inspiriert, so oft
ich auf das Theater trat. Mittelmäßige Stellen wurden zu Gold in meinem Munde."
(4, 16; 284) "He made it a duty for me also in my department to be true, intellectual and
enlivening. Now I seemed to myself even inspired, as often as I came to the theatre. Ordinary passages became gold in my mouth." Moon, 228. But Aurelie turns out to be a

fering approaches to the therapeutically liberating and illuminating function of role-playing, of "Schein" (semblance), in the educational process. The theatre is shown to be a socially and philosophically free space.[80] Everyone is allowed to participate, or exist within its confines: the bourgeois individualist Wilhelm as much as the presumably aristocratic enlightened Abbé, Serlo the professional craftsman of art, the socially heterogeneous Melinas, and even the profoundly anti-social Mignon and the anachronistic Harper. It is also the space in which the different spheres meet and first engage productively, culminating in a member of the Tower Society joining the sphere of theatre to play the ghost of Hamlet's father to great effect, theatrical (for the audience) and emotional (for Wilhelm). Only through his involvement with the theatre does Wilhelm encounter the emissaries of the Tower Society.[81] Wilhelm has instinctively always assumed that the theatre must be such a tolerant and enabling environment. He concludes in his letter to Werner:

---

failure for the Tower. For her, Lothario's teachings are inseparable from his person. When he leaves her she cannot be self-reliant and rational, but falls into a deep self-indulgent melancholy that ends in suicidal depression. All the Tower can do for her now is to provide some spiritual soothing: the doctor from the Tower duly gives her the *Bekenntnisse einer schönen Seele*. With her hyper-sensibility and uncompromising individualism Aurelie is a female Werther, and shares his fate. Like Werther, she represents a typical *Sturm-and-Drang* criticism of the Enlightenment: its detachment of reason from life. Reason and rational education have little effect as abstracts. In her insistence to always connect an idea with a person, ideally a sexual partner, i.e. with the notion of sexual love, Aurelie is again similar to Wilhelm. His passion for the theatre is linked to his passion for Mariane, only after he has met her is he prepared to leave behind his bourgeois background. And he is only prepared to leave the theatre, once he can connect the world of the Tower with potential partners, first Therese, and then, more powerfully, Natalie.

[80] This does not mean that the theatre is itself presented as extra-societal. It may provide a free space, but despite its extra-social qualities, the theatre that Goethe presents is exposed to the changing social and economic conditions of the times, which are moving from feudalism to bourgeois capitalism. No longer an economically secure court theatre of feudal times, Wilhelm's first troupe can only temporarily secure a similarly safe position for a limited period when they are engaged by the Graf for the particular purpose of entertaining the visiting prince. Serlo's company is subject to market forces: Serlo puts on productions for profit and will drop drama in favour of opera if this fills the house more reliably. Similarly, for most of the theatre folk it is a means to make money in order to survive. Art is presented as subservient to business.

[81] If he had not been involved with the actress Mariane, he would not have met the Stranger; if he had not become friendly with Philine and Laertes, he would not have met the Parson; if he had not joined Melina's troupe, he would not have met Jarno.

Ich habe nunmal einmal gerade zu jener harmonischen Ausbildung meiner
Natur, die mir meine Geburt versagt, eine unwiderstehliche Neigung. [...]
Mein Trieb [wird] täglich unüberwindbarer, eine öffentliche Person zu sein,
und in einem weitern Kreise zu gefallen und zu wirken. [...] Du siehst wohl,
daß das alles für mich nur auf dem Theater zu finden ist, und daß ich mich in
diesem einzigen Elemente nach Wunsch rühren und ausbilden kann. (5, 4;
313–14)[82]

The theatre is a free aesthetic space in the sense that Schiller developed
in the *Ästhetische Erziehung*, (although Schiller does not seem to realise
this in his letter dialogue with Goethe).[83] When its economic position is
secure, Goethe's theatre is removed from the realities of social power as
well as the strictures of moral law. According to Schiller, the aesthetic
semblance of art detaches human beings from the coercions of reality
and thus liberates them.

Mitten in dem furchtbaren Reich der Kräfte und mitten in dem heiligen
Reich der Gesetze baut der ästhetische Bildungstrieb unvermerkt an einem
dritten, fröhlichen Reiche des Spiels und des Scheins, worin er dem Menschen die Fesseln aller Verhältnisse abnimmt und ihn von allem, was Zwang
heißt, sowohl im Physischen als im Moralischen entbindet.[84]

It is a space where the distinction between semblance and reality is consciously realised – actors are playing roles –, but where equally the illusion of the identity between semblance and reality is most powerful –
the roles acquire reality through being acted out. Like Wilhelm, Schiller
too identified this liberation with personal development and education.
"Gleich so wie der Spieltrieb sich regt, der am Scheine Gefallen findet,
wird ihm auch der nachahmende Bildungstrieb folgen, der den Schein

---

82 "Now I have an inevitable longing for that harmonious cultivation of my nature which
    my birth has denied me. [...] My inclination every day is becoming more irresistible to
    become a public person, and in a wider circle to please and be influential. [...] You can
    easily see that all this can only be found on the stage, and that only in that element can
    I bestir and cultivate myself according to my wishes." Moon, 251.
83 Perhaps Schiller could not see this connection because Wilhelm's predilection for the
    theatre is connected to an appreciation of the freedom and privileges of the aristocracy,
    which Schiller clearly did not share. Cf. Jacobs, *Wilhelm Meister und seine Brüder*, 76.
84 Schiller, *Ästhetische Erziehung*, 410. "In the midst of the awful realm of powers, and of
    the sacred realm of laws, the aesthetic creative impulse is building unawares a third
    joyous realm of play and of appearance [semblance], in which it releases mankind from
    all shackles of circumstance and frees him from everything that may be called con-
    straint, whether physical or moral." *On the Aesthetic Education of Man in a series of Letters
    by Friedrich Schiller*, translated with an introduction by Reginald Snell, London: Rout-
    ledge & Kegan Paul, 1954, p. 137. Forthwith AE by Snell.

als etwas Selbständiges behandelt." (ibid., 400)[85] Dealing freely with the semblance of reality is the distinctive human activity:

> Da alles wirkliche Daseyn von der Natur, als einer fremden Macht, aller Schein aber ursprünglich von dem Menschen, als vorstellendem Subjekte, sich herschreibt, so bedient er sich bloß seines absoluten Eigenthumsrechts, wenn er den Schein von der Welt zurück nimmt und mit demselben nach eignen Gesetzen schaltet. (ibid., 401)[86]

The aesthetic semblance of art liberates humanity from moral law and the desires of the senses to achieve a synthesis of passion and perception, and of idea and reason. Schiller's theory contains elements of the idea of art as a therapy for the human condition, which is later taken up by psychoanalysis.[87] Through the Abbé, the Tower Society is aware of the therapeutic potential of acting. Playing the Parson in Book 2 the Abbé tells Wilhelm: "Es ist die beste Art die Menschen aus sich heraus und durch einen Umweg wieder in sich hinein zu führen." (2, 9; 127)[88]

The experience of the aesthetic semblance is shown to be educationally productive only for Wilhelm. It does little for Mignon or Aurelie, neither of whom can reach a useful and appropriate understanding of "Schein".[89] Within the sphere of the theatre Wilhelm, however, engages

---

[85] "In the same fashion as the play impulse becomes active in him, and finds pleasure in appearance [semblance], there follows also the imitative creative impulse which treats appearance [semblance] as something absolute." AE by Snell, 126–127. Even in Mignon's transformation into the angel which she plays in Natalie's little play, aesthetic semblance effects a liberation and gives Mignon an idea about her destiny. But in her pre-rational state, Mignon's is the dark inversion of Schiller's hopes, instead of fulfilled humanity she prepares for death.

[86] "Since all actual existence derives its origin from Nature, as an extraneous power, but all appearance [semblance] comes originally from Man, as percipient subject, he is only availing himself of his absolute proprietary right when he separates the appearance [semblance] from the essence and arranges it according to his own laws." AE by Snell, 127.

[87] Otto Rank suggested that writing literature and acting are two complementary ways of coping with, and sorting out, unconscious problems. Cf. *Das Inzest-Motif in Dichtung und Sage. Grundzüge einer Psychologie dichterischen Schaffens.* 2nd edn, 1st edn 1912, Leipzig/Vienna, 1926, p. 216. Quoted in David Roberts, *The Indirections of Desire. Hamlet in Goethes "Wilhelm Meister",* Heidelberg: Carl Winter, 1980, p. 221.

[88] "It is the best way of bringing people out of themselves, and by a circuitous route back into themselves." Moon, 103.

[89] One of the pre-conditions for an education by theatre is the willingness to leave behind social ties and position. From earliest boyhood Wilhelm chooses the theatre as a means of liberation to disengage himself from his bourgeois background, to shed his class-bound skin and develop his true self. Those who are firmly rooted in their respective so-

with Shakespeare and begets his son Felix, both crucial conditions for his further development. The discovery and acknowledgement of Felix as his son by Mariane, the acceptance of his own fatherhood, indeed settles Wilhelm's integration into society. But it only provides the potential of happiness, rather than its actual achievement.

> Er sah die Welt nicht mehr wie ein Zugvogel an, [...]. Alles, was er anzulegen gedachte, sollte dem Knaben entgegenwachsen, und alles, was er herstellte, sollte eine Dauer auf einige Geschlechter haben. In diesem Sinne waren seine Lehrjahre geendigt, und mit dem Gefühl des Vaters hatte er auch alle Tugenden eines Bürgers erworben. (8, 1; 539)[90]

Wilhelm Meister-criticism has pointed out at length how studying and performing *Hamlet* aids Wilhelm in sorting out his antagonism to the bourgeois world and values of his father.[91] But through engaging with Shakespeare Wilhelm also becomes aware of his own identity as a modern individual. The figure of Hamlet functions as the bad example of modernity, with which Goethe initially associates Wilhelm, but which he then lets him leave behind. During the performance Wilhelm experiences the role as if it is happening to himself, which is the basis for its therapeutic effect. It produces the first stirrings of Wilhelm's rise above the Hamletian problem: after the cathartic first night, *Hamlet* becomes quite boring,[92] and eventually the parallels he saw between himself and Shakespeare's character fade. Although there is a note of authorial irony

---

cial spheres, such as the Graf, Wilhelm's father and also Jarno, cannot profit from the theatre because they see it as a sub-social sphere, socially unacceptable in its shady frivolity. It is doubtful whether the latter three could benefit from any art. Wilhelm's father cannot see any point in art, selling his own father's substantial collection to raise funds for his business, and Jarno admits that art is not his métier (8, 5; 588). For the Graf, art is entertaining decoration or panegyric. When he wants to determine the design of Minerva's dress he reveals himself as a pedantic collector of historical details (3, 7; 182–3).

90   "He no longer looked upon the world as a bird of passage [migrating bird, MO]. [...] Everything which he thought of laying out should grow to meet the boy, and everything which he restored [produced, MO] should last for several generations. In this sense his years of apprenticeship were ended, and with the feeling of the father he had gained all the virtues of a citizen." Moon, 430.

91   Cf. David Roberts. *The Indirections of Desire*.

92   "So schlich der Tag nun weiter, und Wilhelmen war noch keiner jemals so alltäglich vorgekommen. [...] Das Interesse an Hamlet war erschöpft, und man fand es eher unbequem, dass er des folgenden Tages zum zweitenmal vorgestellt werden sollte." (5, 13; 353) "So the day passed on and never had one seemed to Wilhelm so dull. [...] The interest in *Hamlet* was exhausted and they found it rather inconvenient that the play had to be performed for the second time the following day." Moon, 283–4.

in this description, mocking Wilhelm's conceitedness, Wilhelm considers himself stronger than Hamlet (and indeed moves on).

> Je mehr ich mich in die Rolle studiere, desto mehr sehe ich, daß in meiner ganzen Gestalt kein Zug der Physiognomie ist, wie Shakespeare seinen Hamlet aufstellt. [...] Zuvörderst ist Hamlet blond [...] als Däne. [...] Die Königin spricht: Er ist fett. [...] Kann man sich ihn da anders als blond und wohlbehäglich vorstellen [...]. Paßt nicht auch seine schwankende Melancholie, seine weiche Trauer, seine tätige Unentschlossenheit besser zu einer solchen Gestalt als wenn Sie sich einen schlanken braunlockigen Jüngling denken [like Wilhelm himself], von dem man mehr Entschlossenheit und Behendigkeit erwartet? (5, 6; 329)[93]

The Abbé is well aware of the (liberating and instructive) therapeutic effect of the aesthetic semblance of art, and of the impact of super-rational, religious experiences, such as the direct revelations that can be provided through it. He aims to combine religious and aesthetic structures in the initiation ritual he devises for Wilhelm, which is based on oracular, pseudo-religious acts. They take place in a disused chapel. The ritual is also a form of theatre: Wilhelm is made to sit down in front of an altar behind which a curtain opens and closes to reveal, in a frame, the Tower's different messengers, i.e. the Stranger, the Parson, the Officer, and Hamlet's father, one by one. The curtain and the frame are reminiscent of the contemporary "Illusionsbühne". All address him with pearls of wisdom and admonitions. Finally the Abbé appears (as himself) announcing that Wilhelm has passed his apprenticeship.

In the presentation of the initiation ritual Goethe alludes to the history of modern drama, and by extension to the cultural-intellectual process of modernity. Furthermore he blends the specifically ancient and modern origins of dramatic art to give an account of the spiritual function of such art. The oracular nature of the utterances and the formerly sacred space allude to the origin of ancient classical theatre in the religious rites accompanying the cult of Dionysos as well as to the origin of modern European theatre in Christian mystery and miracle plays. The-

---

[93] "The more I make a study of the part, the more I see that in my whole form there is no feature of my physiognomy such as Shakespeare presents Hamlet. [...] In the first place, Hamlet is fair [...] as a Dane. [...] The Queen says: He is fat [...]. Can you imagine him otherwise than fair and plump? For dark people in their youth are seldom in this condition. His fluctuating melancholy also, [his soft sadness, MO], his irresolute activity suits better with such a figure than with a slender, dark-haired, young man from whom you would expect more decision and activity." Moon, 263–64.

atre, ancient and modern, developed from the human desire to embel-
lish religious rites as well as the human need to give the supernatural religious content a concrete form, to give the imagination a (revelatory)
picture. But the presentation equally alludes to popular culture: The
"leere, dunkle Öffnung" (7, 9; 531)[94] in which the figures appear can also
be taken to hint at the puppet theatre of popular tradition, which is another ancestor of the modern stage. In addition Goethe suggests that the
Abbé has taken lessons from Northern Europe's most eminent modern
dramatist: the fast-moving mysteriousness of the appearances and utterances, which Wilhelm watches in bafflement and confusion, have something of the magic lantern, to which Jarno likens Shakespeare's plays
(3, 8; 192). On its own the reference to the magic lantern links the
Abbé's production (and by implication Shakespeare) to populist entertainment, i.e. the popular magic lantern shows of the late 18th and early
19th centuries, which hovered on the borderline between charlatanism,
entertainment and artistic mind-expansion.[95]

In the novel the evocation of the origin and history of dramatic art
is not restricted to the sphere of the Tower, it also occurs in the sphere of
the theatre itself. At the party after the successful première of *Hamlet*
Mignon's wild behaviour is likened to that of a Maenad, the braccantic
female revellers of the cult of Dionysos (5, 12; 350), the origin of Greek
drama. Immediately prior to this she had, sitting in a large arm-chair,
been compared to a "Pulcinellpuppe [...] aus dem Kasten"[96] who looks
over the edge of the table in front of her and begins, together with Felix,
to "perform a play", which makes the connection to the indigenous
modern origin of theatre in puppet performances. The difference is that
the Abbé is likely to use these evocations deliberately and consciously in
his ceremony, whereas in the theatre sphere they occur unpremeditated
and unconsciously. By alluding to the different original elements of theatre, Goethe suggests that the latter have accompanied human society
and culture throughout its history in different forms. "Theatre" thus appears as an element of human culture that humanity cannot do without.
For the Abbé, theatre has a function in the educational process. It facilitates self-exploration, but is ultimately geared towards achieving an ex-

---

[94] "empty dark opening".
[95] For a detailed analysis of the nature and influence of magic lantern shows at this time
cf. Rob Elliss, "E.T.A Hoffmann and the Cult of Natural Magic", PhD-thesis Nottingham, 2003.
[96] "puppet from its box".

ternally defined level of understanding of purpose. For Wilhelm, on the
other hand, it *is* education itself by facilitating self-realisation.

The Abbé's approach to the theatre and its enabling use of "Schein" is
subtly criticised through a link with Mignon's (lack of) understanding of
it. The Abbé and Mignon share an objective: both want to disconnect
Wilhelm from the theatre. Mignon: "Lieber Vater! Bleib auch du von
den Brettern!" (3, 7; 184)[97] When Wilhelm signs Serlo's contract she is
quietly and gently trying to pull his hand away from the paper. (5, 4; 315)
And Mignon assists the Tower's efforts directly when she looks after
the mysterious veil featuring the cryptic appellation "Flieh, Jüngling,
flieh!"[98], which the ghost leaves behind, making sure Wilhelm takes it
with him. Mignon's and the Tower's ultimate rejection of the theatre is
rooted in their shared notion that it threatens the perception of reality.
In the case of the Tower it distorts and obscures what they consider real
and important (Wilhelm is to understand the theatre's illusory nature
and grow out of it). In the case of Mignon it dominates and then dis-
solves reality into a labyrinth of unconnected identities. Mignon abhors
the theatre as a predatory machine that deprives her of her dignity and
identity as Wilhelm's chattel. She refuses to do the egg dance on stage
and tells Wilhelm "es [das Kind Mignon] sei nunmehr sein und werde
nicht mehr auf das Theater gehen." (3, 7; 184)[99] Presumably for the
same reason Mignon hates the stage make-up, which she over-zealously
washes off her face. But Mignon has no rational sense of her own identity – which is why she cannot tell whether the make-up has come off –
she can only realise herself by being dependent. Mignon cannot tell
semblance from reality, all semblances have the same reality. Given this
disposition, acting must appear as a shameless usurpation, an unbear-
able prostitution. The Tower Society does not understand this aspect of
Mignon's character. Natalie makes her act the angel in her didactic piece
indented to dispel the myth of Father Christmas and angels in the minds
of her young charges. As the Abbé uses the theatre in the case of Wilhelm, Natalie utilises art for the purposes of enlightenment. The Tower
Society confidently uses appearance to reveal its illusion and foster recognition of what they consider reality. But Mignon cannot play a role,
she transforms into it, refusing to take off her costume after her performance, in expectation of the final transformation, which is death. "So läßt

[97] "Dear Father, do thou too stay away from the boards." Moon, 148.
[98] "Flee, young man, flee!"
[99] "She was now his and would go no more upon the stage." Moon, 148.

mich scheinen, bis ich werde". (8, 2; 553)[100] It is the final relief towards which she gropes in her unenlightened darkness of pain. Although coming from diametrically opposed directions, the Tower Society's view of the theatre and role-playing is as flawed as Mignon's. Neither have an appropriate approach to the use and meaning of semblance (*Schein*), either ignoring is true validity or equating it with reality.

In the wake of Schiller's interpretation, Wilhelm's choice of vehicle for his individuation, the theatre, has been overwhelmingly interpreted as a mistake.[101] But it has become evident that it *is* Wilhelm's vehicle of education, used by the Tower Society as well as himself. There is good reason for regarding Wilhelm's inclination towards the theatre as based on real talent on his part and as a true expression of his individuality that already surfaced in early childhood. The fact that the Abbé accepts Wilhelm's inclination, uses Wilhelm's particular language to educate him, endorses this. One the other hand, another explanation of the Abbé's indulgence of Wilhelm's individual foible could be sought in the Abbé's own leaning towards theatrics. Erwin Seitz, however, has argued that in the *Lehrjahre* the theatre is presented as deliberately misunderstood as an insubstantial diversion, because genuine appreciation of it was still lacking in the Germany of the 1770s and 80s.[102] So the theatre presented as a positive vehicle that is nevertheless widely misunderstood would reflect the contemporary situation Wilhelm found himself in. In this light the Abbé's French identity could explain why he is well disposed to the stage: he comes from a country with a mature theatrical tradition.

In Wilhelm's and the Tower's views two concepts of education clash. This clash hinges on the new notion of individuality, which prioritises individuation over uniformity. Wilhelm's concept, which originates in *Sturm-und-Drang* thinking, is treated ironically by the author. The Tower's concept, which is more beholden to earlier Enlightenment notions of the purpose of education, is identified as dated. Jarno reveals that the Society's practice of teaching others according to their maxims,

---

[100] "Such let me seem, till such I be." Moon, 441, quoting Thomas Carlyle's translation of the verse.

[101] Cf. Jacobs, *Wilhelm Meister und seine Brüder*, 75; Gerth, "'Das Wechselspiel des Lebens'. Ein Versuch, *Wilhelm Meisters Lehrjahre* (wieder) einmal anders zu lesen" *GJB* 113 (1996), 105–20, esp. 106–111, or Blessin, "Die radikal-liberale Konzeption von *Wilhelm Meisters Lehrjahren*" *DVjs* 49 (1975) Sonderheft, 190–225, 196 ff.

[102] Erwin Seitz, "Die Vernunft des Menschen und die Verführung durch das Leben" *GJB* 113 (1996) 121–37. In the same article Erwin Seitz made a case for Wilhelm's talent for the theatre as an undiscredited feature of his individuality.

which they considered infallible – "Wir fingen an nur die Fehler der anderen und ihre Beschränkungen zu sehen, und uns selbst für treffliche Wesen zu halten." (8, 5; 589)[103] – belongs to a past era: "Alles, was Sie im Turme gesehen haben, sind eigentlich nur noch Reliquien von einem jugendlichen Unternehmen, bei dem es anfangs den meisten Eingeweihten großer Ernst war." (8, 5; 588)[104] Their views have been reformed by the Abbé who made them see the self-righteous ineffectiveness of such methods and introduced the priority of individuation into the socialisation process. But the Tower Society's concept of education, reformed or not, is treated with irony, too. The Society advocates that human beings should rely on their own reason – their own individual moral dictates – to lead purposeful lives, but interferes in individual lives like an external agency,[105] which, certainly in the case of Wilhelm, exerts its influence through mysterious, fate-like interventions. This hardly encourages the pupil to believe that the world is a rational place in which the individual fulfils a transparent and clearly understood purpose.

This double ironisation is made possible because on both sides of this educational divide self-reliance and independence seem to stand in conflict with notions of preordained guidance, be they educational guidance (fabricated or real) or providence. The notions of guided improvement by teaching and of self-reliant understanding are both Enlightenment concepts. By setting them against each other, Goethe makes the problematic nature of these Enlightenment tenets visible and sets a dialectical process in motion. The claim that reason is supreme and universal, which makes educational guidance not just useful, but a moral duty and gives providence a rational predictability, became questionable because of the emerging supreme subjectivity of the individual and the historical relativity of values. In turn, the individual claims freedom and independence from any external coercion, because the universal validity of external rules has become doubtful. So (universal) rational expectation is replaced by (individual) unpredictability. Individuality is

---

[103] "We began to see only the faults of others and their limitation[s MO], and to regard ourselves as splendid people." Moon, 470.

[104] "All which you have seen in the Tower are still only the relics of a youthful undertaking, at which there was great earnestness for most of the initiated at the outset." Moon, 469.

[105] It subscribes, or at least subscribed, to the theoretical concept of an apprenticeship in life.

unpredictable because it does not readily conform to a uniform pattern (people are different). Individuality instead develops according to its own inherent pattern. If this pattern is considered to be inherently set, this mindset would encourage a belief in fate, which in turn can lead to a belief in the dominance of an external agency, negating all previously achieved freedom. If education was to have a point in an intellectual situation where the rational expectation of uniformity had been dismissed and the submission to fate was to be avoided, the relation between reason and individual had to change. Previously it had been assumed that reason could be transferred into the individual by teaching. Now, i.e. since Kant, reason is inherently part of the individual, a part that needs to be developed by learning. Wilhelm clearly resents, and rejects, *being taught*. He is, however, not averse to *learning*, particularly when he believes that life and his own inclinations and experiences are his teachers. Crucially, the unpredictably individual can only be *experienced*. Wilhelm is deeply affected by the instructions of the Tower, and he learns from them, but he does not let himself be taught by them. For example when he reads Shakespeare at their behest, he learns about himself from this experience, but the outcomes of this learning are not what the Tower intended.

Thus Goethe exposes the internal dialectic not just of the Enlightenment notions of education and reason, but also of certain *Sturm-und-Drang* ideas. This suggests that in Goethe's view neither the Enlightenment nor *Sturm und Drang* has a truly successful concept of education. Goethe gives the merest hint of a synthesis: in any concept of education that is to be useful under current conditions there must be room for full, but guided, individuation. Enlightenment notions must take account of the rebellious *Sturm-und-Drang* demands of the individual and incorporate the new. The Abbé comes close to this. His concept of learning through error allows the individual a great measure of freedom. His appreciation of different individuals having different dispositions and needing different types of education is not far removed from Wilhelm's ideal of individual dispositions and purposes. The Abbé modified the Tower Society's rigid notions of teaching, of apprenticing and passing individuals, and moved them on towards a new awareness of unique individuality, which corresponds precisely to the emerging awareness of the historicity of reason: the right thing may be very different things under different circumstances. But, as we have seen, the Abbé does not go unchallenged. The *Stiftsdame* comments on his practices as "sonderbarer Versuch" (peculiar experiment) and criticises his anti-devotional (and anti-Cartesian) approach.[106] Her criticism could be dismissed as growing from a superseded consciousness which even precedes that of the Enlightenment. The *Stiftsdame* does not believe the human being capable of prospering when freed from external guidance: "Daß ich immer forwärts, nie rückwärts gehe, [...] läßt sich das alles aus der menschlichen Natur, deren Verderben ich so tief eingesehen habe, erklären? Für mich nun einmal nicht." (6, 452)[107] Natalie's critical remarks must weigh more heavily. She is not convinced that her sister and her youngest brother have benefited from the Abbé approach to education. (8, 3; 559) She has her own views about education, teaching, and guidance and finds universal laws necessary. (8, 3; 566) These criticisms highlight the risky nature of the Abbé's project, which is also evident in his educational failures. Goethe himself remained, it seems, rather uncertain, when he later mused to Eckermann that he must have favoured, rather like Wilhelm, guidance from above, be that God or fate. "Im Grunde scheint doch das Ganze nichts anderes sagen zu wollen, als daß der Mensch, trotz aller Dummheiten und Verwirrungen, von einer höheren Hand geleitet, doch zum glücklichen Ziele gelange."[108]

The uncertainty regarding the efficacy of education, which resulted from the new awareness of individuality and historicity, was of course responsible for the emergence of the "new" genre that the *Lehrjahre* represent: the *Bildungsroman*.[109] The importance, and the problematic nature,

---

[106] "Was ich nicht an diesen Erziehern billigen kann, ist, daß sie alles von den Kindern zu entfernen suchen, was sie zu dem Umgange mit sich selbst und mit dem unsichtbaren, einzigen treuen Freunde führen könne." (6, 451) "But that which I cannot approve of in these instructors is that they seek to withdraw from the children everything which could lead them to intercourse with themselves and with the invisible, only, faithful Friend." Moon, 359.

[107] "That I am always advancing, never going backwards [...]. Can all this be explained from human nature, into the corruption of which I have seen so deeply? For me, now, not at all." Moon, 359.

[108] Zu Eckermann, 18 Jan 1825. Quoted in Jacobs, *Wilhelm Meister und seine Brüder*, 82. "In the end the whole thing does not seem to want to say anything other than that the human being, despite all foolishness and confusion, is guided by Providence [a higher hand] and reaches a happy end."

[109] That it originates in the historical situation and intellectual and aesthetic climate of the *Goethezeit* is well established: Jürgen Jacobs asserts "daß man als 'Bildungsroman' eine bestimmte historische, in der Goethezeit entstandene Gattung zu verstehen habe, kann heute als communis opinio bezeichnet werden." Jacobs, *Wilhelm Meister und seine Brüder*, 14.

of individual "Bildung" rise to prominence in an intellectual and social situation that Jürgen Jacobs characterised as follows:

> Eine Aporie bildet den Hintergrund zur Problematik des Bildungsromans: der Widerspruch zwischen der Ablehnung des festen überlieferten Normenbestandes einerseits und dem gleichwohl fortbestehenden Bedürfnis nach beglaubigten Normen auf der anderen Seite. Dabei verlangt das Subjekt, daß ihm das neue Gesetz nicht als fremdes und äußeres entgegentritt, sondern daß es gewissermaßen auf dem Weg durchs Innere gewonnen wird.[110]

This new education was not achieved without difficulty, a difficulty representing the specific topic of the *Bildungsroman*: "die Identitätssuche im Spannungsfeld zwischen privater Innerlichkeit und gesellschaftlicher Wirklichkeit, zwischen Individuierung und Sozialisation".[111] The *Bildungsroman* attempted to record the bridge-building between the disconnected entities of subject and world, which was to be effected through a gradual process of interlocking. Evidently the *Bildungsroman* tackles the same problem as German Idealism in the wake of Kant's division. Jacobs even described Hegel's *Phenomenology* as "ein ins Philosophische transponierter Bildungsroman".[112] Like Idealism, the *Bildungsroman* is based on the belief in the possibility of achieving a harmonious reconnection.[113] This reconnection is conceived as a process – *Bildungsromane* are

---

[110] Jacobs, *Wilhelm Meister und seine Brüder*, 18. Gerhart Mayer summarised as follows twenty years later: "Die neue, individualistische Bildungsidee entstand während der späten Aufklärung [...]. Der einzelne, aus tradierten ständischen Bindungen mehr und mehr entlassen, begann die gesellschaftlichen Normen und Wertvorstellungen als problematische Fremdbestimmung zu empfinden. Schmerzhaft erfuhr er infolge der rasch voranschreitenden Säkularisierung des christlichen Weltbildes, verbunden mit dem Vordringen des kausal-mechanistischen Denkens, den Verlust der metaphysisch fundierten Seinsordnung. Der bürgerliche Mensch suchte daher nach einem neuen Leitbild, um seine persönliche Identität bestimmen und ein gefestigtes individuelles Weltverhältnis begründen zu können. Die Idee des zur Humanität gebildeten Individuums, in der Aufklärung wenig konkretisiert, gewann gegen Ende des Jahrhunderts Inhalt und Kontur." Mayer, *Der deutsche Bildungsroman*, 21–2.

[111] Mayer, *Der deutsche Bildungsroman*, 21–2.

[112] Jacobs, *Wilhelm Meister und seine Brüder*, 19.

[113] Cf. Jacobs, *Wilhelm Meister und seine Brüder*, 18: "harmonierende Tendenz"; Mayer, *Der deutsche Bildungsroman*, 22: "Die neue Bildungsidee [gewann] [...] ihre Dignität als Schlüsselbegriff der Epoche, als Leitbild humaner Vollendung, gestalthafter Integration der sittlichen Persönlichkeit." In an earlier article Mayer had identified the "menschliche Gestaltwerdung" as a gradual process "towards the idea" that passes through the stages of "Selbstfindung" and "Selbstbegrenzung" until it finally reaches "Selbstgestaltung". The process proceeds by rhythmic change of opposites (diastole and systole). "*Wilhelm Meisters Lehrjahre*. Gestaltbegriff und Werkstruktur" *GJB* 92

always histories –, the process of education represents its gradual achievement. The disparity between subject and world, which is experienced as alienation and overcome by a new, arduously acquired harmony, is fundamentally caused by the awareness of historicity, the temporality of which destroys permanence, but promises change. It is alleviated by a new, striven-for ideal.[114] By refusing to present a unified and universally applicable concept of human improvement though education Goethe takes account of the complex situation that has arisen regarding education due to the emergent awareness of historicity. Like the unpredictable in the individual and in history, Goethe's novel ultimately resists complete rational reduction.[115]

That Goethe engages in *Aufklärungskritik* is well recognised. When criticising the (French) Enlightenment was once – through to the early 20th century – regarded as the individuating signature of German *Geist*, it became after 1945 *de rigeur* to establish that the two great men of Weimar stood firmly in the Enlightenment tradition, which seemed the only way to save them from being implicated in the "German catastrophe". In the animated *Klassik*-debate of the last thirty years more differentiated views have emerged, which recognise that the ideas of the *Goethezeit* depended on as well as diverged from Enlightenment thought.[116] But no interpre-

---

(1975), 140–64. The process of "Gestaltwerdung" that Mayer describes thus shares all key elements with the Hegelian realisation of consciousness, including the dialectical method.

[114] Hegel himself noted the current preoccupation with the development of the hero in contemporary novels and, in his *Ästhetik*, set it in relation to his own notion of the philosophical development of the human intellect in history. Although there are some crucial differences, individuals, just like larger collective historical forces, realise their purpose in the world and, fulfilling it, contribute to the overall progress.

[115] Even such a dedicated champion of the positive achievements of the *Lehrjahre* as Bildungsroman as Gerhart Mayer, who set out to define the "general criteria of the process of human education" (Mayer, "Gestaltbegriff und Werkstruktur", 140) presented in the novel, a process which results in human "Gestaltwerdung", concluded long ago that this human *Gestalt* is "unfathomable" (ibid., 164).

[116] T.J. Reed has argued that the *Lehrjahre* culminate in an abolition of the Kantian notion of rational independence and self-reliance, that human beings have the rational capacity to think and decide for themselves, in favour of an oligarchic guardianship of the truly enlightened. (T.J. Reed, "Revolution und Rücknahme: *Wilhelm Meisters Lehrjahre* im Kontext der Französischen Revolution" *GJB* 107 (1990) 27–43, 39–40.) He explains Goethe's authoritarian turn with the latter's abhorrence of the French Revolution, Goethe preferred "lieber de[n] absolutistischen Regen als die revolutionäre Traufe" (ibid., 36). This restorative tendency occasioned by the Revolution, which wanted to cancel anything potentially revolutionary, was already identified by Giuliano Baioni,

tation focuses on the emergence of historicity as a key factor in Goethe's treatment of Enlightenment ideas. In assessing dependence and divergence in this context much hinges on whether Goethe is thought to discredit the *Sturm-und-Drang* ideas in his novel or not. My reading suggests he achieves a preliminary synthesis of these ideas with the Enlightenment notions within a historically dynamic dialectical framework. Their differences are embedded within the historical development of modernity and their propositions ironised by highlighting similarities or one-sidedness.

The Social Dialectic: Aristocracy and Bourgeoisie

The socio-political development presented in the *Lehrjahre* is also powered by a dialectical dynamic, which Goethe locates in the relationship between the aristocracy and bourgeoisie. In Goethe's day these two social classes faced each other in a social antagonism which was largely responsible for the main political and social event of this period, the French Revolution. (In the context of this investigation this antagonism functions as a dichotomous opposition.) In Wilhelm's encounter with the world of the Graf Goethe presents this social and political opposition as unproductive. But in the mirror-imaging between Lothario and Wilhelm he suggests a beginning dialectical synthesis. The latter pair represent new social types who could be model citizens of an improved future world. Wilhelm is the bourgeois who gains entrance into a circle of enlightened aristocrats, and Lothario the enlightened aristocrat who promotes bourgeois domesticity and engages in the bourgeois business of economic productivity by securing and converting his property, with

who nevertheless argued that rather than abandoning Enlightenment thought Goethe tried to rescue it by restricting its meaning to the realm of the aesthetic and obliterating its radical political potential. "[Goethe und Schiller] vermitteln dem bürgerlichen 19. Jahrhundert die hohe humanistische Tradition der europäischen Aufklärung. Aber diese ausschließlich ästhetische Mission, die sie angesichts der Realität der Revolution ihrer Klasse gegenüber vollbringen zu müssen glaubten, hatte die Tendenz, alle jene fortschrittlichen und revolutionären Fermente zu beseitigen, die von ihrem Sturm und Drang aus an die jungen Vertreter der frühromantischen Schule weitergegeben wurden." (Baioni, "Gesellschaftsidee", 83). Klaus Gerth, on the other hand, stressed the priority of fate over the "optimistic and rational spirit of the Enlightenment" in the *Lehrjahre*, which he argues is an elementary feature of Goethe's *Weltanschauung* (Gerth, "'Das Wechselspiel'", 119). This would suggest that Goethe's criticism of the Enlightenment results from his individual disposition rather than the historical context.

the public-spirited proviso that the greater community (the state) benefits from his possessions and transactions in the form of taxes or lettings.

Lothario went through a process of education that was similar to what
the Abbé envisages for Wilhelm. During his "cultivation" he, too, spent
some time in a space outside parental and class control, to which he had
felt irresistibly drawn since childhood, just as Wilhelm to the theatre. For
Lothario it was the world of soldiering and weapons, to which he felt a
"unüberwindliche Neigung" (4, 16; 282),[117] which he indulged when he
served in the American War of Independence.[118] Like Wilhelm, he was
able to combine indulging this childhood projection of himself with the
idea of serving a social cause of liberation. In Wilhelm's case it was the
founding of a German national theatre, in Lothario's it appears to have
been social and political liberation. Fighting on the side of the break-
away colonies, as a soldier of the revolution so to speak, he must have
been in the company of people who believed in revolutionary republican
political ideals. Lothario's key experiences of "Bildung" took place in
America, i.e. in a socially "free" space, or at least one on the road towards
social emancipation, struggling to leave the European class structure behind along with its colonial ties. But during his life of freedom governed
by vague ideals Lothario realised that his true task was to be accomplished at home, and he returned to an active life in his own society with
the motto "Hier oder nirgends ist Amerika!" (7, 3; 464).[119] He explains:

> Das ist ein Hauptfehler gebildeter Menschen, daß sie alles an eine Idee, wenig
> oder nichts an einen Gegenstand wenden mögen. Wozu habe ich Schulden
> gemacht? Warum habe ich mich mit meinem Oheim entzweit? meine Ge-
> schwister so lange sich selbst überlassen? als um einer Idee willen. In Amerika
> glaubte ich zu wirken, über dem Meere glaubte ich nützlich und notwendig
> zu sein; war eine Handlung nicht mit tausend Gefahren umgeben, so schien
> sie mir nicht bedeutend, nicht würdig. Wie anders seh' ich jetzt die Dinge,
> und wie ist mir das Nächste so wert, so teuer geworden. (7, 3; 464)[120]

---

[117] "insurmountable inclination".

[118] The *Stiftsdame* recalls that "der älteste Sohn meiner Schwester schien seinem Großvater
[...] zu gleichen, [...] auch liebte er, wie jener, der sich immer als ein braver Offizier ge-
zeigt hatte, nichts so sehr als das Gewehr." (6, 449) "The eldest son of my sister seemed
like his grandfather [...] [like him, who had always shown himself to be a brave officer,
he too loved nothing more than guns, MO]". Moon, 357.

[119] "Here or nowhere is America!" Moon, 369.

[120] "That is the great mistake of cultivated men, that they direct everything to one idea,
less or not all [nothing, MO] to an object. Why have I contracted debts? Why have I
quarrelled with

This is the state of mind the Tower Society would like Wilhelm to attain. Like Wilhelm, Lothario is suspicious of one-sided rational understanding, which he believes diminishes the heroic and inspirational capacities of the human being.

> Zu einer gewissen gleichen fortdauernden Gegenwart brauchen wir nur Verstand, und wir werden auch nur zu Verstand, so daß wir das Außerordentliche, was jeder gleichgültige Tag von uns fordert, nicht mehr sehen, und wenn wir es erkennen, doch tausend Entschuldigungen finden es nicht zu tun. Ein verständiger Mensch ist viel für sich, aber fürs Ganze ist er wenig. (7, 3; 464)[121]

Lothario's critique of rationality is, unlike Wilhelm's, primarily concerned with society. The community, not so much the individual, is limited by a dominance of reason. After his period of education, during which he was allowed to indulge himself and make his own mistakes, Lothario seems to have left behind most of his earlier focus on individual self-realisation. Any pursuit of individualism is now limited to the sexual sphere, in which he still follows his individual interests recklessly.

Initially Lothario comes across as the more accomplished and rounded character compared to Wilhelm. The latter certainly experiences himself as inferior, and lavishes abject devotion on the nobleman. "Dieser Mann verdient jede Art von Neigung und Freundschaft, und ohne Aufopferung läßt sich keine Freundschaft denken. Um seinetwillen war es mir leicht ein unglückliches Mädchen zu betören, um seinetwillen soll es mir möglich werden der würdigsten Braut zu entsagen." (8, 4; 574)[122] The Tower Society sets up Lothario as an ideal. Jarno tells Wilhelm:

---

my uncle and for so long forsaken my brothers and sisters, save only for an idea? I thought of doing work in America, beyond the sea. I thought I should be useful and necessary; if a line of action was not surrounded by a thousand dangers, it did not appear to me to be important or worthy. How differently do I now look at things, and how has what is nearest to me become of so much worth and so dear." Moon, 369.

121 "For a certain equable continuous mode of life we want only understanding and nothing more, so that we do not see the extraordinary things which each indifferent day demands of us, and if we do recognise them, yet we find a thousand excuses for not doing them. A man of understanding is much for himself, but little for the general whole." Moon, 369.

122 "This man is deserving of every kind of affection and friendship, and without sacrifice no friendship can be thought of. For his sake it was easy for me to delude an unhappy girl, for his sake it shall be possible for me to renounce the [most] worthy bride." Moon, 458; brackets my addition.

Lernen Sie zum Beispiel Lotharios Trefflichkeit einsehen, wie sein Überblick
und seine Tätigkeit unzertrennlich miteinander verbunden sind, wie er immer
im Fortschreiten ist, wie er sich ausbreitet und jeden mit fortreißt. [...] Vielleicht könnte Lothario in einem Tage zerstören, woran dieser jahrelang gebaut
hat; aber vielleicht teilt auch Lothario, in einem Augenblick, andern die Kraft
mit, das Zerstörte hundertfältig wieder herzustellen. (8, 5; 593–4)[123]

Lothario was instantly popular with early readers. Friedrich Schlegel
calls him "den interessantesten Menschen im ganzen Buch", and found
Jarno's characterisation appealing enough to repeat as his own.[124] Schiller was almost as enthusiastic. When he suggested to Goethe that the
mesalliances at the end needed further explanation he reckoned that this
should be given by Lothario, because "dieser ist der aristokratischste
Charakter. [...] Zugleich gäbe dieses eine Gelegenheit, [...] Lotharios
vollendeten Charakter zu zeigen."[125]

Although he does not feature in many scenes, Lothario's dashing yet
kind, self-assured yet passionate nature and his inspiring charisma obviously had a lot of appeal. He appears as a successful construct of the
ideal German male: the cultured soldier, brave and enthusiastic, with
impeccable manners and a sober yet stylish dress sense who under his
tough manly exterior hides a sensitive nature. "Seine Unterhaltung [war]
belehrend und erquickend; oft bemerkte man Spuren einer zarten Fühl-
barkeit, ob er sie gleich zu verbergen suchte, und, wenn sie sich wider
seinen Willen zeigte, beinah zu mißbilligen schien." (7, 7; 498–9)[126] Aurelie reports that he loved to be addressed with the German version of

---

[123] "Learn, for example, to comprehend Lothario's excellence, how his penetrating glance
and activity are inseparably bound up with one another, how he is always moving onwards, how he gains ground and carries each one along with him. [...] Perhaps Lothario could in one day destroy what the doctor has built in long years; but perhaps
Lothario in one moment might communicate power to others to restore again a hun-
dredfold what has been destroyed." Moon, 474.

[124] "Lothario ist vollendet, seine Erscheinung ist einfach, sein Geist ist immer im Fortschreiten, und er hat keinen Fehler als den Erbfehler aller Größe, die Fähigkeit auch
zerstören zu können. Er ist die himmelstrebende Kuppel." "Über Goethes Meister",
Kritische Friedrich-Schlegel-Ausgabe vol. 2, 146. "Lothario is perfect, his appearance is
simple, his spirit is constantly advancing, he has no fault save the hereditary fault of
greatness, the ability to also destroy. He is the dome stretching towards the skies."

[125] An Goethe, 5 July 1796, *Goethe-Schiller Briefwechsel*, 123. "He is the most aristocratic
character [...]. At the same time this would provide the opportunity [...] to present
Lothario's perfect character."

[126] "His conversation [was] instructive and enlivening; often traces of a tender sensibility
were to be noticed, though he quickly endeavoured to conceal them, and if it showed
itself against his will, he seemed almost to disapprove of it." Moon, 397.

his Christian name. (4, 16; 284) His bride describes herself a "German girl", who tells Wilhelm the story of their relationship sitting under a "deutsche Eiche"(German oak-tree). But Goethe subtly undermines his appeal; he is not quite the good German hero, which pinpoints some of the difficulties of the nascent German identity. Aurelie tells of Lothario's (very un-German) "French" behaviour. Although it is not surprising that as an 18th-century German aristocrat Lothario writes excellent French, the occasion on which he uses this language is interesting. Despite the fact that he can express himself beautifully in this native German according to Aurelie, he falls into French when he intends to leave her. For the nationally minded Aurelie this is a dishonourable and shameful act.

> Während der Zeit unserer freundschaftlichen Verbindung schrieb er Deutsch, und welch ein herzliches, wahres, kräftiges Deutsch! Nun da er mich los sein wollte, fing er an Französisch zu schreiben, was vorher manchmal nur im Scherze geschehen war. [...] Was er in seiner Muttersprache zu sagen errötete, konnte er nun mit gutem Gewissen hinschreiben. Zu Reservationen, Halbheiten und Lügen ist es eine treffliche Sprache; sie ist eine perfide Sprache. (5, 16; 367)[127]

Her beautiful German knight has turned into a faithless, shallow, "perfidious" French lover.[128] And she launches into a denunciation of the French language that anticipates many of Fichte's later criticisms. In every respect the story of Aurelie leaves a blemish on Lothario's heroic character, a blemish that is rooted in his reckless sexual individualism, the one area in which he refuses to submit to the demands of the communal good, which has often been commented on with reproving con-

---

[127] "During the time of our friendly union he wrote in German, and what a heartfelt, true, forcible [strong, MO] German! Now that he wished to be free from me, he began to write in French which previously he had sometimes done only in fun [jest, MO]. [...] That which he blushed to utter in his mother tongue, he could now write with a good conscience. It is a fine language for equivocation, double-entendre and lies; it is a perfidious language!" Moon, 295.

[128] "Ich finde, Gott sei Dank! kein deutsches Wort, um perfid in seinem ganzen Umfang auszudrücken. [...] Perfid ist treulos mit Genuß, mit Übermut und Schadenfreude. [...] Französisch ist recht die Sprache der Welt, wert, die allgemeine Sprache zu sein, damit sie sich nur alle untereinander recht betrügen und belügen können!" (5, 16; 367–8) "I find, thank God, no German word to express in all its compass this 'perfide' of theirs. [...] 'Perfid' means faithless with pleasure, with insolence and malice. [...] French is rightly the language of the world, worthy of being the universal language, so that all may have it in their power to deceive and betray one another." Moon, 295.

sternation.[129] His womanising has been explained as the legacy of his
aristocratic background, which no doubt it is, but he manages to combine it with most bourgeois views on gender difference. While Lothario's desire to marry the illegitimate Therese certainly proves that he
has progressive egalitarian views regarding social origin, he is adamant
that the woman's realm is the home and the man's the world, which is
a notion typical of 18th- and 19th-century bourgeois thinking. (It also of
course points towards the social and political inequality of women inherent in it.) He says he finds it strange

> Daß man es dem Manne verargt, der eine Frau an die höchste Stelle setzen
> will, die sie einzunehmen fähig ist: und welche ist höher als das Regiment des
> Hauses? Wenn der Mann sich mit äußern Verhältnissen quält, [...] überall
> von Umständen abhängt, und ich möchte sagen, nichts regiert, indem er zu
> regieren glaubt. [...] Indessen herrscht eine vernünftige Hausfrau im Innern
> wirklich. [...] Wie wenig Männern ist es gegeben, gleichsam als ein Gestirn re-
> gelmäßig wiederzukehren, und dem Tage, so wie der Nacht vorzustehn! sich
> ihre häuslichen Werkzeuge zu bilden, zu pflanzen und zu ernten, zu verwah-
> ren und auszuspenden, und den Kreis immer mit Ruhe, Liebe und Zweckmä-
> ßigkeit zu durchwandeln. [...] So ist sie von niemand abhängig und verschafft
> ihrem Manne die wahre Unabhängigkeit, die häusliche, die innere. (7, 6;
> 486–7)[130]

His characterisation of female activities likens women to elements of
nature, which underpins the stereotypical division of woman as nature
and man as mind. The woman's debilitating dependence on her man
in economic and social terms in this scenario does clearly not occur to
Lothario as it did to Mary Wollstoncraft at very much the same time.
Thus he promotes the ideal of patriarchal bourgeois domesticity, which,
again, identifies him as a bourgeois aristocrat. As Lothario has no notion
of true equality between men and women, he cannot have any proper

---

[129] Cf. Gerth, 113. Karl-Heinz Hahn, "Adel und Bürgertum im Spiegel Goethescher Dichtungen zwischen 1790–1810" *GJB* 95 (1975) 150–62, 157.

[130] "That we blame the man who sets the woman in the highest place which she is capable
of occupying; and what is higher than the government of the house? If the man tor-
ments himself with other [external, MO] relations, [...] everywhere he is dependent
on circumstances and, I might say, governs nothing, while he imagines he is governing.
[...] To how few men is it given to return regularly as a star, and to stand in front of [to
rule, MO] the day as well as the night; to form their domestic tools, to plant and
to reap, to preserve and to spend, and to wander through the circle always with calm,
love and suitability [practicality, MO]. [...] Thus she is dependent on nobody, and
procures for her husband that true independence, the domestic, the inward." Moon,
387–8.

understanding of Romantic love. He is not in love with Therese, she is simply the right person for the job of his wife. In his many affairs he only ever seems to be in lust. The Romantic lover on the other hand, like Wilhelm, seeks the soul-mate in his partner, which reflects the Protestant origins of the priority of equal male-female companionship in the face of hierarchical constraints and arrangements (which is a different strand of early bourgeois, early modern thinking). This kind of companionship alludes to the fully-fledged modern form of Romantic love. Lothario's lack of understanding of this kind of Romantic love and his belief in socially stabilising gender difference combine with his successful overcoming of his youthful revolutionary (*Sturm-und-Drang*) ideas – which made him abandon his family and fight in America – to reduce his once dangerous revolutionary capacity for social restructuring. He now represents the tamed revolution.

The direction of social development presented in the novel has been interpreted as consolidatory and backward-looking, rather than socially progressive. The bourgeois Wilhelm rebelliously demands liberation from his social confines only to seek acceptance in aristocratic circles, which, just like Wilhelm's choice of the theatre, has been widely interpreted as a misguided notion that illustrates the retardedness of his social and political understanding. The fact that Wilhelm in the end does join the ranks of the progressive aristocracy through his marriage to Natalie, Goethe's "solution" that bourgeoisie and *Reformadel* should unite on aristocratic terms,[131] has been taken to indicate the author's counter-revolutionary restorative intentions, which supposedly amount to a similar political retardation, given the post-revolutionary context in which Goethe was writing.[132] There can be little doubt that Goethe was anti-revolutionary, as is borne out not just in Wilhelm's social journey, but also in the development of Wilhelm's mirror-image Lothario who arrives at a consolidatory position from the opposite direction. The radical aristocrat gives up his revolutionary convictions (his juvenile but productive error) for more evolutionary and oligarchic ideas. But whether such an anti-revolutionary stance can automatically be equated

---

[131] Baioni, "Gesellschaftsidee", 107; Ulrich Stadler, "Wilhelm Meisters unterlassene Revolte. Individuelle Geschichte und Gesellschaftsgeschichte in Goethes *Lehrjahren*" *Euphorion* 74 (1980), 360–74, 373.

[132] Stadler quotes Hans Mayer, *Goethe: ein Versuch über den Erfolg*, Frankfurt aM: Suhrkamp, 1973, p. 98. He himself asserts that Goethe holds on to a pre-revolutionary theory in post-revolutionary times. Cf. Stadler, "Wilhelm Meisters unterlassene Revolte", 373–4.

with reactionary views, which spring from the conviction that progress-ive social change is not necessary, undesirable even, is far less clear.

Careful reading of Wilhelm's letter to Werner shows that Wilhelm does not *just* indulge in backward-looking fantasies of the grandeur and pomp projected by the aristocracy, but also hints at increased levels of personal freedom and political power, which he wishes to claim for him-self.

> Nur dem Edelmann [ist] eine gewisse allgemeine, wenn ich sagen darf perso-nelle, Ausbildung möglich. [...] Wenn der Edelmann im gemeinen Leben gar keine Grenzen kennt, wenn man aus ihm Könige und königähnliche Figuren erschaffen kann; so darf er überall mit einem stillen Bewußtsein vor seines-gleichen treten; er darf überall vorwärts dringen, anstatt daß dem Bürger nichts besser ansteht, als das reine stille Gefühl der Grenzlinie, die ihm gezo-gen ist. (5, 3; 312–3)[133]

Only the aristocrat enjoys freedom and equality. The bourgeois is hemmed in by limits which force him, irrespective of his individual na-ture, to conform to a prescribed one-sided function to such an extent that they alienate his humanity in an exploitative manner.

> Jener [der Edelmann] soll tun und wirken, dieser [der Bürger] soll leisten und schaffen; er soll einzelne Fähigkeiten ausbilden, um brauchbar zu werden, und es wird schon vorausgesetzt, daß in seinem Wesen keine Harmonie sei, noch sein dürfe, weil er, um sich auf eine Weise brauchbar zu machen, alles übrige vernachlässigen muß. (5, 3; 313)[134]

Wilhelm appears to have a fairly clear notion of the need to emancipate the bourgeoisie by extending the aristocracy's rights and freedom to other classes, by democratising their privileges, on the grounds that all (or at least most) human beings have human and civil rights. From this emancipatory angle the initially rather curious term "scheinen" in con-nection with aristocratic privilege – "jener [the aristocrat] darf und soll

---

[133] "A certain general, and if I may say so, personal cultivation is only possible for the nobleman. [...] Since the nobleman in common life knows no limits, since from him kings or king-like figures could be created, he can enter everywhere with a silent con-sciousness as before his equals; he can press forward everywhere, while nothing more becomes the citizen [bourgeois commoner, MO] than the absolutely quiet feeling of the limits which are drawn around him." Moon, 250–51.

[134] "The former [the nobleman] is to ask and make [? influence and act, MO], the latter is to effect and procure [? work and make, MO] – he is to cultivate individual capabil-ities so as to become useful, and it is already presupposed that there is no harmony in his manner of existence nor that there can be, because he is obliged to make himself useful in one direction and must, therefore, neglect everything else." Moon, 250–51.

scheinen, dieser [the bourgeois] soll nur sein" (5, 3; 313)[135] – can be explained. Rather than being an expression of Wilhelm's immature desires to present (mere) appearances, and apart from ambiguously alluding to dazzling glamour, it is possible to associate the term with liberation in Schiller's sense. For Schiller the capability of operating with the semblance of aesthetic representation, which is completely free from utility and profit, distinguishes the human being from non-rational nature. And only through the understanding and operation of the "ästhetischer Schein" can human beings liberate themselves from physical and historical constraints and realise their full humanity.

So the consolidatory tendency, which corresponds exactly to the ordering tendencies of the classical ideals of *Humanität* and *Bildung* as they were defined in the 19th century, is balanced by suggestions in the text that a solution to bourgeois emancipation must be found, that, in effect, only the *methods* of the French Revolution were wrong. The triple mesalliance at the end to some extent validates Wilhelm's aspirations. Schiller spotted the revolutionary (rather than consolidating) implications of these marriages, and was worried about them, because he considered them to run counter to his interpretation of the novel's general tendency. He thought they needed further explaining ("Ich gebe Ihnen zu bedenken, ob der falschen Beurteilung nicht noch durch ein paar Worte 'in Lotharios Munde' zu begegnen wäre."), because he took the book to have "so gar nichts Sansculottisches", on the contrary, "es scheint der Aristokratie das Wort zu reden".[136]

Wilhelm, however, is only concerned with his own individual liberation. Unlike Lothario, he develops no revolutionary intentions on a social scale and appears pessimistic about the prospect of social change, instead he takes whatever route towards *individual* liberation open to him. This accurately reflects the negligible social and political clout of the middle classes in comparison to the political power and maturity of the nobility.

> An diesem Unterschiede [...] ist die Verfassung der Gesellschaft selbst schuld; ob sich daran einmal etwas ändern wird und was sich ändern wird, bekümmert mich wenig; genug, ich habe, wie die Sachen jetzt stehen, an mich selbst

---

135 "The former has a right to seem, the latter only to exist." Moon, 251.

136 An Goethe, 5 July 1796, *Goethe-Schiller Briefwechsel*, 123. "You may wish to think about whether a few words from Lothario might not, after all, countermand wrong judgements." "The book has no Sansculotte element, indeed it seems to promote the views of the aristocracy."

zu denken, wie ich mich selbst und das, was mir ein unerläßliches Bedürfnis ist, rette und erreiche. (5, 3, 313)[137]

Goethe suggests that the path towards social improvement via aesthetics and culture is dictated by (Germany's) social and political conditions rather than being a matter of free choice.

Form: Friedrich Schlegel's *Universalpoesie* and Herder's *Volkspoesie*

Goethe's novel is famous for its symbolic density, its repeated mirrorings and juxtapositions that create a web of complex interrelated meaning. This complex form makes possible the presentation of the complex dialectics within their timescapes outlined in the previous chapters. No spheres or characters are isolated from the rest, or even mere opposites. Opposites are set up and connected, which makes visible their common origin and as well as the inevitably historical process of their becoming (opposites), and the potential path towards their prospective synthesis. The relations between Mignon and the Harper and the Tower Society are the crucial example of this practice. On the other hand, opposites derived from distinct origins are linked by parallels which suggest a structural similarity that may lead to future synthesis. The mirror-imaging of Wilhelm and Lothario and the relationship between the Abbé's and Wilhelm's concepts of education are examples of this. These inter-relations create a complex network of internal dynamics that depicts a reality in constant flux. Frequently the images contain fragmentary allusions to archetypal situations, a practice that Hannelore Schlaffer has aptly called "Diaphanie",[138] and which extends the fluidity beyond the historical past to an ontological one.

This fluidity of constantly shifting ground corresponds to the experience of existing in a world that is conditioned by impermanence, the

---

[137] "This difference is caused [...] by the constitution of society itself; whether it will ever be changed and how it will be changed troubles me but little. As matters now stand I have enough to do to think of myself and consider how I can save myself and reach that which is indispensable for me. [Enough, as matters now stand I need to think of myself and how I can save and reach that which is indispensable to me, MO]." Moon, 251.

[138] H. Schlaffer, *Wilhelm Meister. Das Ende der Kunst und die Wiederkehr des Mythos*. Stuttgart: Metzler, 1980, p. 3. Similarly identified by David Roberts at the same time. Roberts, *The Indirections of Desire*, 224.

pre-condition of the awareness of historicity. Such a fluid structure, deeply chaotic to the individual inhabiting it, yet revealing a never-ending spiral of mirrorings to the observing reader, is Goethe's response to the destabilising progress of time.[139] It manages to focus on the multi-facetted potential of the moment without denying the moment's place in a progressive chain of events, and achieves what Martin Swales called the "*Nacheinander* of plot and the *Nebeneinander* of human totality and potential".[140] Its complexity may ultimately have baffled the author himself when he remarked with hindsight of the *Lehrjahre*: "Es bleibt daher dieses eine der incalculabelsten Produktionen, man mag sie im Ganzen oder in ihren Teilen betrachten; ja, um sie zu beurteilen, fehlt mir beinahe selbst der Maßstab."[141] At the same time the reflection of characters and situations in counterparts or archetypes creates, through recognition by the reader, a symbolism that suggests harmony and completeness even though these suggestions never achieve lasting stability. Although the characters are realistic, the setting contemporary and the coincidences just that, everything is in time revealed to be symbolic. This essentially mythic quality has made the text such a happy hunting ground for psychoanalytical, structuralist and deconstructionist interpretations. Through the symbolic method a chaotic reality acquires the potential of structure, order and meaning, through its fluidity it desists from being fully conclusive.[142] Goethe manages to combine fluidity with symbolism – the symbolism is born out of the fluidity – without allowing one to cancel out the other.

This structural form is responsible for Friedrich Schlegel's enthusiasm for the book, because it corresponds to, possibly even conditioned, his emerging theory of progressive universal poetry.[143] Goethe's text cer-

---

139 With his structural interlockings and repeated mirrorings, Goethe clearly achieves an integration of subjective viewpoint and objective breadth without having crudely delineated voices. Reality appears exactly as Wilhelm experiences it, full of mysterious coincidences and options, which he tries to order. But at the same time the reader is aware that Wilhelm's point of view is not the only one.

140 Martin Swales, *The German Bildungsroman from Wieland to Hesse*, Princeton, N.J.: Princeton University Press, 1978, p. 157.

141 Quoted by Gerth, "'Das Wechselspiel'", 105.

142 Hannelore Schlaffer pointed out that Goethe's practice of "Diaphanie", whereby ordinary reality is constantly shot through with mythic allusions, prevents rational conclusiveness, which in her opinion represents a victory of poetry over prose. Schlaffer, *Wilhelm Meister*, 7.

143 Henry Hatfield suggested that the formulation of *Athenäum Fragment* 116 is indebted to the *Lehrjahre* in general, conceptually and stylistically to the "Lehrbrief" in particular:

tainly does "zwischen dem Dargestellten und dem Darstellenden [...] auf den Flügeln der poetischen Reflexion in der Mitte schweben, diese Reflexion immer wieder potenzieren und wie in einer endlosen Reihe von Spiegeln vervielfachen." It has "was ein Ganzes in ihren Produkten sein soll, alle Teile ähnlich organisiert".[144] Over thirty years after he published the *Lehrjahre*, and ironically at the height of the "Romantiker-streit", Goethe endorsed crucial aspects of Schlegel's theory to grasp the totality of modern reality when he wrote to K.J.L. Iken in 1827: "Da sich gar manches unserer Erfahrungen nicht rund aussprechen läßt, so habe ich seit langem das Mittel gewählt, durch einander gegenübergestellte und sich gleichsam ineinander abspiegelnde Gebilde den geheimeren Sinn dem Aufmerkenden zu offenbaren."[145] Already in 1810 Goethe had noted down in his diary that when describing (a) life, "satisfying totality" could only be created through a combination of detached irony and restrictive one-sidedness:

> Ironische Ansicht des Lebens im höheren Sinne, wodurch die Biographie sich über das Leben erhebt. Superstitiose Ansicht, wodurch sie sich wieder gegen das Leben zurückzieht. Auf jene Weise wird dem Verstand und der Vernunft, auf diese der Sinnlichkeit und der Phantasie geschmeichelt, und es muß zuletzt, wohl behandelt, eine befriedigende Totalität hervortreten.[146]

The *Lehrjahre* must have galvanised Schlegel's ideas about the necessity and characteristics of the novel as a new genre that corresponded to his notions of modernity, because it could be modern and mythic, prosaic and poetic at the same time. It was the medium in which modernity could bring forth its own myth. Schlegel's review focused on the formal

---

"To sum up, one can perhaps say that Schlegel attributed to poetry the varied and magnificent powers which Goethe ascribed to mankind as a whole." "*Wilhelm Meisters Lehrjahre* and 'Progressive Universalpoesie'" *Germanic Review* 36 (1961) 221–229, 229.

[144] Athenäumfragment 116, *Kritische Friedrich-Schlegel-Ausgabe*, vol. 2, 182–3. "What is supposed to be a complete whole in all its products, [it has] all of its parts organised similarly."

[145] 27 Sept., quoted by Schlaffer, *Wilhelm Meister*, 7. "As many matters of our experience cannot easily be put into words, I have for a long time chosen to juxtapose creations that are opposite and, as it were, reflect one another in each other as a means to reveal a more secret meaning to the attentive reader."

[146] Diary entry 15 May 1810. Quoted by Mayer, "Gestaltbegriff und Werkstruktur", 162. "[An] ironic view of life in a higher sense, through which biography rises above life. [A] superstitious view, through which it retreats back towards life. The former way appeals to understanding and reason, the latter to the senses and the imagination, and in the end, if it is done well, a satisfying totality must emerge."

method of Goethe's text rather than the aim of the action.[147] Schiller, one remembers, was pleased with what he considered the limiting closure, but had doubts as to whether it really was as definite as he would have wished. He remained worried about the comedy-like ending, its *ex-machina*-like character, which he felt was unrealistic. Both Schlegel and Schiller sensed that Goethe's ending was provisional, preliminary, that decisions are deferred, and that the future remains unknown. By refusing to define the future, Goethe leaves the unpredictability of history intact. Through the novel's capacity to express, and satisfactorily contain, the complex conditions of a world aware of its own preliminary nature, which Schlegel defined and which Goethe delivered, Schlegel's theory and Goethe's novel acquire the particular "modernity" that Martin Swales identified as a characterising feature of the German *Bildungsroman*,[148] but which really underlies much of the intellectual and aesthetic German endeavours around 1800.

Goethe chose to address vital contemporary intellectual and social concerns. His topics are the relations between the mythic and the (dominant) rational, between the individual and (dominant) society, and between the middle classes and the (dominant) aristocracy. Every relationship in this list is the result of a completed and the basis of a projected new historical development and contains the struggle for the redefinition of the current dominance. The struggles occur in the contexts of paradigm shifts in the late 18th-century on the philosophical, aesthetic

---

[147] Ernst Behler suggested that Friedrich Schlegel could praise the form and developing content of the novel without misunderstanding or wilfully misinterpreting the ending. As Behler pointed out, Schlegel left his interpretation of the end of the novel vague in his review of 1798, to avoid a clash with his notion of ideal poetry to which he clearly thought this work could aspire (and which would forbid any sort of limiting closure). Ernst Behler, "Wilhelm Meisters Lehrjahre and the Poetic Unity of the Novel in Early German Romanticism", *Goethe's Narrative Fiction. The Irvine Goethe Symposium*, Berlin/New York: de Gruyter, 1983, pp. 121–2. Schlegel rejected what Behler considered Goethe's "classical restraint" (ibid., 121). Behler claims that different notions of poetic unity explain this difference. Schlegel himself distinguished between esoteric and exoteric poetic unity in 1803. The exoteric variety is limited to the "Ideal des Schönen im Verhältnisse des menschlichen Lebens", the limitation of the classical, while its esoteric counterpart expands to include also "the world and nature" (ibid., 122). Because of its exoteric limitations, its apparent closure, Goethe's *Wilhelm Meister* was not Romantic in Schlegel's sense. It is well known that the book fared badly among Romantic thinkers in the new century. Most famous is Novalis' stinging criticism, which sees in Goethe's novel only a "novel against poetry".

[148] Swales, *The German Bildungsroman*, 147.

and social level. These shifts are carried by the emerging middle classes who were reaching a critical stage of self-awareness and wished to liberate themselves from current power structures. It is their situation, purpose and future that Goethe's novel addresses. Stefan Blessin has made a case for regarding the emerging principles of the free market economy as the structural basis for the events in Goethe's novel.[149] Blessin pointed out that the central problem of accommodating the autonomy of the individual with a social model based on reason and prosperity is common to the contemporary philosophies of history and the classical theory of national economy (Adam Smith). As it is also defined as the central issue of the *Bildungsroman*, the latter precisely reflects the intellectual and economic problems of the time. Following Baioni's characterisation of Wilhelm and Werner as the "two paradigmatic souls of the bourgeoisie"[150] and Swales' assertion that the *Bildungsroman* "embodies some of the deepest aspirations of bourgeois society"[151], one feels inclined to regard the *Lehrjahre* as presenting the drama of the middle classes.

For the rendition of this drama Goethe chose the middle classes' own preferred literary genre. While the novel was, despite his *Werther*, still to some extent regarded as sub-literary in the later 18th century – Friedrich Schlegel's theory of the novel as *the* modern form of literature was only formulated at the very end of the century –, it represented, as *Trivialroman*, a commercially highly successful genre, read by the literate book-buying bourgeoisie. Goethe chose a populist, "low cultural" medium that had particular resonance with the audience whose problems it addresses. The dominant force in terms of concerted activity in the novel is the Tower Society. For its organisational structure Goethe borrowed the popular element of the Secret Society from the "trivial novel", tapping into populist literature and using its forms and elements for his poetic purposes. This is a stock *Sturm-und-Drang* practice that Goethe had already employed in the *Urfaust*, and would continue to use for the completion of *Faust I*. It is akin to the practice of writing *Kunstballaden*. In both cases popular, simple structures that may have a long tradition – which in this case would be the prose tale – are adapted for modern artistically sophisticated creations with the intention of making the art work particular, i.e. part of a viable tradition which was shared by its

---

[149] Stefan Blessin, "Die radikal-liberale Konzeption von *Wilhelm Meisters Lehrjahren*" *DVjs* 49 (1975) Sonderheft, 190–225.

[150] Baioni, "Gesellschaftsidee", 111.

[151] Swales, *The German Bildungsroman*, 148.

audience. In the case of the novel, these simple popular structures also have a "folksy" dimension in the sense that they develop "unconsciously" as a sub-literary genre in response to popular demand. What results is, according to the concept of *Volkspoesie*, art that engages the human being not just on the rational or aesthetic level, but through their particular milieu. In this respect Goethe's novel is (Kunst-) *Volkspoesie* for the middle classes.

The German Dimension: The Socio-Economic Conditions of the Post-National

It is evident that Goethe's novel is responding to the intellectual and poetic challenges of its time and is part of the intellectual landscape of the closing years of the 18th century in Germany. The *Bildungsroman* has for a long time been defined as a specifically German response to the general as well as the specifically German intellectual and historical situation around 1800. Martin Swales considered it a German speciality that must appear "alien" and "foreign" to English readers (but would nevertheless make very profitable reading for them).[152] This insistence on a sharp demarcation from the Western European tradition has a critical tradition reaching back to the 19th century, which emphasised the German self-definition as a *Kulturnation* reliant on *Bildung* as it had developed around 1800. In the later 19th century, as literary studies had established themselves as an academic subject, the idea of Wilhelm's progress towards a classical ideal of the understanding of life, which largely relies on Schiller's take on *Wilhelm Meister* in particular and on Hegel's take on the *Bildungsroman* in general, became a critical commonplace. Wilhelm Dilthey, who is generally credited with introducing the first theory of the *Bildungsroman* into German literary studies, although he did not coin the phase, asserted in 1870 that "Göthes Werk [*WM*] zeigt menschliche Ausbildung in verschiedenen Stufen, Gestalten, Lebensepochen."[153] In 1906 he fleshed out these stages:

> Von dem Wilhelm Meister und dem Hesperus ab stellen sie alle den Jüngling jener Tage dar; wie er in glücklicher Dämmerung in das Leben eintritt, nach verwandten Seelen sucht, der Freundschaft begegnet und der Liebe, wie er

---

[152] Cf. Swales, *The German Bildungsroman*, 146–7.
[153] Quoted from Dilthey's *Leben Schleiermachers* I by Jacobs, *Wilhelm Meister und seine Brüder*, 11.

nun aber mit den harten Realitäten der Welt in Kampf gerät und so unter
mannigfachen Lebenserfahrungen heranreift, sich selber findet und seiner
Aufgabe in der Welt gewiß wird.[154]

The notion of *Wilhelm Meister* as the classic example of a *Bildungsroman*
has its origin in the same intellectual milieu as the notion of *Deutsche
Klassik* and is equally part of the effort to consolidate a German national
identity. In the wake of Dilthey's definitions regarding the *Bildungsroman*, the latter became seen as evidence of the nation of poets and
thinkers. Rolf Selbmann speaks of an "ideologische Verhärtung des Gat-
tungsbegriffs"[155] when in 1906 H. A. Krüger defined the (contemporary)
German *Bildungsroman* as:

> Eine Romanart, die ein ganz ausgesprochen nationales Gepräge trägt, wie sie
> eigenartiger und individueller kein anderes Volk aufzuweisen hat, den deut-
> schen Bildungsroman, der im letzten Jahrhundert ganz eigentlich der Roman
> der Dichter und Denker war und voraussichtlich auch bleiben wird.[156]

Karl Vietor still spoke of the "klassische Bildungsroman der Deutschen"
in 1949.[157] In the past half-century the notion that Wilhelm has been
formed to conform to a classical ideal, that he has learnt anything, has
found many detractors, and with good reason. It seemed that Novalis'
negative assessment of the outcome of the novel now appeared much
more to the point than Schiller's. The interpretation of Wilhelm's successful integration into a "classical" ideal of purposeful living had become seen as part of the anti-Western German self-definition that created the *Klassiklegende* of the Bismarck-era, which was implicated in
facilitating the development towards Nazi rule. The classical ideal had
become suspect, and could only be saved by being turned into an Enlightenment ideal. But even that was a difficult rescue mission: an ideal
of ordered harmony could hardly find favour with the next generation
of critics who, imbued with the revolutionary zeal of the 1960s, set out
to question all traditional structures of hierarchy and order.[158]

---

[154] Quoted by Jacobs, ibid., from Dilthey's Hölderin-essay *Das Erlebnis und die Dichtung.*
[155] Selbmann, *Der deutsche Bildungsroman*, 18.
[156] H.A. Krüger, "Der neuere deutsche Bildungsroman" *Westermanns Monatshefte* 51. Jahr-
gang, vol. 101, part 1 (1906) 257–72, 270. Quoted by Selbmann, *Der deutsche Bildungsroman*, 18.
[157] K. Vietor, *Goethe. Dichtung – Wissenschaft – Weltbild.* Bern, 1949, p. 131. Quoted by Seitz,
"Vernunft des Menschen", 121.
[158] First cautious doubts regarding the classical ideal had already been raised by Max
Wundt in 1913 (cf. his *Goethes "Wilhelm Meister" und die Entwicklung des modernen Lebens-*

The perceived absence of direct political and social engagement became seen as indicative of the political immaturity of the Germans, which became disastrously evident in the first half of the 20th century when the same Germans showed themselves willing to embrace totalitarianism rather than parliamentary democracy. The particular political and economic situation in late 18th-century Germany, which made political participation difficult for the economically prospering middle classes, was time and again identified as the cause for the German preoccupation with inwardness. And this inwardness was regarded as a key factor in paving the way for the rise of the Nazi dictatorship, because the cult of inwardness was said to have bred the lack of political interest and sophistication that led to a rejection of rational modern notions of citizenship and liberalism by the Germans.[159] Superficially it seems as if the early theorists dealing with the German situation, identity and purpose, such as Schiller and the Schlegels, had themselves stylised this absence of direct political and social engagement as proof of cultural purity and that they celebrated national and political retardation. No doubt there is an element of making a virtue out of a necessity in their insistence on the priority of culture. But first and foremost Schiller and Fichte regarded the lack of German involvement in international power politics as an enabling condition that opened up perspectives and created possibilities for the Germans that others did not have. And these possibilities were decidedly political in the long term, because the aim was the creation of a better, even a perfect, society and state. Education must precede politics, but does not replace politics. That some of these ideas, which all revolve around the German mission in world history, have been the basis from which totalitarian theories of politics and statehood have developed is a different matter.[160] Although it may appear immature from a Western viewpoint, it is short-sighted to allege that the German self-definition of around 1800 is politically backward-looking.

Increasingly the *Bildungsroman*, as the story of an individual development that is focused on intellectual and philosophical issues, became

ideals, Berlin: Göschen, 1913) in the climate of *Jugendstil* which first discovered German Romanticism as a viable alternative to German *Klassik*.

[159] In his conclusion, Swales traces this line of thought and then rejects it, arguing that the poetic and intellectual complexity of the *Bildungsroman* already problematises these issues. Swales, *The German Bildungsroman*, 146–60, esp. 156/7.

[160] Cf. Bernd Fischer, *Das Eigene und das Eigentliche: Klopstock, Herder, Fichte, Kleist. Episoden aus der Konstruktionsgeschichte nationaler Intentionalitäten*, Berlin: Erich Schmidt, 1995, pp. 230–270.

identified as an indicator of how the German development diverged from Western patterns. Indeed the *Bildungsroman* even came to be regarded as the German "substitute" for the *Gesellschaftsroman*, or social novel.[161] In places like Britain and France the social novel was taken to demonstrate a well-developed awareness of social and political processes. Substituting it with the *Bildungsroman* suggests the lack of the latter. More specifically, it has been argued that the final version of the *Lehrjahre* represents a response to the French Revolution, and functioned as a safety valve, suggesting a turning-away from political questions to the "safer" ground of education and culture.[162] From this perspective the *Bildungsroman* becomes the anti-politicising tool of reaction, a piece of what Jürgen Habermas identified as the "Öffentlichkeitsersatz"[163] of the politically disenfranchised German bourgeoisie. The notion of national and political retardation has haunted the German self-understanding and its appreciation by others ever since the bourgeois rising was suppressed in 1819 and failed again in 1849. It stands in the background of most academic discussions ever since Helmut Plessner formulated his influential thesis on this matter.[164] To be sure, placing the *Bildungsroman* in such a German "Sonderlingsecke"[165] has been questioned, but primarily on the premise that novels of individual development in other national contexts also include internal development. For example, the structure which integrates individuation and socialisation is the recognised basis of the Victorian novel. Parallels are rarely drawn the other way round: that the German *Bildungsroman* is politically and socially self-conscious.

Critics have claimed that the *Lehrjahre* illustrate a lack of understanding of political and social developments because they are assumed to have a counter-revolutionary (pro-Ancien Régime) message. Along the same line of interpretation the *Lehrjahre* cannot claim to be a *Gesell-*

---

161 Cf. Wilhelm Voßkamp, "Der Bildungsroman als literarisch-soziale Institution. Begriffs- und funktionsgeschichtliche Überlegungen zum deutschen Bildungsroman des 18. und beginnenden 19. Jahrhunderts." in Christian Wagenrecht, ed., *Zur Terminologie der Literaturwissenschaft*. Germanistische Symposienberichtsbände 9, Stuttgart: Cotta, 1988, pp. 337–52. Also Olaf Reincke, "Goethes *Wilhelm Meisters Lehrjahre* – ein zentrales Kunstwerk der klassischen Literaturperiode in Deutschland" *GJB* 94 (1977) 137–187, 186.
162 Reed, "Revolution und Rücknahme".
163 Habermas, *Strukturwandel der Öffentlichkeit. Untersuchungen zu einer Kategorie der bürgerlichen Gesellschaft*, 4th edn, Neuwied/Berlin: Luchterhand, 1969, p. 17.
164 Plessner, *Die verspätete Nation*.
165 Selbmann, *Der deutsche Bildungsroman*, 23.

schaftsroman in the sense of those English and French specimen because they do not describe a vigorous struggle between rivalling classes. The parameters of this definition deserve to be questioned. Goethe's novel indeed does not describe a confident and established middle class engaged in doing things rather than thinking them. But he *does* depict a dynamic of social rivalry, which is borne out in the social dialectic examined above. Everything in Goethe's novel has a social *as well as* a philosophical and a historical dimension: Wilhelm's bourgeois background, the Tower Society's aristocratic origin, the theatre's extra-social position within society. Goethe depicts contemporary German society with great precision. That ideas about citizenship are voiced only by the aristocrats, Lothario and Jarno, i.e. by members of the politically experienced class in Germany, does not necessarily mean that Goethe promoted a return to the practices of the *Ancien Régime*, but it reflects his belief that aristocrats are most likely to engage in such considerations at this time. What might appear as Goethe's lamentable withdrawal from the real social issues of his time into an unpolitical aesthetic domain of culture and education and his seemingly conservative answer can be interpreted in a very different way. Stefan Blessin argued in his provocative – equally illuminating and one-sided – interpretation of the *Lehrjahre* that Goethe was fully aware of the irreversible social and political change the French Revolution had brought and was searching for a way in which this change could be progressively accommodated in a modern bourgeois society without the need for a violent revolution. According to Blessin Goethe's solution is the following: he makes market forces the organising principle of his novel, which do not need, nor have any room for a public authority such as a constitutional state. He concluded that Goethe presents the abolition of feudalism in favour of a radical form of bourgeois economic liberalism, which has transcended the need for the power of the state.

> Für den Autor der Lehrjahre [heißt] die Alternative nicht: ancien régime oder Französische Revolution, [...] sondern die Verwirklichung bürgerlicher Freiheiten mit oder ohne Gewalt. In dieser Frage hat sich Goethe für eine liberale Tradition entschieden, die das Marktprinzip mit Gewaltlosigkeit identifiziert. [...] Die den Lehrjahren zugrundeliegende [Machtausübungs-]Konzeption folgt weder der einen [Hobbes] noch der anderen [Locke] Seite, weil in ihr genaugenommen gar kein Platz für eine dem Marktgeschehen übergeordnete öffentliche Gewalt ist.[166]

---

[166] Blessin, "Radikal-liberale Konzeption", 215–16.

This interpretation relates directly to my findings regarding post-national German identity. While my interpretation does not primarily see the key reason for the nature of this identity in a radical application of the liberal tradition of the market principle, but in the awareness of historicity, it is not difficult to see the connection between these two reasons. Both focus, or rely, on individual contributions in a world in constant flux. The *particular* is vital for anything to happen, or to progress, but it can never assume dominance, because it is always countered by another particular. In either case Goethe shows himself post-national in the same sense as the theorists discussed in chapter 3. By suggesting that the political structure of the (constitutional nation) state may not be the aim of historical, social, and now economic development, he almost foreshadows the post-national capitalist world of globalisation and multi-nationals. While the capitalist free market is clearly not of German origin, Goethe may well have recognised that its international implications on an economic level corresponded precisely to the German self-definition as post-national on the intellectual level. By skipping the national stage the Germans may leap ahead to the international stage of universal, or global, humanity.[167]

Most critics agree that Goethe sought a non-violent solution to the intellectual and social crisis that gripped Europe in the last decade of the 18th century. Evidently such a search is not necessary reactionary. An abhorrence of the violent developments in France was not restricted to the German thinkers of Weimar classicism, it was equally widespread in socially and politically advanced Britain. By expressing and presenting a concern for the development of the contemporary individual's inner self Goethe indeed shares a German preoccupation, but this does not preclude a social dimension in the novel, nor does this betoken an unwillingness, or inability, to engage with political issues. What Goethe depicts is not so much unpolitical as *not exclusively* political. Into the depiction of contemporary society Goethe weaves the presentation of the contemporary intellectual landscape and its cultural history, which presents a picture of reciprocal dynamics between historical, intellectual and social conditions.

---

[167] Such an aim would be similar to Hegel's, i.e. a fully integrated world, but their paths towards it are very different.

Chapter 5

Historicity as Identity: The German Myth of Modernity in Goethe's *Faust I*[1]

Faust I grew from the basis of a *Sturm-und-Drang* text concerned with addressing contemporary problems through culturally original and relevant materials into a fully-fledged representation of the cultural historicity of modernity. This development was driven by the desire to approach universals by integrating historical particulars into a temporally progressive and cumulative structure. It produced a complex mythic timescape, which stretches throughout modernity, but frequently also alludes to pre-modern elements, both classical-ancient and Northern-archaic. Contained in this timescape Goethe presents complex constellations within modernity between the "original" and the "advanced", and between ancient and modern. These constellations are expressed as synchronic dichotomies and dialectical progressions at the same time. The primary focus is not, as has often been claimed, on a universal human identity, but on the emergence of a modern identity. (The concept of a universal humanity was, however, linked to modern humanity as a future prospect.) The intellectual objective of integrating historical particulars was shared by the German Idealists and the Early Romantics, and the two founders of Weimar classicism, whose thinking was suspended between the former two. Weimar classicism aimed at integrating a precise historical awareness of its own cultural position and condition with a desire for the more time-resistant structural aspects of humanity. The German intellectual situation was by contemporary thinkers believed to be particularly well suited to achieve such an integration of historicity and identity within a modern framework. It was to

---

[1] Here only "Der Tragödie erster Teil" will be treated because its genesis covers the different periods discussed in this study.

be an integration that deliberately went beyond particular and national limits, although this openness is itself an aspect of its particularity.

This belief in certain time-resistant aspects of humanity – what tends to be referred to as "das Reinmenschliche" – has frequently been taken to indicate the ahistorical, conservative (even reactionary) nature of German classicism.[2] Conceptually this interpretation is supported by the notion that any classicism must necessarily be ahistorical because it is by definition based on a belief in universal – i.e. unchangeable – values. But German classicism is a special case, occurring after the crisis of rationality had made unquestioned adherence to universal ideals impossible and carried by people who as young men had been instrumental in bringing this crisis to a head. Goethe and Schiller may have been horrified by the course the French Revolution took and may have turned their backs on direct political involvement and the immediate reorganisation of society through any form of executive force, but they did not forget their early lessons about the importance and power of historical change.

French classicism had to cope with the Enlightenment notion of continuing progress and improvement. French classicism managed to do this during the late 17th and early 18th century because this classicism and the enlightened belief in eventual perfectibility shared the conviction that the constancy of human nature and the constancy and knowability of truth are immutable. German classicism emerged in a far more precarious situation regarding intellectual stability. It had to cope with the increasing unreliability of both these constancies, which only leaves two options: unmitigated relativism or a historically conditioned notion of perfectibility, which only allows for the historically limited perfection of particulars along the way.

Under such conditions any aspect of humanity persisting through time must be approached through the lens of historical awareness. One may attempt to strip humanity to its core, but at the same time humanity can only be presented as within its specific historical situation, which in Goethe's case is modern. The modern historical situation was defined through a double relation to antiquity: *both* as modern in

---

[2] Goethe's political activities at the Weimar Court indeed evince political conservatism. Cf. W. Daniel Wilson, *Geheimräte gegen Geheimbünde. Ein unbekanntes Kapitel der klassisch-romantischen Geschichte Weimars*, Stuttgart: Metzler, 1991. But they cannot be equated with the intellectual concerns and artistic expression that dominate this work of literature.

contrast to ancient *and* as modern in *succession* to ancient, which is the basis for the historical dialectic examined in this study. This historical dialectic involves recourse to the "original-natural" of modernity, i.e. to materials, such as myths or folk-tales, that are seen as connected to the origins of modern culture. Such materials offer the opportunity to present the original nature of modernity in relation to its subsequent historical development. On the one hand this suggests structural equality between ancient and the modern culture: both have distinct cultural origins which define them. On the other hand, setting Northern and ancient mythic elements in context to each other and designating them as pre-modern provides modernity with two predecessors, so identifying its historical position as successor integrated into historical development. By contributing to a precise positioning of *ancient* and *modern* in cultural history this practice also makes it possible to point towards the place and purpose of modernity in "universal history" as it appears in contemporary philosophical theories of world-history. Any form of universal humanity only reveals itself through its disparate parts as they occur in time and space, none of which are alike. If these parts can be related to each other without losing their distinctive character, a complete – albeit preliminary and prospective – picture of (European) humanity and its history would emerge.[3]

Goethe's *Faust* presents the modern condition in exactly this way: by dealing with its historical genesis and development. Its historically dialectical nature (i.e. being original *and* advanced) makes this presentation fluid and shifting, which has resulted in the wide divergence of interpretation in *Faust*-criticism over two centuries. But in recent times an instance of agreement has established itself: that Goethe's play presents the drama – or is it the tragedy? – of modernity. Separated by twenty years, Werner Keller and Hans-Jürgen Schings give the same definition: Faust "steht repräsentativ für den modernen Menschen" (Keller)[4], repre-

---

[3] Undoubtedly, in Goethe's day European humanity would have represented universal humanity as the (European) world was thoroughly Euro-centric (despite becoming increasingly aware of "other" cultures, such as Far Eastern ones). Two hundred years later the ancient-modern cultural paradigm can only be taken to represent European humanity. Even though the *Goethezeit* thinkers may have believed they were treating universal humanity, it is evident that they constructed this humanity historically, without a presupposed constancy of features.

[4] W. Keller, "Der klassische Goethe und sein nicht-klassischer Faust" *GJB* 95 (1978) 9–28, 27.

sents "das Unglück des modernen Charakters schlechthin" in a "Tragödie des rigoros Modernen" (Schings).[5] Keller's and Sching's modernity is
marked by the despair caused by the perpetual frustration of unbound
subjective desire for the impossible, which has of course been a key aspect of the definition of (Romantic) modernity since Goethe's day. In
the definitions of Schlegel and Schiller, however, this "difficult" modernity was in the end redeemed by its problematic features. Keller and
Schings, on the other hand, define a problematic modernity that in
Faust only finds negative expression. Both critics arrive at the conclusion
that the Faust-figure is intended not as a model, but as a warning.
Schings declared that "[Fausts] Unruhe stellt sich frontal und fundamental [...] gegen die Prinzipien der klassischen Lebenskunst. Unbegreiflich, [...] wie man da einen Triumph des Strebens wahrhaben
möchte, wo er in Wahrheit seine ganze 'Unseligkeit in diesem Leben' of-
fenbart".[6] Schings here alludes to the glorification of Faust's titanic and
unrestricted striving, which has played such a problematic role in the interpretation of Faust as a model of a specifically modern German identity.[7] Keller's and Sching's evaluations mark a key shift in *Faust*-criti-
cism: that from hero to problem-figure, which in West German research
has been prevalent since the end of the Third Reich.[8] However, seeing
Faust as deeply problematic is not at all unprecedented. Contemporary
reactions after the publication of the 1808-version contained many critical and shocked voices.[9] But this critical approach evaporated once the
Klassik-Legende had been created. The problematic view of the Faust-
figure that has dominated the last few decades corresponds to a similar
shift in *Wilhelm Meister*-criticism, whereby the *Bildungsroman* par excellence comes to be seen as the story of an education the outcome of
which is hard to pin down, a view that was most radically and pro-

[5] J. Schings, "Fausts Verzweiflung" *GJB* 115 (1998) 97–123, 97 and 99. Cf. also Benno von
    Wiese quoted in Neil Brough, *New Perspectives of Faust. Studies in the Origins and Philos-
    ophy of the Faust Theme in the Dramas of Marlowe and Goethe.* Frankfurt aM: Peter Lang,
    1994, p. 194.
[6] Schings, "Fausts Verzweiflung", 121–22.
[7] "Liegt nicht gar in dieser Verwechslung die Einbruchstelle für die Ideologie des 'Fau-
    stischen' mit ihren bekannten Folgen?" Schings, "Fausts Verzweiflung", 99.
[8] Cf. Karl R. Mandelkow, "Wandlungen des Faust-Bildes in Deutschland"; Jane K. Brown,
    Meredith Lee, Thomas P. Saine, ed.s, *Interpreting Goethe's "Faust" Today*, Columbia, SC:
    Camden House, 1994, pp. 239–51.
[9] Cf. Hans Schwerte, *Faust und das Faustische. Ein Kapitel deutscher Ideologie*, Stuttgart: Klett,
    1962, pp. 42–54.

vocatively formulated in Karl Schlechta's thesis of Wilhelm's "Abstieg". Such critical, or even negative, evaluations of the "message" presented by Goethe pose a double problem for a positive evaluation of German intellectual and literary history in a post-1945 context. Such negative evaluations undermine the prescriptive dominance of *Klassik* as a specific and particular German achievement, which it had acquired in the wake of the *Klassik-Legende*. Such undermining may appear justified when it is assumed that this specific and particular German *Klassik* is implicated in the German deviation from (West-)European values, which culminated in the Nazi dictatorship. But the irredeemably negative evaluations of Wilhelm as a non-achiever and of Faust as the symbol of an "unhappy modernity" also undermine the rescue attempts mounted on behalf of Weimar classicism. Interpretations aimed at rescuing *Klassik* claimed that it had been wrongly appropriated by the propagators of the *Klassik-Legende* and the *Deutsche Bewegung* as anti-Enlightenment and thus wrongfully implicated in the anti-Western German hubris, and suggested that it was instead a continuation (or German version) of the Enlightenment.[10] The negative evaluations make an association with optimistic Enlightenment notions of progress difficult, thus damaging the safety net that the pro-Enlightenment interpretations have extended. These interpretations also turn the key works of *Klassik* into examples of non-*Klassik* when they claim that these works present an insoluble problematic. And indeed, both Keller and Schings arrived at the conclusion that the Faust-figure contradicts Goethe's "classicism". Keller solved the "classical" problem by suggesting that Faust has to be seen both in relation and in contrast to Wilhelm Meister, with whom he forms a classical unit of two opposing halves.[11] (For Keller Wilhelm has remained a success.) Such an integration of *Klassik* and non-*Klassik* follows the same pattern as recent endeavours to integrate counter-Enlightenment into

---

[10] Cf. Gottfried Willems' (much debated) article "Goethe – ein Überwinder der Aufklärung?" *Germanisch-Romanische Monatsschrift* 40 (1990), 22–40, J. A. McCarthy, "Klassisch Lesen" *Jahrbuch der deutschen Schillergesellschaft* 36 (1992) 414–32, and also Dieter Borchmeyer, "Wie aufgeklärt ist die Weimarer Klassik?", ibid., 433–440. And T.J. Reed, "Die Geburt der Klassik aus dem Geist der Mündigkeit" *Jahrbuch der deutschen Schillergesellschaft* 32 (1988) 367–74.

[11] "Der sich selbst verabsolutierende Faust, der seine unbeschränkte Freiheit nicht in freie Selbstbeschränkung umwandeln kann, wird überdies relativiert in der Spiegelung durch Wilhelm Meister. [...] Erst die Vereinigung der Gegensätze [...] ergibt die Lebenstotalität – die humane Ganzheit des Menschen, auf die es Goethe ankommt." Keller, "Der klassische Goethe", 27/8.

Enlightenment in the sense of an unavoidable internal dialectic,[12] thus reiterating the problematic nature of modernity as Goethe and his contemporaries saw it.

Goethe's works surely have the scope to accommodate both perspectives: they present figures that are achieving heroes and deeply problematic characters at the same time. This puts Goethe's writings at the forefront of literary and intellectual developments at the turn towards the 19th century and also gives them their modern, even post-modern, qualities. If Goethe's works refuse to bow to any one clear ideal, this already indicates that the time of static ideals was irrevocably past.[13] The shifts in interpretative focus identified above are thus less an indication of increasing clarity about Goethe's "real" aims, but reflect the changing circumstances that make one "side" appear more prominent at any one time (which of course is also a key quality of truly *mythic* materials).

However, to return to the common denominator in most Faust-interpretations, if Goethe deals with modernity, or with modern humanity, how exactly does he *construct* this modernity in *Faust I*? Surprisingly little attention has been given to this question. A close look at the origins of the different strands of material that make up *Faust I* will serve as a first orientation.

The Materials of *Faust I*

With the Faust-material Goethe chose a modern myth that is set against the spiritual background of Christianity. The Faust-legend originates in the 16th-century, the time of the Reformation, of the spreading impact of Renaissance ideas and the beginning of the scientific revolution, and it proliferated throughout the next 200 years. Reading widely in the older Faust-literature, Goethe was well aware of the historical roots of his material.[14] Neil Brough has pointed out that the Faust-story belongs in the context of the 16th-century devil-literature in Germany, the rise of

---

[12] Cf. Christop Jamme, "Klassische Aufkärung oder aufgeklärte Klassik?" *Jahrbuch der deutschen Schillergesellschaft* 36 (1992) 414–46. And also *Aufklärung und Idealismus*, ed. by C. Jamme and G. Kurz, Stuttgart: Klett-Cotta, 1988.

[13] Martin Swales summed this up in his "Goethe's Analysis of Modernity", *Goethe at 250=Goethe mit 250. Goethe Symposium*, Munich: Iudicium, 2000, pp. 9–18, 11.

[14] He located the legend's origin in the 16th century, its "Ausbildung" the 17th. Cf. Letter to Zelter, 16/11/1829, quoted by Ann White, *Names and Nomenclature in Goethe's Faust*, London: University of London, Bithrell Series vol. 3, 1980, p. 96.

which Brough links to the religious controversies the Reformation engendered.[15] The self-reliance of the individual soul, propagated by the
Reformation, which occurs in the Renaissance context of emerging individualism and subjectivism, necessarily brings in its wake the direct
confrontation between man and the devil. When Goethe began work on
his drama in the early 1770s, his choice of material was in keeping with
the *Sturm-und-Drang* aspiration to create a relevant modern poetry that
reached beyond the contemporary to the historical origins of modern
identity. Such aspirations suggested material from the newly defined
original period of modernity, which was considered to stretch from the
decline of the Roman Empire to the Reformation. The sensitive and historically minded reworking of such material could be the basis for effecting a reconnection of contemporary culture to the natural-original,
which was considered desirable in Herder's newly developed *Sturm-und-
Drang* concept of literature, and would continue to be important in
Friedrich Schlegel's Romantic concept of poetry as well as in Schiller's
aesthetic education. It is well known how dark and nebulously Northern
his material appeared to Goethe after he had first put it aside. But in the
folk-tale of the man who bartered his soul to the devil Goethe found all
he needed to present the current intellectual crisis of modernity. His
own additions to the traditional Faust-material, i.e. the witches and the
Gretchen-story, make visible the pre-history, emergence, and resulting
nature of modernity, i.e. the additions take account of the material's historicity.

Already in *Urfaust* Goethe had attached the story of Margarete/
Gretchen to the traditional Faust-material. While the connection of
these two stories was entirely his own idea, Goethe probably picked up
the key-elements of Gretchen's story, including her name, from a
number of related popular ballads.[16] "Margaret's Ghost", "Sweet William's Ghost" and "Sweet William and Fair Margaret" all revolve around
the same characters and deal with love, betrayal, desertion, haunting,
and black magic. All feature in Thomas Percy's *Reliques*, a book that
Goethe is known to have revered from the early days of his friendship
with Herder in Strasbourg. In "Margaret's Ghost" and "Sweet William
and Fair Margaret" the deserted girl haunts her lover as a ghost, which
may be the inspirational seed for the idol's appearance in *Walpurgisnacht*.
In "Sweet William's Ghost" the lover returns at night as a somewhat sat-

---

[15] Brough, *New Perspectives of Faust,* 36.
[16] Cf. Ann White, *Nomenclature,* 73.

anic, ghost-like figure to take the girl away with him, a departure that
manifests itself in her death. Thus "Sweet William's Ghost" deals with
the issue of breaking the social and religious rules governing sexual conduct (i.e. having a lover at all, and a satanic one to boot), which are also
key topics in Goethe's story of Gretchen. This ballad may also have
given Goethe the idea for Faust's appearance in the dungeon.[17] Both the
Margaret of "Sweet William and Fair Margaret" and Gretchen take up
with a lover who has (access to) a spiritual dimension beyond ordinary
reality and ordinary life. In both cases this dimension comes across as
doom-laden and possibly satanic. While Margaret is taken away by her
devilish lover on a magical horse in the night, Gretchen declines a similar offer at the end of her story on earth. Undoubtedly Goethe made
Gretchen's story a great deal more realistic, i.e. less gothic – despite the
many gothic elements in *Faust I* and the Gretchen-tragedy[18] – than those
of her ballad-sisters, but it is not difficult to see how the ballads present
key elements of Gretchen's story seen through the metaphysical, metaphorical and sensationalist lens of the popular imagination. Percy,
Herder and Goethe took these British ballads to be extant remnants of
old post-classical European traditions, which to them meant that they
were not only naturally, inherently, modern, but also expressed modern
conditions historically. They are hence similar in cultural originality to
the Faust-story. These ballads treat the topic of Romantic love, which
defies not just social and religious dictates, but rationality and ultimately earthly life. Thus they were suited to the contemporary taste of
the Gothic and of *Empfindsamkeit*, but they also express the uncompromising nature of Romantic love, which is defined as distinctly modern.[19]
Missing in those ballads is the deserted mother's infanticide. With this
element Goethe added a contemporary social and legal problem to the
Gretchen-plot, which as the story of the corruption of innocence was
also in tune with a prominent 18th-century preoccupation that decisively
influenced the emerging genre of the contemporary social bourgeois tragedy. So in both Faust's and Gretchen's case Goethe uses (historical)
folk-traditions to explore contemporary problems. By connecting the
Faust-material with the Gretchen-story he links the problems of the

---

[17] "Sweet William's Ghost" was of course reworked as one of the most popular *Kunstbal-laden* of the time, Bürger's "Lenore" (1773).
[18] Cf. Jane and Marshall Brown, "Faust and the Gothic Novel", *Interpreting Goethe's "Faust" Today*, pp. 68–80.
[19] Cf. *Lehrjahre*-chapter, "Mignon and the Harper".

modern intellect with the problems appertaining to the modern concept of love, a connection that spans the philosophical-spiritual and the sensual-natural aspects of modern humanity. But how exactly are these two strands brought together?

In the gradual re-workings that finally resulted in *Faust I*, Faust's involvement with the devil – or the tragedy of the scholar – and his involvement with women and society – the tragedy of Gretchen – are linked through material that Goethe drew from the hinterland of Christian superstition: the world of witchcraft. Again, this material is historically distinctly modern in origin; its heyday coincides with the rise of the Faust-story at the beginning of the early modern period when interest in (and fear of) witches resulted in a European-wide witch-hunting hysteria. In Goethe's day the witch topic also had a folksy dimension: although witchcraft was still punishable by law during Goethe's lifetime,[20] the belief in witches was being relegated to the uneducated classes. More recently anthropology has identified in the practices of witchcraft the remnants of ancient rituals, while psychology recognises in the demonisation of witches a social mechanism for the suppression of the subconscious. Goethe already uses the witch material in exactly these two ways. Thus the intellectual condition of modernity is linked to its emotional counter-part, i.e. the modern concept of Romantic love, through material exploring "origins", i.e. early cultural activities and pre- and non-rational mental regions.

The witch-scenes serve to open the Gretchen-action (*Hexenküche*) and to initiate its closure (*Walpurgisnacht*). They form a contrast to Faust's world of the intellect, by presenting the sensual in the shape of femininity. They put Faust in touch with the woman who will be his delight, his victim, his scourge and, eventually, his saviour. In these two scenes Gretchen does not appear as herself, but as an apparition,[21] foreshadowing her appearance in the flesh in the subsequent scenes. These metaphysical appearances identify her connection with this sphere as

---

[20] The last two executions of convicted witches took place in Germany in 1749 and 1774 respectively. Cf. Albrecht Schöne, "Faust, Paralip. 50", *Johann Wolfgang von Goethe*, ed. by Heinz Ludwig Arnold, Munich, Text und Kritik Sonderband, 1982, p. 195.

[21] I feel free to choose one of the possible identifications of the beautiful woman Faust sees in the mirror in the witch's kitchen. It is evident that no final decision on whether it is Helena or Gretchen can be inferred from the text, i.e. Goethe must have intended the ambiguity, and the choice. Within the context of *Faust I*, Gretchen obviously makes more sense.

only *imagined*, illustrating her intense effect on the imagination of the protagonist, who is the medium for these apparitions. *Hexenküche* introduces the theme of the sexual and makes Faust's amorous adventure possible: sexual relations are the topic of the Gretchen-story that follows. *Walpurgisnacht* summarises Faust's progress as a questing human being, and predatory lover, and forces Faust to face some of the consequences his striving has produced.

In *Hexenküche* Faust encounters, for the first time it would appear, the world of the feminine as it exists under patriarchal conditions. In a male-run world the female has two functions: as sexual object and as keeper of the kitchen. As keeper of the kitchen the witch-woman has a certain degree of autonomy and authority. She is the head of this establishment, runs her servants (the "Magd" and "Knecht") and is referred to by them as "Frau", the original meaning of which is "lady" in the sense of denoting a social position of power.[22] But in the greater scheme of things, the lady of the kitchen is subject to male dominance as Mephisto makes clear by asserting his power in traditional patriarchal terms, i.e. through violence in general and the threat of sexual subjugation in particular. Thus femininity is clearly presented as oppressed and exploited: Mephisto uses the witch's skills and powers, which he lacks, for his own purposes. The witch is as dependent on her male lord, as confined within the rigid structures of her society, as is Gretchen.[23]

But in this scene the feminine is not just oppressed and exploited, it also emerges as the "other" of (male) rationality and logic.[24] Mephisto understands the witch's "Hokuspokus" as little as Faust, except that he knows it has its uses: Mephisto, unlike Faust, is fully aware that the non-

---

[22] The witch's housewifely activities and her relation to Mephisto echo descriptions of successful housekeeping put forward by Lothario in *Lehrjahre*. She brews her potions which quietly ferment over time. This female business of quietly producing sustenance is reminiscent of Lothario's praise of the crucial female role in a well-run house. "Wie wenig Männern ist es gegeben, […] sich ihre häuslichen Werkzeuge so zu bilden, zu pflanzen und zu ernten, zu verwahren und auszuspenden." (*Lehrjahre*, 7, 6; 487).

[23] The demonic darkness of the scene is alleviated by the comedy elements which suggest a parody of patriarchal conditions. This is a safe, i.e. non-revolutionary undertaking, because this underworld of devils and witches is a carnival-like "world upside-down".

[24] Cf. Barbara Becker-Cantarino, "Hexenküche und Walpurgisnacht. Imagination und Dämonie in der frühen Neuzeit und in *Faust I*" *Euphorion* 93 (1999) 193–225. "Das Andere der Vernunft […] wehrte sich gegen die rationale Verdrängung und ist – so meine These – von Goethe in der Figur der Hexe und deren Welt rekodiert worden." Ibid., 194.

rational has its place in the human make-up. Mephisto also knows about the history of the modern European witch. By addressing her as "Sibyl" he alludes to her earlier status as wise-woman and prophetess. Thus Mephisto's address of the witch as sibyl conjures up an echo of antiquity in modernity.

Her arts enable Faust to experience life in its fullness. The original Sibyl provided Aeneas with the mythical Golden Bow that enabled him to enter the underworld. While the Sibyl of Cumae's act provided the Greco-Roman hero with an enlightening experience, under modern Christian conditions the witch's assistance can, on the surface, only provide a licence to sin for Faust, a shift that is in keeping with the demonisation of the wise-woman in Christian modernity. Significantly her "Kunst ist alt und neu"[25] (l. 2559),[26] but in her present incarnation, Mephisto suggests, she is connected to Christian modernity by representing the dark flip-side of Christianity. She is indebted to the theory of the trinity. "Es war die Art zu allen Zeiten, / Durch Drei und Eins, und Eins und Drei / Irrtum statt Wahrheit zu verbreiten." (ll. 2560–62)[27] The witch's cultural descent not only hints at the descent of the modern from the ancient, and the oppositional relation between the two, but equally suggests the presence of something archaic underneath the surface of modernity. This archaic in humanity is the sexual and the non-rational, which, anarchic and untamed, represents a constant challenge to the established order. The natural, in its pre-rational and pre-modern state, is original (and constructive, as the Sibyl) *as well as* anarchically archaic (and destructive, as the witch) depending on how it is handled by the culture and society surrounding it.[28]

---

[25] Johann Wolfgang Goethe, *Faust. Der Tragödie erster Teil,* Stuttgart: Reclam, 1986, repr. 1995. Reclam's edition is based on the Weimerer Ausgabe of 1887. References are in the following giving in line numbers.

[26] "The art's both new and old." *Johann Wolfgang von Goethe. Faust. Part One.* Translated with an introduction by David Luke. Oxford/New York: Oxford University Press, 1987, p. 80. Forthwith Luke. Wherever the line references are identical they will not be repeated.

[27] "Let error, not the truth be told- / Make one of three and three of one; / That's how it always has been done." Luke, 80.

[28] Goethe hints, most historistically, that even this manifestation of the archaic is subject to the erosive impact of time. The Sibyl of legend is an extremely old woman who lives through much of history, but did not enjoy immortality. At her own request, the Sibyl of Cumae had been granted the life-span of a thousand years, which still leaves her bound by time, a historical creature who has no claim to eternal validity.

The witch-theme amalgamates a culturally precise position with deeper archaic layers. The witch is clearly rooted in Christian superstition, i.e. located in modernity. In her pernicious and satanic dimension, she is even more precisely placed in the early modern context of witch-hunting hysteria, which belongs to the same context as the increasing interest in the devil in the wake of the Reformation, which generated the original Faust-story. The early modern period saw witches as colluding with blasphemy, but also involved in forbidden activities indulging in orgiastic excesses or using magical powers to achieve "unnatural" or "improper" ends. On the other hand, with the onset of modernity in the narrower sense, i.e. Goethe's time, and its intellectual interest in cultural history, the witch-figure became recognised as the demonised version of the wise-woman of ancient, pre-Christian times, whom the Christian religion's claim to supremacy could not tolerate, because she represented links to an ancient (in both senses) religious mysticism.[29] Such a view suggests the existence of a pre-Christian cultural nucleus within modern culture that stretches the roots of modernity down into a pre- or even non-modern identity. The "other" comes into view as part of a dichotomy, as evil, and as part of a historical development, as the non-rational, at the same time, setting in motion a two-fold dialectic dynamic.

With the witch-matter Goethe drew on legendary material from a crucial period of modernity, i.e. when a historically grounded cultural self-consciousness first emerges in European thought. He perceived in this material an archaic nucleus that allowed him to use its figures and practices to represent that which modern-Christian culture had come to deem as suspect: the non-rational and subconscious workings of the mind (which had dominated an earlier stage of humanity) and the sen-

---

[29] This historical "deconstruction" of Christian-medieval and early modern legendary materials and folk customs into archaic and mythic elements, which is not just a scientification, but also a secularisation, was stimulated by Herder's investigations into *Volkspoesie* and culminated in Jacob Grimm's *Deutsche Mythologie*, first published 1835 and expanded in 1844. Herder's investigations were originally inspired by the desire to provide modernity with its own cultural origin that would ground its identity as safely as that of antiquity had been grounded by classical mythology. Grimm's efforts were based on the assumption that an equivalent mythology must lie buried underneath the cultural superstructure of Christianity, which had to take up a relation to the culture which it was supplanting. This relation can tentatively be described as suppression through appropriation.

sual experiences of the body celebrated in ancient rituals.[30] This gives the modern material a universal ("rein-menschlich") oppositional dimension – rational/non-rational, conscious/subconscious, mind/senses – without abandoning its historical particularity because Goethe suggests that beyond the dichotomy there is a historical relation between the two. It also makes modern culture genuinely equivalent to the combination of specificity and universality that Goethe and his contemporaries so admired in the ancients. In this light it can be no coincidence that Goethe first conceived the *Hexenküche* in Italy. Through this practice he effects a mythologisation of modernity by means of its own indigenous materials.

The three stands of material that Goethe drew on in *Faust I* – Faust-legend, Gretchen-story, witch-culture – are culturally modern-Christian, all three treat contemporary issues alongside the historical origin and development of modernity, and all three reveal modernity to be in crisis. The legend of the Renaissance alchemist-magician who enters into a pact with the devil is used to explore the problems of the disillusioned Enlightenment thinker. The story of the deserted Margaret of the folk ballads is used to address problems in contemporary society – unwed mothers turning infanticides and the exploitation of one social class by another – and to explore the nasty consequences attendant on the titanic individualism propagated by the *Sturm-und-Drang* rebels. Finally, the devil and his witches reveal archaic layers in intellectual-rationalist modern culture and in the modern psyche that allow a treatment of the "other" of rationality, of the non-rational and subconscious, a positive evaluation of which had recently – since *Sturm und Drang* – begun to help question the rule of reason. These choices of material and their treatment result in a complex construction of the present in relation to its past, developed out of the past and in contrast to it, which achieves a sense of history as well as an ever-lasting present. It is a present that is, and always has been, dialectically productive.

---

[30] The sensual-physical was suspect throughout Christian modernity including the medieval period. The suspicion of the non-rational has been prevalent since the rise of rationalism from the 16th century onwards, i.e. from the beginning of what in current historical terminology is referred to as modernity. It could be argued that medieval mysticism not only condoned, but encouraged non-rational experiences through its celebration of spiritual ecstasy. It is, however, important to note that the latter were considered to have a direct relation to the divine, not the individual, which makes them externally instigated, rather than sub-conscious. When the sub-conscious was dark and impenetrable, i.e. not illuminated by divine intervention, it was evil.

Faust and Mephisto

The simultaneous construction of oppositional as well as synthetic relations, such as have been traced between and within the strands of material, is also evident in the relations between the three main characters. Each one forms an opposition with each other one, but in each opposition similarities can be traced that suggest a potential synthetic relationship between each pair. For Faust and Mephisto this is well known, but little attention has been given to the *historical* nature of their similarities.

It is well recognised that the tragedy of the scholar which unfolds in the "Night"- and "Study"-scenes pinpoints a crucial aspect of modernity as it was being defined around 1800. Conditioned by the spiritual dictates of Christianity, which focus on a world beyond the concrete that can only be striven for, the scenes present an individual in the process of completing his liberation from these dictates, while remaining unmistakably marked by this conditioning. Goethe presents the whole process of liberation, or secularisation, by amalgamating its start, i.e. the Reformation, and finish, the Enlightenment, when he suggests both a 16th-century as well as an 18th-century background to these scenes. The Gothic architecture of the room places Faust vaguely at the end of the medieval period, his reference to Nostradamus's prophecies more precisely in a 16th-century context (or later). The fact that he is a university teacher, but does not seem to be a cleric, again suggests a post-medieval background. On the one hand Faust is the early modern Renaissance scholar who is emancipating himself from the prescriptive dogmatism of medieval Christianity. His attempt to translate the Gospel of St. John allusively links him with Martin Luther and reformatory religious activity in the 16th century. On the other hand, much of what he says betokens the disillusionment of a frustrated rationalist and empiricist, who has renounced faith, but found no illumination in rational investigation and empirical research.

> Und [ich] sehe, daß wir nichts wissen können!
> Das will mir schier das Herz verbrennen.
> Zwar bin ich gescheiter als alle die Laffen,
> Doktoren, Magister, Schreiber und Pfaffen;
> Mich plagen keine Skrupel noch Zweifel,
> Fürchte mich weder vor Hölle noch Teufel –
> Dafür ist mir auch alle Freud entrissen,
> Bilde mir nicht ein, was Rechts zu wissen,

Bilde mir nicht ein, ich könnte was lehren,
Die Menschen zu bessern und zu bekehren. (ll. 364–73) [...]
Beschränkt von diesem Bücherhauf,
Den Würme nagen, Staub bedeckt, [...].
Mit Gläsern, Büchsen rings umstellt,
Mit Instrumenten vollgepfropft,
Urväter Hausrat drein gestopft –
Das ist deine Welt! Das heißt eine Welt!
Und fragst du noch, warum dein Herz
Sich bang in deinem Busen klemmt? (ll. 402–411)[31]

He has come to question the Protestant aspiration of converting the erring flock to the true religion as well as the Enlightenment tenet of improvement by teaching, of achieving perfectibility by increasing knowledge. He has left behind the original (and formative) spirituality of modernity, i.e. (Catholic) Christianity, but also appears to be dissatisfied with its intellectual legacy, Protestant and Enlightenment thought. Rather like Augustin in the *Lehrjahre*, he has gone through much of what modernity had to offer spiritually and intellectually. The characteristic feature of the modern individual, the striving for a "higher" fulfilment, is still his most prominent trait. For him, this higher fulfilment consists of achieving perfect, complete knowledge. "Daß ich erkenne, was die Welt / Im Innersten zusammenhält." (ll. 382–3)[32] But he rejects the piecemeal nature of the results that intellectualising and empirical research produces. Nature, he concludes, will not be understood by dissection, but by empathy and experience.

Ach! könnt ich doch auf Bergeshöhn
In deinem [des Mondes] lieben Lichte gehn,
Um Bergeshöhle mit Geistern schweben,

---

31 "And I see all our search for knowledge is vain, / And this burns my heart with bitter pain. / I've more sense, to be sure, than the learned fools, / The masters and the pastors, the scribes from the schools; / No scruples to plague me, no irksome doubt, / No hell-fire or devil to worry about- / Yet I take no pleasure in anything now; / For I know I know nothing, I wonder how / I can still keep up the pretence of teaching / Or bettering mankind with my empty preaching. [...] Hemmed in by books to left and right / Which worms have gnawed, which dust-layers choke, / [...] These glasses, boxes, instruments, All stuffed and cluttered anyhow, / Ancestral junk – look at it now, / Your world, this world your brain invents! / And you still ask why your heart / is pent and pining in your breast." Luke, 15–16.

32 "To grant me a vision of Nature's forces / That bind the world, all its seeds and sources / And innermost life." Luke, 15.

Auf Wiesen in deinem Dämmer weben,
Von allem Wissensqualm entladen,
In deinem Tau gesund mich baden! (ll. 392–97)[33]

The Faust-character expresses very precisely the doubts regarding rationalism and the emphatic wish to commune with nature holistically, which
characterise *Sturm-und-Drang* ideas. But Faust reckons that direct access
to nature is denied him, hence the subjunctive mood of impossibility in
"Oh, sähst du" (l. 386) and "Ach! könnt ich doch".[34] He is too much of
an intellectual, or of a rational human being, to assume he could simply
(re-)join the natural world. He believes the only way out of his dusty
walled-up dungeon and towards perfect knowledge, which his rational
and empirical enquiry has found barred, is through "die Magie". He turns
to the magic signs in the prophecies of Nostradamus to try to access the
beauty of the cosmos.[35] The magical fulfils a twofold purpose: to produce
the desired revelation and make rational enquiry redundant: "Die Kräfte
der Natur rings um mich her *enthüllen*" (l. 438), followed by "Jetzt erst *er-
kenn* ich …" (l. 442). This revelation is to be achieved not through intellectual speculation or inquiry but sensual and emotional experience as
the italicised words in the following lines make clear: "Ha! welche Wonne
fließt in diesem Blick" (l. 430), "Ich *fühle* junges […] Lebensglück" (l. 432),
and "das arme *Herz* mit Freude füllen" (l. 436).[36] Already here, before his
discussions with Mephisto, Faust edges towards replacing thought with
experience. Although the aim is still acquiring knowledge,[37] it is now to

---

33 "Oh, take me to the hilltops, there / To wander in the sweet moonlit air, / By mountain
   caves, through fields to roam, / Cleansed by book-learning's fog and stew / And healed
   by bathing in your dew!" Luke, 16.

34 "If you could see" and "if only I could".

35 Although Nostradamus was an astrologer at the French court, the Church had always
   remained dubious about astrology (astronomy even), because it was too close to sooth-
   saying. That acquiring knowledge from magical sources is not sanctioned by religious
   and social laws and has to be done in secret is clearly suggested by the "Bürgermädchen"
   in "Vor dem Tor", who will not associate with the witch-like sooth-sayer in public, but
   uses her services clandestinely to find out about her prospective husband. This is historical packaging which derives from late medieval morality literature and was still
   prevalent in the later 18th century, placing the plot in a precise early modern context.

36 "The powers of Nature all about me are revealed"; "at last I understand", Luke, 17. "Ha!
   What joy flows in this look"; "I feel a youthful happiness to be alive", "to fill the poor
   heart with joy". Luke's translation does, for obvious reasons, not stick as closely to the
   original wording as would be required to make my point.

37 Faust hopes "die Magie" will lead to the sphere of spirits, of "Geister", from whom Faust
   expects revelation. "Ob mir durch Geistes Kraft und Mund / Nicht manch Geheimnis

be acquired through revelation, which is a non-rational means. This revelation derives from experience. (In this Faust is quite like Wilhelm, and Goethe takes up the educational dialectic he had addressed in the *Lehrjahre*.) Favouring revelation through experience achieved by extra-rational means is at the same time a throwback to medieval mysticism *and* a leap to contemporary late 18th-century notions regarding the human powers beyond reason. It is in any case a rejection of 17th- and early 18th-century rationality. Faust now considers true knowledge to exist only in a sphere inaccessible to rational analysis.

But what exactly is meant by "Magie"? This is the crucial point as the rest of the drama takes place under the aegis of (Mephistophelian) magic. The white magic Faust practises with magic signs, and in his attempt to exorcise the Mephistophelian poodle, is only the gateway to Faust's involvement with its black counterpart represented by the satanic sphere of Mephisto. In both contexts the term "Geist" is frequently used. It always denotes the non-concrete, the realm beyond objects, which animates the latter. In the drama *Geist* is a neutral entity. Always beyond the concrete reality of rationally definable objects, it can refer to the divine or the satanic sphere as well as to that of the senses. Spirits can be equally good or bad; Wagner refers on the one hand to "Geistesfreuden" (l. 1104) and to the dangerous "Geisterzahn" (l. 1130)[38] on the other in his conversation with Faust "Vor dem Tor". Their realm may be beyond human rationality, but it is not inaccessible to human experience. *Geist* and *Geister* have their home in the imagination. Neither concrete, i.e. empirically verifiable, nor rational, they inhabit the above and below of human rationality. They are a concrete experience of the non-concrete in the mind, an imaginary concretisation of extra-rational phantoms.[39]

Faust's first foray into the realm of the spirits, during which he grapples with the principles of, first, nature and, then, history, and which he undertakes without any external help, ends in failure. His unsatisfactory experiences reinforce his view of the limited and flawed nature of contemporary human understanding. The initially fulfilling experience of the beauty of the universe, which the sign of the macrocosm

---

würde kund" (ll. 378–379). "Calling on spirits and their might / To show me many a secret sight." Luke, 15.

[38] "Joys of the spirit" and "the ghost's tooth".

[39] Cf. similar (but not identical) findings by Ritchie Robertson in "Literary Techniques and Aesthetic Texture in *Faust*", *A Companion to Goethe's Faust: Parts I and II*, ed. by Paul Bishop, Rochester, NY: Camden House, 2001, pp. 1–27, 20/21.

affords, fades when it occurs to him that what he sees is only a representation. "Welch Schauspiel! Aber ach! Ein Schauspiel nur! / Wo faß ich
dich, unendliche Natur?" (ll. 454–5)[40] Faust decides that nature, the universe, is too large for him to grasp. As an alternative he appeals to the
Erdgeist who is associated equally with earth and world, i.e. the human
realm, *and* with nature as humanity experiences it. The *Erdgeist* describes
himself as the "loom of time". He is the sum – past, present and future –
of human history.

> In Lebensfluten, im Tatensturm
> Wall ich auf und ab,
> Webe hin und her!
> Geburt und Grab,
> Ein ewiges Meer,
> Ein wechselnd Weben,
> Ein glühend Leben,
> So schaff ich am sausenden Webstuhl der Zeit,
> Und wirke der Gottheit lebendiges Kleid. (ll. 501–09)[41]

But Faust cannot cope with the magnitude of history either, and his
dreams of aspiring to the status of a human divinity are shattered.
Neither nature nor history can be mastered by him as an individual,
neither by the human reason of an Enlightened rationalist nor by the
textbook magic of an early modern alchemist. This ultimate failure
sends him into a suicidal depression, which gives him another idea of
achieving liberation. Death may be the gate through which deliverance
into a higher sphere can be effected. Here Faust reveals himself as conditioned by a religious culture: he is a firm believer in an afterlife that
has all the hallmarks of a spiritual paradise, where he will be equal to the
godhead. But his vision of the afterlife has been purged of the terrifying
Christian notion of reward and punishment. It will not be held against
him that he has meddled in the black arts, or that he has taken his own
life. This double vision illustrates to what extent Faust is imbued with
the history of Christian ideas. On the one hand he makes the Protestant
attempt to emancipate himself from rigid church dogma, the human
quest for knowledge must not be blocked by religious considerations.

---

[40] "How great a spectacle! But that, I fear, / Is all it is. Oh, endless Nature, where / Shall I
embrace you?" Luke, 17.
[41] "In life like a flood, in deeds like a storm / I surge to and fro, / Up and down I flow! /
Birth and the grave / An eternal wave, / Turning, returning, / A life ever burning: /
At Time's whirring loom I work and play / God's living garment I weave and display."
Luke, 19.

But on the other he subscribes to the residual Catholic notion that divine grace is unfathomable. And Christianity clearly still has a hold over him: he is brought back from the brink of suicide by the Easter Mass, i.e. by deeply rooted memories of the spiritual origin of his culture, which is Christianity's promise of salvation symbolised by the Resurrection and celebrated at Easter.

But for Faust magic remains the only way forward. Mephisto's magic will lead him into the (non-rational) worlds beyond the academy, into the world of Gretchen and sexual love, but also into the world of spirits and the non-rational regions of human experience and the self. This choice represents a reconnection to a lost original-natural element, because such encounters with what is beyond what the human mind can grasp rationally was lost to the scientists of the Enlightenment. Such encounters had been available to the medieval mind in the religious ecstasy of prayer and, artistically, in the mystery and morality plays, to the tail end of which tradition the original Faust-story is still indebted. And they had also been available to the ancient mind in the ancient myths and tragedies set in a world ruled by divine powers. It is no coincidence that Faust's assistant Wagner, an unreconstructed *moderne* who, like Faust, wants to know everything, but still believes he can find out through painstaking research and the accumulation of facts, thinks Faust is reciting from a "Greek tragedy" when he overhears Faust arguing with the *Erdgeist*. Their ensuing discussion gives Faust the opportunity to launch a presentation of *Sturm-und-Drang* notions of poetic values, which are based on Herder's assessment of Shakespeare.[42] This allusive

---

[42] Faust voices some standard *Sturm-und-Drang* complaints about the a-historical nature of contemporary thought and literature. "Was ihr den Geist der Zeiten heißt, / Das ist im Grund der Herren eigner Geist, / In dem die Zeiten sich bespiegeln. / Da ist's denn wahrlich oft ein Jammer! / Man läuft euch bei dem ersten Blick davon, / Ein Kehrichtfaß und eine Rumpelkammer, / Und höchstens eine Haupt- und Staatsaktion / Mit trefflichen pragmatischen Maximen, / Wie sie den Puppen wohl im Munde ziemen." (ll. 577–85) "And what you learned gentleman would call / Its spirits, is its image, that is all, / Reflected in your own mind's history. / And what a sight it often is! Enough / To run a mile from at first glance. A vast / Old rubbish-dump, an attic of the past, / At best a royal tragedy – bombastic stuff / Full of old saws, most edifying for us, / The strutting speeches of a puppet-chorus!" Luke, 21. This echoes in some detail Herder's assessment from the early 1770s, especially from his Shakespeare-essay, of the ills of contemporary literature and particularly French tragedy. Not surprisingly it is taken verbatim from the *Urfaust*, i.e. originates in the *Sturm-und-Drang* orbit and unmistakably bears the imprint of its aesthetics. (Cf. Goethe, *Sämtliche Werke* vol. 5, *Die Faustdichtungen*, Munich: dtv, 1977/Zürich: Artemis, 1950, "Urfaust", pp. 9–65, p. 15, ll. 225–32.) Herder had attacked

focus on the revelatory powers of the poetic imagination – ancient tragedy, medieval mystery play and Shakespeare's drama – also suggests, notwithstanding its capitalist ironisation in the *Vorspiel*,[43] that this poetic imagination may succeed where faith and reason have failed. The "Magie" is not just the magic of the devil, but also the magic of the poetic, which can command the services of devils, witches and spirits to illuminate and explore existence. The magic of the poetic imagination succeeds because poetry can create a universal, but diverse totality, as even the profit-oriented *Theaterdirektor* knows well:

> Drum schonet mir an diesem Tag
> Prospekte nicht und nicht Maschinen. [...]
> So schreitet in dem engen Bretterhaus
> Den ganzen Kreis der Schöpfung aus,
> Und wandelt mit bedächt'ger Schnelle
> Vom Himmel durch die Welt zur Hölle. (ll. 233–42)[44]

Faust represents the modern intellect from its origin and throughout its historical development. From its spiritual base in Christianity it devel-

---

in very similar terms the "puppet"-nature of the characters who declaim pretty but meaningless verse in an irrelevant "Staatsaktion". They always remain contemporary French people although they are inappropriately dressed up as characters from a different and distant culture. This inappropriate use of the past, the raiding of the "Rumpelkammer", included for Herder the continued use of the dramatic unities, against which he set Shakespeare as an appropriate example of modern drama, who had dispensed with the unities and created a wealth of actions in different places, which in Herder's view appropriately represented the historical condition of modernity.

43 For the reader-spectator of the 1808-version the case for this kind of new dramaturgy has already been presented by the *Theaterdirektor* in the *Vorspiel*. Against the Poet's dream of a universal poetry of humanity he demands the rather Shakespearean wealth of material and diversity of action for a diverse modern audience. "Besonders aber laßt genug geschehen! [...] / Die Masse könnt Ihr nur durch Masse zwingen, / Ein jeder sucht sich endlich selbst was aus. / Wer vieles bringt, wird manchem etwas bringen; [...] / Gebt ihr ein Stück, so gebt es gleich in Stücken!" (ll. 89–99) "And let's have enough action, above all! [...] Mass alone charms the masses; each man finds / Something to suit him, something to take home. / Give much, and you'll have given to many minds; [...] And let your piece be all in pieces too!" Luke, 5. *Sturm-und-Drang* aesthetics are revealed as appropriately modern also in the bourgeois-capitalist sense. While the *Theaterdirektor* gives no indication of understanding Herder's point of Shakespeare's new unity (of history) that is hidden beneath the surface diversity, i.e. of being able to identify new intellectual trends, he nevertheless has a sound grasp of contemporary tastes and needs.

44 "So make sure now we have machines / And plenty of spectacular scenes! [...] Thus on these narrow boards you'll seem / To explore the entire creation's scheme – / And with swift steps, yet wise and slow / From heaven, through the world, right down to hell you'll go!" Luke, 9.

oped through the Renaissance and the Reformation towards Enlightenment notions, which are now found to be unsatisfactory. It is to be reformed by reconnecting to a pre-rational, original-natural capacity of
human understanding and conceptualising, i.e. magic, through which
he believes he can achieve fulfilment.

It is a commonplace that Mephisto is constructed as an oppositional
counterpart to Faust, who nevertheless shares crucial characteristics
with him, an interpretation that has given rise to the idea of Mephisto as
Faust's *alter ego*. Mephisto provides Faust with access to the world
beyond Faust's study, i.e. to the regions of the sensual, the subconscious
and the non-rational. While Faust can access the regions of pantheistic
meditation, where he communes with universal nature and universal
humanity, on his own, as he does in *Nacht*, and again in *Wald und
Höhle*,[45] he is incapable of experiencing the real and particular without
help, because he is too disconnected from original-natural concreteness.
In this he is the stunted creature of a cerebral and bloodless rationality
that was the target of much *Sturm-und-Drang* criticism. But Faust is at the
same time a *Sturm-und-Drang* character in that he recognises his debility
and wishes to overcome it, a project for which he seeks help. That such a
facilitator is, at least at surface level, cast as the devil is on the one hand
in keeping with the modern-Christian origin of the material Goethe has
chosen. It is the hallmark of Christianity to consider all involvement
with physical desires and experiences, and the manifestations of their
workings in the subconscious, as sinful and linked to evil. But the choice
of the evil tempter also fits in well with some of the no-go areas of enlightened rationalism. Despite being interested in the (rationally explicable) workings of the subconscious, rationalism was by definition dubious of the irrational, which it considered retarded and barbarous. The
devil was just as much the bogeyman of rationalism because he symbolised the legacy of barbarous irrationality in humanity, which needed to
be overcome.

---

[45] I would argue that the spirit addressed in *Wald und Höhle* is the "Erdgeist". Crucial imagery is repeated, e.g. the face in the fire, and the reference to the moon-lit landscape
(cf. ll. 386 and ll. 3235–39), which Faust then desired, and which now appears as a gift
received. The idea that Faust has made some progress in terms of experience since he
has become involved with "Magie" is evident from ll. 3218–27, while the imperfect
nature of Faust's project is nevertheless clear (ll. 3240–50), which suggests this scene
continues the conversation of ll. 460–513.

But quite contrary to his Christian origin, Mephisto introduces himself as part of the original chaos which is darkness and which independently produced light out of darkness. This is a notion from antiquity that, in a more complex form, features prominently in Hesiod's *Theogony*.[46] It makes Mephisto part of the primordial matter and energy of the universe, which is not only distinct from the Christian Creation, but also associates him with forces predating the "Lord" and his arch-angels in the *Prologue*. But, as this is Mephisto's self-presentation, perhaps he simply wishes to indulge in some self-aggrandisement, because in the same *Prologue*, which precedes his words to Faust, he is clearly integrated into the world order of the Lord. Yet the ancient, and also archaic, notion of an original dark and fertile chaos, which is common in primitive mythologies, goes well with Mephisto's function as link to the dark and chaotic regions of the sensual and the subconscious. In this context these two identifications, *ancient* original chaos and the *modern*-Christian devil, are historically successive and dialectically complementary rather than contradictory. In this Mephisto's history resembles that of the wise-woman-turned-witch: such primitive mythologies were always demonised by the Christian Church. Again Goethe manages to flash up the whole of European cultural history, in which ancient times precede the modern period, in one figure and thus to allude to the existence of an anthropological human force in its different historical manifestations. He contrives to suggest a universal human phenomenon without negating or even impairing the essentially historical nature of humanity.

But on top of being chaos and the devil, Mephisto has yet another string to his bow. Initially he introduces himself to Faust the thinker in a more intellectual manner.

> [Ich bin] Ein Teil von jener Kraft,
> Die stets das Böse will und stets das Gute schafft. [...]
> Ich bin der Geist, der stets verneint!
> Und das mit Recht; denn alles, was entsteht,
> Ist wert, daß es zugrunde geht. (ll. 1335–40)[47]

In the first three lines Mephisto represents the negative part of the productive Fichtean (and later Hegelian) dialectic of the mental acquisition

---

[46] Cf. Ulrich Hoffmann, "Mephistophes: 'Ich bin ein Teil des Teils, der anfangs alles war'. Anmerkungen zu Goethes Faust, Vers 1349–58" *GJB* 109 (1992) 57–60.
[47] "Part of that Power which would / Do evil constantly, and constantly does good [...] I am the spirit of perpetual negation; / And rightly so, for all things that exist / Deserve to perish." Luke, 42.

and experience of the world, which is to lift Faust's self-centred subject out of its isolation. In the latter two he realigns himself with the notion of universal life cycles prevalent in ancient cosmologies that place a dark indefinition of chaos at the beginning of the world. As the force of negation Mephisto, whose aim is to re-introduce original nothingness, has already in the *Prologue* complained about the productiveness of the dialectic.

If the Fichtian notions of intellectual processes and development are to be applied to Faust, there has to be one important qualification. The Fichtean principle is not applied absolutely, but historically: Faust is clearly no unconscious ego, like for example Mignon, who has not yet begun the intellectual process. *He* is in need of Mephisto's dynamising effect not so much because of his individual psychology, but because of his position in intellectual history (although the latter has of course shaped the former). The frustrated rationalist and empiricist needs to be led out of the Cartesian isolation by reconnecting to the world. Not surprisingly this introduction of Mephisto was not part of the text of the *Urfaust* or the *Fragment*, but only appears in the version published in 1808, i.e. was written after Goethe had engaged with the intellectual endeavours of Idealism in the 1790s.[48] So in his double identity as a part of original chaos and as the force of negation Mephisto is both pre-Christian and post-religious, associated with ancient mythology and post- (or at least very late) Enlightenment philosophy. He alludes, on the one hand, to a memory of the archaic and, on the other, to the latest development in modern thinking. The connection between the two is the productive potential inherent in both. Mephisto represents historical continuity as well as historical change. Change due to the dynamics inherent in negativity, and continuity in that this negativity is ever-present. His appearance in history changes with the times. He describes himself:

> Auch die Kultur, die alle Welt beleckt,
> Hat auf den Teufel sich ersteckt;
> Das nordische Phantom ist nun nicht mehr zu schauen;
> Wo siehst du Hörner, Schweif und Klauen?
> Und was den Fuß betrifft, den ich nicht missen kann,
> Der würde mir bei Leuten schaden;
> Darum bedien ich mich, wie mancher junge Mann,

---

[48] It is well known how dubious Goethe was about Fichte's philosophical theories. Cf. for example J.R. Williams, "Goethe and the Idealists. Der Teufel als Wille und Vorstellung", *Goethe at 250*, 121–30.

Seit vielen Jahren falscher Waden. […]
Er [Junker Satan] ist schon lang ins Fabelbuch geschrieben;
Allein die Menschen sind nichts besser dran,
Den Bösen sind sie los, die Bösen sind geblieben. (ll. 2495–2509)[49]

Mephisto is the only one capable of putting Faust in touch with areas of experience he cannot access himself: the subconscious and society governed by sexual relations. It is not surprising that the areas of the subconscious and society are linked, and inaccessible to Faust the scholar of the Enlightenment. Both are resistant to reason, not (fully) controlled by the rational. Already demonised by Christian doctrine, they had traditionally been the spaces where evil flourished.

Cartesian subjectivism and Renaissance individualism focus on the rational in the human make-up. But at the same time as the rational becomes championed intellectually, i.e. from Descartes on, particularly as the secularising and demystifying drive of modernity accelerated, this evil, the negative, the destructive, the doubting force becomes identified as constructive. It became indispensable in the process of dialectical dynamics, which emerged as the answer to the problem of time and value around 1800. The Mephisto-figure does not only visualise this historical development, but also its ambiguous outcome: dialectical progression on the one hand, the spectre of unbridled materialism and relativism on the other.

Mephisto is in every respect the lynchpin of Part 1 as Goethe published it in 1808. Apart from providing horizontal connections, i.e. on the historical level, he also links the different vertical levels of the play. He inhabits the different human worlds of Faust and Gretchen as well as the witch-milieu, and he has access to the sphere of the *Prologue*, so moving between the sub-terrainian and the celestial spaces as well as the world of humanity. This ubiquity makes him potentially the most complex character, but he tends to be seen in relation to the eponymous hero, i.e. as a fascinating foil.[50]

---

[49] "Besides, civilization, which now licks / Us all so smooth, has taught even the Devil tricks; / The northern fiend's becoming a lost cause – / Where are his horns these days, his tail, his claws? / As for my foot, which I can't do without, / People would think me odd to go about / With that; and so, like some young gentlemen, / I've worn false calves since God knows when. […] The name has been a myth too long. / Not that man's any better off – the Evil One / They're rid of, evil is still going strong." Luke, 78.

[50] There have always been exceptions. Mme de Staël thought that he was the hero of the piece. Quoted in Harald Weinrich, "Der zivilisierte Teufel", *Interpreting Goethe's Faust Today*, pp. 61–67, 61.

If the horizontal levels of the play relate to time, the vertical ones, from Heaven to Hell, may be taken to relate to values, which in their outward guises appear as Christian values. But Christianity is treated critically, as a culturally powerful legacy that is nevertheless a historically (almost) superseded entity. Karl Eibl has recently made a case for the Lord's general withdrawal from the world, which in his view amounts to a liberation of humanity in the sense of leaving them out in the cold on their own.[51] This could be taken to reflect the increasing secularisation of human affairs from early modern times onwards. Such a reduction of divine power, limiting the Lord's involvement to the act of creation, gives Mephisto the free rein he enjoys with humanity. This divine retreat is given a fairly precise historical setting. In the *Prologue* the Lord appears as a feudal over-lord who grants audiences to his subjects, or perhaps is on a royal progress. Mephisto appears as the jester at his court. Eibl detected overtones of the absolutist ruler who enacts his own majesty in the ritual of the levée in the presentation of the Lord.[52] It has been notoriously hard to determine who is supposed to be in charge of what is happening in Faust's world. Is it the Lord, who through the instrument of Mephisto intends to lead his subject Faust "in die Klarheit", an interpretation that has not found much critical favour recently?[53] Or is it Mephisto, whose power has increased since the divine withdrawal? Or neither? One illuminating approach comes from within Goethe's oeuvre itself. When read in connection with the *Lehrjahre*, both the Lord and Mephisto appear as two sides of the same coin. Both wish to educate Faust, and both display striking parallels with the Abbé of the *Lehrjahre*. The Lord shares with the Abbé a belief in the beneficial function of errors in the process of human education. From this perspective, Faust's tribulations may appear as the benign education undergone by protagonists in comedies. And it has indeed been argued that a "perspective of comedy" was imposed on the tragic fragment.[54] Faust's eventual salvation also supports this point. At the same time there are notable parallels between the Abbé and Mephisto. The Lord identifies Mephisto

---

[51] Karl Eibl, "Zur Bedeutung der Wette im Faust" *GJB* 116 (1999) 271–280, 274–5.

[52] Eibl, "Bedeutung der Wette", 274.

[53] Cf. C. E. Schweitzer, "Gretchen and the Feminine in Goethe's *Faust*", *Interpreting Goethe's Faust Today*, pp. 133–141.

[54] Eberhard von Zezschwitz has argued that the witch-scenes are derived from comedy structures. He judges that only through comedy could the *Sturm-und-Drang* fragment be integrated into a "classical" framework. Cf. Zezschwitz, *Komödienperspektive in Goethe's "Faust I"*, Bern: Peter Lang, 1985.

as a divine tool that keeps the human lot, for their own educational good, on their toes: he is the "Schalk" (l. 349), amusing, harmless, yet effective. This term is also applied to the Abbé in the *Lehrjahre* (cf. 8, 5; 594). It is Mephisto who tells Faust that "die Zeit ist kurz, die Kunst ist lang" (1787),[55] which is a key passage from Wilhelm's "Lehrbrief". Furthermore, it would appear that the word "Schalk" had a very particular meaning for Goethe.[56] In the novella *Die Guten Weiber* (1801) Goethe examines the aspect of "radikales Negatentum" which he associates with this term. In the "Theatervorspiel" "Was wir bringen" of the following year Goethe tells the story of a traveller who imposes himself on a circle of characters promising entertainment, conversation and making the impossible possible. He is suspected of being a magician, charlatan or even sorcerer, but eventually reveals himself as Hermes/Mercury, the classical "Schalk"-figure. Von Zezschwitz has convincingly highlighted the allusions to Mephisto in this piece.[57] In the *Lehrjahre*, the "divine spirit" and the "Schalk" are united in the figure of the Abbé. In *Faust* the two are split up into Lord and Devil. In its kaleidoscopic shifts between representing paradise and a brainwashing tyranny, the "Himmel" in *Faust I* shares more than a passing resemblance with life inside the Tower Society. Mephisto is clearly an instrument of the Lord, but the Lord, like the Tower Society, is not sanctioned as a divine absolute.[58] Not least, the spectator-readers must remain sceptical regarding any suggestion of a simple morality play, because unlike any character in *Prologue, Gelehrtentragödie* or *Gretchentragödie* they are privy to the "Vorspiel", which, by presenting the former as the products of the human imagination, reduces the Lord to a figment of this imagination. A figment that has been made up to satisfy the fickle audience whose attention span is short. The theatre director, who is ultimately responsible for the Lord's appearance, is presented as a thoroughly contemporary bourgeois capitalist who is fully conversant with the dynamics of the market and who feels subject only to *its* powers.

The good-evil dialectic between the Lord and the Devil relates to the neutrality of *Geist* discussed earlier. Both crucially exist in the non-concrete, rationally inaccessible sphere of human experience. And both ef-

---

[55] "Time is short, and art is long." Luke, 54.
[56] Cf. Zezschwitz, *Komödienperspektive*, 221 f.
[57] Ibid.
[58] To muddy the waters further, Mephisto is of course not only the Lord's *alter ego*, but also Faust's.

fect a form of rebirth for Faust: When Mephisto engineers Faust's rebirth, his new life, in the *Hexenküche*, this rebirth by witchcraft was prefigured by Faust's return to life from the brink of suicide occasioned by the Easter Mass. This counters the witchcraft with a christological dimension, effecting exactly the dialectical connection between the divine and the satanic that is also hinted at in the closeness between Mephisto and the Lord.

If Faust represents the modern rational intellect which has become dissatisfied with reason and Mephisto the non-rational other of the human make-up, then Goethe has chosen to represent this dichotomy embedded in its historical development. The historical development of the manifestations of the non-rational is presented as having its own dialectical dynamic, which lets Mephisto appear as shifting between ancient chaos, devil and modern philosopher (just as the witch shifts between wise-woman and sibyl). These shifts demonstrate the kaleidoscopic nature of value, which is occasioned by the historical process and intensified by the dialectical tension between the divine and the satanic, which is implied, albeit by reference to another work, in the parallels between the Lord, Mephisto and the Abbé. Faust is surrounded by evolving value systems, which set him adrift in the flow of time.

The dichotomous relationship between Mephisto and Faust is bridged by a similarity between the two, which is of course the basis for all *alter ego*-theories, but which in this context is more illuminatingly treated as a potential for a dialectical synthesis. The two share a key characteristic: irrepressible striving to achieve a seemingly impossible aim, the realisation of which would alter the current conditions that both experience as dissatisfying and meaningless. Both are striving for the ultimate. Mephisto is just as convinced that he can win his bet as is Faust. Mephisto's win would grant him, it would appear, world rule.[59] With such a titanic desire, Mephisto's aspirations are the same as Faust's. Their experience of meaninglessness is closely related to their experience of time. Both are acutely aware of the rush of time, which is potentially meaningless, because it can only provide *experience*, i.e. the unpredictable without purposeful structure. It never seems to provide the revelation Faust longs for, or the lasting success Mephisto desires. For Faust it only offers a gratification of the senses, for Mephisto preliminary victories that remain partial.

---

[59] Cf. Karl Eibl, "Bedeutung der Wette", 271–80.

Des Denkens Faden ist zerrissen,
Mir ekelt lange vor allem Wissen.
Laß in den Tiefen der Sinnlichkeit
Uns glühende Leidenschaften stillen! [...]
Stürzen wir uns in das Rauschen der Zeit,
Ins Rollen der Begebenheit!
Da mag denn Schmerz und Genuß,
Gelingen und Verdruß
Miteinander wecheln, wie es kann. (ll. 1748–58)[60]

Significantly "Freude" (l. 1765, "joy") is not involved in such "Genuß" ("enjoyment"). Faust's creativity is permanently denied.

In jedem Kleide werd ich wohl die Pein
Des engen Erdelebens fühlen. [...]
Was kann die Welt mir wohl gewähren?
Entbehren sollst du! sollst entbehren!
Das ist der ewige Gesang,
Der jedem an die Ohren klingt, [...]
Den Tag zu sehn, der mir in seinem Lauf
Nicht *einen* Wunsch erfüllen wird, nicht *einen*,
Der [...]
Die Schöpfung meiner regen Brust
Mit tausend Lebensfratzen hindert. (ll. 1544–61)[61]

Mephisto's (negative) creativity is equally thwarted.

Was sich dem Nichts entgegenstellt,
Das Etwas, diese plumpe Welt,
So viel als ich schon unternommen,
Ich wußte ihr nicht beizukommen,
Mit Wellen, Stürmen, Schütteln, Brand –
Geruhig bleibt am Ende Meer und Land!
Und dem verdammten Zeug, der Tier- und Menschenbrut,

---

[60] "The thread of thought is torn, / Books sicken me, I'll learn no more. / Now let us slake hot passions in / The depths of sweet and sensual sin! [...] Let us plunge into the rush of things, / Of time and all its happenings! / And then let pleasure and distress, / Disappointment and success, / Succeed each other as they will; / Man cannot act as if he is standing still." Luke, 53.

[61] "The earth's a prison – one cannot get away / From it, whatever clothes one wears. [...] What satisfaction can life hold? / Do without, do without! That old / Command pursues us down the years / Endlessly echoing in our ears [...] To think that when this day has passed / I'll not have had one single wish fulfilled, / That even my presentiments of joy / Will die of nagging scruples, and life's mess / Of trivial impediments destroy / My active soul's creativeness." Luke, 48.

Dem ist nun gar nichts anzuhaben:
Wie viele hab ich schon begraben!
Und immer zirkuliert ein neues, frischen Blut. (ll. 1363–72)[62]

Time's passing does not bring progress.[63] This is one of the reasons for
their shared near-nihilistic outlook at the beginning of the play. The
other is their equally shared dim view of human rationality, Faust's is

---

[62] "The Something, this coarse world, this mess, / Stands in the way of Nothingness, /
And despite all I've undertaken, / This solid lump cannot be shaken – / Storms, earth-
quakes, fire and flood assail the land / And sea, yet firmly as before they stand! / And as
for that damned stuff, the brood of beasts and men, / That too is indestructible, I've
found; / I've buried millions – they're no sooner underground / Than new fresh blood
will circulate again." Luke, 43.

[63] There is a counter-position to that of Faust and Mephisto in relation to time, but it is
shown as dated. Although the inhabitants of the heavenly sphere, the Lord and Arch-
angels, are aware of the rush of time, too – ("Und schnell und unbegreiflich schnelle /
Dreht sich umher der Erde Pracht; / Es wechselt Paradieseshelle / Mit tiefer, schauer-
voller Nacht." (ll. 251–54) "The glorious earth, with mind-appalling / Swiftness, upon
itself rotates, / And with the deep night's dreadful falling / Its primal radiance alter-
nates." Luke, 9–10) –, from their divine perspective, the rush of self-perpetuating eternity is most satisfying. "Der Anblick gibt den Engeln Stärke / Da keiner dich ergründen
mag, / Und alle deine hohen Werke / Sind herrlich wie am ersten Tag." (ll. 267–70)
"And each of us, uncomprehending, / Is strengthened as we gaze our fill; / For all thy
works, sublime, unending, / Retain their first day's splendour still." Luke, 10. From
their divine vantage-point, the meaninglessness of perpetual death and destruction is
obliterated by perpetual rebirth, as Mephisto knows to his cost. The destructive storms
Michael refers to do not seem to affect the picture, and one can always look the other
way (cf. ll. 265/66). It may of course simply be a question of their respective positions,
and attendant degrees of security: what presents itself as beautiful eternity in heaven, is
experienced as pointless yet perpetual impermanence on earth. But more crucially, the
two spheres are disconnected. For those on earth there is no longer a meaningful connection between (Christian) Heaven and Earth. This represents the loss of religious certainty, or increasing secularisation, which has gone hand in hand with intellectual liberation and philosophical progress. However, conditions in heaven are subtly presented
as historically dated. None of the Heavenly Host experience any kind of intellectual
revelation, they (have to) remain content with their state of submerged mystical contemplation of universal beauty. *They* view life on earth still in an ancient-archaic context. The notion of conceiving existence on earth as eternal cycles of rebirth is historically at home in ancient, pre-Christian cultures. Christianity conceives of time on earth
in a linear eschatological fashion, which means that any experience of eternity is lost to
humans in this life. (One might argue that, as this scene seems to take place in heaven,
this is the Christian eternity beyond earthly time, but it is clearly the earthly Creation
itself which is praised by the archangels, which is supposed to be subject to the Apocalypse, i.e. to destructive termination.) This confirms from a different angle Karl Eibl's
view of the Lord as superannuated. Modernity, although it may currently be at a loss intellectually, has long achieved emancipation from religion.

based on disillusionment ("Des Denkens Faden ist zerrissen ..."), Mephisto's on disrespect.

> Der kleine Gott der Welt bleibt stets vom gleichen Schlag,
> Und ist so wunderlich als wie am ersten Tag.
> Ein wenig besser würd er leben,
> Hättst Du ihm nicht den Schein des Himmelslichts gegeben;
> Er nennt's Vernunft und braucht's allein
> Nur tierischer als jedes Tier zu sein. (ll. 281–86)[64]

The double meaning of the German "Schein" leaves open whether Mephisto suggests that the Creator has given humanity a portion of true divine understanding, i.e. the *light* of divine reason, or just the *appearance* of it. Both Faust and Mephisto agree that reason is a failure. There will be no human progress in its name, perfectibility is a sham. At first sight this attitude seems to negate any historical perspective because human nature is constant in its partially enlightened dumbness. Yet these views of reason and (im)perfectibility represent the negative corollary of the Enlightenment idea of reason and progress. Faust's frustrations confirm, on the level of individual experience, Mephisto's general findings. This marks both Faust and Mephisto as critics of the Enlightenment ideal of reason.

Their striving to overcome dissatisfaction, failure and despair identifies them both as modern creatures. In keeping with their modern mindset, they are restless and do not stop yearning for the fulfilment of their highly ambitious desires. Although Faust says he does not really believe it is available, he strives for complete fulfilment, first in terms of total knowledge, then in terms of total experience. And Mephisto pursues a goal that is equally boundless: the overthrow of the heavenly order and the reinstatement of nothingness. Both, irrespective of their respective experience of failure so far, want to wrestle something from their frustrating existence, so each engages in his respective gamble. Their shared project is the achievement of meaning under the conditions of meaninglessness, which presupposes a dialectical dynamic. The linear nature of the Christian concept of time is ultimately responsible firstly for their tenacious belief in the merits of striving and secondly for the experience of time as pointless onward movement. Originally Chris-

---

[64] "The little earth-god still persists in his old ways, / Ridiculous as ever, as in his first days. / He'd have improved if you'd not given / Him a mere glimmer of the light of heaven; / He calls it Reason, and it only has increased / His power to be beastlier than the beast." Luke, 10.

tianity offered a reward for dedicated striving by promising a final resolution, which constituted the revelatory intersection between time and eternity, between the Here and the Beyond. But, when stripped of its eschatological trappings, the Christian concept of time leaves behind exactly this pointless onward movement. And as creatures of advanced modernity both Faust and Mephisto have lost their belief in Christianity's religious promise as well as in the Enlightenment's intellectual promise of reason. But, at the same time, as moderns conditioned by Christianity they still desire an irreversible caesura, an end in every sense of the word. They are not content with endlessness and want to give time a telos. For them there can be no satisfaction as long as there is no result. Faust laments: "So tauml ich von Begierde zu Genuß, / Und im Genuß verschmacht ich nach Begierde." (ll. 3249–50)[65] Both have to cope with the critical situation that the emergence of historical awareness has produced. The ancient concept of cyclical eternity cannot satisfy a mind conditioned by a culture based on linear time, either. Eternal cycles and eternal onward movement are equally pointless. Both want to break through to eternity *while on earth*, and repudiate the Christian marginalisation of earthly existence. This amounts to an attempt to reclaim the (imagined) natural-original paradise on earth, each after his own fashion, as nothingness for Mephisto, and as fulfilment in the here and now for Faust. For both it is an escape from time within time itself.[66]

That their project is thoroughly conditioned by the newly discovered problematic nature of time is most evident in the presentation of their respective bets, the stakes of which have been formulated along very innovative lines. While the content of their stakes is quite different, Faust's is individual, Mephisto's is universal,[67] their formal aspects are identical. The options for both are *either* be fully satisfied, i.e. win, *or* carry on indefinitely, i.e. lose. And in this lies a significant change regarding the purpose of existence and activity, a circumstance that in decades of discussions of the "wagers" has not been appreciated and which is directly related to the impact of the awareness of historicity on values.

---

[65] "Thus from my lust I stumble to fulfilment, / And in fulfilment for more lust I languish." Luke, 103. In my view "fulfilment" does not work in this context.

[66] Both solution attempts are astutely (post-)modern: no new religion or philosophy, their time is past, because they will only be surpassed by time.

[67] The content of their choices of telos is crucially different. Mephisto's aim is timeless nothingness, an eternal death. Faust desires the ecstatic moment which he hopes will contain "an" eternity because time loses its significance. Mephisto's is still a universal solution, which betokens his origin in the divine sphere, whereas Faust's is individual.

Whereas before, under a system of universal values, the highest stake would be the risk of death, of ceasing to have the opportunity to strive, now it is the risk of having to carry on indefinitely (and probably pointlessly) on earth. Activity has threatened to become pointless, because it has become difficult to be certain of aims or purposes, whereas before, activity could be directed towards universal constants. In terms of reward and punishment, which are implicit in the wagers, the "continuing indefinitely" constitutes the New Hell on Earth, whereas a complete cessation of activity, a final coming to rest, is the New Heaven on Earth. This change in approach of course reflects the process of increasing secularisation (that any form of Heaven on Earth should be contemplated at all), but this secularisation is itself conditioned by the discovery of the problematic of time, which has eroded the constancy of spiritual values. Nihilistic relativity is only symptomatically based on the loss of religious metaphysical meaning. It is not possible without the new problematic of time. This change in approach to success and failure, to punishment and reward, represents the new historicist world-picture with all its problems. Goethe dramatised the contemporary problem of the relations between time and value. He does not propose any solutions to this problem, which affects the individual and universal spheres.[68] Except neither Faust nor Mephisto are ever shown to capitulate.

Gretchen and Faust

Gretchen and Faust also stand in opposition to each other, yet are subtly linked by a similarity. She, too, is embedded in the historical development of modernity. Faust's relationship with Gretchen is suspended in a dialectical dynamic that has dichotomous features as well as a historical-cultural dimension. The dichotomous features rely on the (time-honoured) division between the intellectual and the unintellectual-natural, while the similarity is based on Gretchen's capacity for rebellious striving. Gretchen's femininity is allusively associated with three key definitions of femininity that modern culture had produced: madonna, whore, and nature.

In his Mephisto-engineered encounters with the world Faust first experiences the "kleine Welt" of personal and sexual relations in a social context. In *Faust I* sexual relations remain the key theme once they have

---

[68] The harmony of the *Prologue* is identified as pre-modern. Cf. note 63.

been introduced in *Hexenküche* and *Auerbach's Keller* (where the revelling students reject politics in favour of their love lives as a topic of conversation). The course of the Faust-Gretchen relationship leaves open the question whether a love relationship could generate the bliss that Faust is convinced he can never experience, yet still seeks, (and Gretchen finds) or whether an affair will at best be a diversion in the "Rollen der Begebenheit" and at worst a punishable offence against social codes. Faust experiences their relationship as based on overwhelming sexual desire, on loving adoration (in Gretchen's bedroom), as a predictable episode (in *Wald und Höhle*) and as a sexual-commercial transaction (just before Valentin's murder)[69] at different times, which encompasses most of the options of how male-female encounters are commonly presented. Gretchen's experience of their relationship is equally varied, but different.

Gretchen's story takes place in the domestic spaces of her house, her neighbour's house and garden, and in the social spaces of street, church and public well. Faust is in every respect an intruder into the ordered world of the town which is tightly controlled by social and religious codes.[70] Reputations and damnation are easily risked. Marthe complains:

> Es ist, als hätte niemand nichts zu treiben
> Und nichts zu schaffen,
> Als auf des Nachbarn Schritt und Tritt zu gaffen,
> Und man kommt ins Gered, wie man sich immer stellt. (ll. 3198–3201)[71]

Gretchen, too, is worried:

> Ich war bestürzt, mir war das nie geschehn;
> Es konnte niemand von mir Übels sagen.
> Ach, dacht ich, hat er in deinem Betragen
> Was Freches, Unanständiges gesehn? (ll. 3169–72)[72]

The older interpretation of Gretchen as pure or natural innocence being corrupted has more recently been replaced by discussions over whether

---

[69] "Nicht ein Geschmeide, nicht ein Ring, / Meine liebe Buhle damit zu zieren? [...] / Mir tut es weh, / Wenn ich ohne Geschenke zu ihr geh." (ll. 3670–75). "Was there no jewellery you could find? / My mistress loves those golden toys. [...] it makes me sad to go / Without a gift to her, you know." Luke, 116.

[70] During the Gretchen-action only Faust is seen to have access to spaces beyond the town walls, in *Wald und Höhle* and *Feld*, and to the Brocken Mountain in *Walpurgisnacht*.

[71] "It's as if they all had nothing else to do, / Day in, day out, / But try to sniff their neighbours' business out. / It's wicked! But one can't escape their talk." Luke, 101.

[72] "It was a shock – you see, it never had / Happened before. No one ever says bad / Things of me, and I thought: did I somehow / Seem lacking in modesty just now?" Luke, 100.

Gretchen can be conclusively associated with the sphere of the witches
in the drama, discussions that were sparked by Albrecht Schöne's recon-
struction of a "complete" *Walpurgisnacht*, which included materials from
the *Paralipomena*.[73] Gretchen is certainly presented as a heterogeneous
character comprising aspects of the saintly and the witch-like, both of
which are linked to her femininity. Twice, she is associated with culturally potent images of mother and infant. The first image is that of
Gretchen with her baby sister on her lap, which occurs in her own account of her relationship with her younger sibling, in which she is the
surrogate mother (ll. 3133–35). This image alludes to the Holy Virgin
with whom Gretchen shares her virginal motherhood. The second image
is that of Gretchen as infanticide, the mother who kills her baby, which
associates her with folk beliefs about witches, among whom child kill-
ings and child sacrifices were believed to be a common practice. Infanticide was a contemporary problem that was being discussed in its social
and legal contexts, which might be taken to indicate that it had become
dissociated from its historical connections with witches.[74] While the
topic of infanticide may have been approached in this "enlightened"
fashion, the notion of the "unnatural" and "evil" that remained attached
to a crime which tended to occur in the wake of sexual misdemeanour
(nearly all infanticides were unmarried and had killed their illegitimate
babies) made it easy to connect it with satanic powers. In the 1772 case
of the Frankfurt infanticide Margarete Susanna Brandt, a case famously
well known to Goethe, the accused testified that she had obeyed orders
by the Devil.[75] That such testimony must objectively be considered the
last resort of a cornered and frightened interviewee strengthens, rather
than undermines, the argument that in terms of associative background,

---

[73] The debate of the past twenty years has recently been summarised by Peter Delvaux
("Hexenglaube und Verantwortung. Zur Walpurgisnacht in Goethe's *Faust I*" *Neophilologus* 83 (1999) 601–16) and Barbara Becker-Cantarino ("Hexenküche und Walpurgisnacht"). It was started by Albrecht Schöne in his *Götterzeichen, Liebeszauber, Satanskult.
Neue Einblicke in alte Goethetexte* of 1982, who suggested that Gretchen is associated with
the sphere of the witches (not that she actually is presented as a witch) which nevertheless sparked a lively controversy. For a counter-account to Schöne cf. Christoph Müller,
"Gretchen als Hexe? Eine Anmerkung zu Albrecht Schönes Rekonstruktion der Walpurgisnacht" *Euphorion* 87 (1993) 347–64.

[74] As C. Müller argued in "Gretchen als Hexe", 356.

[75] Cf. Schöne, "Faust. Paralip 50", 193. (This is the "Vortragsfassung" of the Walpurgis-
nachts-essay in his *Götterzeichen, Liebeszauber, Satanskult. Neue Einblicke in alte Goethetexte*.) Also referred to by Müller, "Gretchen als Hexe", 356.

the infanticide and the witch (as helpmate of the Devil) were still closely linked in the later 18th century, particularly in the popular imagination.

Madonna and witch are the allusive extremes surrounding the Gretchen-figure. They suspend her in the same dialectical tension between divine and satanic that has already been noted in the depiction of the Lord and Mephisto, and that recurs in the allusive connection between the Cathedral-scene and *Walpurgisnacht*. With these allusions Goethe draws on the two crucial cultural, and potentially dialectical, concepts of femininity that Christian modernity has produced. In the drama, both are *images* of her that only exist in the spectator-reader's imagination. They are suggested rather than presented as part of the dramatic action, which makes them the associative backdrop to the Gretchen-figure and identifies them as cultural constructions of femininity at the same time. These cultural associations point to the functional dialectic of the Gretchen-figure in relation to Faust. She intercedes on Faust's behalf for his eventual salvation – the "eternally feminine" is to save the renegade male, after all –, but at the same time she is the *be-witch-ing* female who leads Faust astray in a double sense. Mephisto tries to integrate her into his plans for Faust by attempting to use her as a sexually corrupting force (with only limited success). On the other hand (or at the same time) Gretchen leads Faust away from Mephisto (his educator appointed by the Lord) and attempts to integrate him into her own scheme of things (with disastrous consequences).

Within such cultural parameters, the female lead of the play *actually* appears as both innocently virtuous and sexually interested, successfully combining the madonna-whore opposition, which translates the imagined link between madonna and witch from the moral into the sexual field. Given this combination Gretchen is not just the archetypal essence of modern-Christian femininity, but also clearly a male fantasy. Gretchen is virtuous in that she seems to have no history of sexual activity and behaves as a devout Christian. But even from her first encounter with Faust, which is also the spectator's first encounter with her, it is clear that she is sexually confident. She is well able to parry Faust's ironically insolent chat-up line with a retort that demonstrates semantic and linguistic self-assurance in this situation. "Bin weder Fräulein, weder schön, / kann ungeleitet nach Hause gehn."[76] (ll. 2607–8)[77] And her ef-

---

[76] "I'm not a lady and I'm not sweet, / I can get home on my own two feet." Luke, 81.

[77] It is unlikely that Gretchen says this "innocently", i.e. as a face-value statement of fact. In the Dungeon-scene she admits that she knows she was beautiful. "Schön war ich

fect on Faust is exactly that of a tease. He responds to, and enjoys, what
he experiences as the mix of virtue and challenge (ll. 2611–19). Gretchen
retains a sexual forwardness until the end. When in the dungeon scene
Faust's mind is on other matters and he neglects to kiss her, she immediately approaches him and initiates sexual contact with a hint of challenge and the unmistakable air of sexual self-confidence. "Küsse mich! /
Sonst küß ich dich!" (*Sie umfaßt ihn.*) (ll. 4491–2)[78]

Although Gretchen never loses her archetypal and functional
qualities in relation to the Faust-character, she is developed as a character with her own agenda, much like Mephisto in whom dramaturgical
functionality is also combined with an individual agenda. (Faust lacks
such functionality if one disregards his relationship with the Lord.)
Gretchen's agenda is two-pronged: she strives for (sexual) satisfaction
and individual liberation. This dual, but linked dimension of the
Gretchen-figure is indicated by the two different names by which she is
referred to in different scenes by the author.[79] She is *Gretchen* in her sexual relation to Faust, who experiences her as the natural innocent with
an instinct for sex. She is *Margarete* when she focuses on her goal of individual liberation. Her change of name goes hand in hand with her
sexual activity. The name Gretchen is used for the first time when her
sexual intentions are made explicit (at the spinning wheel) and used
continuously after she has slept with Faust,[80] only to be dropped again
in the Dungeon-scene, in which she develops her individual tragic
greatness.[81]

---

auch, und das war mein Verderben." (l. 4434) "I was pretty too, and that's the reason
why." Luke, 143.

[78] "Oh kiss me now! / Or I'll show you how! [She embraces him.]" Luke, 145.

[79] Bernhard Greiner, who surprisingly seems to be the first to investigate the meaning of the
two names, interprets the duality as the expression of a development through which the
female protagonist acquires the tragic prerequisite of freedom in the face of unreflective
determination, which allows her to become a fully realised tragic heroine. Greiner sees
this in direct connection to Goethe's classical aesthetics, in which a connection of the
two spheres of free will and necessity was to be effected. Cf. Greiner, "Margarete in Weimar: Die Begründung des *Fausts* als Tragödie" *Euphorion* 93 (1999) 169–91.

[80] This duality was already worked into the *Urfaust* and maintained in the *Fragment*. In the
Urfaust her sexual intentions are made even clearer in the song at the spinning wheel:
"Mein Schoos, Gott! drängt sich nach ihm hin" ("Urfaust", 49, l. 1098).

[81] In this respect she should really be referred to as Margarete in critical discussions treating this aspect of her character (that she is not, and has never been, reveals much about
the perspective of the interpreters), but it may be too late to change established usage,
even if the point is not a pedantic one.

Gretchen is aware of her sexuality, her own desires and her effect on men, but she also knows the limitations that social and religious rules impose on her existence. When she is confronted with the jewel casket she reveals herself as an adept reader of her situation. Her relative poverty and her bourgeois station add more restrictions to a female existence already restricted and hemmed in by cultural archetypes. "Darf mich, leider, nicht auf der Gassen, / Noch in der Kirche mit sehen lassen."[82] (ll. 2883–4)[83] She appears curious and adventurous ("Ich denke wohl, ich mach es auf!" (l. 2789)),[84] opening the casket although she is at first convinced it is not for her. Her curiosity is also responsible for her sexual forwardness. She senses there are pleasures beyond the fences erected by the rules she is expected to live by, and she would like to try them. She enjoys the taste of glamour and importance that the wearing of the jewels afford her (ll. 2796–7), and resents the fact that this has to be done in secret. Just like Faust in his dusty study, Gretchen wants to break out of her limited existence. (ll. 3406–11) Both experience different modes of "incarceration". Faust calls his study a "Kerker" and realises that Gretchen exists in a similarly locked-up world. Gretchen comes to experience the full force of social and religious restrictions in the cathedral-scene, where walls and vaults constrict her breathing, and she finally ends up in a real dungeon. The difference is that Faust's restrictions are intellectual and internal, whereas Gretchen's are external and real. Faust has no intention of accepting the restrictions he perceives, whereas Gretchen in the end does submit to hers. But initially, before she has learnt of suffering and guilt, she is as ready to be rebellious as Faust. She worries about misbehaving, and she knows when she is doing it, but in the end this does not stop her. "Ich war recht bös auf

---

[82] "But I can't wear them in the street, or go / To church and be seen in them, you know." Luke, 90.

[83] She also comes across as materialistic and vain, which has been interpreted as a suggestion that she is in danger of becoming guilty of two deadly sins: superbia (vanity) and avaritia (avarice), which will bring luxuria (unchasteness) and acedia (despair) in their wake. Albrecht Schöne referred in this context to an essay by Birgit Stolt entitled "Gretchen und die Todsünden", in which the author identified these four deadly sins in Gretchen's behaviour in this context. Quoted by Christoph Müller, "Gretchen als Hexe", 350. While I find it difficult to see her as so intrinsically corrupt from the beginning, these suggestions of human failings in the form of the deadly sins place her in cultural and historical terms, yet again, precisely in the context of medieval and early modern Christianity, which is also the cultural-historical home of the Faust-matter.

[84] "I think I'll open it." Luke, 87.

mich, / Daß ich auf Euch nicht böser werden konnte." (ll. 3177–78)[85]
Goethe suggests that bourgeois girls like her resent the social rules that
restrict them, which is borne out in the scene at the well. Lieschen is not
horrified by some ethical evil in Bärbelchen's conduct; she resents that
Bärbelchen got the chance to be with her boy-friend, while she herself
had to stay in under her mother's vigilant eye. She is jealous, not morally outraged, and glad that Bärbel does not get away with the unfair advantage she enjoyed. (ll. 3563–69) When Gretchen, who we know is like
Lieschen inclined to sexual fantasies at the spinning wheel (which were
toned down in the 1808-version), reveals that she used to come down ex-
cessively hard on such digressions herself (l. 3577), one wonders whether
her former self-righteous indignation was not based on jealously, too.

For her rebellion in search of liberation she chooses the path of love
and sexual relations, which is in keeping with her sex and social station.
The only way in which a bourgeois girl could effect a change in her situation, could leave parental control and remain within society, would be
through love and marriage. Brought up under patriarchal conditions,
she must believe that women define themselves through relationships
with men. How much she associates Faust's love with freedom and liberation becomes clear in the dungeon-scene, where she believes his presence sets her free more effectively than stepping outside the prison-cell
ever could (ll. 4461–63 and ll. 4472–74). Gretchen's agenda is two-
pronged: she is looking for sexual fulfilment and an escape from an oppressive and exploitative home, represented by her pious and demand-
ing mother. Love (and marriage) promise both.

Yet rebelliousness and submission remain in the balance with
Gretchen and form Gretchen's internal dialectic. Despite her desire for
liberation Gretchen does not want to leave society and religion behind
(which distinguishes her from Faust): she will not countenance an existence outside society. While she is looking for the freedom to choose personal fulfilment in a loving relationship, she still wants Faust to be
a traditional god-fearing believer, hence she asks the *Gretchen-Frage*
(l. 3415) and makes her own opinion clear (l. 3421). She refuses to leave
the dungeon, or the town, because she does not want to be a social out-
cast, or condemned to eternal damnation (ll. 4544–49). However, she
does not submit to the dictates of religion and society fully. To the last
she is not prepared to consider her relationship with Faust as sinful, she

---

[85] "In fact I got quite cross with myself, too, / For not being quite cross enough with you."
Luke, 100.

remembers it as "ein süßes, ein holdes Glück" (l. 4531) and "glückliche Zeiten" (l. 4573),[86] which must count as a considerable rebellion against the rules because her involvement with Faust is responsible for the deaths of her entire family, mother, brother, and child. In this constellation lies the basis for her tragedy. Her awareness and use of freedom lead her into conflict with the necessities of her world. It is a conflict she cannot survive: her world crushes her as punishment for the errors she has committed while pursuing her free will. In this constellation of accepting her guilt (submission) but cherishing her defiance also lies the solution to her tragic conflict, and to her internal dialectic. The Dungeon-scene reveals tragic Margarete as fulfilled Gretchen.[87]

While the Dungeon-scene provides a resolution to Gretchen's conflict, it rehearses its struggle in its imagery. The scene is based on the close connection of sex and violence and their spiritual equivalents of love and death, which reflects the socially destructive and personally tragic potential of Gretchen's relationship with Faust as well as its spiritually and physically fulfilling potential.[88] Gretchen mistakes her lover for her executioner (ll. 4427–8), a (mis)apprehension she does not fully revise until the end: Faust's touch remains violent to her (l. 4437 and l. 4576–7). But the exchangeability works both ways: she says that the dawning day of her execution should have been her wedding day (ll. 4580–1). Despite her fear of being hurt, she comes out from her hiding position and throws herself on the floor at her lover-executioner's feet in a gesture of submission and invitation, writhing around with the physical intensity of an animal. The term used in the stage direction is "wälzen" (l. 4425), which connotes rolling and turning almost in the sense of wallowing. She offers herself to the violence as much as she may offer sexual favours – a violation of her integrity – for an hour's grace. The connection lies in the fact that sex with Faust has violated and de-

---

[86] " ... so blessed, a joy so sweet", "good times", Luke, 146–47.

[87] In the Dungeon-scene Margarete reappears as liberated and empowered by her relationship with Faust. Here she is in charge, controls the action, and Faust. In a reversal of their roles she resists him as he resisted her catechising, and finally withdraws from him as he did from her. In her society she can only achieve this level of empowerment through the acceptance of her own death, which is the typical path (and fate) of sentimental 18th-century heroines in such situations. The impact of her appearance on Faust (and the spectator) results from her situation as a character *in extremis*. Her near-madness lifts her out of her intellectual and social inferiority to Faust.

[88] In the *Urfaust* the sexual element was even more pronounced, in the *Fragment* the scene was omitted.

stroyed her socially, while it has made her strong enough to accept (and possibly even pass) her (own) judgement, because it made her fulfilled. When she relives her relationship with Faust, it becomes clear that she found the eternal moment of happiness, which makes her impervious to time and mortality. Her words recall the wording of Faust's bet with Mephisto: "O weile!" (l. 4479) It is this fulfilment that makes her ready and able to take responsibility for her actions and submit to the demands of heaven and earth. Her fulfilment is physical and spiritual rather than intellectual. The idea that women are fulfilled by love identifies the femininity Goethe presents as traditional. But more interesting in this context is the fact that she is capable of such complete fulfilment at all, because it makes her a somewhat *un*-modern creature.

Margarete's tragic greatness is developed in the Dungeon-scene where she chooses the physical destruction and spiritual redemption which her world offers to her over a life haunted by unatoned guilt in a spiritual wilderness of freedom, even if she would share this life with her beloved. Without repudiating it, she turns her back on the all-consuming nature of (modern) Romantic love. In this Margarete's tragedy is not fully modern, she does not reach what Friedrich Schlegel called the "maximum of despair" of a Hamlet, or a Faust, which is insoluble. She remains protected by a spiritual certainty that was lost when the process of modernity scaled unprecedented self-reflexive heights.[89] Her rebellious search for liberation occurs in the instinctive and sense-dominated sphere of sexual love, on which she reflects in the ballads she sings. Characteristically her expression of self (individual will and identity) comes in balladesque song, like Mignon's, which since Hamann was considered the original, i.e. pre-intellectual form of human expression. She is redeemed by her spiritual trust as well as by the sensual fulfilment she has experienced. Thus she represents the naïve under modern conditions. The Gretchen-figure's background in folk balladry underlines her status as a natural in modernity, as the modern naïve, which she is for Faust. It is blended with her role as (ancient) tragic heroine (which Margarete is for herself) in the tragedy focused on the infanticide, which bears the hallmarks of ancient classical tragedy. In the figure of Gretchen Goethe successfully synthesises aspects of both historical manifestations of Schiller's

---

[89] One may of course wonder whether the killing of her child may not represent such inaugmentable despair, but the difference is that she, unlike the modern characters listed above, is able to resolve her conflict rather than be overwhelmed by it.

naïve, the ancient as well as the natural.[90] It is clear that her "naturalness" in a "realistic" reading of the text results from her (extreme) cultural and social conditioning, which she cannot transcend intellectually, which in turn keeps her safe from nagging doubts. The woman as "natural", as instinct-driven and un-intellectual, is, after madonna and whore, the third key image of femininity in European culture.

The interpretation of Gretchen as pre-modern is not new. Most recently it has been formulated by Martin Swales.[91] It is not entirely clear whether Swales defines this pre-modernity as medieval or ancient. Both interpretations are possible after all. This highlights the shifting nature of modernity as it has emerged in this context: as contrasting opposite to antiquity as well as synthetic successor that incorporates historically past, but original features. The contrast of ancient and modern is necessary to achieve modern independence. The dialectic of modernity, however, holds the key to modern self-transcendence, the solution to the modern problem of incompleteness. For Faust, both Gretchen and Mephisto represent oppositions to this own identity. Together Gretchen and Mephisto surround Faust with a dialectical tension that incorporates the divine-satanic, the natural-spiritual and the intellectual-sensual.

Walpurgisnacht and *Dom*

Faust and Gretchen are both modern individuals who undergo a non-rational experience during which they are confronted with unresolved issues. For Gretchen this is triggered by a religious service, for Faust by a satanic ritual. In both cases the presentation goes on to suggest that the moral meaning of the rituals could be inverted, which initially suggests an internal dialectic of the rituals, which in turn opens up space for the historical evolution of values.

Thematically *Walpurgisnacht* belongs with *Hexenküche*. Although the prospect of witnessing a witches' Sabbath seems to reawaken Faust's intellectual curiosity – he hopes: "Dort strömt die Menge zu dem Bösen,

---

[90] Whether in such naivety, which is capable of an ancient tragic solution, the figure of Gretchen, and the "eternally feminine", is, from beginning to end, not just a *male*, but equally a *modern* fantasy must be discussed elsewhere.

[91] M. Swales, "Goethe's Analysis of Modernity", *Goethe at 250*, 9–18.

da muß sich manches Rätsel lösen." (ll. 4039–40).[92] This resurfacing of the enquiring scholar occurs, strictly speaking, in a "pre-Walpurgis" setting before Mephisto and Faust have really arrived.[93] At this point Mephisto is clearly not yet in his (witch-)element, he complains about the cold and the poor visibility. Once they *have* arrived, *Walpurgisnacht* is a scene of the senses, dominated by visual, aural and sensory stimuli. It is episodic with its constantly changing personnel and operatic, as J. R. Williams observed, not just in its extensive use of sung lines, but in its first appeal to the senses rather than the intellect. It is clearly marked as an excursion into a non-rational sphere, a "Traum- und Zaubersphäre", which is accessed by the sub- and super-rational language of music, the "Wechselgesang" between Faust, Mephisto, and the *Irrlicht*, which they begin while still in the relatively unmagical setting of a nocturnal hike. The magical sphere is equally that of dream. At the end of the "Wechselgesang" the singers – or is it only Faust? – seem to fall into a swoon or sleep.

> Aber sag mir, ob wir stehen,
> Oder ob wir weitergehen?
> Alles, alles scheint zu drehen,
> Fels und Bäume, die Gesichter
> Schneiden, und die irren Lichter,
> Die sich mehren, die sich blähen. (ll. 3906–11)[94]

A journey into the non-rational world of dreams is a journey into the subconscious. Long before Freud's analysis of dreams – who, along with most early leading psycho-analysts, was for obvious reasons intrigued by

---

[92] "The mob streams up to Satan's throne; / I'd learn things there, I've never known." Luke, 128.

[93] The contemplating scholar-Faust, who claimed that "des Denkens Faden ist zerrissen" (l. 1748) and who wanted to throw himself into the "Rollen der Begebenheit" (l. 1755), has already resurfaced in *Wald und Höhle*, where he appears to commune once more with the *Erdgeist* and refers to key ideas from the *Nacht*-scene. These extended intrusions of the scholar-action into the Gretchen-story were written after Goethe's Italy-experience. However, a "witch-moment" already preceded the Dungeon-scene in *Urfaust*: the short "Offen Feld" ("Urfaust", p. 62:"Was weben die dort um den Rabenstein? [...] [Es ist] Eine Hexenzunft!"). This suggests that the involvement of witches might have been planned long before *Hexenküche* and *Walpurgisnacht* were written.

[94] "Are we coming? are we going? / Are we standing? There's no knowing! / All is whirling, all is flowing! / Rocks and trees with weird grimaces / Shift their shapes and change their places; / Wild fires wander, teeming, growing." Luke, 124.

Goethe's writings[95] – Goethe focuses on the sexual dynamics of the human subconscious, which he presents using traditional images taken from depictions of a Christian hell.

The atmosphere of the world Faust and Mephisto enter is violent, physical and sexual: against imagery of fire and storm the witches appear, cloaked in intense, not to say revolting, physicality. The language that describes their ascent deals in images of sexual activity. This sexuality is presented as evil, dirty, disgusting and rude, which is in keeping with the Church's view and propaganda of the threatening sexuality of witches and gives the scene its modern-Christian colouring. The "Hexenchor" discusses, divided into two separate halves, male and female approaches to the "Böse" and then joins together in more explicit allusions to sexual activity. At this point the judgmental presentation of sexuality changes by alluding to an older archaic interpretation: the suggestion that they "cover the earth" hints at the celebration of sexuality in fertility rites. The connection between dirt and fertility is re-enforced by the suggestion that cleanliness is associated with infertility. "Wir möchten gerne mit in die Höh. / Wir waschen, und blank sind wir ganz und gar; / aber auch ewig unfruchtbar." (ll. 3987–9)[96] The notion of fertility is explicitly referred to by the recurring term "mother", equally applied to the figure of Baubo and the sow she rides, although it is at the same time negated by the allusions to stillbirth or abortion in ll. 3974–77.[97] Baubo actually straddles both the spheres of fertility and of evil sexuality. Identified as Demeter's nurse in classical mythology she is linked to childbirth and breastfeeding. But already in the Orphic tradition Baubo is associated with obscenity and lewdness, and in the 18th century her name connoted female lasciviousness. Ann White points out that the name Baubo is also connected to Hecate, who, also closely connected with Demeter, was the goddess of night (especially nightly terrors and nightmares) and

---

[95] Cf. Paul Bishop, "Intellectual Affinities between Goethe and Jung, with special reference to *Faust*" *PEGS* 69 (1999) 1–19, and Sabine Prokhoris, *The Witch's Kitchen: Freud, Faust and the Transference*, trans. by G. M. Goshgarian, Ithaca, NY: Cornell University Press, 1995.

[96] "We want to come, but we don't know how. / The water washes us bright and clear, / But we're barren forever, we're still stuck here." Luke, 126.

[97] Hexen. Chor. "Der Weg ist breit, der Weg ist lang, / Was ist das für ein toller Drang? / Die Gabel sticht, der Besen kratzt, / Das Kind erstickt, die Mutter platzt." ("The way is wide, the way is long; / The devil take this crazy throng! (? MO) / The broomstick scratches, the pitchfork pokes, / The mother bursts, the baby chokes." Luke, 126).

(black) magic,[98] and as such could be taken to foreshadow the Gretchen-apparition in what could be seen as Faust's guilty nightmare.

This again associates the witch-sphere with an archaic pre-Christian culture, which is partly ancient-classical, partly Northern-archaic, and which had been demonised by the Christian Church. As in *Hexenküche* there are blasphemous allusions, which seem to target Christianity in general.[99] The pre-Christian background suggested by the Baubo-figure can be extended to the entire scene's aspects of (excessive) revels, intoxication and theatrics, which allude to the classical cult of Dionysus, the god of revels and wine, whose cult developed into Greek theatre. The god's rites were celebrated with much music, singing and dancing. Rituals performed in his honour included, at the excessive end, the tearing to pieces of sacrificial animals and the eating of their raw flesh, which has a distant echo in the witches' legendary infanticides. The ancient references here function as allusions to an ancient-archaic culture that still survives in a new cultural context, but has been driven underground. It is a double layer of "ancient" cultural history, which can still surface in "modern" times, but at the same time presents an "underground" layer of the individual psyche. The constitution of the individual mind mirrors the cultural and intellectual development of (modern) humanity as a whole.

As in *Hexenküche*, before the sexual can be approached directly, as it will in the dance with the young Eve-like witch ll. 4128ff, the contemporary social sphere of humanity has to be entered. To dispel Faust's intellectual curiosity Mephisto appeals to Faust's sexual instincts and the hedonistic atmosphere. "Man tanzt, man schwatzt, man kocht, man trinkt, man liebt; / Nun sage mir, wo es was Bessers gibt?" (ll. 4058–9)[100] When they enter the party-zone they encounter, not mythic-anthropo-

---

[98] White, *Nomenclature*, 108. In classical mythology, Hecate first appears (in Hesiod) as a powerful, but benign force who ruled over earth, sea and sky. Only by the 5th century BC had she become the menacing queen of sorcery and nightly terrors. Cf. Jenny March, *Cassell Dictionary of Classical Mythology*, 179.

[99] J. R. Williams reports that ll. 3987–9 have been "tenuously identified with the Roman Catholic priesthood", ll. 3996–9 with the Protestant Church. Cf. *Goethe's Faust*, London: Allen & Unwin, 1987, 112. The Catholic Church always felt stung by the drama and duly picked up the gauntlet. Hans Schwerte pointed out that Catholic theology has fought an uncompromising battle against the play and the "Faustian" ever since the appearance of the former. Cf. *Faust und das Faustische*, 44.

[100] "One can dance here, talk, drink, make love or cook a meal; / Just tell me where you'll get a better deal!" Luke, 128.

logical creatures, but real human beings, namely a general, a minister, a parvenu, a writer and the proctophantasmist. All these figures are being behind the times. They have all lost their power. The former four are associated with the *Ancien Régime*, the latter, a parody of Friedrich Nicolai, with dogmatic Enlightenment. The former represent a social, the latter an intellectual belatedness. Their resigned dejection is reminiscent of scenes from the Bastille during the Terror, when in overcrowded open-plan conditions political prisoners of both sexes, i.e. (alleged) supporters of the *Ancien Régime*, would await trial, judgement or execution and amuse themselves in whatever fashion they saw fit.[101] As in *Hexenküche*, the contemporary social situation is presented as problematic and precarious, mirroring the intellectual conditions of modernity and the individual situations of Faust and Gretchen. The remainder of the scene revisits the Gretchen-story, which is surfacing as a traumatic nightmare for Faust, by alluding to key events in their relationship through displaced objects. The reference to dead offspring in l. 3977, killed at foetal or infant stage, amid references to fertility,[102] precede the wares of the Trödelhexe, which include a "Kelch", "Schmuck", "Schwert" and "blutiger Dolch" (ll. 4104–8) and allude to the poisoning of Gretchen's mother, Faust's tempting gifts for Gretchen, the killing of her brother Valentin, and presumably Gretchen's defloration respectively. Faust's and Mephisto's dance with the witches recalls the two pairs gallivanting in Marthe's garden. This increasingly dense web of allusion leads to Faust's vision of Gretchen as the bound prisoner with her head possibly already detached. This spectre of Gretchen appears here evidently against Mephisto's wishes who desperately tries to distract Faust by drawing his attention to the impending theatre performance. In an ironic twist he repeatedly has to appeal to reason against magic in his effort to drag Faust away from the vision. "Das ist die Zauberei, du leicht verführter Tor!" (l. 4199)[103]. This recalls Mephisto's original reluctance to let Faust get involved with Gretchen.

Whether or not *Walpurgisnacht* was once designed as a counter-scene to the *Prologue*, whether it could function as such a counter if it had re-

---

[101] Or perhaps they have not been detained yet. Thomas Zabka locates them in a "nach-revolutionäres Walpurgis-Bordell" in his "Dialektik des Bösen. Warum es in Goethes Walpurgisnacht keinen Satan gibt" *DVjs* 72 (1998) 202–26, 215.
[102] Williams suggested that this alludes to "voluntary or involuntary abortion". Williams, 112.
[103] "Gullible fool! That's the enchanter's art!" Luke, 133.

tained the worship of Lord Urian that has survived in the *Paralipomena*, a
suggestion I find convincing, must remain speculation, as Goethe chose
not to make this relation explicit. But it is obvious that *Walpurgisnacht*
stands in a clear relation to the Cathedral-scene, in connection with
which it creates, yet again, a dialectical tension between the divine and
satanic. Both *Walpurgisnacht* and *Dom* present communal rituals in
which the participants worship their spiritual leaders. Like *Walpurgisnacht*, *Dom* is a thronging scene; the stage directions read "Gretchen
unter vielem Volk" and with its intense musical element – the choir and
the organ – it is no less overpoweringly operatic. In the Cathedral-scene
Gretchen is confronted with the subconscious landscape of her soul in
the same way that Faust is in *Walpurgisnacht*. In keeping with Gretchen's
general character *her* scene is considerably less complex. It remains
within the confines of Christian and bourgeois dimensions, which define her existence. In both cases these encounters are presented as dark,
threatening and apocalyptic. In the Cathedral-scene the reference to the
biblical apocalypse is obvious. "Die Posaune tönt! / Die Gräber beben! /
Und dein Herz, / Aus Aschenruh zu Flammenqualen / Wieder aufge-
schaffen, / Bebt auf!" (ll. 3801–07)[104] In *Walpurgisnacht* such references
are more hidden, but numerous.[105] In psychoanalytical terms the apocalyptic can be interpreted as the surfacing of the subconscious, which is
always accompanied by a (temporary) dissolution of the rational personality. The Cathedral-scene is dominated by the disturbing accusations of
the "evil spirit" and the invisible cathedral choir singing those equally
threatening sections of *Dies Irae* of the Requiem Mass that deal with
judgement. Gretchen experiences the walls and vaults as claustrophobic,
and faints. While it is possible to read the scene "realistically", i.e. interpret its "evil" voice and the fainting as the result of pregnancy-induced
hormonal imbalance, it is more often seen as a representation of

---

[104] "The Last Trumpet scatters its sound! / The graves shudder open! / And your heart /
That was at rest in its ashes / Is resurrected in fear, / Fanned again to the flames / Of its
torment." Luke, 120.

[105] Cf. Eberhard von Zezschwitz. He interprets them in the context of Goethe's "trauma-
tische Gesellschaftsperspektive" (passim) in close connection to the French Revolution. This social-political interpretation of the apocalyptic in *Walpurgisnacht* is certainly feasible, but it can only with difficulty account for the apocalyptic in the
Cathedral-scene, which may obscure the link between these two scenes, which is,
among other similarities, established by the shared imagery of the apocalypse. In the
Cathedral-scene the social aspect can only be applied on the individual level: Gretchen
experiences the scene as judgement, which destroys her *social* existence irreparably.

Gretchen's bad conscience, which has been activated by the church environment which encourages the sinner to reflect on his or her actions.
But why is it an *evil* spirit? If it facilitated her repentance, would it then
not be a good spirit? The Evil Spirit connects the Cathedral-scene to
Walpurgisnacht. The two scenes are linked through the judgement of
Gretchen. The condemnation of Gretchen by the Spirit leads directly to
her spectral appearance in *Walpurgisnacht*: the sinner who is on her way
to, or has already faced, judgement and punishment. If the "Hochge-
richt"-apparition from the *Paralipomena* had been used, this connection
would have been (even) more obvious. If one accepts that the "idol"
is Gretchen, she is here executed by the "grau- und schwarze Brüder-
schaft",[106] which can be interpreted as a reference to the monks of the
Franciscan and Dominican orders, which carried out most of the early
modern Inquisition and were responsible for its bloody practices.[107] The
Evil Spirit suggests a bloodthirsty and satanic dimension in a Church
that can be gruesomely punitive and violent. The Evil Spirit represents
the internal dialectic of the religious and social mechanisms to control
individual desires and aspirations, which gives these mechanisms their
equally divine and satanic qualities and reflects the tension that has
already been traced surrounding the figures of Mephisto and the Lord.
The dichotomy between Gretchen the pious sinner in church and
Gretchen as idol at the Witches' Sabbath represents the crux on which
the interpretation of Gretchen as witch or as saintly victim and sacrifice
hinges. Explicitly she is neither, as she is neither madonna or witch. But
again Goethe has blurred the associative and allusive boundaries in
order to create a productive dialectic between these two scenes. On the
one hand this dialectic represents a historical and cultural criticism of
the Christian (Catholic) Church put forward by the Enlightened mind.
On a more general interpretative level the religious images of service and
idol represent intrusions of imposed external control into the individual's life, checking disruptive, rule-breaking desires. But desire and control do not only face each other in a dichotomic opposition, they are
also linked through a dialectic of their own in which the boundaries between the divine and the satanic are blurred, as just they are regarding
the control mechanisms. Both Faust's and Gretchen's desires are equally
inspired by the need to strive to progress and be liberated, but at the

---

[106] "Paralipomena", Goethe, *Die Faustdichtungen*, 538–619, 556.
[107] Cf. Albrecht Schöne, "Faust. Paralip. 50", 194; and Müller, "Gretchen als Hexe", 351,
quoted in Delvaux, "Hexenglaube und Verantwortung", 602.

same time they are driven by the reckless selfishness of individual grati-fication. On the one hand Faust's desires represent a legitimate rebellion against the Enlightenment tyranny of an increasingly dysfunctional con-cept of rationality, on the other they lead to reprehensible acts of social and religious immorality. On the one hand they represent the modern intellect being attracted to and sincerely trying to embrace the natural in an attempt to achieve a union, (which fails). On the other hand the modern intellect is seen to exploit and abuse the natural, although he is unable to destroy its independent spiritual essence. Similarly Gretchen's desires represent the legitimate search for (female) fulfilment and liber-ation from an oppressive situation, but are shown to lead to acts of ex-treme wrong-doing. In her unintellectual naturalness she readily defies religious and social codes in the name of Romantic love, but at the same time her unintellectual spirituality steers her away from being tempted into the total freedom of a spiritual wasteland. Again Goethe links historical and seemingly universal dimensions: their desires represent stages in intellectual and social development, but at the same time mark turning-points between good and evil. These historical and universal (or dichotomic) dimensions are linked through dialectics: this double dialectics between and within desire and control is again presented in the historical-cultural context of modernity, in which reason overcame punitive and limiting religion, but the ensuing tyranny of rationality was challenged by a demand for liberation from all "unnatural" confines. But at the same time it was becoming clear that such liberation harbours the danger of leading to the spiritual wasteland of moral relativity.

Mephisto and Gretchen

The relations between these two characters are based on the same struc-tures as those which exist between the other two pairs: an initial dichot-omy turns into a potential dialectical synthesis. At the beginning Me-phisto and Gretchen appear as the opposition of corrupting Devil versus pious good-natured innocent, which can even be extended to evil versus good. This opposition is expressed through their evident dislike of each other. Mephisto is not very keen on Gretchen's involvement with Faust (ll. 2626ff) or on her appearance in the *Walpurgisnacht*. He knows she is ultimately incorruptible. Gretchen repeatedly makes clear her abhor-rence of Mephisto (ll. 3469–82, ll. 3489–98). His presence and Faust's involvement with him are the crucial reasons why she will not run away with Faust at the end (ll. 4601–10). It even appears as if Mephisto and Gretchen are the two key influences on Faust pulling him in opposite directions, into moral and spiritual bankruptcy and towards a pious life of the righteous and blessed. In this "pulling" lies the similarity between the two: both have designs on Faust and want to integrate him into their own plans. Although it suits Faust to be integrated into both their schemes, he ultimately resists them both. Both Mephisto and Gretchen quite clearly realise the other's intentions regarding Faust. Gretchen senses that while Faust is with Mephisto he cannot really be with her. Mephisto clearly understands that Gretchen is looking for the "right" husband (ll. 3522–27). When the ending of *Faust II* is taken into account, it can be argued that both Mephisto and Gretchen are appointed by the Lord for different functions in relation to Faust, Mephisto to test him and Gretchen to save him. The allusive similarities between them further underline the kaleidoscopic nature of value in Faust's world: there is a dialectic of good as well as dialectic of evil.

What is the prospective synthesising solution to the dialectics of modernity? In *Faust I* none of the three main characters succeeds in their quest to find final fulfilment under the defacing tyranny of time. Faust's and Mephisto's, and even Gretchen's (although she achieves a form of fulfilment that eludes the other two), projects continue. Faust's turning to the Here and Now can only superficially be read as a return to ancient (and happier) sensibilities. We do not see him setting up a bulwark of time-resistant human experience *against* the flow of time. Instead, we see him working *within* time. *Faust* remains the drama of modernity, which treats its constitutive elements: the linear time-scapes and individualistic anthropology (each soul matters) bequeathed by Christianity, which have emerged from the intellectual process of secularisation as historicism and individualism. Goethe dramatised this process as well as these elements. *Faust* presents modernity within its historical setting, as succeeding, negating and transforming antiquity. It can be regarded as a drama of (European) humanity in the one respect that, because it incorporates antiquity as a "before", it presents the compass of (European) history as it was understood at the time. But the modernity Goethe presents and examines also has a Northern pre-history, a Northern "antiquity". The ancient-classical and the Northern are both part of the tension between the cultured and the archaic, which is a version of the difference – qualitatively and historically – between the intellectual and the natural. This is the basis for the heterogeneity of modernity, which takes the memory of "ancient-ness" as the starting-point of understanding itself. So the Northern-ancient wise-woman and the classical-ancient Sibyl stand in the same relation to the modern intellectual Faust. He is suspended between a desire for the real and an aspiration towards the ideal, between a desire for the natural and an aspiration towards the spiritual, between a desire for the sensual and a capacity for the intellectual, between a desire to be united with the original and an aspiration to know the previously unknowable and unimaginable.

> Zwei Seelen wohnen, ach! in meiner Brust,
> Die eine will sich von der andern trennen;
> Die eine hält, in derber Liebeslust,
> Sich an die Welt mit klammernden Organen;
> Die andre hebt gewaltsam sich vom Dust
> Zu den Gefilden hoher Ahnen. (ll. 1112–17)[108]

Modernity stands in a dialectical relationship with its ancient and archaic predecessors. It is heterogeneous in origin, before it has even developed its modern identity. It is (understood as) a successor by definition. This is why its identity can only be fully grasped from a historical perspective. Because of the modern mind's awareness of the past as intrinsically different, the essence of modernity must be conceived as dialectically dynamic. Goethe achieves a depiction of this identity by presenting this historical dialectic.

The initial question with which I approached *Faust* must be raised again. Can this historical dialectic be squared with a Goethean classicism based on an ideal of the "Reinmenschlich"? Gerhard Schulz summed up *Faust* in his impressive literary history of the Goethe-period when he wrote:

> Goethe's *Faust* ist ein Abbild der Konstruktionen, die sich unter deutscher Perspektive der aufgeklärte, zum "reinen Selbstbewußtsein", zur Herrschaft über die Dinge und die Geschichte strebende Mensch schafft, um mit den Problemen seiner Existenz unter eben den Voraussetzungen seiner Aufgeklärtheit fertigzuwerden.[109]

Given this assessment of Goethe's drama it appears at first sight curious that Schulz introduced his assessment with the remarks that *Faust* is

---

[108] "In me there are two souls, alas, and their / Division tears my life in two. / One loves the world, it clutches her, it binds / Itself to her, clinging with furious lust; / The other longs to soar beyond the dust / Into the realm of high ancestral minds." Luke, 36.

[109] Schulz, *Die deutsche Literatur zwischen Französischer Revolution und Restauration*, vol. 2, Munich: Beck, 1989, pp. 678–9.

"schlechterdings kein Spiegel europäischer Gesellschafts-, Wirtschaft- und Kulturgeschichte [...], sondern die Geschichte [...] ist Spiegel einer Persönlichkeit, deren geschichtliche Koordinaten sehr viel weiter sind."[110] Schulz aims to protect the universally human, and hence finds history in *Faust* limited, which allows him to claim the drama for an allegedly Goethean "world literature" (679). Such an interpretation is symptomatic of the desire to prevent "reinmenschlich" from becoming fully historicised. Significantly the challenge to the modern mind is its "Aufgeklärtheit", which was also pinpointed by Beiser, Frank and Jamme as the key reason for the intellectual crisis at the end of the 18th century,[111] *not* the situation of historicity. But as the characteristics and condition of modernity are presented as *defined* by their historical evolution, timelessness can never be its (lasting) outcome. When Goethe conducts and presents a theoretical examination of modernity with historicity in mind, he is in tune with the latest contemporary philosophical and aesthetic theory, i.e. with the notion to base theory on history. If A. W. Schlegel intended to link theory and history through the means of analytical critique, Goethe achieved the same through synthetic *Diaphanie*. What results is a myth of modern identity as a historically dialectic process. *Faust* is of course the result of specifically German historical and intellectual, and by implication, political and economic conditions. But these conditions were conducive to grasping the wider issues of modernity in such a general sense that the drama has retained its appeal beyond Germany and the *Goethezeit*. In the shape of a modern myth, *Faust I* represents the process of modernity becoming consciously defined as conditioned by historicity.

Formal Aspects: "Philosophical Tragedy"
and modern *Volkspoesie*

The double bind of being aware of historical particularity but still desiring to approximate to a universal theory also finds expression in key formal aspects of *Faust*. Again it is Friedrich Schlegel's theoretical explorations of the nature of modern poetry that pinpoint them. *Faust* does not only *treat* the tragedy of modernity, it is *formally* a modern tragedy by being un-classical in every respect. *Faust* explodes the dramatic unities in

---

[110] Schulz, *Die deutsche Literatur* II, 678.
[111] Cf. Chapter 2.

an unsurpassable manner, including heaven and earth and, self-consciously, the practicalities of producing drama. It disregards tragedy's demand for the tragic protagonist's (usually violent) death as the solution of the tragic conflict: in *Faust II* Faust dies of old age and his demise is not tragic since he is evidently saved. The latter circumstance has provoked comparisons with medieval mystery and morality plays, which are the indigenous origin of modern European drama. But the post-medieval twist in Goethe's drama is the disconnection between "works" and reward. For *Faust I* the ending is even more revolutionary: Faust is condemned to "go on" in restless unhappiness.

The disregard for the unities is of course a direct result of intending to present the modern historical world, for which, as contemporary ideas suggested, Shakespearean tragedy was the artistic blueprint. *Faust I*, however, *contains* the tragedy of Gretchen whose tragic conflict and end is of Aristotelian-Lessingian proportions: she is destroyed through the irreconcilable opposition between her will and desires and the laws of her world. She, too, is spiritually saved of course. But her social and physical destruction following her tragic error are presented in such stark terms and accompanied by such heart- and mind-rending suffering that she clearly acquires tragic greatness in the classical sense. The Gretchenstory with its elements of ancient tragedy is a phase Faust experiences and then leaves behind. The ancient is again embedded in the cultural experience of modernity.

While Gretchen's tragic conflict is resolved on the conceptual level by her tragic death, on the social level by her execution, and on the spiritual level by the voice from above, Faust's problems, his accumulating errors and disappointments, drag ever on in the New Hell on earth. For him there is no tragic death or hope of Christian redemption, no solution, and no answer – at least at this point –, which exemplifies the infinity of the modern existence governed by time. Faust's is a state of perpetual despair, assuaged temporarily by the project of reaching the "moment". ("So tauml' ich von Begierde zu Genuss, / Und im Genuss verschmacht ich nach Begierde"). In this *Faust* conforms to Friedrich Schlegel's notion of the new philosophical tragedy, which Schlegel thought represented the nature of modern literature.[112] Its key interest

---

[112] "Diese Dichtart [philosophical tragedy] [ist] [...] eins der wichtigsten Dokumente für die Charakteristik der modernen Poesie." Friedrich Schlegel, *Studium, Kritische Friedrich-Schlegel-Ausgabe* vol. 1, 246. "This type of poetry [...] [is] [...] one of the most important documents for the characterisation of modern poetry." *Study of Greek Poetry*, 32.

was not beauty, which he defined as the key concern of the "aesthetic tragedy" of ancient times, but an understanding and knowledge of its own desperate situation. Hence it is "didactic" (ibid., 245). It expresses the individual and subjective realisation of the "purposelessness of life", of the "complete emptiness of all existence",[113] which for Schlegel was the characteristic feature as well as the continuing challenge of modern art.

> Ihre eigne natürliche Entwicklung und Fortschreitung führt die charakteristische Poesie zur philosophischen Tragödie, dem vollkommnen Gegensatze der ästhetischen Tragödie. Diese ist die Vollendung der schönen Poesie, besteht aus lauter lyrischen Elementen, und ihr endliches Resultat ist die höchste Harmonie. Jene ist das höchste Kunstwerk der didaktischen Poesie, besteht aus lauter charakteristischen Elementen, und ihr endliches Resultat ist die höchste Disharmonie [der zerrütteten Natur im dissonierenden Weltall, dessen tragische Verworrenheit sie im getreuen Bilde schrecklich abspiegelt]. Ihre Katastrophe ist tragisch; nicht so ihre ganze Masse: denn die durchgängige Reinheit des Tragischen (eine notwendige Bedingung der ästhetischen Tragödie) würde der Wahrheit der charakteristischen und philosophischen Kunst Abbruch tun.[114]

Beyond a basic didactic interest, however, the philosophical tragedy presents the fate of the modern individual in a "universalising" fashion (what Schlegel calls "idealisch"), which is as far as modernity can transcend its historically conditioned particularity. Schlegel pinpoints precisely the impossibility of creating the universally "Reinmenschlich" under modern conditions. For Schegel the blueprint for such a philosophical tragedy, the fully-fledged theory of which he considered still outstanding in the mid-1790s, was *Hamlet*. But he already suspected that the *Faust-Fragment* of 1790 would, if it were to be finished, surpass Shakespeare's tragedy in terms of representative modernity. "Wenn der

---

[113] "Zwecklosigkeit des Lebens" and "vollkommene Leerheit alles Daseins", ibid., 251–2.

[114] Ibid., 246. The text in brackets is taken from the editor's footnotes giving variant (later) versions. "Its own natural evolution and progression leads characteristic poetry to philosophical tragedy, which is the complete opposite of aesthetic tragedy. Consisting of nothing but lyrical elements, the former is the culmination of the poetic arts – it results ultimately in utmost harmony. Consisting of nothing but characteristic elements, the latter is the greatest work of didactic poetry – it results ultimately in the utmost disharmony [the utmost disharmony of nature destroyed in a dissonant universe, the tragic confusion of which it reflects terrifyingly in a faithful representation; MO]. Its catastrophe is tragic; this is not true of it in its entirety: for the thorough purity of the tragic (which is a necessary precondition of aesthetic tragedy) would harm the truth of characteristic and philosophical art." *Study of Greek Poetry*, 32.

'Faust' vollendet wäre, so würde er den Hamlet [...] weit übertreffen. Was dort nur Schicksal, Begebenheit – Schwäche ist, das ist hier Gemüth, Handlung und Kraft."[115] In *Hamlet*, individuality is still manifest only as weakness rather than strength. Fate and event, one ancient, one epic concept, both of which still somewhat contaminate the modern tragedy in Shakespeare, have in Goethe's fragment been turned into modern and dramatic categories. With the turn to "Gemüt, Handlung, Kraft" the modern focus on the will of the individual and on the independent and creatively striving mind and heart is fully realised. In the context of this study this cannot be surprising.

Faust does not only satisfy Friedrich Schlegel's demands for a new and appropriately modern poetry, but also Herder's notions of *Volkspoesie*. Goethe's drama does not just represent modernity from the philosophical side, where history is used to derive theory, but from the purely historical side, where all theory is subject to the historicist perspective, in the way that Herder formulated in his essay on Shakespeare. The three strands in *Faust*, the Faust-material, the Gretchen-story, and the witches, all have their origin in folk poetry. While *Wilhelm Meister* in its bourgeois and realistic setting remained *Volkspoesie* for the middle classes, *Faust* represents an example of a generally modern *Volkspoesie*, which prioritises the historical, yet raises it to philosophical levels by using materials of modern cultural origin for a depiction and analysis of modernity as a whole. This is sound Herderian cultural practice, quarrying relevant cultural traditions and heritage – one's own cultural antiquity – to produce uniquely illuminating and effective poetry of, and for, the present. While the ancients only had to turn their myths into aesthetic artworks, which *eo ipso* expressed the universal human truths of their cultural particularity, the moderns had to adapt their materials from a historicist view-point, i.e. treat the dimension of time, which had become recognised as a constituent feature of the modern identity, to approximate to any universal statement about their condition. In 1773 Herder provided a ground-breaking analysis of the difference between ancient and modern identity and culture and from this analysis he abstracted a blueprint for cultural relevance that incorporated the awareness of historicity and thus could accommodate the process of time. Its aim was not to create ideals of the "Reinmenschliche", but to make visible the particular of the universal. This is exactly what Goethe achieved in *Faust* with regard

---

[115] "Göthe. Ein Fragment." (1796). Quoted by Keller, "Der klassische Goethe", 9.

to modernity. Against this background it would indeed be mistaken to interpret the "Faustian", whether in its positive, ideologically driven self-aggrandisement or its negative dangerousness, as nationally German in a traditional sense.[116] The detailed description of the undaunted and irrepressible human spirit that is awe-inspiring in its audacity and vision, but equally frightening in its scope and relentlessness is clearly identified as *modern* in nature, or as the Schlegels called it, as *Romantic*. However, the analysis of this poetically distilled modern spirit is presented by the author as confined in historical and individual particulars: set in the fading Christian world ordained by the *Prologue*, which is bound by the specifics of making late 18th-early 19th-century drama, as the *Vorspiel* indicates, it is lastly the product of an individual imagination which is conscious of its individual history, as the "Zueignung" suggests.

In the wake of ideological criticism such as Schwerte's substantial study little further effort has been made to re-examine the connections between Goethe's *Faust* and a German identity. And yet the interpretation of modernity that *Faust* presents is crucially dependent on the German intellectual situation. But, although (and because!) it is conditioned and governed by a particular "national" situation, it is less an expression of "Faustian Germanness" than it is an assessment of the origin and development of European modernity that aims at transcending the national within a modern context, which is in line with contemporary post-national definitions of Germanness.

---

[116] Cf. Schwerte, *Faust und das Faustische*, 7–26.

Conclusion

The New Universality and the German *Kulturnation*

This study shows that in German thought and literature around 1800 the concepts of historicity, of modernity and of German identity are inseparably linked. These links provide important pointers to the relationships between the traditionally defined "phases" of the *Goethezeit*, to the relationship between the Enlightenment and the evolving German concept of modernity and they allow conclusions regarding the theory of the German *Sonderweg*. They provide new insights into the concept of the German *Kulturnation*, which was first defined by Friedrich Meinecke a century ago.[1]

It has become clear that the modern German identity, as it became defined at this time, entailed a distinct sense of universality, of non-particularity that was characterised by openness and cultural absorbency. Universality was in this case not to be understood as undefined generality, or a static theoretical abstraction, but as a heightened awareness of the definite particularity – regarding merits and demerits – of others and their contribution to the whole of humanity's achievements, which could be assessed, appropriated and transformed by the absorbent German "spirit" on the historical road to a composite and complete human

---

[1] The discussion about the validity and meaning of the notion of *Kulturnation* was re-ignited following the most recent German unification-process. This discussion remained indebted to Meinecke's definition because it did not challenge his notion that a *Kulturnation* is a vegetative pre-modern entity. Cf. B. Giesen, ed., *Nationale und kulturelle Identität*, Frankfurt aM: Suhrkamp, 1991; O. Kallscheuer/C. Leggewie, "Deutsche Kulturnation vs. französische Staatsnation. Eine ideengeschichtliche Stichprobe" in H. Berding, ed., *Nationales Bewußtsein und kollektive Identität*, Frankfurt aM: Suhrkamp, 1994, pp. 112–62; H. Peitsch, "Is Kulturnation a synonym for national identity?" *Studies in 20ᵗʰ-Century Literature* 26 (2) 2002, 445–59.

identity.[2] What results in terms of national identity is not so much a non-national or supra-national than a *post*-national identity, because it is based on the claim to have a clear understanding of the characteristics and functions of other national identities, which are considered as the elements of the gradually emerging whole (of humanity). From this perspective any specifically defined national identity is a concept of limited validity. Its clearly defined particularity renders it vital to the whole, but makes it too specific to represent the whole.

This notion of universality results from a preoccupation with temporal impermanence engendered by the dynamics of the historical process. This preoccupation in turn results from the acute awareness of historicity, which rose to unprecedented prominence in German thought towards the end of the 18th century. Shattering the hitherto dominant frameworks of post-medieval European thought, i.e. the constancy of reason, values and ideals, it forms the background to the unfolding crisis of rationality in the last third of the 18th century. This crisis has commonly been attributed to the growing awareness that reason, due to its self-analytical nature which eventually turns against its own foundations, is not, and cannot be, adequately grounded metaphysically. But this is only one aspect of the problem. The difficulty of grounding reason adequately is equally due to the increasing awareness of historicity, which necessitated a reconfiguration of the relation between theory and history – or ideal and time – in an attempt to accommodate ideals with the notion of historical change. This reconfiguration produced the dialectical process as the tool with which such an accommodation could be effected. The awareness of historicity predisposes the thinker to conceive of the historical process as stages in a development, in which, dialectically and successively, differences clash and are assimilated. As well as accommodating value with time, dialectics drives and structures this developmental process. The most crucial of all historical developments to ponder was the road towards perfect humanity, a legacy of the Enlightenment notion of perfectibility, which now turned into the process towards consummate universality. German literary, cultural and philosophical theory of this period is focused on intellectual development in this direction. No matter whether the thinkers involved emphasised the origin or the end of the development, they all held that the *experience of*

---

[2] Such a view of one's own identity obviously harbours dangers, as it may pave the way for notions of superiority. But at the same time this definition is designed to fulfil the functional capacity to facilitate progress and improvement.

the ongoing process between the two is the only tangible reality. The crux of this intellectual development is always the experience of initial difference, which results in alienation, and the subsequent increasing connectedness between world and consciousness, which results in increased self-understanding and self-reflexivity. This process responds to, and produces, a constantly changing environment. The emphasis is always on examining and understanding the ways in which world and consciousness connect. Self-conscious reflexivity triggers (initial) alienation, which in turn triggers, and is overcome by, increased self-conscious reflexivity. This process became the basis for the definition of modernity, and by extension of (intellectual) history as a whole. Reflexivity was seen as the original cause for the alienating disconnection between world and consciousness, but at the same time it promised a solution to this problem, as its ever-increasing reflexive capacity would eventually fully integrate the world into consciousness, which would result in complete understanding. Initial difference and eventual assimilation and integration were productively linked in the dialectical process, providing a framework to accommodate opposites (as universals) in any given present, while revealing them as dialectical elements, and part of an achieved or prospective synthesis, in the sequential historical process.

The historical process is based on and powered by difference, a realisation that sprang from the German Quarrel of the Ancients and the Moderns, but which had been prepared by the original *Querelle* in France a century earlier. The difference between ancient and modern is the original historical difference that gave rise to modern historical thinking *per se*. It spawned the preoccupation with the concept of the original-natural, the lost or obscured ideal, which could be defined, but not re-achieved. This concept forms the basis for the modern definitions of ancient as well as modern identity. It is also the basis for modern cultural nostalgia and modern criticisms of rationality and civilisation. At the same time it lies at the heart of the contemporaneous theories of cultural and intellectual progress and the "improvement" of rationality, civilisation and humanity. The idea of progress and the notion of universality, which are both key concepts of Enlightenment thinking, are thus retained, but crucially modified by the awareness of historicity. The new universality comes to represent increasing integration rather than permanent constancy. Progress now refers to transformation rather than augmentation. Humanity remains conceived of as universal in tendency, but this constancy of human nature, another Enlightenment tenet, does not denote a reduction to a mechanical formula or a common denominator, but refers to an integrated inclusiveness, a compositeness, in which all parts are equally represented. Crucially, these parts of the human make-up, integrated but distinct, were subject to historical influences and could thus appear differently at any given time.

These concerns regarding the relation between particularity and universality in the historical process and in human nature form the basis for the new theories in philosophy, and for the new concepts of literature and culture, which develop at this time. The manner of the gradually decreasing disconnection between consciousness and world, or thought and experience, or the abstract and the concrete, was the key topic of Idealist philosophy from Fichte to Hegel. As to literature and culture, Herder's concept of *Volkspoesie* and Schillers "aesthetic education" both criticise the Enlightenment for championing a one-sided rationality based on theory and abstraction, which they consider humanly incommunicable and unintelligible. This rationality is to them an isolated fragment of humanity masquerading as the essence of humanity. They argue that, because human reality is based on temporal flux and historical change, the abstract and timeless have no real bearing. Even if the abstraction has been understood theoretically, it still needs to be *experienced* in order to be fully grasped and to impact on behaviour and consciousness. To make it possible to experience the abstract, and thus make it humanly relevant, it must be linked to something concrete. At any time in its development the universal must retain a basis in the particular and temporal. Herder saw this link in local or national tradition, Schiller in the aesthetic experience of the beautiful, and Friedrich Schlegel in the pulling together of the distinct elements of human synthetic creativity and analytical understanding, of the human capacity for both memory and projection. His "progressive Universalpoesie" represents an approximation to such an integrationist progressive universality, which makes the dynamic process itself supreme: poetry must also be its own critique, as it must carry within it its own history and point to its own future. It must be its own mythology and its own critical analysis at the same time. Crucially, the connection between the abstract and the concrete, which makes the experience of the abstract possible, is always conceived of as *cultural* in nature.

So the notion of historicity changes not only the view of universals, but also of the particular, for which it defines an essential need, closely relating it to any notion of universality and making it equally important. The once abstract universal, no longer theoretical and static, becomes a composite of succeeding particulars (in order to become complete), while the concrete particular becomes seen as vital to communicate and experience any form of abstraction. Thus both, universal and particular, remain in constant flux. Making the abstract experienceable in time and space, i.e. giving it human reality, bridges the divide between world and consciousness and can help perform the assimilation between the two. While there remain differences between these three thinkers – Herder focuses on the origin and the process, Schiller on the process and its aim, for Schlegel the aim increasingly recedes beyond the bounds of human reality which makes him focuses on the process itself –, the uniformity of the question they faced and the similarity of their answers regarding the historical dynamic which they considered underlay all literary development and any future literary achievement, point to a fundamental intellectual coherence not just of the 1790s, but of the period that has traditionally been divided into *Sturm und Drang, Klassik* and *(Früh-)Romantik*. All the thinkers discussed here were profoundly interested in accommodating the effects of historicity. These effects, and the nature, of historicity were perhaps easiest to grasp, and easiest to swallow, from a German perspective. In the German cultural and intellectual context of the time historicity (only) challenged theoretical concepts, many of which had been imported, rather than an established identity inherently reliant on these concepts. In fact the premise of flux and impermanence inherent in the notion of historicity was congenial to the German lack of established national unity and political coherence.

Two of Johann Wolfgang Goethe's major works, *Wilhelm Meisters Lehrjahre* and *Faust I*, reflect these concerns precisely, in form as well as content. The *Lehrjahre* pivots on the crisis of rationality. The novel investigates the relationship between *Sturm-und-Drang* and Enlightenment ideas on art and education, which form the basis for a dialectical clash. But at the same time this clash is integrated into the intellectual development of modernity from its original and constitutive roots in the Middle Ages to Goethe's present. Embedded in its historical context, the dialectical clash is on the one hand made to appear as stemming from a universal and irreducible duality in human nature. But at the same time it appears to be conditioned by the successive progress of a particular historical development (i.e. that of modernity). The clash appears as an ancient-modern dialectic within modernity, giving modernity its own natural-original roots. Thus Goethe presents an historical dialectic that accommodates (previously) universal positions within its dynamic. Their claim to being absolute universal values is historicised rather than abandoned.

As a *Bildungsroman*, however controversial this concept may have become, the *Lehrjahre* depicts the endeavour, successful or not, to understand the ways in which world and consciousness connect in an environment that is socially and intellectually in flux. The *Lehrjahre* revolves around dichotomies that are at the same time dialectical successions (and potential syntheses), which are realised in historical as well as individual form: the concept of natural modernity vs. the concept of intellectual modernity, the Enlightenment notion of individuation and socialisation vs. that of *Sturm und Drang*, social concepts of personal freedom and independent rulership vs. social dependence and economic productivity. Grappling with the problem of Enlightenment values in an historistically aware world gives Goethe the opportunity to pinpoint the Enlightenment's dialectic – which in itself is evidence of the intrinsic modernity of the Enlightenment: it is heterogeneous, and hence dialectically productive – and place its ideas in a dialectically dynamic relationship with *Sturm und Drang*, and potentially Romantic, ideas.

Faust I grasps the history and historicity of modernity in mythic terms. Modernity is set *in contrast and in succession* to classical as well as Northern antiquity. Again the modern condition is shown to have its own internal dialectic. European cultural history is not only a development from antiquity to modernity, but also from archaic anarchy bound by a sensual immersion in the here and now to modern rationality. But by the same token, the successive nature of this development (or progress) is dialectically challenged by the suggestion of the simultaneity of the successive conditions. The non-rational and archaic are a constant presence within modernity. As in the *Lehrjahre*, the dynamic is based on historical dialectics and seemingly universal dichotomies at the same time. History (the past) not only *determines*, but also *exists in* the present. The present *contains* the past. For example, *Faust I* contains in the Gretchen-story a modern tragedy fashioned on ancient-classical structures. This represents the assimilation and integration of difference in the dynamic between consciousness and world in reverse-angle view: the present *has* assimilated the past, the assimilation of difference *has* been instrumental in producing the new (present) condition, but the past condition has retained an independent existence in a transformed shape. It now forms the alien "other" necessary to move the historical process further on. Thus the figure of Faust, the disillusioned Enlightened thinker who turned *Sturm-und-Drang* rebel, encounters his "others": the non-rational, the natural, and that which is sensually experienced. From these encounters he emerges into a historically open space. The original has been superseded in order to re-emerge as the other. Universal opposites are historicised. As in the *Lehrjahre*, these processes work on the historical as well as the individual level, in this case at the same time.

Both works present an accommodation of universal values with time, they also effect a representation of the dynamic connections between past (history) and present, which defines the present without limiting it, i.e. the present remains open to change. *Faust I* is darker in outcome than the *Lehrjahre*. It *leaves open*, in the fashion the young Friedrich Schlegel described, what the novel seemingly harmonises, as Friedrich Schiller hoped. Both works suggest a link between oppositional and successive constellations, which makes possible the integration of value and time. These connections within time are based on the historical dialectic: on continuity as well as discontinuity, on superseding as well as assimilation and re-emergence.

Although Goethe's works evince a decidedly German perspective regarding the meaning and purpose of modernity, he refused to define a particular German identity, or the particularity of Germanness. Instead there is a focus on the cultural, which places the "Reinmenschliche" in its cultural and historical context. But this now appears less as an inability or unwillingness due to an anti-national, unpolitical or conservative stance, but as the result of an awareness of the German suitability for a post-national approach. In the cultural and philosophical theories discussed here, *the cultural* was considered the defining feature of humanity, from the beginning to the end of the intellectual and historical process, which makes it an evolving essence that can successfully relate norms to time. In its constant presence but changing appearance it precedes, supersedes, and expresses any form of (human, national, or other) particularity, i.e. it is particular and universal at the same time, which makes it an exact match for the post-national synthetic universality of German identity. Formulating such a view of humanity and definition of identity at a time when great importance was attached to the construction of specific national identities, which could be utilised politically, indeed constitutes a German *Sonderweg*. But it is not a case of deliberately creating separatist difference, but of integrating European particulars. This was to be the identity and the purpose of the *Kulturnation*. Defined by Friedrich Meinecke in 1907 as a unified human community based not on political statehood but on shared culture, it derives from the ideas of culture, its nature and function, developed around 1800. In the understanding of the *Goethezeit* thinkers a *Kulturnation* would have been an original concept of human community, since culture, or cultural and spiritual education and understanding, had to precede politics, if political progress was to work and last. At the same time it would have been considered the consummate concept of human community, as culture will supersede politics, in particular the political conception of the nation state. The *Kulturnation* reflects the original nature of humanity as well as the desired destination of humanity. (It is probably worth pointing out that this process was not considered to occur automatically, but as the result of human efforts to understand the conditions and purpose of humanity and make progressive choices.) The *Kulturnation* and its conception of culturally and historically conditioned humanity was compatible with the contemporary notions of the *Weltbürger* and *Weltliteratur*. It expresses the post-national vision and the focus on historicity which underlay the definition of modern German identity at the time. Evidently, this definition of identity was quite different from the nationalism that eventually prevailed.

Bibliography

Primary Sources

Fichte, Johann Gottlieb, *Reden an die deutsche Nation*, *Fichtes Werke*, vol. 7, ed. by Immanuel H. Fichte, Berlin: Veit, 1845–46, repr. Berlin: De Gruyter, 1971, pp. 257–501.

Johann Gottlieb Fichte. Addresses to the German Nation, edited with an introduction by George Armstrong Kelly, originally translated by R.F. Jones and G.H. Turnbull (1922), New York: Harper & Row, 1968.

Goethe, Johann Wolfgang, *Faust. Der Tragödie erster Teil,* Stuttgart: Reclam, 1986, repr. 1995 (follows *Weimarer Ausgabe* of 1887).

Goethe, Johann Wolfgang, *Die Faustdichtungen, Sämtliche Werke in 18 Bänden*, vol. 5, Munich: Deutscher Taschenbuchverlag, 1977/Zürich: Artemis, 1950 (unchanged reprint of Artemis-edition, ed. by Ernst Beutler et al., Munich: Deutscher Taschenbuchverlag, 1949).

Johann Wolfgang von Goethe. Faust. Part One, translated with an introduction by David Luke, Oxford/New York: Oxford University Press, 1987.

Goethe, Johann Wolfgang, "Shakespeare und kein Ende!" *Morgenblatt für gebildete Stände*, 12 May 1815, *Johann Wolfgang Goethe. Schriften zu Literatur und Theater*, ed. by Walter Rehm, (*Gesamtausgabe der Werke und Schriften in 22 Bdn*, vol. 15) Stuttgart: Cotta, 1963, pp. 994–1008.

Goethe, Johann Wolfgang, *Wilhelm Meisters Lehrjahre, Sämtliche Werke in 18 Bänden*, vol. 7, Munich: Deutscher Taschenbuchverlag, 1977/Zürich: Artemis, 1950.

Wilhelm Meister. Apprenticeship and Travels, translated from the German by R.O. Moon, 2 vols, London: Foulis & Co., 1947.

Goethe-Schiller. Briefwechsel, ed. by Walter Killy, Frankfurt aM/Hamburg: Fischer, 1961.

Hegel, Friedrich, *Ästhetik*, 2 vols, ed. by Friedrich Bassenge, Berlin/Weimar: Aufbau-Verlag, 1965.

Hegel, Friedrich, *Phänomenologie des Geistes, Georg Wilhelm Friedrich Hegel's [sic] Werke, vollständige Ausgabe durch einen Verein von Freunden des Verewigten*, vol. 2, 2nd edn, ed. by D. Johann Schulze, Berlin: Dunker und Humblot, 1841.

Hegel's Phenomenology of Spirit, translated by A.V. Miller with Analysis of the Text and Foreword by J.N. Findlay, Oxford: Oxford University Press, 1977.

Herder, Johann Gottfried, *Alte Volkslieder, Herders Sämmtliche Werke*, vol. 25, ed. by Carl Redlich, (= *Herders Poetische Werke* vol. 1) Berlin: Weidmannsche Buchhandlung, 1885, pp. 1–126.

Herder, Johann Gottfried, *Auch eine Philosophie der Geschichte zur Bildung der Menschheit, Herders Sämmtliche Werke*, vol. 5, ed. by Bernhard Suphan, Berlin: Weidmannsche Buchhandlung, 1897, pp. 475–594.

Herder, Johann Gottfried, *Auszug aus einem Briefwechsel über Oßian und die Lieder alter Völker, Herders Sämmtliche Werke*, vol. 5, pp. 159–207.

Herder, Johann Gottfried, *Briefe zur Beförderung der Humanität*, Achte Sammlung, *Herders Sämmtliche Werke*, vol. 18, ed. by Bernhard Suphan, Berlin: Weidmannsche Buchhandlung, 1883, pp. 67–140.

Herder, Johann Gottfried, "Shakespear", *Herders Sämmtliche Werke*, vol. 5, pp. 208–231.

Herder, Johann Gottfried, "Über die Würkung der Dichtkunst auf die Sitten der Völker in alten und neuen Zeiten", *Herders Sämmtliche Werke*, Berlin: Weidmannsche Buchhandlung, 1877–1913, vol. 8, ed. by Bernhard Suphan, pp. 334–436.

Herder, Goethe, Frisi, Möser, *Von deutscher Art und Kunst. Einige fliegende Blätter*, mit einem Nachwort von Hans Dietrich Irmscher, Stuttgart: Reclam, 1968, 2nd edn 1988, repr. 1995.

Schelling, Friedrich Wilhelm Joseph, *Das System des Transzendentalen Idealismus, Schellings Werke*, vol. 2, nach der Originalausgabe in neuer Anordnung von Manfred Schröter, Munich: Beck, 1927, pp. 327–634.

System of Transcendental Idealism (1800) by F.W.J. Schelling, translated by Peter Heath with an introduction by Michael Vater, Charlottesville: University of Virginia Press, 1978.

Schiller, Friedrich, "Deutsche Größe", *Schillers Werke, Nationalausgabe*, begründet von Julius Petersen, vol. 2 I (Gedichte), ed. by Norbert Oellers, Weimar: Hermann Böhlau Nachfolger, 1983, pp. 431–36.

Schiller, Friedrich, *Schillers Werke, Nationalausgabe*, vol. 2 II (Anmerkungen zu Band 2 I), ed. by Georg Kurscheidt and Norbert Oellers, Weimar: Hermann Böhlau Nachfolger, 1993.

Friedrich Schiller, *Über die ästhetische Erziehung des Menschen in einer Reihe von Briefen, Schillers Werke, Nationalausgabe*, vol. 20.I, ed. by Benno von Wiese unter Mitarbeit von Helmut Koopmann, Weimar: Hermann Böhlau Nachfolger, 1962, pp. 309–412.

Friedrich Schiller. On the Aesthetic Education of Man in a Series of Letters, edited and translated with an Introduction, Commentary, Glossary of Terms by Elizabeth M. Wilkinson and L.A. Willoughby, Oxford: Clarendon Press, 1967.

On the Aesthetic Education of Man in a series of Letters by Friedrich Schiller, translated with an introduction by Reginald Snell, London: Routledge & Kegan Paul, 1954.

Schiller, Friedrich, *Über Naïve und Sentimentalische Dichtung, Schillers Werke, Nationalausgabe*, vol. 20.I, pp. 413–503.

Friedrich von Schiller. Naïve and Sentimental Poetry and On the Sublime. Two Essays, translated and with an Introduction and Notes by Julius A. Elias, New York: Frederick Ungar, 1966; *Naïve and Sentimental Poetry*, pp. 83–190.

Schlegel, August Wilhelm, *Geschichte der Romantischen Literatur, August Wilhelm Schlegel. Kritische Schriften und Briefe*, vol. 4, ed. by Edgar Lohner, Stuttgart: Kohlhammer, 1965.

Schlegel, August Wilhelm, *Vorlesungen über dramatische Kunst und Literatur*, 2 vols in 1, ed. by G.V. Amoretti, Bonn/Leipzig: Kurt Schröder Verlag, 1923.

Lectures on Dramatic Art and Literature by August Wilhelm Schlegel, translated by John Black, 3rd edn, rev. by A.J.M Morrison, London: Bell & Sons, 1894.

Schlegel, August Wilhelm, *Vorlesungen über Schöne Literatur und Kunst, Vorlesungen über Ästhetik I*, ed. by Ernst Behler (*August Wilhelm Schlegel. Kritische Ausgabe der Vorlesungen*, vol. 1) Paderborn: Schönigh, 1989, pp. 179–783.

Schlegel, Friedrich, *Gespräch über die Poesie, Kritische Friedrich-Schlegel-Ausgabe*, ed. by Ernst Behler unter Mitwirkung von Jean-Jaques Anstett and Hans Eichner, vol. 2, ed. by Hans Eichner, Munich/Paderborn/Vienna: Schönigh/Zürich: Thomas Verlag, 1967, pp. 284–351.

Schlegel, Friedrich, *Fragmente, Kritische Friedrich-Schlegel-Ausgabe*, vol. 2, pp. 147–272.

Friedrich Schlegel. Dialogue on Poetry and Literary Aphroisms, translated, introduced and annotated by Ernst Behler and Roman Struc, University Park/London: Pennsylvania State University Press, 1968.

Schlegel, Friedrich, *Über das Studium der Griechischen Poesie, Kritische Friedrich-Schlegel-Ausgabe*, vol. 1, ed. by Ernst Behler, Paderborn/Munich/Vienna: Schönigh/Zürich: Thomas Verlag, 1979, pp. 217–367.

Friedrich Schlegel. On the Study of Greek Poetry, translated, edited and with a critical Introduction by Stuart Barnett, Albany, NY: State University of New York Press, 2001.

Schlegel, Friedrich, "Über Goethes Meister", *Kritische Friedrich-Schlegel-Ausgabe*, vol. 2, pp. 126–146.

Schlegel, Friedrich, *Kritische Friedrich-Schlegel-Ausgabe*, vol. 18, ed. by Ernst Behler, Munich/Paderborn/Vienna: Schönigh/Zürich: Thomas Verlag, 1963.

Secondary Sources

Alt, Peter-André, *Schiller. Leben-Werk-Zeit*, 2 vols, Munich: Beck, 2000.

Anderson, Benedict, *Imagined Communities: Reflections on the Origin and Spread of Nationalism*, London: Verso, 1983.

Baioni, Guiliano, "*Märchen – Wilhelm Meisters Lehrjahre – Hermann und Dorothea*. Zur Gesellschaftsidee der deutschen Klassik" *Goethe-Jahrbuch* 92 (1975) 73–127.

Becker-Cantarino, Barbara, "Hexenküche und Walpurgisnacht. Imagination und Dämonie in der frühen Neuzeit und in *Faust I*" *Euphorion* 93 (1999) 193–225.

Behler, Ernst, *German Romantic Literary Theory*, Cambridge: Cambridge University Press, 1993.

Behler, Ernst, "*Wilhelm Meisters Lehrjahre* and the Poetic Unity of the Novel in Early German Romanticism", *Goethe's Narrative Fiction. The Irvine Goethe Symposium*, ed. by William J. Lillyman, Berlin/New York: de Gruyter, 1983, pp. 121–122.

Beiser, Frederic, *The Fate of Reason: German Philosophy from Kant to Fichte*, Cambridge MA: Harvard University Press, 1987.

Belhalfaoui, Barbara, "Johann Gottfried Herder: Shakespeare – ein Vergleich der alten und neuen Tragödie" *Deutsche Vierteljahrsschrift* 61 (1987) 89–124.

Berger, Stefan, "The German Tradition of Historiography 1800–1995", *German History since 1800*, ed. by Mary Fulbrook, London: Arnold, 1997, pp. 477–92.

Bishop, Paul, "Intellectual Affinities between Goethe and Jung, with special reference to *Faust*" *Publications of the English Goethe Society* 69 (1999) 1–19.

Blessin, Stefan, "Die radikal-liberale Konzeption von *Wilhelm Meisters Lehrjahren*" *Deutsche Vierteljahrsschrift* 49 (1975) Sonderheft, 190–225.

Bodmer, Johann Jacob, *Von den vortrefflichen Umständen für die Poesie unter den Kaisern aus dem schwäbischen Hause* (1743), *Das geistige Zürich im 18. Jahrhundert: Dokumente und Texte von Gotthart bis Pestalozzi*, ed. by Max Wehrli, Zürich: Atlantis, 1943, pp. 67–76.

Borchmeyer, Dieter, *Weimarer Klassik. Portait einer Epoche*, Studienausgabe, Weinheim: Beltz Atheäum, 1998.

Borchmeyer, Dieter, "Wie aufgeklärt ist die Weimarer Klassik? Eine Replik auf Beiträge von John A. McCarthy und Gottfried Willems" *Jahrbuch der deutschen Schillergesellschaft* 36 (1992) 433–440.

Brinkmann, Richard, "Romantische Dichtungstheorie in Friedrich Schlegels Frühschriften und Schillers Begriffe des Naiven und Sentimentalischen" *Deutsche Vierteljahrsschrift* 32 (1958) 344–71.

Brough, Neil, *New Perspectives of Faust. Studies in the Origins and Philosophy of the Faust Theme in the Dramas of Marlowe and Goethe*, Frankfurt aM: Peter Lang, 1994.

Brown, Jane and Marshall, "Faust and the Gothic Novel", *Interpreting Goethe's "Faust" Today*, ed. by Jane K. Brown, Meredith Lee, Thomas P. Saine, Columbia, SC: Camden House, 1994, pp. 68–80.

Delvaux, Peter, "Hexenglaube und Verantwortung. Zur Walpurgisnacht in Goethe's *Faust I*" *Neophilologus* 83 (1999) 601–16.

Eibl, Karl, "Zur Bedeutung der Wette im Faust" *Goethe-Jahrbuch* 116 (1999) 271–280.

Eichner, Hans, "Friedrich Schlegels Theorie der Literaturkritik" *Zeitschrift für deutsche Philologie* 88 (1969) Sonderheft, 2–19.

Elliss, Rob, "E.T.A Hoffmann and the Cult of Natural Magic", PhD-thesis University of Nottingham, UK, 2003.

Fiedler, Leslie A., *Love and Death in the American Novel*, Cleveland, 1962.

Fischer, Bernd, *Das Eigene und das Eigentliche: Klopstock, Herder, Fichte, Kleist. Episoden aus der Konstruktionsgeschichte nationaler Intentionalitäten*, Berlin: Erich Schmidt, 1995.

Fischer, Bernhard, "Goethes Klassizismus und Schillers Poetologie der Moderne: *Über Naïve und Sentimentalische Dichtung*" *Zeitschrift für deutsche Philologie* 113 (1994), 225–245.

Frank, Gustav, "*Sturm und Drang*: Towards a new Logic of Passion", *Counter-Cultures in Germany and Central Europe*, ed. by Steve Giles and Maike Oergel, Oxford/Bern: Peter Lang, 2003, pp. 25–42.

Frank, Manfred, *Das Problem "Zeit" in der deutschen Romantik: Zeitbewußtsein und Bewußtsein von Zeitlichkeit in der frühromantischen Philosophie und in Tiecks Dichtung*, (1st edn 1972) Paderborn: Schönigh, 1990.

Frank, Manfred, *Der kommende Gott: Vorlesungen über die neue Mythologie*, Frankfurt aM: Suhrkamp, 1982.

Friedrich, Karin, "Cultural and Intellectual Trends", *German History since 1800*, ed. by Mary Fulbrook, London: Arnold, 1997, pp. 88–105.

Gellner, Ernest, *Nations and Nationalism*, Oxford: Blackwell, 1983.

Gerth, Klaus, "'Das Wechselspiel des Lebens'. Ein Versuch, *Wilhelm Meisters Lehrjahre* (wieder) einmal anders zu lesen" *Goethe-Jahrbuch* 113 (1996) 105–20.

Giesen, Bernhard, ed., *Nationale und kulturelle Identität: Studien zur Entwicklung des kollektiven Bewußtseins in der Neuzeit*, (1st 1991) 2nd edn, Frankfurt aM: Suhrkamp, 1992.

Gilles, Klaus F., *Goethes "Wilhelm Meister": Zur Rezeptionsgeschichte der Lehr- und Wanderjahre*, Königstein/Ts: Athenäum, 1979.

Grab, Walter, "Burschenschaften im Kontext national-revolutionärer Emanzipationsbewegungen anderer Länder 1815–1825", *Das Wartburgfest und die oppositionelle Bewegung in Hessen*, ed. by Burghard Dedner, Marburg: Hitzeroth, 1994, pp. 11–29.

Greiner, Bernhard, "Margarete in Weimar: Die Begründung des *Fausts* als Tragödie" *Euphorion* 93 (1999) 169–91.

Grimm, Reinhold, Hermand, Jost, eds., *Die Klassiklegende. 2nd Wisconsin Workshop*, Frankfurt aM: Athenäum, 1971.

Grimminger, Rolf, *Die Ordnung, das Chaos und die Kunst. Die neue Dialektik der Aufklärung,* (1st 1986) Frankfurt aM: Suhrkamp, 1990.

Grosse-Brockhoff, Anneke, *Das Konzept des Klassischen bei Friedrich Schlegel und August Wilhelm Schlegel*, Cologne/Vienna: Böhlau, 1981.

Habermas, Jürgen, *Der philosophische Diskurs der Moderne*, Frankfurt aM: Suhrkamp, 1985.

Habermas, Jürgen, *The Philosophical Discourse of Modernity*, translated by Frederick Lawrence, Cambridge: Polity Press, 1987, repr. 1994.

Habermas, Jürgen, *Strukturwandel der Öffentlichkeit. Untersuchungen zu einer Kategorie der bürgerlichen Gesellschaft*, 4th edn, Neuwied/Berlin: Luchterhand, 1969.

Hahn, Karl-Heinz, "Adel und Bürgertum im Spiegel Goethescher Dichtungen zwischen 1790–1810" *Goethe-Jahrbuch* 95 (1975) 150–62.

Hatfield, Henry, "*Wilhelm Meisters Lehrjahre* and 'Progressive Universalpoesie'" *Germanic Review* 36 (1961) 221–229.

Hewitt, M.A., "(Re)zoning the Naïve: Schiller's Construction of Auto-Historiography" *European Romantic Review* 14 (2003), 197–202.

Hobsbawm, Eric, Ranger, Terence, eds., *The Invention of Tradition*, Cambridge: Cambridge University Press, 1983.

Hoffmann, Ulrich, "Mephistophes: 'Ich bin ein Teil des Teils, der anfangs alles war'. Anmerkungen zu Goethes *Faust*, Vers 1349–58" *Goethe-Jahrbuch* 109 (1992) 57–60.

Iggers, Georg, *The German Conception of History: The National Tradition of Historical Thought from Herder to the Present*, Middletown CT: Wesleyan University Press, 1968.

Ill-Sun, Joo, *Goethes Dilettantismus-Kritik. Wilhelm Meisters Lehrjahre im Lichte einer ästhetischen Kategorie der Moderne*, Frankfurt aM: Peter Lang, 1999.

Jacobs, Jürgen, *Wilhelm Meister und seine Brüder. Untersuchungen zum deutschen Bildungsroman*, Munich: Fink, 1972.

Jamme, Christoph, "Aufklärung via Mythologie. Zum Zusammenhang von Naturbeherrschung und Naturfrömmigkeit um 1800", *Idealismus und Aufklärung: Kontinuität und Kritik der Aufklärung in Philosophie und Poesie um 1800*, ed. by Christoph Jamme and Gerhart Kurz, Stuttgart: Klett-Cotta, 1988, pp. 35–58.

Jamme, Christoph, "Klassische Aufkärung oder aufgeklärte Klassik?" *Jahrbuch der deutschen Schillergesellschaft* 36 (1992) 414–46.

Jauss, Hans Robert, *Literaturgeschichte als Provokation*, Frankfurt aM: Suhrkamp, 1970.

Johnston, Otto W., *The Myth of a Nation. Literature and Politics in Prussia under Napoleon*, Columbia, NC: Camden House, 1989.

Kallscheuer, O./Leggewie, C., "Deutsche Kulturnation vs. französische Staatsnation. Eine ideengeschichtliche Stichprobe", *Nationales Bewußtsein und kollektive Identität*, ed. by H. Berding, Frankfurt aM: Suhrkamp, 1994, pp. 112–62.

Keller, Werner, "Der klassische Goethe und sein nicht-klassischer Faust" *Goethe-Jahrbuch* 95 (1978) 9–28.

Keppel-Kriems, Karin, *Mignon und Harfner in Goethes "Wilhelm Meister": Eine geschichtsphilosophische und kunsttheoretische Untersuchung zu Begriff und Gestaltung des Naiven*, Frankfurt aM/Bern/New York: Peter Lang, 1986.

Kluckhohn, Paul, *Die Auffassung der Liebe in der Literatur des 18. Jahrhunderts and in der Romantik*, (1st 1922) 3rd unchanged edition, Tübingen: Niemeyer, 1966.

Korff, H.A., *Geist der Goethezeit. Versuch einer ideellen Entwicklung der klassisch-romantischen Literaturgeschichte*, 5 vols, Leipzig: Weber, 1923–57.

Kuhn, Thomas, *The Structure of Scientific Revolutions*, Chicago/London: Chicago University Press, 1962.

Koselleck, Reinhart, "Das 18. Jahrhundert als Beginn der Neuzeit", *Epochenschwelle und Epochenbewußtsein*, ed. by Reinhart Herzog and Reinhart Koselleck, Munich: Fink, 1987, pp. 269–82.

Langewiesche, Dieter, "Nation, Nationalismus, Nationalstaat: Forschungsstand und Forschungsperspektiven" *Neue Politische Literatur* 40 (1995) 190–236.

Lovejoy, O.A., "Schiller and the Genesis of German Romanticism" *Modern Languages Notes* 35, repr. in O.A. Lovejoy, *Essays in the History of Ideas*, Baltimore: John Hopkins Press, 1948, pp. 228–253.

McCarthy, John A., "Klassisch Lesen: Weimarer Klassik, Wirkungsästhetik und Wieland" *Jahrbuch der deutschen Schillergesellschaft* 36 (1992) 414–32.

Mandelkow, Karl Robert, "Kunst- und Literaturtheorie der Klassik und Romantik", *Europäische Romantik I*, ed. by Karl Robert Mandelkow in Verbindung mit Ernst Behler, (*Handbuch der Literaturwissenschaft* vol. 14, ed. by Klaus von See) Wiesbaden: Athenaion, 1982, pp. 49–82.

Mandelkow, Karl Robert, "Wandlungen des Faust-Bildes in Deutschland", *Interpreting Goethe's "Faust" Today*, ed. by Jane K. Brown, Meredith Lee, Thomas P. Saine, Columbia, SC: Camden House, 1994, pp. 239–51.

March, Jenny, *Cassell Dictionary of Classical Mythology*, (1st 1998) London: Cassell, 1999.

Martin, Wayne, *Idealism and Objectivity: Understanding Fichte's Jena Project*, Stanford, CA: Stanford University Press, 1997.

Mayer, Gerhart, *Der deutsche Bildungsroman. Von der Aufklärung bis zur Gegenwart*, Stuttgart: Metzler, 1992.

Mayer, Gerhart, "*Wilhelm Meisters Lehrjahre*. Gestaltbegriff und Werkstruktur" *Goethe-Jahrbuch* 92 (1975) 140–64.

Meinecke, Friedrich, *Die Entstehung des Historismus*, (1st 1936) ed. by Carl Hinrichs, vol. 3 of *Werke*, Munich: Oldenbourg, 1959.

Mennemeier, Franz Norbert, *Friedrich Schlegels Poesiebegriff dargestellt anhand der literaturkritischen Schriften*, Munich: Fink, 1971.

Minden, Michael, *The German Bildungsroman. Incest and Inheritance*, Cambridge: Cambridge University Press, 1997.

Muhlack, Ulrich, *Geschichtswissenschaft im Humanismus und in der Aufklärung. Die Vorgeschichte des Historismus*, Munich: Beck, 1991.

Müller, Christoph, "Gretchen als Hexe? Eine Anmerkung zu Albrecht Schönes Rekonstruktion der Walpurgisnacht" *Euphorion* 87 (1993) 347–64.

Müller-Seidel, Walter, *Die Geschichtlichkeit der deutschen Klassik. Literatur und Denkformen um 1800*, Stuttgart: Metzler, 1983.

Naschert, Guido, "Friedrich Schlegel über Wechselerweis und Ironie (Teil 1 und 2)", *Athenäum. Jahrbuch für Romantik* 1996, 47–90 (Teil 1); 1997, 11–36 (Teil 2).

Nohl, Hermann, *Die deutsche Bewegung. Vorlesungen und Aufsätze zur Geistesgeschichte 1770–1830*, ed. by O.F. Bollnow and F. Rodi, Göttingen: Vandenhoek & Ruprecht, 1970.

Oergel, Maike, "Revolutionaries, Traditionalists, Terrorists? The *Burschenschaften* and the German Counter-Cultural Tradition", *Counter-Cultures in Germany and Central Europe: From Sturm und Drang to Baader-Meinhof*, ed. by Steve Giles and Maike Oergel, Bern/Berlin: Peter Lang, 2003, pp. 61–86.

Oergel, Maike, "The German Identity, the German *Querelle*, and the Ideal State. A Fresh Look at Schiller's 'Deutsche Größe'", *Schiller. National Poet – Poet of Nations. A Birmingham Symposium*, ed. by Nicholas Martin, forthcoming.

Oxford Companion to Philosophy, ed. by Ted Honderich, Oxford/New York: Oxford University Press, 1995.

Peitsch, H., "Is Kulturnation a synonym for national identity?" *Studies in 20th-Century Literature* 26 (2) 2002, 445–59.

Plessner, Helmuth, *Die verspätete Nation. Über die Verführbarkeit des bürgerlichen Geistes*, (1st 1935/1959) Frankfurt aM: Suhrkamp, 1992.

Prokhoris, Sabine, *The Witch's Kitchen: Freud, Faust and the Transference*, translated by G. M. Goshgarian, Ithaca, NY: Cornell University Press, 1995.

Pyritz, Hans, *Goethe-Studien*, ed. by I. Pyritz, Cologne: Böhlau, 1962.

Reed, T.J., "Die Geburt der Klassik aus dem Geist der Mündigkeit" *Jahrbuch der deutschen Schillergesellschaft* 32 (1988) 367–74.

Reed, T.J., "Revolution und Rücknahme: *Wilhelm Meisters Lehrjahre* im Kontext der Französischen Revolution" *Goethe-Jahrbuch* 107 (1990) 27–43.

Reill, Peter Hanns, "Herder's Historical Practice and the Discourse of Late Enlightenment Science", *Johann Gottfried Herder: Academic Disciplines and the Pursuit of Knowledge*, ed. by W. Koepke, Columbia, SC: Camden House, 1996, pp. 13–21.

Reill, Peter Hanns, *The German Enlightenment and the Rise of Historicism*, Berkeley/Los Angeles/London: University of California Press, 1975.

Reincke, Olaf, "Goethes *Wilhelm Meisters Lehrjahre* – ein zentrales Kunstwerk der klassischen Literaturperiode in Deutschland" *Goethe-Jahrbuch* 94 (1977) 137–187.

Roberts, David, *The Indirections of Desire. Hamlet in Goethes "Wilhelm Meister"*, Heidelberg: Carl Winter, 1980.

Robertson, Ritchie, "Literary Techniques and Aesthetic Texture in *Faust*", *A Companion to Goethe's Faust: Parts I and II*, ed. by Paul Bishop, Rochester, NY: Camden House, 2001, pp. 1–27.

Schings, Hans-Jürgen, "Fausts Verzweiflung" *Goethe-Jahrbuch* 115 (1998) 97–123.

Schlaffer, Hannelore, *Wilhelm Meister. Das Ende der Kunst und die Wiederkehr des Mythos*, Stuttgart: Metzler, 1980.

Schlechta, Karl, *Goethes "Wilhelm Meister"*, Frankfurt aM: V. Klostermann, 1953.

Schneider, W., "Vom Weltweisen zum Gottverdammten. Über Hegel und sein Philosophieverständnis", *Idealismus und Aufklärung. Kontinuität und Kritik der Aufklärung in Philosophie und Poesie um 1800*, ed. by Christoph Jamme and Gerhart Kurz, Stuttgart: Klett-Cotta, 1988, pp. 201–16.

Schöne, Albrecht, "Faust, Paralip. 50", *Johann Wolfgang von Goethe*, ed. by Heinz Ludwig Arnold, Munich: Text und Kritik Sonderband, 1982.

Schulz, Gerhard, *Die deutsche Literatur zwischen Französischer Revolution und Restauration*, 2 vols, Munich: Beck, 1983–89.

Schweitzer, C. E., "Gretchen and the Feminine in Goethe's *Faust*", *Interpreting Goethe's "Faust" Today*, ed. by Jane K. Brown, Meredith Lee, Thomas P. Saine, Columbia, SC: Camden House, 1994, pp. 133–141.

Schwerte, Hans, *Faust und das Faustische. Ein Kapitel deutscher Ideologie*, Stuttgart: Klett, 1962.

Seitz, Erwin, "Die Vernunft des Menschen und die Verführung durch das Leben" *Goethe-Jahrbuch* 113 (1996) 121–37.

Selbmann, Rolf, *Der deutsche Bildungsroman*, 2nd edn, Stuttgart: Metzler, 1994.

Simpson, James, *Goethe and Patriarchy: Faust and the Fates of Desire*, Oxford: European Humanities Research Centre, 1998.

Stadler, Ulrich, "Wilhelm Meisters unterlassene Revolte. Individuelle Geschichte und Gesellschaftsgeschichte in Goethes *Lehrjahren*" *Euphorion* 74 (1980) 360–74.

Strich, Fritz, *Klassik und Romantik oder Vollendung und Unendlichkeit: ein Vergleich* (1st 1922), 2nd edn, Munich: Meyer & Jessen, 1924.

Swales, Martin, "Goethe's Analysis of Modernity", *Goethe at 250 = Goethe mit 250. Goethe Symposium*, ed. by T.J. Reed et al., Munich: Iudicium, 2000, pp. 9–18.

Swales, Martin, *The German Bildungsroman from Wieland to Hesse*, Princeton, N.J.: Princeton University Press, 1978.

Szondi, Peter, "Das Naïve ist das Sentimentalische: Zur Begriffsdialektik in Schillers Abhandlung" *Euphorion* 66 (1972) 174–206.

Voßkamp, Wilhelm, "Der Bildungsroman als literarisch-soziale Institution. Begriffs- und funktionsgeschichtliche Überlegungen zum deutschen Bildungsroman des 18. und beginnenden 19. Jahrhunderts.", *Zur Terminologie der Literaturwissenschaft*. Germanistische Symposienberichtsbände 9, ed. by Christian Wagenrecht, Stuttgart: Cotta, 1988, pp. 337–52.

Voßkamp, Wilhelm, ed., *Klassik im Vergleich. Normativität und Historizität europäischer Klassiken*, Stuttgart/Weimar: Metzler, 1993.

Weber, Heinz-Dieter, *Friedrich Schlegels Transzendentalpoesie. Untersuchungen zum Funktionswandel der Literaturkritik im 18. Jahrhundert*, Munich: Fink, 1973.

Wehler, Hans-Ulrich, *Nationalismus. Geschichte, Formen, Folgen*, Munich: Beck, 2001.

Weinrich, Harald, "Der zivilisierte Teufel", *Interpreting Goethe's "Faust" Today*, ed. by Jane K. Brown, Meredith Lee, Thomas P. Saine, Columbia, SC: Camden House, 1994, pp. 61–67.

White, Ann, *Names and Nomenclature in Goethe's Faust*, London: University of London, Bithrell Series vol. 3, 1980.

Willems, Gottfried, "Goethe – ein Überwinder der Aufklärung?" *Germanisch-Romanische Monatsschrift* 40 (1990) 22–40.

Williams, John R., "Goethe and the Idealists. Der Teufel als Wille und Vorstellung", *Goethe at 250 = Goethe mit 250. Goethe Symposium*, ed. by. T.J. Reed et al., Munich: Iudicium, 2000, pp. 121–30.

Williams, John R., *Goethe's Faust*, London: Allen & Unwin, 1987.

Wilson, W. Daniel, *Geheimräte gegen Geheimbünde. Ein unbekanntes Kapitel der klassisch-romantischen Geschichte Weimars*, Stuttgart: Metzler, 1991.

Wundt, Max, *Goethes "Wilhelm Meister" und die Entwicklung des modernen Lebensideals*, Berlin: Göschen, 1913.

Zabka, Thomas, "Dialektik des Bösen. Warum es in Goethes Walpurgisnacht keinen Satan gibt" *Deutsche Vierteljahrsschrift* 72 (1998) 202–26.

Zezschwitz, Eberhard von, *Komödienperspektive in Goethe's "Faust I". Dramentechnische Integration eines Sturm und Drang-Fragments in den Ideenzusammenhang der Klassik*, Bern: Peter Lang, 1985.

Index of Names